TRAVERSI, D
Approach to Shakespeare
VI to Twelfth Night

N

AN APPROACH TO SHAKESPEARE

I

HENRY VI TO TWELFTH NIGHT

BY THE SAME AUTHOR

Shakespeare: The Last Phase
Shakespeare: From Richard II to Henry V
Shakespeare: The Roman Plays
An Approach to Shakespeare II:
Troilus and Cressida to The Tempest

AN APPROACH TO SHAKESPEARE

I
HENRY VI
TO
TWELFTH
NIGHT

DEREK TRAVERSI

Third edition
revised and enlarged
in two volumes

HOLLIS & CARTER
LONDON SYDNEY TORONTO

PUBLISHER'S NOTE

The edition used as a basis for the act, scene, and line
references printed next to the quotations in the text is the
Oxford University Press *Complete Works of Shakespeare*,
edited by W. J. Craig.

This edition © Derek Traversi 1968
SBN 370 00257 1
Printed and bound in Great Britain for
Hollis & Carter Ltd
9 Bow Street, London, WC2
by William Clowes & Sons Ltd, Beccles
Set in Monotype Bembo
First published 1938
Second edition revised and enlarged 1957
Third edition revised and enlarged 1968

AUTHOR'S NOTE TO THIRD EDITION

The present study, *Henry VI to Twelfth Night*, is conceived as a supplement to my earlier book, originally published as *An Approach to Shakespeare* as long ago as 1938 and re-issued, in a considerably extended form, in 1957. It has long been apparent to me that this study suffered by being concentrated exclusively on the later stages of Shakespeare's dramatic career. I hope that the present book may go some way towards correcting the balance. In the companion volume, *Troilus and Cressida to The Tempest*, I have re-written the work already published to take account of changes of view or emphasis in the intervening years and to include discussion of all the plays not originally covered.

There has been, inevitably, some overlap with the earlier book, and with other previous publications. Chapter IV on the Sonnets reproduces, with some amendment, what I first wrote in 1938, and Chapter VII on the later series of English History Plays largely sums up the argument of my book, *Shakespeare: From 'Richard II' to 'Henry V'*, first published by Messrs. Hollis and Carter in England and by the Stanford University Press in the United States in 1958. Chapter III on the Early Comedies also owes a good deal to an essay on the same plays published in the *Writers and Their Work* series (Longmans and the British Council) in 1960. Eleven plays, however, are studied entirely for the first time and I hope that the argument as a whole will throw some light on the development of the dramatist's art in its earlier stages.

The book was conceived, and largely written, during a semester spent in the autumn and early winter of 1965 as Visiting Professor at Swarthmore College, Pennsylvania. I am conscious of a great debt of gratitude to my colleagues and friends there, and also to my seminar students in discussion with whom not a few of the points here made were formulated or clarified. The views expressed are, of course, entirely my own, but without these advantages the book might well not have been written.

DEREK TRAVERSI
Rome, November 1967

CONTENTS

INTRODUCTION

IT IS PERHAPS worth recalling at the outset of this study that its origins lie in a very short and perhaps rather dogmatic essay originally published thirty years ago and entitled, like the present volume, *An Approach to Shakespeare*. The point of departure for this essay was an assertion that the great nineteenth-century tradition of Shakespearean study—running from Coleridge and Goethe to Bradley's *Shakespearean Tragedy*[1]—had reached 'something like the limits of its usefulness'. Little more, it was suggested, remained to be discovered in that particular direction; nor, at the time of writing, were the assumptions which this school of criticism had taken for granted entirely acceptable. More particularly, the Victorian insistence upon *character*, when carried to the point of excluding other aspects of an essentially *dramatic* action, had its foundation in the subjectivism of 'Romantic' thought. *Hamlet* the tragedy—to take the stock example—became, when considered in the light of this tradition, a fruitful mirror for the dissatisfactions of the romantic self, and even the greatest students of the plays—who gave us a great deal that was very valuable—found it difficult to avoid confusing Shakespeare's aims with their own, often quite different concerns. Above all—and to this we shall return—this type of criticism found its theatrical counterpart in a conception of the stage, and of the dramatic action as a whole, which tended to distort Shakespeare's intentions and even to make some of the greatest plays[2] almost impossible to represent.

This, however, as the introduction to the 1938 essay also suggested, was not the whole of the story. 'We all know that to discuss Hamlet's life *outside* the limits of the play, to attempt to deduce the manner of his upbringing in order to explain his subsequent behaviour, is an illegitimate extension of the critic's proper function. Nor can we share the confidence with which some writers fathered their own philosophies on to Shakespeare's work. But, although we are certain that the old outlook was incomplete and sometimes misleading—just as we know that the sumptuous and realistic productions, which were its theatrical equivalent, were not the last word in the production of the plays—we are far less sure what is to replace them.' The essay went on to say that many valuable lines of approach had been opened out since the beginning of the century; we might now add, thirty years later, that many more have become available. Among these is a notable advance in our knowledge of the Elizabethan background of thought in cosmology, psychology, rhetoric, and in ideas on literature in general and drama in particular, which has the negative virtue of discouraging us from reading the plays too directly in the light of subsequent experience. Side by side with this, and largely complementary to it is the remarkable growth in our understanding of Elizabethan stage conditions and of their relevance for a proper understanding of the plays; already in 1938, it was possible to mention the pioneer work of Granville Barker,[3] and a great deal has been accomplished in this direction in subsequent years. Finally, the introduction to the original essay mentioned the rise of a double-edged approach to the plays in the kind of *interpretation* proposed by Professor Wilson Knight and still a relatively new development in the thirties.

Each of these 'approaches', however, though important and fruitful, brought with it its accompanying dangers. The increased modern interest in Elizabethan thought and knowledge has led us back, truly and significantly, to the contemporary setting of the plays and so has helped, among other things, to avoid the nineteenth-century errors of misplaced emphasis; but—it must be added—the criticism which has followed from this approach has shown itself apt to ignore the element of essential *discontinuity* which separates a genius from the commonplaces of his age. A writer of Shakespeare's stature is of his time in the ideas he uses, and we shall always be unwise to forget this; but he uses these ideas in ways of his own, which are not necessarily those of his time alone. Shakespeare's plays on English history, for example, lean heavily upon contemporary notions concerning such subjects as monarchy, its origins, its *rôle*, and its justification; but to interpret the series of chronicles from *Richard II* to *Henry V* as no more than exercises in Tudor patriotic propaganda is, in my submission, seriously to underestimate their originality. What truly emerges from these plays—as I shall seek to show[4]—is a thoroughly personal vision, increasingly tragic in its implications, of man as a political being; so that, properly read, they speak to us not less than they did to the late sixteenth-century, and speak moreover in ways that very few minds of that age—with the possible exception of Machiavelli—would have fully understood. To compare Shakespeare, as a mature dramatist, to almost any other Elizabethan writer is to be made aware of the degree to which he evades, escapes from the current Elizabethan limitations. Such a writer, in other words, and to adapt a critical commonplace, both is of his time and transcends it. The scholar is by the very nature of his task inclined to stress those aspects of a Shakespeare that relate him to his own times. In the process of so doing he helps to save us from committing fundamental errors of appreciation; but the critic—if I may be allowed, *for my present purpose alone*, to separate him from the scholar—is there to redress a necessary balance, the failure to appreciate which will prevent a response to his subject's true originality.

Something of the same kind, though to a lesser degree, can be said of an 'approach' too exclusively limited to a knowledge of the theatre and, more particularly, of contemporary stage conditions. As I suggested in 1938, Granville Barker's very considerable contribution to our understanding of Shakespeare as a working dramatist was to some extent limited by the tendency to rest on established judgements where both poetry and the definition of characters were concerned. He stressed, in the body of his work, an important truth, and one that his immediate predecessors had tended to neglect; but it was possibly too much to expect that he should also transform our understanding of other and not less important aspects of Shakespeare's work to correspond to that truth and to produce a new vision in its totality. His Hamlet and his Othello, were, in other words, still close to those proposed by Bradley, though our view of the stage on which these characters appeared was re-vivified, largely transformed, by the line of study which he did so much to originate.

The third of our new lines of 'approach', as seen thirty years ago, was that which led finally to the methods of 'interpretation' largely associated with the work of Wilson Knight. The effect of these methods was to move away from the more traditional readings in terms of character or 'philosophic' content to another, by which a given play was regarded, to use Wilson Knight's own phrase, as 'an expanded metaphor'. In the light of this contention the critic's task became very largely that of tracing in the plays significant threads and patterns of imagery within a 'spatial unity', recurrent themes through whose study and correlation the full 'meaning' of the work as a whole was to emerge. This line of approach can be associated, on a more academic level, with that of Professor Caroline Spurgeon, who—in a pioneer study published at this time[5]—card-indexed and catalogued Shakespeare's images, following up the repetition of particular images in a given play, and who even claimed as a result to be able to tell us something about the writer's own tastes and prejudices. Because, for example, the dramatist can be shown repeatedly to associate spaniels with cloying flattery, and because this association tends to produce in his poetry a sense of almost physical revulsion, we are asked to conclude that Shakespeare the man—that dim and unsatisfactory abstraction—felt a particular dislike for this species of dog, and perhaps for dogs in general. Whether this deplorably un-English trait contributes anything to an appreciation of his work remains uncertain.

To leave the matter thus is clearly to be less than fair to what Professor Spurgeon, and her method as developed by others in various directions, in fact achieved. The best parts of her study were valuable and important: how important we are perhaps now prevented from seeing by the fact that not a few of her discoveries have become common currency in later criticism. It helps us to understand *Troilus and Cressida*, for example, to know that there can be found in it a notable concentration upon imagery of taste; it is relevant to the study of *Macbeth* to remember that images of ill-fitting clothes appear repeatedly in the course of the play. These real discoveries called for a development which Professor Spurgeon herself was not always ready to give them: a development that, in one way or another, takes us beyond the card-index, beyond the more or less mechanical collation and counting of the images used, into a response to the poetry as a living and dynamic whole, a whole moreover that looks for its completion beyond itself, through incorporation into the ultimate unity of the dramatic action to which it belongs. This is the incorporation at which Professor Wilson Knight has consistently aimed in what is possibly the most ambitious attempt to interpret Shakespeare that the last half century has produced.

There can be no doubt that Wilson Knight to an eminent degree, and Professor Spurgeon in her own possibly more pedestrian way, have greatly extended our understanding of Shakespeare, and for this we have reason to be accordingly grateful. We shall do well, however, whilst recognizing this, to look a little closely at the 'methods', so to call them, upon which these real discoveries are said to be based. In the case of Professor Spurgeon we shall see at once that the 'method', in its essence, consists of card-indexing and counting images with a view to establishing their relative frequencies and drawing the corresponding conclusions. The image 'X' appears so many times and the image 'Y' so many: from the preponderance of either we can draw all kinds of conclusions, which seem to be 'scientifically' based, perhaps about the dramatist's own tastes and certainly, it is suggested, about the intentions which underlie a given play. We shall find, I think, on reflection, however, that the poetic image, even if we accept it as a kind of ultimate constituent of poetry, is not readily susceptible to this kind of treatment. Some images belong primarily to literary convention, others impress us as deeply personal in their effect; some, again, belong exclusively to the dramatic personage in whose mouth they are placed and to the situation in which he finds himself, others seem to answer more directly to the expression of the author's own experience. Above all, the poetic image is, more particularly as used by Shakespeare, a living and not a dead thing; and it lives, not dissected and placed in a card-index, but in a context, in relation to the intensity with which it is conceived (which varies greatly from one case to another), to the rhythm of the verse that conveys it, and to the total conception of the play in which it is found. Images, in fact, cannot be abstracted from their context, or counted up by a mechanical process as if they were all identical or similar in value. They live, develop, and change by their very nature, and it is precisely the life, the development, and the change which escape classification and call for the critic, or more simply the theatre-goer, to make his similarly living response. If the result is, as it must surely be, something less than a scientific certainty, that may be considered by some a pity; but the rest of us may derive some encouragement from the reflection that there are certain areas of life (it may well be the most important) which are, of their very nature, irreducible to the card-index and its overgrown and monstrous successor, the computer.

The case of Wilson Knight, which I have associated with that of Professor Spurgeon only on account of the tendency of both to start from a consideration of the poetic image and its function in the complete dramatic effect, is a good deal more complex. Whether we accept his conclusions or not, there is nothing of the card-index or the computer about Professor Wilson Knight's work; and it is just and necessary to say that there has been probably no writer on Shakespeare, in the period which here concerns us, who has opened out more new fields of vision to an understanding of the dramatist in his full life and complexity. Practically everyone who has since written on Shakespeare has had occasion to express his disagreement with many of Wilson Knight's conclusions, in which highly personal applications of ideas derived in varying degree from Nietzsche and from Christian tradition play a large part; but practically all those who have done so have also repeated or developed findings that he was the first to express. And yet, we must add, when all the debts have been fairly acknowledged, the numerous insights recognized for what they are, we often find ourselves asking, as we read or re-read these studies, how exactly all this was achieved. The moments of vision are unquestionably there, many and true (and not always recognized as a source by those who have subsequently used them): but there too, surely, are an almost fantastically confused set of religious, 'philosophical', and patriotic preoccupations often based, scarcely less than in the case of the card-indexers, upon an extraordinarily naive conception of what image and metaphor really are. The interrelation of these two aspects—remarkable, genuine insights and the tendency to force the text to say what the critic wants it to say—is not difficult to illustrate. An entire book by Wilson Knight— *The Shakespearean Tempest*[6]—sets out to show, for example, the existence through all the dramatist's work of a music-tempest opposition, and traces the presence of this line of imagery in every play that he wrote. The intuition is, beyond doubt, valid and important. The opposition between these two sets of constantly repeated images is *there* and, moreover, *means* something for our understanding of Shakespeare. In the proving of it, however, we are asked to believe that images taken from the early *Henry VI* plays are as valuable, have much the same degree of significance, as others from the unquestioned masterpieces, from *King Lear* and *The Tempest*; and that a burlesque piece spoken by Bottom in his first rehearsal for the Pyramus and Thisbe interlude in *A Midsummer Night's Dream*[7] has to all intents and purposes as much meaning as others drawn, for example, from the undoubtedly Shakespearean part of *Pericles*. This is surely absurd. Similarly in *Antony and Cleopatra*, perhaps the supreme test for a balanced criticism of Shakespeare, the romantic estimate of Antony in terms of 'vitality', 'transcendance', and 'immortality' is stressed by Wilson Knight, if not exclusively, certainly unduly in relation to the merciless realism that accompanies the poetry at each stage in the development of the action. This is, no doubt, for the excellent reason that Wilson Knight himself feels the play in this way; and, so feeling, he has indeed greatly extended our understanding of Shakespeare, but has also on occasion fallen into traps, one-sided and finally confused judgements which are the opposite of our author's dispassionate clarity and balanced strength.

One other tendency in modern Shakespearean studies, related to though not directly deriving from Wilson Knight's work, can appropriately be mentioned at this point. This is the tendency, observable to-day in many academic quarters, to read into the plays explicit statements of Christian belief and morality. The greater writers of the nineteenth-century tended, on the whole, to underestimate the Christian content of Shakespeare's thought, and it is perhaps in reaction to this that many writers in our own time have tended to present him as a moralist of orthodox tendencies and even, on occasions, as something of a theologian. This reaction, if such it is, towards a new orthodoxy has no doubt been carried too far in Shakespearean criticism, and has ended in producing a set of mechanically orthodox readings which are at least as far from what the plays actually offer as the interpretations to which they are opposed. Once again, Shakespearean criticism can only benefit in this situation from the capacity to draw and to maintain necessary distinctions. In view of the admitted lack of external evidence it seems clear that little can usefully be said concerning Shakespeare's personal beliefs, and certainly none of his plays were written to illustrate religious dogmas or to point preconceived moral judgements; on the other hand, it is surely no more than natural that a writer of his time and place should be aware of Christian tradition as an influence moulding his thought and that he should even seek, more especially in his later plays, to present in terms of a highly personal reading of that tradition some of his final conclusions about life. The relation of the final romances, in particular, to Christian notions of repentance, atonement, and 'grace', is certainly in no sense a matter of simple transcription or direct reflection; but for taking the romances seriously in my final chapter, for reading them as something more than poetic fantasies in dramatic form, I offer no apology. The seriousness and originality of these plays seems to me to be clearly written on practically every page.

In the situation outlined in the preceding paragraphs it seems that the student of Shakespeare will do well to consider his own position with some care. Once again my short introduction of 1938 may serve, even in its one-sided incompleteness, as a starting-point. Following a line that was more novel then than it is now—though, of course, I made no claim to be originating anything[8]—I then suggested a possible 'approach' through the development of language and verse as seen in the entire course of the dramatist's work, beginning with the individual word and taking it on, in the first instance, into its verse setting. Or, as I put it at the time:

If a writer's intention is apparent in his choice of subject and general treatment, it has an even closer relation to the words and phrases in which he expresses himself. The word, as we shall see again and again in dealing with Shakespeare, is the product of the most intimate relations of thought and feeling, nervous sensitivity and conscious emotion. Indeed, word and thought, word and feeling, form part of an indivisible process of poetic creation; and, in the greatest poetry, the relation is felt as an identity, so that it becomes impossible to separate the personal development of an experience from its formal expression in words.[9]

And, since the dangers of a mechanical counting of words and images, referred to above, were already apparent, I added: 'It only remains to add that the individual word cannot be considered apart from the verse in which it performs its function. . . . The development of Shakespeare's versification is revealed in a growing flexibility of response to the increasingly complex implications of the individual word. The various stages in the process by which he masters his experience, projects it fully into his plays, are most easily traced by starting from his continual effort to adapt language and verse structure to the growing pressure of his emotions'.[10]

In the years that have passed since this point of view was put forward both the virtues and the limitations of this kind of 'approach' have become clearer, to the writer at least, than they were at the time of writing. I should not now be inclined to express the argument in quite the same terms as those I first used thirty years ago. In particular I should be less happy now to talk, a little less than precisely, of Shakespeare's 'experience', at least in so far as this might be held to have 'biographical' implications, to be related to facts and circumstances in his life about which we can know nothing: nor am I altogether sure that there is a valid distinction between 'thought' and 'feeling' as elements making up a work of literature, between what I called, rather obscurely as I now find, 'nervous sensitivity' and 'conscious emotion'. I would now say, perhaps more simply, that if it is our aim to define the total impact upon us of a given play, we shall do well to start with the words, the language through which that impact makes itself most immediately felt in any given moment, proceed to the incorporation of the word into the verse structure to which it belongs, see again how this bears fruit in the conveying of such things as character, motive conscious and unconscious, and, finally, draw all these connected and successively expanding aspects of the work with which we are con-

cerned into the complete concept of a *dramatic action*, which is the end
and *raison d'être* of the whole.

In other words, we can now see—perhaps more clearly than I
originally saw—that the kind of 'approach' suggested above is only
useful in so far as it leads beyond itself, linking up with the various
elements which go to make up the complete dramatic reality. No
analysis of the first stage, *the word*, that does not illuminate some part of
the last, the complete *dramatic action*, can be valid; but—and to this
extent I would stand by my original proposal—we shall understand the
action itself better if we proceed initially from the smaller unit to the
larger, from that in which the individual intention first makes itself felt
to the final unity of concept and projection which is the complete work
of art. Or, as I put it in 1957, modifying and extending my intentions
of 1938:

> The application of this general conception will clearly vary greatly from one
> play, or one period, to another. When applied to Shakespeare's early work, it
> is bound to be largely concerned with detecting the birth of tendencies that
> later found full integration in the unity of his mature masterpieces. Only
> gradually will it become apparent how these early intuitions, these first
> motions of personal feeling, are assumed into an adequate dramatic form.
> If we wish to find traces of true individuality in the plays of Shakespeare's
> youth, we must look not to the complete work, which is normally still
> derivative, artificial in conception, but primarily to individual turns of phrase,
> the occasional striking choice of a word or image to be discerned in otherwise
> commonplace passages of verse. From these it is natural to pass to a study of
> the way in which the words thus personally used influence the run of the
> verse itself, expanding into images which are eventually seen to bear signifi-
> cant repetition and to form, with the presentation of character and action
> correspondingly developed, a more subtle and suggestive unity. It is at this
> last point that the poetic merges into the dramatic reality. To proceed from
> the word to the image in its verse setting, and thence to trace the way in
> which a pattern of interdependent themes is gradually woven into the
> dramatic action, unifying and illuminating it, is the most fruitful approach—
> the most accurate and, if properly handled, the least subject to prejudice—to
> Shakespeare's art.[11]

To turn back to this passage, over the intervening years, is to obtain the
sense of a valid, but also a notably one-sided procedure. In the study of
Shakespeare's early work, to which reference is made, it would rather
seem that two simultaneous lines need to be developed. The revealing
personal phrase or image is important, both in itself and in relation to

the character who utters it or to the situation in which it is spoken. But, side by side with it, an equally valid field of study would show Shakespeare developing and extending his conception of a dramatic action in its entirety; it would explore progressively the way in which his dramatic personages throw light upon one another by their comments and reactions, and are defined at least as much by what others say of them as through the impact of their own words. Beyond this again, analysis of the same plays would reveal a dramatist engaged in studying the scope of the dramatic conventions he has accepted, defining the implications of comedy, extending the possibilities of the historical chronicle, even moving from relatively crude beginnings to a more unified and subtle concept of tragedy. All these things, side by side with the attention simultaneously given to the growth of his expressive possibilities in language and verse, show a Shakespeare engaged in realizing the full possibilities, for his own purposes, of an integrated dramatic action.

The stress laid in the preceding argument on the dramatic action implies, as a necessary corollary, awareness that the plays were written for the stage, and for a given type of stage at that. A growing recognition of this reality, indeed, constitutes one of the most fundamental conquests of modern scholarship. Reading in the study can greatly extend our understanding of what Shakespeare wrote, even bringing out points which would normally escape us in the rapid development of a stage action; but in the long run it is to the stage—and to a particular moment in the development of the theatre—that we find ourselves returning, not in a spirit of mere historical reconstruction, but because the conditions of the Elizabethan playhouse need to be present in the mind of those who aim to present the plays in a way that shall be at once modern and—in the deepest sense, one separated from mere historical accident—truly Shakespearean.

Every undergraduate knows that the stage with which Shakespeare was initially familiar, and for which most of his plays were written,[12] descended in a very real sense from the platform used during the Middle Ages to represent the so-called 'miracle' plays. Without entering into details, which are either too familiar to repeat or too intricate to find a place in these introductory remarks, it was like this platform, and unlike most modern stages, in being surrounded on three sides by the public towards which it was deliberately projected. Furthermore, as it seems hardly necessary to remind the reader, it was divided into various parts, corresponding to different dramatic needs and roughly distinguishable, to modern scholarship, by the names of main, back, and apron stages. These arrangements looked very primitive from a nineteenth-century point of view, but—as has again often been shown—they offered certain important advantages; without some appreciation of these Shakespeare's conception of a dramatic action must remain largely obscure. It was, in the first place, a stage on which contact between the actors and the public was remarkably direct and intimate: the stock example is the speaking of Hamlet's soliloquies, difficult to deal with on a modern stage without interrupting the flow of the action, but normal and natural in their effect when considered in relation to the stage for which they were written.

If *intimacy* was the first important advantage this stage offered, *flexibility* was certainly the second. The tripartite division of the stage made it easy to maintain a rapid and uninterrupted flow of action. The stock examples, again, are Romeo addressing Juliet on the balcony, Othello strangling Desdemona on the back stage after the main stage has been cleared of the 'public' action and the separating curtains have been drawn apart. We might add, in *Henry IV, Part I*, the contrast between the court scenes and their burlesque reflection in Eastcheap, between the aristocratic leaders invoking honour on the field of battle and Falstaff passing his comment on that same 'honour' in a spirit at once openly cynical and indicative of life and realism. In each case, dramatic tension and the continuity of the action are maintained to important ends; and the lack of complex scenic effects, apparently an intolerable limitation when considered through nineteenth-century eyes, in fact often supported both. All this is elementary, but it seems important, in considering Shakespeare's work, to remember what a dramatic action is *not*. It is *not*, properly understood, a spectacle to be contemplated externally, still less a photographic imitation of what is sometimes misleadingly called 'real life'. It is rather, on the contrary, a spoken action, non-realist and conventional by its very nature, requiring the *participation* of the audience as a necessary element; indeed, the concept of scenery and decoration as a kind of subsidiary art added to give more visual attraction, is contrary to any serious view of the drama. An outstanding example of the kind of effect at one time lost to the theatre, but abundantly open to Shakespeare, was that of the storm in *King Lear*, where the aged king, in the process of creating the external tempest in the only way open to the poet, through his own words, fuses it with the dramatic projection of his own tragic state. Everywhere present, beneath the apparent poverty of the stage conditions available to

Shakespeare and his contemporaries, was a wealth of opportunity for the more profound poetic effects which the complication of later ages has often threatened to destroy.

To sum up, then: from a knowledge of the Elizabethan and Jacobean theatre it is possible to derive certain consequences which illuminate the Shakespearean conception of poetic drama. In the first place, like his mediaeval predecessors, Shakespeare based his work on what was still, in its underlying presuppositions, a popular and social conception of the stage and of dramatic art. It is true that by the sixteenth-century the participation of the craft guilds, which had been the most obvious sign of this participation, had given way to a more individualistic spirit; but the tradition that considered dramatic representation as a collective act, from which none need be excluded, however illiterate or lacking in social pretensions he might be, was still sufficiently alive to find reflection in Shakespeare's work. We shall not fully understand *Hamlet* if we do not see in the hero's tragedy, besides the intricate analysis of spiritual motives which it certainly conveys, the melodramatic and blood-thirsty story of revenge which so attracted the Elizabethan public. We shall not grasp *all* of the force of *Macbeth* if we only consider the drama of contrary impulses which moves the hero to his choices against a universal background of redemption and damnation, and forget the simple story of crime and punishment, of the destruction that evil brings upon itself, which is an essential part of the complete effect. Shakespeare's greatest plays have, in reality, something of the universal appeal of myth, of the expression of a universal consciousness deeply implanted in the popular mind and accessible, though in varying degrees and ways, to all levels of society. They appeal in different fashions to different levels of understanding, related to one another by the very fact of their common participation, but not identical. There is something in these great plays for the illiterate as for the intellectual, and it is part of their greatness that the immense field of experience they offer to the latter is still intimately related to the primary emotions which constitute the chief popular appeal of the drama.

Secondly, and possibly even more important: the very structure of the theatre in which these works were shown was such as to concentrate attention, not on a spectacle or on the character interpretation of a single actor, however gifted, but on the *action*, in which the artists appeared on the raised and central platform of the stage as inter-mediaries between the conception of the author and the public, requiring of the latter not only that they watch and listen, but that they participate in the development taking place before them. This sense of *participation*, which had been alive in the Middle Ages as part of a frankly religious manifestation, survived in the sixteenth-century in a form akin to that encouraged by myth and legend. In the case of Shakespeare's great tragedies, we are required to participate in the fortunes of the central protagonist—a king, a hero, deliberately exalted above common humanity—either directly or through the comments and reactions of those who surround him: the result is an emotional effect akin to that to which Aristotle, in his basic treatise on dramatic poetry, gave the name of *katharsis* or purification.

Finally (and here we return to our starting point and justify our proposal to use sensitivity to living language as a point of departure), this essentially public action is *poetic* in nature, though not—I need hardly say—tied to any particular form of versification. In the best works of the Elizabethan theatre poetry, the vehicle of emotion, and the drama into which it flowers constitute a single and inseparable whole, fused in a unity that goes beyond its separate elements and to which we give the name of *poetic drama*. The personal emotions of the poet extend themselves to the public emotions of the theatre, establishing contact with society through the highly conventional and unrealistic medium of the stage. This example has a permanent validity, in so far as the possibilities of the theatre, properly considered, lie primarily neither in psychological accuracy of portrayal nor in realistic truth to the surface appearances of life. They lie, rather, elsewhere. Of all artistic forms, the drama is perhaps the most thoroughly conventional, the one that requires from the author the highest degree of identification with the special conditions which its very existence implies. This apparent limitation can, however, if properly understood and accepted, constitute a source of life; because it permits the poetic impulse, with which it is so intimately related, to flower with the greatest intensity, and because it provides the poet with a field of action that, unequalled in emotional depth, transcends the expression of purely personal sentiment. The dramatic poet is as fully poetic, as intense in his expression of emotion, as any other writer in verse; and, in addition, his chosen form obliges him to pass beyond the purely personal, to aim at the creation of a world that, in so far as it is outside himself, is beyond the accidents and prejudices of his own experience. To create is, artistically speaking, to bring into the light an obscure personal emotion, giving it the external appearance of form; the example of Shakespeare shows us how dramatic necessity can be united, continuously and harmoniously, to the ends of personal expression. The theatrical conventions of to-day have changed in many ways since the sixteenth-century, and we should not wish to re-create them in a spirit of mere historical accuracy; but the permanent lessons of the Shakespearean theatre are still available, still actual, and still waiting to be re-applied.

I

THE EARLY
CHRONICLE PLAYS

1 Henry VI—Part I

THERE IS a tendency among modern writers on Shakespeare to find
the early series of plays on the reign of Henry VI a good deal more
impressive than previous generations would have allowed. Recent
stage revivals[1] have brought out a powerful unity in the general conception, suggesting the presence—once strongly denied—of a single
author in the treatment of the chronicle material of all three plays; and
the discernible variations of style seem more purposeful, more deliberate in their intended effect, than was formerly believed. The author
of these plays, whom we may reasonably concede to have been
Shakespeare, was possibly the first Elizabethan dramatist to make
coherent and meaningful use, on this scale, of chronicle material and, in
the process of so doing, to advance an interpretation of historical events
which, full as it undoubtedly is of traditional and patriotic echoes, is
already notably personal and, moreover, develops remarkably in the
process of its unfolding.[2]

In spite of this revaluation, we may agree that the First Part of
Henry VI is considerably less coherent in its general effect, less marked
by the clear presence of a dominating intention, than the later and more
individual plays that followed. The series opens with a formal evocation of the death of Henry V, and its treatment of subsequent events
turns largely upon two closely related consequences of this loss: on the
one hand, what amounts to a prolonged elegiac lament for the dying
chivalry of England and, on the other, the growth in England itself of
the savage internal rivalry which ruined the great King's patriotic and
warlike achievement. The obsessive presence of these two themes is
conveyed through an episodic, pageant-like conception of drama
which is notably less coherent in its effect than the action of the two

plays to follow: but, whilst we may admit this inferiority, we may yet find the two aspects of this first play more closely and meaningfully interwoven in the development of the action than may immediately appear.

As a first step we may note that Lord Talbot, who is undoubtedly on any account the 'hero' of this first chronicle, is celebrated indeed in his heroism—the messenger in the opening scene refers to him as 'valiant Talbot', 'undaunted spirit', and his whole later history confirms this estimate—but also that the culminating emotional moments of the action are habitually associated with death, so as to constitute a lament for the older generation of English chivalry in the moment of its passing. In this mood, the play shows us the death of Salisbury—'this woeful tragedy' (I. iv. 77)—and that of Bedford—'Undaunted spirit in a dying breast' (III. ii. 99)—both celebrated by Talbot almost in anticipation of his own end. Above all, we are shown Talbot's own death, with which it seems that positive virtue passes finally and irreparably from the life of England:

> How are we *park'd* and *bounded in a pale*,
> A little herd of England's timorous deer,
> Mazed with a yelping kennel of French curs!
> If we be English deer, be then in blood;
> Not rascal-like, to fall down with a pinch,
> But rather, *moody-mad* and *desperate* stags,
> Turn on the bloody hounds with heads of steel
> And make the cowards stand aloof at bay.   (IV. ii. 45)

Not all the stress laid here upon defiant heroism can conceal a sense of desperation, of fighting against hopeless odds; and indeed Talbot's last words, when the moment to pronounce them inexorably faces him, balance the craving for immortality against a persistent, almost obsessive sense of vanity and impermanence, which will later receive much finer expression in the final speech of the dying Hotspur:

> Thou *antic death*, which laugh'st us here to scorn,
> Anon, from thy *insulting tyranny*,
> Coupled in bonds of *perpetuity*,
> Two Talbots, winged through the lither sky,
> In thy *despite* shall 'scape *mortality*.   (IV. vii. 18)[3]

For perhaps the first of many occasions, more particularly when a reaction against 'mutability', the prospect of annihilation, is in question, a Shakespearean character seems to be engaged here in asserting emphatically the opposite of what he knows to be reality. The positive affirmation towards which Talbot's declaration ostensibly tends is flawed by its own rhetoric, felt to be poised finally against emptiness; we can hardly avoid feeling in these lines the presence of a persistent note of tragic irony which is surely close to the real, the truly intimate spirit of the general conception.

It is in accordance with this spirit, indeed, that even the emphatic celebration of Talbot's warlike virtues exists side by side throughout with a stressed and unnatural ferocity. This is the note which emerges in his threat to the citizens of Bordeaux—

> if you frown upon this proffer'd peace,
> You tempt the fury of my three attendants,
> Lean famine, quartering steel, and climbing fire—   (IV. ii. 9)

where we may feel that he anticipates Henry V before Harfleur,[4] and which, more crudely, finds expression more than once in the savagery of the earlier action:

> Your hearts I'll stamp out with my horse's heels,
> And make a quagmire of your mingled brains;   (I. iv. 108)

the same which is again reflected, in another context, in his description of his breaking loose from captivity:

> Then broke I from the officers that led me,
> And with my nails digg'd stones out of the ground,
> To hurl at the beholders of my shame:
> My grisly countenance made others fly;
> None durst come near for fear of sudden death.
> In iron walls they deem'd me not secure;
> So great fear of my name 'mongst them was spread
> That they supposed I could rend bars of steel,
> And spurn in pieces posts of adamant.   (I. iv. 44)

No doubt we should be unwise to modernize unduly the spirit of lines such as these. Much in them answers to the typical rant of the 'old play', beloved of the Elizabethan groundlings; but, equally surely, we should do wrong to equate Shakespeare's effects here simply with those called forth by those around him, or fail to respond to the presence in this speech of something more, a note of precariousness, a sense of civilized life as balanced on the edge of savagery in a way which the later terms in this series of plays will amply and with full consciousness confirm.

For it is a fact that, Talbot apart, the emphasis throughout this first play is clearly upon a consistent savagery in the living which contrasts with the occasional and precarious chivalry of the dead. It is a savagery, moreover, which stands in the closest relationship to degradation and despair. The squandering by England of her traditional heritage in France is paralleled by bitter quarrelling at home, and Talbot himself is successively the victim of betrayal, first at the hands of the ignoble Fastolfe and then, more gravely, at those of York and Somerset, each exclusively dedicated to the pursuit of his selfish ends (IV. iii, iv). As a result of these divisions victory, won habitually by deceit, falls as though by default to their weak and superstitious foes. Shakespeare's presentation of the French in this play is, indeed, for all its crudity, occasionally more subtle than has sometimes been believed: more subtle even, possibly, than he himself was altogether prepared to recognize. In a play largely devoted to the celebration of Talbot, in whom something of the patriotic virtue of Henry V survives, there could be no place for anything like a modern reading of Joan of Arc. She is accordingly shown in a grotesquely unfavourable light, as devil-inspired, lecherous, and consumed by vanity. Oddly enough, however, we may note even here an occasional moment of greater depth, as though in evasion of the author's plainly declared intention. This is notably apparent in the surprisingly eloquent tone of the lament which she utters over her country's ruin:

> Look on thy country, look on fertile France,
> And see the cities and the towns defaced
> By wasting ruin of the cruel foe.
> As looks the mother on her lowly babe
> When death doth close his tender dying eyes,
> See, see, the pining malady of France.   (III. iii. 44)

The horror and the vanity of war is a theme which rarely failed to move Shakespeare to eloquence, and it is not altogether fanciful to find here a first anticipation, dim and distant indeed, of Burgundy's far greater speech, in *Henry V*,[5] upon the waste which follows upon armed conflict. Scarcely less unexpected is the force, relative though it is, with which Joan is allowed at the last to denounce the vices of her English enemies:

> you, that are polluted with your lusts,
> Stain'd with the guiltless blood of innocents,
> Corrupt and tainted with a thousand vices,

Because you want the grace that others have,
You judge it straight a thing impossible
To compass wonders but by help of devils. (V. iv. 43)

We should not, of course, overstress these apparent anomalies in relation to the play's more obvious purposes: but we may feel that they
foreshadow, even at this early date and in this, one of the most unsubtle
of his plays, something of the characteristic Shakespearean balance and
detachment, that they may show a deeper conception in the process of
coming to life, however tentatively and even incongruously, in the act
of writing.

Perhaps most notable of all, however, in its relation to the later parts
of the series, is the tendency, already observable in this First Part, to
balance pathos against irony. The Henry VI of this play is a marginal
and ineffective figure, not yet endowed to any significant degree with
the tragic depth to which he will later, on occasions, arise; but already a
few of his utterances point beyond weakness and incapacity to a deeper
truth which few of those around him show any sign of grasping:

O, think upon the conquest of my father,
My tender years, and let us not forgo
That for a trifle that was bought with blood. (IV. i. 148)

As a comment on the savage squabbling between the rival 'roses',
which provides the play with one of its most effective scenes (II. iv),
this is not without point. Pathos again, though of a different kind,
makes its presence felt in the words of the imprisoned and helpless
Mortimer, 'Swift-winged with desire to get a grave' (II. v. 15). The
death-wish, indeed, is strong in many parts of this play, and against it is
set, persistently and in disturbing contrast, a notably sardonic quality in
the mutual abusings of the lords and churchmen who so short-
sightedly and rapaciously indulge their absorbing appetite for power:

—Gloucester, thou wilt answer this before the pope.
—Winchester goose, I cry, a rope! a rope!; (I. iii. 52)

attitudes which are contrasted again with the ineffective and despairing
commonsense which prompts the Mayor of London, in the course of
the same scene, to cry: 'Good God, these nobles should such stomachs
bear!' and to reveal his own pacific nature in his wry comment:
'I myself fight not once in forty year' (I. iii. 92). Even La Pucelle
contributes, in her own inelegant way, to an effect of the same kind
when she says of the body of the Lord Talbot, lying at her feet,

> Him that thou magnifiest with all these titles
> Stinking and *fly-blown* lies here at our feet.   (IV. vii. 75)

Once more, we should not overstress the significance of this, answering
as it does closely enough to an avowedly popular mood: but it may not
be altogether fanciful to see at this point something of the spirit of
the future Thersites[6] casting a passing shadow over this earlier and
immeasurably less subtle play.

2   Henry VI—Part II

The above account suggests that *Henry VI, Part I* is, in the main, a crude
piece distinguished by occasional moments of insight. *Part II* is, beyond
reasonable dispute, a more closely-knit and purposeful performance.
Its starting-point is the marriage of the unfortunate Henry VI to Margaret of Anjou, engineered in the course of the previous play by the
Earl of Suffolk, whose last words as the curtain fell on the action of
Part I provide a link with what is to come:

> Margaret shall now be queen, and rule the king;
> But I will rule both her, the king and realm.   (*Part I*, V. v. 107)

The results of the mixture of ambition and lasciviousness thus cynically
revealed dominate the course of the new play.

The first consequence of this unhappy union is the shameful renunciation by Henry VI of those rights in France which his father had so
gloriously maintained and for which Talbot had fought and died.
As Gloucester, who now becomes the mouthpiece of the traditional and
patriotic order, puts it in his rhetorical question,

> Shall Henry's conquest, Bedford's vigilance,
> Your deeds of war and all our counsel die?   (I. i. 97)

The second result, which follows logically from all that has gone before,
is the revival of the 'ancient bickerings' of the outraged and egoistic
lords against the justly hated person of Suffolk; the Cardinal, whom we
saw in no favourable light in *Part I*, gives vent to his intense hatred of
Gloucester, whom Buckingham and Somerset in turn distrust, seeing
in him an obstacle to their own progress towards the power which they
crave for themselves. Beyond these quarrels, which have been carried
over from the earlier play, a new and ultimately more sinister force

declares itself for the first time through the early soliloquies of the Duke of York, who now announces—though to himself alone—that 'A day will come when York shall claim his own' and who is ready to bide his time in the expectation of his opportunity: 'Then, York, be still awhile, till time do serve' (I. i. 249). In the declaration of his secret motives through soliloquy, and in his readiness to wait for the action of time to reveal itself on his side, York represents forces that have no precedent in this series of plays. His reflections, with their novel sense of poise and self-awareness, mark the entry into the series, and indeed into Shakespeare's work, of a new political consciousness which, vastly developed, will eventually produce Richard Crookback[7] and, further still beyond him, illuminate certain aspects of characters as different as Iago and Edmund. The conception represented by York is already beyond the reach of *Henry VI, Part I*; and side by side with it, on a lower level of society, we are shown the new craving for self-advancement inspiring John Hume in his insistent desire for wealth: '*Sort how it will*, I shall have gold for all' (I. ii. 107). Here, expressed in plain and simple terms, is the motivation of the new and exclusive driving energy which has everywhere replaced patriotic chivalry as a guide in life.

In this new world, Gloucester stands, in growing isolation, for loyalty and the rule of law, as Suffolk, Beaufort, and Buckingham join in snarling against him. His essential virtue is revealed on different levels in a series of episodes which amount between them to a projection of the state of English society. His exercise of justice is portrayed in his resolution of the dispute between Horner and his apprentice Peter (I. iii; II. iii), which is in itself conceived as a commentary upon the aristocratic bickerings which surround the throne, his grasp of truth appears in his exposure of the false 'miracle' at St. Albans (II. i), and his personal integrity is shown by his readiness to allow justice to punish his own intriguing wife whom he urges to repent (II. iv). The last of these incidents throws perhaps the clearest light upon his character and his situation. When Elinor, in the moment of her humiliation, warns him bitterly and truly of the 'snares' which his enemies are preparing against him, he replies declaring his readiness to take his stand upon the law:

> I must offend before I be attainted;
> And had I twenty times so many foes,
> And each of them had twenty times their power,
> All these could not procure me any scathe,
> So long as I am loyal, true and crimeless.   (II. iv. 59)

Gloucester's attitude, here and throughout the play, is unexceptionable, and represents in Shakespearean terms the only possible guarantee for an ordered and humane polity; but in the political world which this play is concerned to present it is also singularly vulnerable.

Gloucester, indeed, for all his virtue and integrity—even, we may say, on account of these—is a man whose attitudes are out of date in the world in which he so disturbingly finds himself. The new Queen and his own fellow nobles see him as 'insolent', 'proud', and 'peremptory', presuming upon the virtues which, whilst he maintains his authority, bar their own paths to advancement. They accuse him of their own 'rancorous minds', see him as 'smoothe Duke Humphrey', assert of him—in terms which later Shakespearean politicians will make their own[8]—that 'By flattery hath he won the commons' hearts' (III. i. 28). Against the background provoked by the bitter news of the loss of France, York, seeing that his hour has struck, makes bold to arrest him for treason, and the only reply Gloucester can offer is an exposure of the bitter realities of the present:

> Virtue is choked with foul ambition,
> And charity chased hence by rancour's hand ...
> Beaufort's red sparkling eyes blab his heart's malice,
> And Suffolk's cloudy brow his stormy hate;
> Sharp Buckingham unburthens with his tongue
> The envious load that lies upon his heart;
> And dogged York, that reaches at the moon,
> Whose overweening arm I have pluck'd back,
> By false accuse doth level at my life.   (III. i. 143)

In its incisive intensity and truth to character this is writing of a new kind, and answers as such to a fresh vision of public realities in a world from which all sanctions, human and traditional alike, have been debarred; and in the unhappy King's reaction to his faithful servant's plight, a reaction which his wife Margaret dismisses as so much 'foolish pity',[9] Henry himself moves a little nearer to the centre of the stage, shows signs of becoming a tragic rather than merely an ineffectual figure. Shakespeare is beginning in this play to consider a problem which will exercise him in later and greater works: the problem represented by the existence of the 'good' man in a political order from which pity and humanity have been deliberately excluded. We may agree that Henry remains, as King, ineffectual, whilst sensing also that efficiency, in a world where the appetite for power imposes itself as a

uniquely absorbing imperative, seems more and more to imply the
sacrifice of common humanity and thereby to forge the circumstances
of its own doom.

From the moment of Gloucester's arrest, indeed, the plunge of
society into dissolution is most tensely and realistically conveyed. The
Cardinal, his chief enemy, ruthlessly brushes aside the law to obtain his
death:

> No more of him, for I will deal with him,
> That henceforth he shall trouble us no more;   (III. i. 323)

and this resolution is ferociously commended by the Queen. The Irish
are reported to have risen in rebellion. York, entrusted with the mission
of suppressing them, exposes the 'policy' of those who are glad to
see him away and commends—once more in soliloquy—his own
treacherous determination:

> I fear me, you but warm the starved snake,
> Who, cherish'd in your breasts, will sting your hearts,   (III. i. 343)

as he stresses his consuming desire to obtain 'the *golden* circuit' of which
he obsessively dreams. To this end, he proposes to stir up a movement
of popular rebellion, making use of Cade as an unconscious tool for ends
of his own. A new political force, cunning and thoroughly amoral,
exclusively concentrated upon its desire for power, is moving further
towards its assertive self-awareness.

Gloucester's tragic end is soon reported (III. ii) as the inevitable
culmination of so much savagery. The unhappy King laments his loss,
admitting the self-deception which has helped to bring it about, and the
Queen turns upon him the full ferocity of her disdainful reproach:
'Is all thy comfort shut in Gloucester's tomb?' (III. ii. 78). In uttering
this question, she speaks more truly than she knows, for we shall soon
see that, with Gloucester, hope itself is about to die in Henry's stricken
realm. As a first step the people, hitherto passive in their loyalty, are
reported to have risen 'like an angry hive of bees'; from this turning-
point, we look forward to the full fury of anarchy unleashed. Meanwhile, the horror of Warwick's description of Gloucester's murdered
corpse answers, beyond mere melodrama, to the prevailing spirit of
the action:

> But see, his face is black and full of blood,
> His eye-balls further out than when he lived,
> Staring full ghastly like a strangled man;

His hair uprear'd, his nostrils stretch'd with struggling;
His hands abroad display'd, as one that grasp'd
And tugg'd for life and was by strength subdued;   (III. ii. 168)

whilst Suffolk, openly accused of murder, answers his accusers with plain and ferocious defiance:

here's a vengeful sword, rusted with ease,
That shall be scoured in his rancorous heart
That slanders me with murder's crimson badge.   (III. ii. 198)

By contrast the people, though driven at last to revolt, rise in a mood which is still one of desperation, in 'mere instinct of love and loyalty' (III. ii. 250). The Queen, on the other hand, is exclusively devoted to the pursuit of her own appetites. She pleads against the banishment of Suffolk, in which she sees the intolerable loss of her lover; and, once she has been deprived of the object of her desire, she is ready in her baffled rage to call upon the forces of 'mischance and sorrow' to ruin all alike. Suffolk's answering outburst, in turn, is more than an expression of spleen, proceeds, as he himself confesses, from the intensity of his thwarted passion: as he tells his royal mistress,

where thou art, there is the world itself,
With every several pleasure in the world,
And where thou art not, desolation.   (III. ii. 362)

As a final contribution to this accumulation of horrors, and in fitting response to the description of the dead Gloucester, we are given the picture of Beaufort, the most ruthless of his enemies, lying on his own deathbed in what we may reasonably call a dim anticipation of Macbeth's later and far more subtle guilt:

Died he not in his bed? where should he die?
Can I make men live, whether they will or no?
O, torture me no more! I will confess.
Alive again? then show me where he is:
I'll give a thousand pound to look upon him.
He hath no eyes, the dust hath blinded them.
Comb down his hair: look, look, it stands upright,
Like lime-twigs set to catch my winged soul.   (III. iii. 9)

Death comes habitually, in this play, unnaturally and horribly, the appropriate reflection of unnatural horror in the behaviour of evil and short-sighted men.

The rest of the play, which is seen in this way to be centred upon Gloucester's criminal murder, brings an appropriate retribution upon those who have contrived it for ends of their own. The guilty and supremely worthless Suffolk dies at the hands of a mere anonymous Captain. Before he is despatched, his vain appeal in the name of the 'noble' blood which his conduct has so consistently belied receives an adequate answer:

> Pool! Sir Pool! lord!
> Ay, kennel, puddle, sink; whose filth and dirt
> Troubles the silver spring where England drinks.
> Now will I dam up this thy yawning mouth,
> For swallowing the treasure of the realm:
> Thy lips that kiss'd the queen shall sweep the ground;
> And thou that smild'st at good Duke Humphrey's death
> Against the senseless winds shalt grin in vain.   (IV. i. 70)

Meanwhile, in Cade's rebellion, the principal theme of the following episodes, the historical panorama is notably broadened as the populace that once listened loyally to Gloucester, and applauded his judgements, degenerates into the uncontrolled and predatory mob. The transformation, indeed, is not a pretty one, and Shakespeare does not spare us its brutal significance; but, in considering its full impact, we should not forget that it was York who originally instigated Cade to rise in the pursuit of ends of his own. Clearly enough, the rebellion now afoot is a repudiation of law, learning, society, and natural order. As such it is beyond all possible defence; but it is proper to add that its manifestations, savage and brutal as they are, are yet the response of the people to the brutality and savagery so amply displayed by their supposed 'betters'. The people, indeed, even in the moment of their rage, still revere the memory of Henry V and recognize that England is 'maimed', broken by the conflict in which they participate; though we must add that their own shame is revealed in the ignorance which drives them to the slaying of Lord Say for no better reason that his 'speaking Latin' (IV. vii). Adrift in this sea of desperate and meaningless conflict the king is reduced still further to helplessness, whilst his Queen is glimpsed, gruesomely but with a dreadful fittingness, avidly and passionately clutching Suffolk's severed head (IV. iv).

Rebellion, indeed, is seen in the concluding scenes of this sombre action engaged in generating its own gathering excess, following to their logical conclusion its perverse laws of negation. Cade orders the

records of the realm to be burnt and, as he does so, makes his own full
assertion of anarchy:

> The proudest peer in the realm shall not wear a head on his shoulders, unless
> he pay me tribute; there shall not a maid be married, but she shall pay to me
> her maidenhead ere they have it: men shall hold me *in capite*: and we charge
> and command that their wives be as free as heart can wish or tongue can
> tell. (IV. vii. 125)

In the idiom of this play, this represents anarchy bent upon the satisfaction of its baser instincts, exulting in the immediate prospect of
destruction. Cade '*in capite*', using the power he proposes to seize for
the satisfaction of his baser instincts, is a dreadful parody of true
authority. No political realism, however, accompanies the people in
their headlong career, and so Clifford, as the emissary of the established
'order', finds it easy to separate the rebel leader from his followers by a
rhetorical appeal to the patriotic memory of Henry V. The people
waver in their response, much as they will do later to the rhetoric of
Mark Antony in *Julius Caesar*.[10] They finally abandon the cause of
Cade, who is left a man out of his depth indeed, betrayed and brought
to an ignominious end, but not altogether a sinister figure in his fall; for
with his dying breath he is able to assert that he has been the victim of
adverse circumstances, that 'famine and no other hath slain me'
(IV. x. 63).

At the end of so much bloodshed and ruin, the way is left clear for
York, who has been shrewd enough to foresee this moment and to
bring it about:

> From Ireland thus comes York to claim his right,
> And pluck the crown from feeble Henry's head. (V. i. 1)

'Let them obey that know not how to rule' (V. i. 6): this is the voice of
a new political spirit, and if it implies a real criticism of Henry's weak
and helpless rule, it is none the less true that it will, in due course, bring
an appropriate doom upon its own head. The content of York's
ambition is already implicit in his own words:

> This hand was made to handle nought but *gold*.
> I cannot give due action to my words,
> Except a sword or sceptre balance it:
> A sceptre shall it have, have I a *soul*. (V. i. 7)

The equation of the impulses of the 'soul' with the craving for a
'sceptre' and the power that goes with it: the consuming obsession with

'gold' which York, echoing that already expressed, in more humble terms, by Hume,[11] now raises to the level of the crown: these things, taken together, represent the strength and the final limitation of the new political spirit. Its immediate manifestation is the clash between York and Somerset and the confrontation of Clifford and Warwick. Clifford refers to his rival scornfully in vivid terms of bear-baiting—

> Are these thy bears? we'll bait thy bears to death
> And manacle the bear-ward in their chains—   (V. i. 148)

even as he calls York's son Richard a 'foul undigested lump' (V. i. 157), in a graphic reference charged with menace for the future. The King is left pathetically in the middle of the disputing factions, bemoaning with bitter truth the death of natural virtue—

> O, where is faith? O, where is loyalty?
> If it be banished from the frosty head,
> Where shall it find a harbour in the earth?—   (V. i. 166)

but helpless to impose any semblance of order upon a world empty of valid restraints: a world where the general reaction is summed up in the tone of Richard's final snarl to young Clifford:

> —   . . . you shall sup with Jesu Christ to-night.
> —Foul stigmatic, that's more than thou canst tell.
> —If not in heaven, you'll surely sup in hell. (V. i. 214)

On the battlefield at St. Albans, to which all this implacable rivalry naturally leads, and as York kills Clifford, the victim's son reflects the spirit of this entire action by his final dedication, made against a background of universal anarchy, to war and revenge:

> Fear frames disorder, and disorder wounds
> Where it should guard.   (V. ii. 32)

Such, concisely and intensely stated, is the state of the world, and the only response to it which the speaker can conceive is expressed in terms of a dedication which can only seek to cover ultimate emptiness. 'Let no soldier fly', cries Clifford in his despair, and goes on:

> He that is truly dedicate to war
> Hath no self-love, nor he that loves himself
> Hath not essentially, but by circumstance,
> The name of valour. (V. ii. 37)

Dedication, accordingly, is to be the order of the day, perhaps because outside the gesture of dedication there lies only the prospect of chaos and meaningless disaster; but, we must surely find ourselves asking, dedication to what? The answer is—to nothing, to a vision of general ruin in a world conceived of as beyond remedy vile and worthless. As Clifford goes on to say, clothing his natural grief in a universal resentment:

> O, let the *vile* world end,
> And the premised flames of the last day
> Knit earth and heaven together!
> Now let the general trumpet blow his blast,
> Particularities and petty sounds
> To cease! (V. ii. 40)

This in turn gives way to the speaker's renewed thought of the death of his father, ruthlessly slaughtered, against all the natural pieties, 'in his chair-days': a thought which leads directly to the final statement of appalling and inhuman resolve:

> Even at this sight
> My heart is turn'd to stone: and while 'tis mine,
> It shall be stony. York not our old men spares;
> No more will I their babes: tears virginal
> Shall be to me even as the dew to fire,
> And beauty that the tyrant oft reclaims
> Shall to my flaming wrath be oil and flax.
> Henceforth I will not have to do with pity. (V. ii. 49)

The final statement, with each word brief and tense in its separation, sounds its note of iron in a world of desolation. York's dedication to the ends of power and personal glory have bred at this point their logical and necessary answer. As Clifford declares the turning of his heart, thus unnaturally in the flower of his youth, to the quality of stone, his words look forward to the savage slaughter of Rutland, and of York himself, in the play to follow. Richard, on his side, echoes with his words what has become the pervading spirit of the entire action: 'Priests pray for enemies, but princes kill' (V. ii. 71). As the play ends, Clifford affirms once more his determination to continue the struggle, utters his ambiguous prayer for the future: 'more such days as these to us befall' (V. iii. 33). Many more, indeed, and even more full of unmitigated horror, there are to be.

3 Henry VI—Part III

Enough will have been said by now to suggest that Shakespeare's initial series of plays on English history is more consistent in its design, more purposeful in its presentation of events, than has sometimes been recognized. It foreshadows, indeed, not a few of the points which later plays were to develop. Roughly speaking, it may be said that the *Henry VI* plays turn upon two separate political ideas, each of them amply reflected in the literature of the age. The first of these was the traditional belief, derived from a great body of mediaeval thought and colouring the familiar mediaeval view of tragedy, that sin committed by the individual is eventually repaid in the form of retribution upon the sinner; the second, more modern in its implications and supremely reflected for the sixteenth century in the writings of Machiavelli, relates the prevalence of disorder in the state to elements of weakness and indecision in the attitude of its ruler. Both these notions are developed, insistently and side by side, through the various stages of this series. The first finds expression in the ultimate fate of nearly all the principal contendants for power; and the figure of Henry VI in some sense serves to join the two, since it is clear that he is at once a good man, against whom sin is almost continuously committed, and a feeble ruler who is disposed at times, moreover, to admit that his own claim to the throne is in some respects uncertain.

However this may be, it is clear, as the curtain rises upon *Part III*, that the disorder so thoroughly traced in the preceding plays is everywhere rampant and victorious. The bloody victors of St. Albans display their grisly trophy, the head of Somerset, whilst Richard utters his ominous threats against the King himself: 'Thus do I hope to shake King Henry's head' (I. i. 20). York's attitude at the moment of his triumph finds expression in his own words: 'By words or blows here let us win our right', and his son urges him to 'be resolute' in the pursuit of his ends. On the other side, and scarcely less ominously, Clifford 'mourns in steel', whilst in the middle Henry stands helplessly, recognizing, even as Richard calls upon York to 'tear the crown from the usurper's head', that his own title is 'weak'. As the majority of the nobles turn away from a King who thus stands revealed as unready to defend his own rights Clifford, still dedicated to anarchy and the prospect of revenge, swears to support him 'right or wrong'; whilst Henry, in an impossible gesture of weakness which his Queen at once sees for what it is, seeks peace for himself and his realm by offering the crown to York, 'after my decease' (I. i. 175).

The driving-force of the action, however, is by now increasingly concentrated upon the person of Richard, in whom the elements of passion and savagery which everywhere prevail around him appear to have grown to self-conscious and ominous maturity. In this, indeed, he is seen to be his father's son. His desire for power outdoes that of York in emotional intensity—

> How sweet a thing it is to wear a crown;
> Within whose circuit is Elysium,
> And all that poets feign of bliss and joy—

as it rises to the ferocious dedication of his conclusion:

> I cannot rest
> Until the white rose that I wear be dyed
> Even in the lukewarm blood of Henry's heart.   (I. ii. 29)

It is perhaps not without meaning that Richard associates the lure of the crown with the 'feigning' of poets and so, in a certain sense, with delusion; but it is, at all events, a delusion to which he is passionately and irrevocably committed. Many other personages in this series of plays have *thought* in this way, or something very like it; but none, with the partial exception of York, have declared their motives with this remarkable blend of intense passion and cool clear-sightedness. For this reason alone, if for no other, the immediate future belongs to Richard.

A situation in which motives of this kind so exclusively prevail can only end in slaughter, and this bleak necessity is immediately fulfilled at Wakefield. Clifford at last obtains the revenge to which he has dedicated himself by killing Rutland, 'this innocent child', after he has torn him from his tutor's arms. As he declares in the moment of this macabre triumph, revealing once more the obsessive nature of his motivation:

> The sight of any of the house of York
> Is as a fury to torment my soul;
> And till I root out their accursed line
> And leave not one alive, I live in hell.   (I. iii. 30)

Not, however, until York has himself fallen into his captor's power is the full extent of the ferocity of his enemies revealed. Even in this series of plays, where savagery pressed to its ultimate limits is the habitual order of the day, the baiting of York on his mole-hill adorned with his 'paper crown' in what appears to be a sardonic parody of the Passion of Christ, stands out uniquely in the supreme bitterness of Margaret's revengeful taunting:

> Where are your mess of sons to back you now?
> The wanton Edward, and the lusty George?
> And where's that valiant crook-back prodigy,
> Dicky your boy, that with his grumbling voice
> Was wont to cheer his dad in mutinies? . . .
> Why art thou patient, man? thou shouldst be mad;
> And I, to make thee mad, do mock thee thus.
> Stamp, rave, and fret, that I may sing and dance.
> Thou would'st be fee'd, I see, to make me sport:
> York cannot speak, unless he wear a crown.
> A crown for York! and, lords, bow low to him:
> Hold you his hands, whilst I do set it on.
> Ay, marry, sir, now looks he like a king!   (I. iv. 73)

In these mockings, conceived with an almost visual intensity worthy, in another artistic order, of Hieronymus Bosch or Breughel, there is brought home to us the Nemesis that has appropriately followed upon York's consuming lust for power. It is the same which, in the not long delayed fulness of time, will also bring retribution upon his killers.

Revenge, indeed, begins to take shape at once in the reflections of Richard whose purposes, firm in the acceptance of anarchy as the inescapable law of life and self-consciously dedicated to the ends of power, seek to grow now to the full stature which they will reach by the end of the play. His thoughts at this point are steeped in a detached, even an ironic estimate, of his situation:

> I cannot weep; for all my body's moisture
> Scarce serves to quench my furnace-burning heart:
> Nor can my tongue unload my heart's great burthen;
> For selfsame wind that I should speak withal
> Is kindling coals that fires all my breast,
> And burns me up with flames that tears would quench.
> To weep is to make less the depth of grief:
> Tears then for babes; blows and revenge for me!   (II. i. 79)

This is the definitive birth of a force which York's earlier soliloquies had only foreshadowed, but which now gathers up all the preceding savagery into the power of its concentrated drive.

In contrast to so much dedicated ferocity, the King maintains his precarious foothold, moved by pity to appear a figure at once tragic and politically inept. When Clifford, the latest of his mentors, sweeps aside the motions of compassion:—

> To whom do lions cast their gentle looks?
> Not to the beast that would usurp their den—   (II. ii. 11)

his answer is a significant inversion of a phrase later to be used by Macbeth: 'things ill-got had ever bad success'[12]: the expression, indeed, of a true philosophy, as the course of events will eventually show, but of one which is tragically impotent to influence the immediate present. And so from Wakefield we are brought to Towton, where Clifford once again affirms his brutal dedication to revenge— 'This is the hand that stabb'd thy father York' (II. iv. 6)—whilst Henry utters in terms of pastoral nostalgia an elegiac lament which we need not dismiss as simply ineffectual:

> Gives not the hawthorn bush a sweeter shade
> To shepherds looking on their silly sheep,
> Than doth a rich embroider'd canopy
> To kings that fear their subjects' treachery?   (II. v. 42)

This is no doubt the expression of a hopeless, even finally an irresponsible desire to abdicate, a renunciation from which a King is debarred by the very nature of the office he has assumed. For his refusal to accept responsibility Henry may, as a political figure, fairly be condemned. Machiavelli's 'unarmed prophet'[13] can properly be exposed as such, on Machiavelli's terms; but, in blaming him, we shall also respond to the tragedy implied, in this same scene, by the patterned atrocities unwittingly committed by father against son and son against father, atrocities which lay stress upon a world pitilessly dedicated to self-destruction. Time, however, in these plays, waits for no man. Having uttered his lament, the King is obliged to flee before his victorious enemies and Clifford, his incongruous support, recognizes that

> The foe is merciless, and will not pity;
> For at their hands I have deserved no pity.   (II. vi. 25)

It is now Clifford's turn to die, but whereas he was afforded the opportunity—as we may now remember—to insult, in the person of York, his living enemy, York's sons, Edmund and Richard, joined to

Warwick, can only claim the lesser satisfaction of offering outrage upon his lifeless corpse. The note of sardonic frustration which runs through their insults answers very closely to the present spirit of the action.

From the open savagery of battle we pass immediately to that, more disguised but not on that account less vicious in its implications, which rules the political game. The helpless King, found by the hunters who see in him a welcome if unexpected prey, is taken prisoner in 'the thick-grown brake' (III. i. 1). Meanwhile Edward, the newly-crowned and lascivious King, is engaged in wooing the Lady Grey, a kind of 'merry widow' whose eye is firmly fixed upon her own advancement, whilst his brothers ironically look on. Richard, indeed, already desires Edward's ruin in the pursuit of his own ambitions:

> Would he were wasted, marrow, bones and all,
> That from his loins no hopeful branch may spring,
> To cross me from the golden time I look for! (III. ii. 125)

The expression of this desire is followed by a soliloquy in which the speaker contemplates himself, as he examines his motives, in a characteristic mood of ironic detachment:

> Why, love forswore me in my mother's womb:
> And, for I should not deal in her soft laws,
> She did corrupt frail nature with some bribe,
> To shrink mine arm up like a wither'd shrub;
> To make an envious mountain on my back,
> Where sits deformity to mock my body;
> To shape my legs of an unequal size:
> To disproportion me in every part,
> Like to a chaos, or an unlick'd bear-whelp
> That carries no impression like the dam.
> And am I then a man to be beloved? (III. ii. 153)[14]

The speech, like others which Richard will utter in the later stages of his history, implies an effort to turn deficiency, exclusion from the normal order, into a kind of superiority. It opens with an admission that the speaker feels himself deprived by a trick of invidious fate from the gentle influence of 'love' and considers himself accordingly free from the human obligation to correspond to what he dismisses, with an attempted sneer, as 'her *soft* laws', as a corrupting force acting upon 'frail nature'. In asserting his superiority to this 'frailty' Richard seeks, indeed, a compensation for his exclusion from a human order which, even as he affects to despise it, he in fact envies: but the stress which his own words lay, almost obsessively, upon 'deformity', 'disproportion', 'chaos', and upon their physical reflection in his own body, show clearly enough where the true inspiration of so much confidence and self-sufficiency lies. It is enough to make of Richard, not merely a 'Machiavellian' villain rejoicing in his own capacity to hurt, but the most mature character creation that Shakespeare had at this early stage in his career achieved.

The conclusion to so much keen self-scrutiny is, on the surface at least, the comforting one which the speaker desires. It amounts to a readiness to find congenial the reality which originally moved him to complain against his fate: the reality that the pursuit of power is in effect the only path left open to him:

> since this earth affords no joy to me,
> But to command, to check, to o'erbear such
> As are of better person than myself,
> I'll make my heaven to dream upon the crown,
> And, whiles I live, to account this world but hell,
> Until my mis-shaped trunk that bears this head
> Be round impaled with a glorious crown.   (III. ii. 165)

We need not deny the force of this 'dream', which amounts to an intensifying of York's earlier identification of the crown, the symbol of power, with the richness and the glitter of 'gold'.[15] It is a 'dream' which will bring Richard to the attainment of the ends which his nature craves before finally destroying it. Already, however, the sense that emerges from this, his first fully revealing soliloquy, is that of a monstrous birth, the projection of his own twisted origins into his subsequent career in a world upon which, precisely because it rejects him as 'unnatural', he is determined to impose himself. There is meaning in the self-comparison which uses images finally associated with the evocation of a painful, a monstrous labour, to convey the picture of himself as a kind of beast thrusting through the dense tangles of a wood to emerge to his own kind of disillusioned clarity:

> I, —like one lost in a thorny wood,
> That rends the thorns and is rent with the thorns,
> Seeking a way and straying from the way;
> Not knowing how to find the open air,
> But toiling desperately to find it out,—
> Torment myself to catch the English crown:
> And from that torment I will free myself,
> Or hew my way out with a bloody axe.   (III. ii. 174)

No simple moral explanation can cover the impression which these words of self-analysis convey. What is suggested here is, indeed, something very like a grotesque parody of the natural processes of birth. Richard feels himself a man 'lost', caught in the 'thorns' which surround and tear him as he struggles to free himself, 'straying from the way' in spite of the intensity of his efforts to find it: a man caught by his own admission in a situation which has elements of claustrophobia about it and seeking, even 'toiling desperately' to find the 'open air', turning his inescapable disability into the 'torment' which his absorbing search for power implies. If the 'bloody axe' is the instrument to his hands, which he will wield with ruthless confidence against rivals for the most part as evil, and far more stupid, than himself, it is one which will never bring him to that 'freedom', that liberation from the 'torment' of ambition which he recognizes in himself and which constitutes, even beyond his own understanding, the tragic contradiction of his nature. Such is the 'explanation', psychologically a good deal more complex than its immediate presentation may suggest, which at this point brings Richard to the surface confidence of his final, consciously 'Machiavellian' declaration of political self-sufficiency:

> I can add colours to the chameleon,
> Change shapes with Proteus for advantages,
> And set the murderous Machiavel to school.
> Can I do this, and cannot get a crown?
> Tut, were it further off, I'll pluck it down. (III. ii. 191)

The scene (III. iii) that follows this crucial declaration is, appropriately, an exposure of 'realist' diplomacy in its relation to unconfessed personal motives of passion and craving for power. As such, it too may be said to break new ground which Shakespeare will abundantly cultivate in later plays. Lewis of France, with claims of his own discreetly in view, greets Henry's exiled Queen and promises her relief; but when Warwick enters, representing the present power of Edward, he turns his attention cautiously to the newcomer:

> Is Edward your true king? for I were loath
> To link with him that were not lawful chosen,   (III. iii. 114)

before adding the still more loaded question: 'Is he gracious in the people's eye?'. This is, in fact, a politician whose thoughts are firmly set upon his own possible advantage. Inspired by these considerations, Lewis agrees to give his sister Bona in marriage to Edward, only to learn as soon as he has done so that the royal lecher who now sits on the

English throne has contracted marriage with the widow in whose
pursuit he has been engaged at home. In view of this rebuff Margaret is
restored to the French King's favour, and joined by Warwick in repudiation of the offence to his self-esteem. The movement of the scene, as
Warwick and Margaret, who began it as rivals, are joined in friendship,
is not without subtlety: 'Warwick, these words have turned my hate to
love' (III. iii. 199). The new alliance is at once cemented by the
betrothing of Warwick's eldest daughter at the shortest notice to
Margaret's son[16]; but the best comment on this move in the political
game is provided by Warwick himself, when he frankly declares his
own motives:

> Not that I pity Henry's misery,
> But seek revenge on Edward's mockery.   (III. iii. 264)

Meanwhile, back in England, Richard and his temporary associate
Clarence are equally frank in their ironic comments on Edward's
incontinence and on his 'well-chosen' bride (IV. i. 7); as Richard
puts it:

> God forbid that I should wish them sever'd,
> Whom God hath join'd together.   (IV. i. 21)

It is against this presentation of public realities, ironic in its detachment,
that the action is ready to move to its conclusion.

As an initial step in this process, Edward, whom Richard has first
captured and then released, wins the city of York by a stratagem upon
which Richard himself (who more appropriately, indeed?) makes this
typical comment:

> when the fox hath once got in his nose,
> He'll soon find means to make the body follow.   (IV. vii. 25)

A similar device will be used by John of Lancaster, in *Henry IV*, *Part II*[17],
to obtain a bloodless victory over the rebel armies at Gaultree Forest.
Whilst the civil war thus continues on its sombre and ignoble course,
Henry VI takes his stand on virtue, but this does not save him from
being seized by his enemies in answer to his declarations of good intention. His response is in effect a bitter cry of despair:

> My pity hath been balm to heal their wounds,
> My mildness hath allay'd their swelling griefs,
> My mercy dried their water-flowing tears;
> I have not been desirous of their wealth,
> Nor much oppress'd them with great subsidies,

> Nor forward of revenge, though they much err'd;
> Then why should they love Edward more than me? (IV. viii. 41)

Why, indeed? The answer to this question, whatever it be, is not to be found in this play, which presses forward to its bleak conclusion after the death of Warwick at Barnet (V. ii) and the stabbing of the young Prince after the scolding-match with Edward, Gloucester, and Clarence. As ever in this series, irony and savagery are joined to the last in destructive and inhuman action.

Finally, as a logical culmination to the whole process, Richard murders the helpless Henry to the accompaniment of a last grim gibe at virtue itself: 'Down, down to hell; and say I sent thee thither' (V. vi. 67). This supremely callous act, however, becomes at once the occasion for the most revealing soliloquy that this murderer has yet uttered. Once again Richard contemplates himself, in the light of his deed and those that have gone before, with his characteristic show of detachment—

> I, that have neither pity, love, nor fear—

before he goes on to speak yet again of the 'unnatural' and loveless birth which so obsesses him throughout, to justify himself finally in what is surely, beyond his immediate intention, nothing less than a declaration of his limitation as a human being:

> Then, since the heavens have shaped my body so,
> Let hell make crook'd my mind to answer it.
> I have no brother, I am like no brother;
> And this word love, which greybeards call divine,
> Be resident in men like one another,
> And not in me: *I am myself alone*. (V. vi. 78)

'I am myself alone'. In these few words, with all that they imply, we may find that Shakespeare has made what is so far his first approach to a profound and finally positive statement about life. Richard has declared his manifesto, his programme, which we are called upon to judge in the light of all that we have seen, all that it now illuminates. Evil has become at last, not merely an obscure instinct in the hearts of savage men, but fully self-conscious, self-possessed, and self-aware: but, in the very act of so declaring itself, it has announced its isolation, accepted in its own despite its inescapable human—or inhuman—limitation. As the play ends, and against the next threat to peace, humanity, and nature, which is already foreseen by its conscious agent—'Clarence, thy turn is next, and then the rest'—Edward is left to bring the action to a close by saying, with a feebleness that contrasts with the force of what we have just heard: 'here, *I hope*, begins our lasting joy' (V. vii. 46). What will in fact begin, and be brought to its logical conclusion in the next play, is the consummation of Richard Crookback's advance to power.

4 Richard III

In relation to the series of *Henry VI* plays, of which it is the logical conclusion, *Richard III* represents a new, a more elaborate and finished development. The simple construction of the earlier chronicles, which answers, generally speaking, to the sequence of the events described, is replaced by a more deliberately patterned action, in which the principal themes repeat themselves significantly or stand out in deliberate contrast. Phrase responds deliberately to phrase, either ironically or to intensify by choric emphasis a broad tragic effect; incident recalls incident, either in an intentional accumulation of horror or to stress the presence, beneath so much inhumanity, of an obscure and appropriate Nemesis working itself out through the unfolding of events. At the centre of this variously contrived structure, focussing upon his own person the elements of self-awareness which we have seen emerging, at first tentatively in York and then more firmly in the stages of his own rise to power, stands the dominating figure of its protagonist. With Richard placed at the centre of his play, which he overshadows to a degree that we shall scarcely find repeated in Shakespeare before *Hamlet*, a new type of drama is at once the necessary conclusion of all that has gone before and the expression of a new conception of what the chronicle play implies.

Given this development, and the concept of the dramatic protagonist to which it leads, it is natural that the new play should open with a long and highly individual soliloquy spoken by Richard himself. His definition of his own nature, for which the previous play has prepared us,[18] is principally new in its more controlled and deliberate use of ironic effects. It operates by setting the evident villainy of his intentions against a cool realism which almost, in certain of its pungent phrases and shrewd evaluations, qualifies for definition as comedy:

> I, that am not shaped for sportive tricks,
> Nor made to court an amorous looking-glass;
> I, that am rudely stamp'd, and want love's majesty
> To strut before a wanton ambling nymph;
> I, that am curtail'd of this fair proportion,
> Cheated of feature by dissembling nature,
> Deform'd, unfinish'd, sent before my time
> Into this breathing world, scarce half made up,
> And that so lamely and unfashionable
> That dogs bark at me as I halt by them;
> Why I, in this weak piping time of peace,
> Have no delight to pass away the time,
> Unless to spy my shadow in the sun,
> And descant on mine own deformity;
> And therefore, since I cannot prove a lover,
> To entertain these fair, well-spoken days,
> I am determined to prove a villain,
> And hate the idle pleasures of these days.   (I. i. 14)

The speech, though based on the established attributes of envious villainy, plays down its more obvious rhetorical overtones in the interests of a less grotesque irony and a firmer delineation of character. Although a certain stilted quality survives in the movement of the verse (there is a sense, common to many Elizabethan stage heroes and villains, of the speaker playing up to a dramatically acceptable picture of himself), the general effect is remarkably concise and pointed. Richard's state of mind is conveyed primarily through a series of sharp visual touches—the vision of himself as strutting ludicrously before a 'wanton ambling nymph', as being barked at by the dogs as he passes, as spying his misshapen shadow in the sun—and through the sustained contrast with its implications of contempt and repudiation, between the 'sportive tricks' and exigencies of 'these fair, well-spoken days' and his own situation as an outsider, 'deform'd, unfinish'd', 'scarce half made up' 'lamely' put together and beyond all remedy 'unfashionable'. In this way, by making his envy express a criticism which is felt not to be altogether unjustified, the speaker is in some degree humanized, transformed from the abstract incarnation of a traditional vice exploited for melodramatic effect into something like a person: a being whose nature is twisted indeed by his exclusion from 'love's majesty' (the phrase stands out forcibly by contrast with the sneer that follows it), but who retains in the cool, pungent run of his comments a definite human plausibility. The contrast between this plausibility and the horror of

what Richard actually achieves in the course of the action is a primary
factor in the creation of the play's peculiar irony.

It is in accordance with this ironic intention that the first half of the
action traces the successive stages of Richard's advance towards his
goal. His initial declaration of moral autonomy is almost at once
followed by the removal of Clarence, who has been Richard's associate
in the preceding play and whose downfall was there foreseen, to the
Tower. Richard, having himself instigated it, ascribes the responsibility for this move in characteristically pungent terms to the intrigues
of the Queen and Mistress Shore:

> The jealous o'erworn widow and herself,
> Since that our brother dubb'd them gentlewomen,
> Are mighty gossips in this monarchy.   (I. i. 81)

The critical implication is clear and, once again, not without force; but
the speaker, in making it, is moved not by any kind of public spirit—he
has just declared his complete separation from society—but by the
pleasure which his own superior insight, and the sense of his own
capacity to mould the course of events to the ends he has proposed to
himself, gives him. It is germane to the situation of the politically aware
man, as this play conceives it, that he can only rise further by kicking
away the steps that have led him to his present eminence; it is Richard's
quality to know and accept this truth, as it is his final tragedy to be
inexorably limited by his acceptance of it. With the elimination of
Clarence already in his mind, Richard first promises him the disinterested support of a loyal friend and loving brother and then, left to
himself, makes his sardonic comment upon so much capacity for self-
deception:

> Simple, plain Clarence! I do love thee so,
> That I will shortly send thy soul to heaven,
> If heaven will take the present at our hands.   (I. i. 118)

The ability to *act* the villainies he plans, taking the audience into his
confidence with a kind of cheerful *bonhomie* that contrasts with the real
monstrosity of his intentions, distinguishes Richard from the other
historical personages in this series of plays. Without making him on that
account less horrifying as a human being, it adds a fresh dimension to
the pattern of crime and retribution with which all the political agents
in this ironic melodrama are so obsessively concerned.

Whilst engaged thus in planning death for his brother Richard continues, in his own way, to pursue his concern with life by wooing the
Lady Anne. In their meeting, accusation and irony clash as the object of
these grotesque advances recalls the saintly figure of the martyred
Henry VI to his murderer, who is also, for good measure, the assassin of
her own husband, Henry's son:

> —O, he was gentle, mild, and virtuous!
> —The fitter for the King of heaven, that hath him.
> —He is in heaven, where thou shalt never come.
> —Let him thank me, that holp to send him thither.   (I. ii. 105)

As she spits 'mortal poison' at him in hatred and repulsion, Richard
presses his suit, offering his breast for her to stab, declaring his readiness
to kill himself at her command. His confidence, of course, is fully
justified by the event. Anne surrenders at the end of a protracted verbal
struggle and, as she does so, the cool comment of her wooer expresses
the satisfaction which his success, and perhaps his sense of having
adventured successfully to the very edge of danger, inspires in his keen
twisted mind:

> Was ever woman in this humour woo'd?
> Was ever woman in this humour won?
> I'll have her: but I will not keep her long.   (I. ii. 229)

Once again, as he seems to stand aside from his projects to take us, his
alternately shocked and fascinated audience, into his confidence, Richard
adds a new dimension to his villainy, forces us to share after a fashion in
the detachment from habitual moral judgements which throughout the
first part of the play qualifies the essential savagery of his actions.

A similar impression emerges from his self-presentation to the world
around him. Aware of the hostility that his actions will inevitably
inspire, Richard cultivates the essentially ironic vision of himself as a
'plain' man who laments the refusal of a corrupt and self-seeking world
to take him at his own valuation:

> Because I cannot flatter and speak fair,
> Smile in men's faces, smooth, deceive, and cog,
> Duck with French nods and apish courtesy,
> I must be held a rancorous enemy.
> Cannot *a plain man* live and think no harm,
> But thus his *simple truth* must be abused
> By silken, sly, insinuating Jacks?   (I. iii. 47)

Once more this self-portrayal contains, beneath its essential perversity, a measure of truth. Richard, we may feel, can justly claim a certain superiority to the world of courtly intrigue in which he moves and by which he feels himself rejected: but the exclusion, of course, is also from the natural positives of living, from human sociability as such, and the isolation which he seeks throughout to turn into an asset will bring him in the long run to an appropriate ruin. Meanwhile, however, we can hardly fail to respond to the grimly comic zest which inspires his definition of himself, to those who are already marked down to be the victims of his drive to power, as 'too childish-foolish for this world' (I. iii. 142).

The 'comedy', nevertheless, if such we can call it, is projected, here and throughout, against an oppressive background of doom. Its principal mouthpiece continues to be Henry VI's widow Margaret who, having survived the ruin of all her own cherished ambitions, can now denounce all those who surround her as so many

> wrangling pirates, that fall out
> In sharing that which you have pill'd from me.   (I. iii. 158)

Margaret, however, is by now no more than a survival from the past, a shadow of former pride. Richard is in a position to answer her by recalling her own ferocities, her part in the murder of York and Rutland so cruelly executed in the moment of her precarious triumph; and to this her only reply can be to urge, as though from the spent ashes of her exhausted passion, yet more death upon those who have replaced her on the summit of glory. To Edward IV's reigning Queen she has only this to say:

> If not by war, by surfeit die your king,
> As ours by murder, to make him a king!
> Edward thy son, which now is Prince of Wales,
> For Edward my son, which was Prince of Wales,
> Die in his youth by like untimely violence!
> Thyself a queen, for me that was a queen ...   (I. iii. 197)

The function of Margaret in this play is to give choral emphasis to the pattern of doom that dominates the entire course of the action, and further, in the process of so doing, to expose the essential savagery of Richard's motives:

> Look, when he fawns, he bites: and when he bites,
> His venom tooth will rankle to the death.   (I. iii. 290)

The exposure, however, as coming from one whose life is concentrated upon the sterile savagery of the past, falls upon deaf ears in an equally ruthless present. In replying to these denunciations Richard declares, once more in soliloquy and with typical ironic satisfaction, his determination to outdo the world at its own game of hypocrisy, to

> clothe my naked villainy
> With old odd ends, stolen out of holy writ,   (I. iii. 336)

and to proceed zestfully with his preparations for the elimination of his brother.

The murder of Clarence introduces a further variation into the general panorama of bestiality and horror. The victim's premonitory dream, in particular, insinuates a new projection of poetry into the realm of sub-conscious twilight:

> Lord, Lord! methought, what pain it was to drown!
> What dreadful noise of waters in mine ears!
> What ugly sights of death within mine eyes!
> Methought I saw a thousand fearful wrecks;
> Ten thousand men that fishes gnaw'd upon;
> Wedges of gold, great anchors, heaps of pearl,
> Inestimable stones, unvalued jewels,
> All scattered in the bottom of the sea:
> Some lay in dead men's skulls; and in those holes
> Where eyes did once inhabit, there were crept,
> As 'twere in scorn of eyes, reflecting gems,
> Which woo'd the slimy bottom of the deep,
> And mock'd the dead bones that lay scattered by.   (I. iv. 21)

This transformation of the reality of 'pain', of 'the dreadful noise of waters' and 'ugly sights of death', into a phantasmagorical vision of treasures beyond value scattered at the bottom of the sea, answers to a kind of poetry which the rest of this play, ferociously concentrated upon brutality and lust for power, can hardly parallel. It is, however, profoundly Shakespearean. For this imaginative transformation of the charnel, this wedding of death to a transfigured, shifting opulence on the ocean-bed, it is necessary to look far forward into the dramatist's future poetry: almost as far, we may think even as we establish firmly the essential differences, as the world of Prospero's magic spells and of the 'pearls' into which Ariel's song transmutes the supposedly drowned eyes of Ferdinand's 'lost' father.[19] The effect, of course, is different, beyond comparison less charged with significance and depth; but, having recognized this, we may also see in the poetic elaboration of this dream a content which, in the act of echoing them and taking up their obsessive rhythms, transforms the repetitive patterns of murder and retribution which principally dominate this play.

A further note of profundity, though of a different kind, is somewhat tentatively struck, again at this point, by one of Clarence's murderers in his reflections upon conscience. 'I'll not meddle with it', he concludes;

> it is a dangerous thing: it makes a man a coward . . . it is a blushing shamefast spirit that mutinies in a man's bosom . . . it is turned out of all towns and cities for a dangerous thing; and every man that means to live well endeavours to trust to himself and to live without it.   (I. iv. 138)

The results of this 'endeavour' on the part of man 'to trust to himself', which constitutes precisely Richard's declared programme for living,[20] will be made apparent in many of Shakespeare's tragedies, from the present play to at least as far as *Macbeth*. It implies, in the long run, a forcing of reality, a reversal of 'nature' which brings its own retribution with it; but the realization, in so far as the murderer's words may be said to imply it, is rejected at this point, fails to exercise any influence upon the course of events. Clarence, left in his extremity to plead for mercy in the name of 'the King of kings', is condemned by his own crimes committed in the past, and his murderer's answer is, in terms of this play's retributive pattern, unanswerable:

> How canst thou urge God's dreadful law to us,
> When thou hast broke it in so dear degree?   (I. iv. 218)

The saving qualities of compassion can have no place in an action dominated, almost to repetitive obsession, by the prospect of man's inhumanity to man.

Against this background of gathering horror the King, old and mortally sick, flawed by his own moral worthlessness, exacts a momentary show of reconciliation. Buckingham bows to his will, swearing loyalty in terms which his own conduct will shortly turn to irony, and Richard, as usual, passes his own implicit comment on the worth of this fiction by uttering his grotesque parody of repentance immediately before announcing the death of Clarence:

> I do not know that Englishman alive
> With whom my soul is any jot at odds,
> More than the infant that is born to-night;   (II. i. 70)

so speaks the murderer, and caps his gesture with an avowal more
fantastic still: 'I thank my God for my humility' (II. i. 73). The final
comment on this mockery is conveyed, in the scene which follows,
through the long choric lament of the bereaved and stricken Queens:

> —Oh, for my husband, for my dear lord Edward!
> —Oh, for our father, for our dear lord Clarence!
> —Alas for both, both mine, Edward and Clarence!
> —What stay had I but Edward? and he's gone.
> —What stay had we but Clarence? and he's gone.
> —What stays had I but they? and they are gone.
> —Was never widow had so dear a loss.
> —Were never orphans had so dear a loss.
> —Was never mother had so dear a loss.   (II. ii. 71)

The device of patterned lamentation is familiar and, of course, artificial
in conception and effect; what is new and striking is the intensity with
which it is carried out through the course of the play and, still more, the
contrast between these accumulations of grief and the attitude, at once
ferocious and ironic, tending to a kind of grim comedy, shown by the
murderer. It is, moreover, at the end of these same lamentations that
Richard and Buckingham, who have just joined in public expression of
loyalty to their King, draw secretly together to plan the death of the
young Princes and the seizure of the crown.

At this juncture the King dies, whilst the Citizens express their
expectation of an even grimmer future (II. iii). The Queen and her son,
set against the background of a state pitilessly dedicated to civil strife:

> Blood against blood, self against self—   (II. iv. 62)

seek 'sanctuary' with the Archbishop of York. Sanctuary, however, is a
concept without meaning in the world as this play conceives it, and
Buckingham is at hand to give the politician's reason why it should be
profaned: as he tells the prelate, not without the man of the world's
cynical satisfaction in the contemplation of his supposedly superior
realism:

> You are too senseless-obstinate, my lord,
> Too ceremonious and traditional.   (III. i. 44)

Inevitably, the attitude which these words represent soon prevails.
Richard commits the young Princes to the Tower, Rivers, Vaughan,
and Grey are brought to their doom (III. iii), thus confirming Margaret's prophecy, and Hastings is executed for his loyalty just after he

has expressed, with further unconscious irony, his faith in his murderer's honesty:

> I think there's never a man in Christendom
> Can lesser hide his love, or hate, than he:
> For by his face straight shall you know his heart.   (III. iv. 51)

Richard, meanwhile, is busy advancing his cause by appropriate public
gestures for the benefit of the unwilling citizens, whose support he
requires. These, as reported by Buckingham, are bemused by the course
of events which they find it hard to welcome and cannot aspire to
control:

> Now, by the holy mother of our Lord,
> The citizens are mum, and speak not a word.   (III. vii. 2)

To exercise upon the populace the arts of politic persuasion Richard
offers himself to their view, piously flanked by supporting clerics—
'See where he stands between two clergymen!'—as he allows Buckingham to 'persuade' him to accept the crown.

Thus far the action of the play, concentrated upon the successive
stages of Richard's advance to his goal, have been poised between the
horror which his deeds inspire and a kind of detached, ironic comedy
which the contemplation of his deeds provokes in him and which,
actor-like, he communicates to the audience. As protagonist, he sums
up and gathers into his person the savagery which everywhere prevails
around him; as self-conscious actor of his own career, he passes on to us,
as spectators, a detached and sardonic estimate of his own motives. The
crowning, however, represents a turning-point after which the spirit of
the later action undergoes a notable change. Having obtained the ends
he has proposed to himself, Richard is seen increasingly as the victim of
his own choices. The horrors he has instigated follow him into his new
state, and bind him finally and irrevocably to the consequences of his
own actions in the past. His first act as King (IV. ii) is to order the
murder of the imprisoned Princes who represent an unwitting threat to
his new eminence; the next is to plan the death of the Lady Anne—for
whom, as he has already foreseen,[21] he has no further use—and to
prepare the way for a new marriage by which he hopes to provide for a
rule which, as he admits, 'stands on brittle glass' (IV. ii). At this point
his position shifts from that of the confident outsider, immersed in the
contemplation of his control of the world around him, and begins to
offer notable anticipations of *Macbeth*: anticipations that occasionally

produce remarkable verbal parallels, as when he says, speaking of his own state,

> I am in
> So far in blood that sin will pluck on sin (IV. ii. 63)[22]

Words such as these, which can hardly be related to anything so concretely expressed in the earlier part of the play, indicate a fundamental shift of emphasis in its later development. Richard, hitherto so keenly aware of himself as the agent of his own destiny, is beginning to feel himself the prisoner of his own actions. The voice of natural pity, so elaborately expressed in Tyrrel's account of the Princes' death (IV. iii) is one which he can less than ever afford to recognize, which he needs, even at the cost of forfeiting such humanity as remains to him, rigidly to exclude from his thoughts. There is from now on something increasingly automatic in the royal murderer's grim references to the execution of his plans—'Anne my wife hath bid the world good night'—and even in the attempt to caricature his own behaviour as that of 'a jolly thriving wooer' (IV. iii. 43). For the first time, we sense a man engaged in whistling in the dark to keep up his own courage, to hide even from himself the sense of intimate emptiness which is beginning to hover obsessively on the edge of his thoughts.

For, in spite of these efforts to maintain the façade of ironic confidence, which are essentially a carry-over from the earlier action, the entire mood of the play is very notably changing. Margaret, backed now by the Duchess of York, continues to sound the familiar note of choric doom; but their lamentations, which Richard had once been able to shrug off, with some justification, as hollow echoes from a withered past, fall now with a fresh urgency, a new sense of tragic issues closing in upon the entire action. Seeing in their unhappy state the fulfilment of Margaret's most bitter prophecies, the royal victims of the murderer's ruthlessness feel themselves reduced to the status of participants in a common vanity to which, no doubt, their own sins, and those of their children, have contributed. As always, Margaret is the most explicit:

> I call'd thee then poor shadow, painted queen;
> The presentation of but what I was;
> The flattering index of a direful pageant:
> One heaved a-high, to be hurl'd down below;
> A mother only mock'd with two sweet babes,
> A dream of what thou wert, a breath, a bubble,
> A sign of dignity, a garish flag

> To be the aim of every dangerous shot;
> A queen in jest, only to fill the scene.   (IV. iv. 83)

The old Queen's words answer sufficiently, beyond her own grief and ruin, to a change of emphasis in the entire action, which is concentrated now, not on the political confidence of the protagonist, but upon the doom which radiates from his actions and drags down his entire world with it. The typical mediaeval themes of retribution for past sin and of the fall of the presumptuous from their high estate are in process at this point of being gathered into a final tragic resolution.

It is not, however, by these shadows of the past that Richard feels himself immediately threatened. As he returns at the tail-end of these laments, and as his victims turn upon him with their bitter accusations, they receive only the ironic blast of his reply:

> A flourish, trumpets! strike alarum, drums!
> Let not the heavens hear these tell-tale women
> Rail on the Lord's anointed!   (IV. iv. 149)

The emphasis, however, is now upon concealment, upon the drowning in mere sound of an unpalatable and ominous truth. Against this grotesque background Richard, as though in a final gesture carried over from his former confident self, sets out to woo the Princess Elizabeth and invites to this end the good offices of the Queen her mother. The answer he receives, setting irony against irony in an effect of accumulated bitterness, is indeed damning in its effect;

> What were I best to say? her father's brother
> Would be her lord? or shall I say, her uncle?
> Or, he that slew her brothers and her uncles?   (IV. iv. 338)

Even ironic self-assertion has its limits, and the sombre and menacing weight of the Queen's final denunciation—

> Swear not by time to come; for that thou hast
> Misused ere used, by time misus'd o'erpast—   (IV. iv. 396)

explicitly reveals them. The fact that, before the long and elaborate exchange is brought to an end, Richard's victim has shown herself to be, in accordance with his own cynical expectations, 'Relenting fool, and shallow, changing woman', cannot entirely take the edge from these denunciations or cover the decline in his own original comic energy as the revenges of time begin to take shape against him.

As the scene ends, indeed, confirmation of the changing direction of events reaches the usurper with the news of the Earl of Richmond's return. Richard receives these tidings in a mood which again closely foreshadows that of Macbeth at the end of his tragedy: the mood of a man on edge, veering and changeable, seeking the illusion of relief in what is now rapidly becoming an empty show of decisive action. As his disconnected commands, uttered in haste and stress—'Fly to the Duke': 'Post thou to Salisbury'—mingle with unfinished instructions and impatient gestures—'Why stand'st thou still and go'st not to the Duke?'—his followers are left to grope in ignorance of his intentions, alternately upbraided and confused:

> —First, mighty sovereign, let me know your mind,
>   What from your Grace I shall deliver to him.
> —O, true, good Catesby; bid him levy straight
>   The greatest strength and power he can make,
>   And meet me presently at Salisbury.
> —I go.
> —What is't your highness' pleasure I shall do
>   At Salisbury?
> —Why, what wouldst thou do there before I go?
> —Your highness told me I should post before.
> —My mind is changed, sir, my mind is changed.   (IV. iv. 448)[23]

This is the voice of a man who feels the control of events slipping from him, who has, perhaps for the first time, no clear vision of where or how far he means to go. The pressure of events only strengthens his disorientation. Lord Stanley is already preparing to desert him, and Richard can only seek to counter this defection by holding his son as hostage; the power which has been obtained by acting against the course of nature now seeks to perpetuate itself through the imposition of unnatural fear. By the time the long scene has drawn to a close, the armies of retribution are gathering against the usurper, as they will later gather against Macbeth, and his own followers—here as at Dunsinane —'on both sides do fight'.[24]

Richard's cause, indeed, is already in the process of destroying itself. The treacherous Buckingham, who assisted him in his rise to power, is brought to execution, paying thus for his own sins—

> Wrong hath but wrong, and blame the due of blame—   (V. i. 29)

whilst the armies of Richmond move forward 'without impediment', 'to reap *the harvest* of perpetual peace' and to restore, with the reign of ordered loyalty, the '*summer fields* and *fruitful vines*' (V. ii. 8) which the usurper's excesses have brought to ruin. It is interesting to see that at this point the ideas of peaceful harmony and natural fertility have already found their characteristic Shakespearean association. Faced by this rising tide of restoration, Richard shows himself still a brave man—like Macbeth after him—and one who, like Macbeth again, seeks the shadow of consolation in intense activity: 'For, lords, to-morrow is a busy day' (V. iii. 18).[25] His is an activity, however, which answers to an essentially febrile and incoherent condition. Unlike Richmond, Richard can barely contemplate the foreseen outcome of the action forced upon him. He continues to threaten Stanley, whom he has good reason to mistrust, through the person of his son; but, beyond the steps which immediate necessity imposes upon him, his innermost thoughts are already dominated by the prospect of annihilation, and contemplate what his own vivid phrase describes as 'the blind cave of eternal night', and are ready to make confession of foreboding:

> I have not that alacrity of spirit,
> Nor cheer of mind, that I was wont to have.   (V. iii. 73)

By contrast to this condition we are shown Richmond consecrating himself and his army serenely to 'the just God whose captain I account myself', whilst punishment and restoration join hands in his advancing train.

As night falls, and its ghostly shadows reveal to the rival contendants their contrasted images of the past, Richard is left, in a soliloquy perhaps more searching in its implications than anything Shakespeare had yet written, to pronounce his recognition of the egoist's isolated doom:

> What do I fear? myself? there's none else by:
> Richard loves Richard; that is, *I am I*.   (V. iii. 183)

The assassin's definition of his state is laconic and direct at the last, as befits a man who has awakened from the dream of action and ironic self-assertion in which he has hitherto sought refuge from an awareness of his real condition. The result of a life-long dedication to the egoist's desire for power is seen to be the impossibility of self-evasion, of escape from what now emerge, with dreadful clarity, as the limits of the isolated self. As Richard goes on to confess in his last vain effort to come to terms with the situation in which he finds himself:

> Is there a murderer here? No. Yes, I am:
> Then fly. What, from myself? Great reason why:
> Lest I revenge. What, myself, upon myself?

> Alack, I love myself. Wherefore? for any good
> That I myself have done upon myself?
> O, no! alas, I rather hate myself
> For hateful deeds committed by myself!   (V. iii. 185)

This is a far cry from the initial confidence of the 'Machiavellian' prince, arrogantly dedicated to his own advancement; but it is essential to understand that the end was implied in the beginning, that the whole story answers to an irreversible tragic logic. Before the final bar of a judgement he has never recognized, but which now imposes itself upon him, Richard ends by confessing the isolation which he has chosen for himself and which has now become, by virtue of this very choice, his inescapable limitation:

> I shall despair. There is no creature loves me;
> And if I die, no soul will pity me:
> Nay, wherefore should they, since that I myself
> Find in myself no pity to myself?   (V. iii. 201)[26]

To the last Richard is haunted by the thought of exclusion from the world of 'love', which he recognizes in his own despite as the natural sign of human solidarity and in the absence of which life presents itself to the egoist as empty, simply void of meaning. This is perhaps the Shakespearean equivalent, more human and less 'metaphysical', of the vision of hell which haunted Faustus in Marlowe's great play, where it also produces a last great speech confessing to irreparable loss.[27] It is significant that now, for the first time, Richard confesses that he is *afraid*. 'O Ratcliff, I fear, I fear'; and when his servant seeks to restore him to confidence—'Nay, good my lord, be not afraid of shadows'—he can only confess that 'shadows to-night' have struck more 'terror' into his soul than the 'substance of ten thousand soldiers'.

Once again, the nature of this confession is full of meaning. In terms of an obliterated distinction between 'substance' and 'shadow', reality and illusion, the moral duality which everywhere accompanies Shakespearean evil is already presented in the form of a psychological rift, a split in the personality which is the necessary consequence of perverse and unnatural choices. It is worth noting that Richmond has, at this same moment, received the visitation of

> The *sweetest* sleep, and *fairest boding* dreams
> That ever entered in a drowsy head,   (V. iii. 228)

and that he is in a position to tell those who follow him;

> I promise you, my soul is very *jocund*
> In the remembrance of so fair a dream.   (V. iii. 233)

As so often, and so surprisingly, occurs in this play, we sense anticipations of the vastly enriched world of *Macbeth*.

It is no more than appropriate, accordingly, that in his final oration to his soldiers, Richmond should lay stress upon the return to natural order which his victory will bring with it:

> If you do free your children from the sword,
> Your children's children quit you in your age;   (V. iii. 262)

whilst his rival, in contrast, can only seek relief in the illusion, finally self-engendered and self-maintained, that the presages of nature are empty of significance:

> Not shine to-day! Why, what is that to me
> More than to Richmond?   (V. iii. 286)

The battle once joined becomes for him a last means of escaping from reality, whilst 'conscience' is dismissed, in accordance with the 'philosophy' that has consistently ruled his life, as 'but a word that cowards use'.[28] 'Our strong arms be our conscience, swords our law': but the end of this show of confidence is seen, on its own confession, to be at best dubious:

> March on, join bravely, let's to't pell-mell;
> If not to heaven, then hand in hand to hell.   (V. iii. 313)[29]

After this last flourish, made less to encourage his followers than to conceal from himself the sense of his own vanity, Richard in a final rousing speech revives for a moment some of his undoubted qualities as a leader of men in his lively dismissal of the enemy before him as

> A sort of vagabonds, rascals, and runaways,

seeing in them no more than

> these bastard Bretons, whom our fathers
> Have in their own land beaten, bobb'd, and thump'd.   (V. iii. 334)

To the last he acts bravely in his despair. As his followers report:

> The king enacts more wonders than a man,
> Daring an opposite to every danger:
> His horse is slain, and all on foot he fights,
> Seeking for Richmond in the throat of death.   (V. iv. 2)[30]

All this frenzied activity answers finally, as we have already seen reason
to suspect, to an attempt at self-evasion, a reaction against recognized
vacancy. As we follow Richard to his death, we can hardly avoid
establishing a further parallel with Macbeth at the end of his tragedy,
equally facing retribution in the person of Macduff. Like Macbeth, he
succumbs to the death which the nature of his own choices has finally
implied. Richmond is duly crowned (V. v), making his appeal to
'smooth-faced peace' and announcing, with the final conquest of evil
after its perverse impulse has been at last exhausted, the end of civil
strife and the restoration of 'smiling plenty' and 'fair prosperous days'.
Shakespeare's first series of chronicle plays has been brought, with the
fulness of time, to its logical and impressive conclusion.

II
TITUS ANDRONICUS

AT APPROXIMATELY the same time as he was engaged on his first series of chronicle plays, Shakespeare embarked, with *Titus Andronicus*, upon his first venture in tragedy. The piece, though hardly attractive on first acquaintance, is more interesting than may immediately appear. Seneca and Ovid share a great part of its literary inspiration between them, not always to its dramatic advantage. Seneca lends his authority to the monotonous pattern of reiterated savageries which dominates the action; and Ovid, to whom Shakespeare was showing his devotion at about this time in the elaborate sensual decoration of *Venus and Adonis* and the more complex moral conflicts of *The Rape of Lucrece*,[1] contributes a scarcely less reiterative thread of images which, largely concentrated upon the story of the rape of Philomel and the revenge of Procne, is alternatively decorative, moralizing and sensational. Throughout the play, emblematic artifice and ferocious melodrama share between them a tragedy which is crude in its construction and largely monotonous in its striving after effect; but it is fair to add that the monotony answers to a definite unity of style and conception, through which we glimpse at times anticipations of greater plays to come.

For the first time in his dramatic career, Shakespeare makes use of the unique prestige that, for a sixteenth-century mind, surrounded the name of Rome. The opening scene, stiff and immobile with rhetoric, presents the election of the Roman emperor. Whilst Saturninus and Bassianus declare their readiness to accept the verdict of the people, Titus speaks with measured solemnity of his country and with elegiac, almost necrological emphasis, of his own dead:

> There greet in silence, as the dead are wont,
> And sleep in peace, slain in your country's wars! (I. i. 90)

Against the physical background provided by the massive funeral monument of the Andronici, his son Lucius demands revenge upon 'the proudest prisoner' of the defeated Goths, seeking permission to 'hew' his limbs and 'sacrifice his flesh'. The demand is an ominous inversion of the initial contrast between Roman civilization and Gothic barbarity. This is made clear when the captive Queen Tamora pleads eloquently for her son's life:

> O, if to fight for king and commonweal
> Were piety in thine, it is in these.
> Andronicus, stain not thy tomb with blood.
> Wilt thou draw near the nature of the gods?
> Draw near them then in being merciful. (I. i. 114)

The appeal, addressed to the natural 'pieties' which a Roman might be expected to revere, falls upon deaf ears. Lucius mercilessly presses his vengeful demands: 'Let's *hew his limbs* till they be clean consum'd'. His words show what Tamora is justified in calling 'irreligious piety', and cause her son Chiron to ask pertinently: 'Was ever Scythia so barbarous?'. As his brother Demetrius joins him in invoking the vengeance of the gods, Lucius returns with his freshly blooded sword, announcing with sombre satisfaction that 'Alarbus' limbs are *lopp'd*', and Titus celebrates a peace which he associates, most typically, with the release which his own slaughtered sons have found in dying for their country's cause:

> In peace and honour rest you here, my sons:
> Rome's readiest champions, repose you here in rest!
> Secure from worldly chances and mishaps!
> Here lurks no treason, here no envy swells,
> Here grow no damned drugs; here are no storms,
> No noise, but silence and eternal sleep:
> In peace and honour rest you here, my sons! (I. i. 150)

Whilst Titus, in words which recall those to be spoken, to a very different end, by Duncan's murderer,[2] thus builds upon bloody vengeance his own world-weary, death-directed meditations, the public affairs of Rome slip beyond his control into savagery and ruin.

Life, indeed, continues on its course in spite of these deathward reflections. As Titus' daughter Lavinia enters, she greets her father with a significant inversion of the words he has just spoken: 'In peace and honour *live* Lord Titus long!', and is received by him as his 'cordial' whilst he weeps 'tears of joy'; for a precarious moment the poetry of the play seems to move from death towards a sense of continued life. Death, however, is already firmly enthroned. As the hero rejects the

imperial nomination which he might have used for the furthering of
peace, Saturninus appeals openly to the sword—

> Andronicus, would thou wert shipp'd to hell,
> Rather than rob me of the people's hearts!—   (I. i. 206)

and Titus makes the fatal error of confirming him with his support.
The consequences of his decision are immediately apparent. In the very
act of taking Lavinia for his Queen, Saturninus reveals his true nature
by lusting after Tamora; and Bassianus, when he claims Lavinia for
himself, equally sets his own will above the due processes of law. The
affirmation of self-will becomes everywhere supreme. When Bassianus
announces his determination 'to do myself this reason and this right',
Titus' brother Marcus supports him by saying 'This prince in justice
seizeth but his own', and Lucius, fresh from the cruel vengeance he has
exacted from the Goths, adds emphatically: 'And that he *will*, and *shall*,
if Lucius live'. Titus, for his part, clings obstinately to his own unwise
decisions and actually ends by killing the son who stands in his way to
the accompaniment of a typical egoistic brag:

> What, villain boy,
> Barr'st me my way in Rome!;   (I. i. 290)

and when Lucius is reasonable enough to point out that he has committed this deed in 'wrongful quarrel', his only reply is the unnatural
gesture which leads him to disown his own flesh: 'Nor thou, nor he,
are any sons of mine'.

The consequences of Titus' error, and of so much blind self-will,
soon emerge. Secure in the possession of arbitrary power, Saturninus
renounces Lavinia—'that changing piece'—and takes 'lovely Tamora'
for his Queen. Innocence and lust are visibly personified in these two
brides, and the tyrant, following the laws of his own nature, makes the
appropriate choice. Titus, faced by this proof of perversity in the man
to whose election he has been instrumental, clings to his error, even to
the point of refusing burial in the family tomb for the son he has just
slain; when his sons finally persuade him against this unnatural decision,
his consent is grudgingly and morosely given: 'Well, bury him, and
bury me the next!' (I. i. 386). Saturninus, meanwhile, pursuing his
tyrannical path and seeking to eliminate his rival, accuses Bassianus of
'rape' in the person of his discarded bride, but is persuaded by Tamora
to 'look graciously', in feigned friendship, upon Titus; her real aim is
to be avenged upon the Andronici for the sacrifice of her own child.

The brutality committed by the Romans upon Alarbus is to be repaid in full measure before the play reaches its desolate conclusion.

The appearance of Aaron, immediately after this long and heavily stylized opening, brings a new sense of life to the play. The part is full of self-conscious overtones, ironies which lend a distinctive quality to its obvious melodrama. Aaron is the theatrical 'villain', thoroughly aware of his own evil and dedicated to the pleasure it affords him. Recognizing his own situation as an 'outsider', he glories in feeling himself precariously poised over an abyss. His first words place Tamora on the perilous eminence from which they will both eventually fall:

> Now climbeth Tamora Olympus' top,
> Safe out of fortune's shot, and sits aloft. (II. i. 1)

To scale 'Olympus' top' is to invite the resentment of the gods; but, meanwhile, Aaron is ready to share his mistress' exaltation and to enjoy the sensation of holding her subject to his will, 'fetter'd in amorous chains'. For Aaron, precisely because he moves beyond the limits of society, love is an instrument to power, and in this spirit he encourages Chiron and Demetrius to carry out their designs upon Lavinia. Both are fully qualified to be his pupils. They share a common cynicism in their lust, which finds lively expression in Demetrius' attitude to their proposed victim:

> She is a woman, therefore may be woo'd;
> She is a woman, therefore may be won; ...
> What, man! more water glideth by the mill
> That wots the miller of: and easy it is
> Of a cut loaf to steal a shive, we know! (II. i. 82)

This is the language, incisive and popular in its effect, which we have been accustomed to hear from the mouth of Richard Crookback[3]; it reflects, basically, the same 'outsider's' attitude to life. With this suitable material to his hands, Aaron proposes the ravishment of 'the dainty doe' Lavinia, to be carried out far from the social habitations of man, which are 'full of tongues, and eyes, and ears', in the solitude of the woods, 'ruthless, dreadful, deaf, and dull'. His conclusion, spoken with typical imaginative energy,—

> There speak, and strike, brave boys, and take your turns;
> There serve your lust, shadow'd from heaven's eye,
> And revel in Lavinia's treasury— (II. i. 129)

announces the transfer of the action to a new setting and to ferocity of another kind.

The scenes which now follow constitute in some sense the imaginative centre of the whole play. In the recesses of the forest, and in the energies of the hunt, the principal characters are taken out of their normal public selves—as they will later be, though to very different ends, in Shakespeare's great comedies, in the Forest of Arden[4] and the sheepfolds of Bohemia[5]—and revealed in the intimacy of their contrasted reactions. For Titus, hunting is still a jocund, essentially a civilized occupation which contrasts with Aaron's sinister evocations of gloom and obscure horror:

> The hunt is up, the moon is bright and grey,
> The fields are fragrant, and the woods are green:
> Uncouple here, and let us make a bay,
> And wake the emperor and his lovely bride,
> And rouse the prince, and ring a hunter's peal,
> That all the court may echo with the noise.   (II. ii. 1)

This might be a first intimation, slight and even crude by comparison, of the spirit in which Theseus and Hippolyta will set forth for the chase in *A Midsummer Night's Dream*.[6] It represents, for the last time in this play, a set of sociable, positive emotions which are shortly to be plunged into palpable darkness. A hunt of a very different kind, indeed, is already afoot as Aaron, who has already referred to the 'wide and spacious' forest walks as 'Fitted by kind for rape and villainy' (II. i. 116), lays his stratagem by burying 'sweet gold' (II. iii. 8) at the roots of the forest tree.

As he is joined, immediately after this, by Tamora, the woods assume another aspect, become the setting for the triumphant sensuality which she is ready to share with her lover:

> My lovely Aaron, wherefore look'st thou sad,
> When everything doth make a gleeful boast?
> The birds chant melody on every bush;
> *The snake lies rolled in the cheerful sun*;
> The green leaves quiver with the cooling wind,
> And make a chequer'd shadow on the ground;
> Under their sweet shade, Aaron, let us sit,
> And, whilst the babbling echo mocks the hounds,
> Replying shrilly to the well-tuned horns,
> As if a double hunt were heard at once,
> Let us sit down and mark their yellowing noise;
> And, after conflict such as was supposed
> The wandering prince and Dido once enjoy'd,

When with a happy storm they were surpris'd,
And curtain'd with a counsel-keeping cave,
We may, each wreathed in the other's arms,
Our pastimes done, possess *a golden slumber*;
Whiles hounds and horns and sweet melodious birds
Are unto us as is a nurse's song
Of lullaby to bring her babe asleep.   (II. iii. 10)

This is surely one of the most impressive speeches of the whole play.
Turning to fresh use the Ovidian conventions already familiar in *Venus
and Adonis*, it shows us the woods from another point of view, not
altogether unlike that already expressed by Titus, but directed to a very
different end. Through the evocation of the gay 'melody' of the birds,
the green leaves 'quivering' in the breeze and making their cool
'chequer'd shade' whilst the 'well-tuned' horns of the hunters contribute their sociable note to the complete picture, we are brought to
the hidden embraces of Aeneas and Dido and so to the bliss enjoyed by
Aaron and Tamora themselves, 'each wreathed in the other's arms',
locked in the real if transitory possession of their 'golden slumber'. The
classical conventions, evoked with considerable intensity and skill, provide the background for a sensuality which, like the 'snake' coiled
deceptively in 'the cheerful sun', at the heart of what seems so much
idyllic peace, is dangerously and enticingly alive.

Aaron, however, is not concerned with these 'venereal signs', for his
obsessions lie elsewhere:

Vengeance is in my heart, death in my hand,
Blood and revenge are hammering in my head;   (II. iii. 38)

and, apart from this, he 'never hopes more heaven than rests in thee'.
Meeting this dangerous pair as they wander through the wood Bassianus and Lavinia are imprudent enough to taunt Tamora as Aaron's
mistress; and she, as her sons rally around her, introduces yet another
variation upon the forest theme, investing it with a new and sinister
quality congruent with the dark deed of passion she now urges upon
them in pursuit of her revenge:

A *barren* detested vale, you see it is;
The trees, though summer, yet forlorn and lean,
O'ercome with moss and *baleful* mistletoe:
Here *never shines the sun*: here *nothing breeds*,
Unless the nightly owl or fatal raven:
And when they showed me this abhorred pit,

> They told me, here, *at dead time of the night,*
> A thousand fiends, a thousand *hissing snakes,*
> Ten thousand swelling *toads,* as many *urchins,*
> Would make such fearful and confused cries,
> As any mortal body hearing it
> Should straight fall mad, or else die suddenly.   (II. iii. 93)

The presence here of all the familiar trappings of melodrama should not obscure the fact that an effect of some subtlety, in relation to the episode as a whole, is being pursued. The serpent of sensuality, basking in the 'cheerful' sun, has turned into a sinister image of revenge, dweller in a labyrinth of darkness. The whole nature of the wood has changed to meet this new mood; neither the scene of joyous hunting nor of intense sensual gratification, it has become the home of 'barrenness', 'where nothing breeds', where deeds of death and destruction are consummated in the dark dead of night.

This transformation of conventional poetry, and all that it implies in terms of moral desolation, is one of the most striking features of the play. It is confirmed in action when Tamora accuses Bassianus of seeking to rape her, and her sons kill him before turning savagely on Lavinia:

> Drag hence her husband to some secret hole,
> And make his dead trunk pillow to our lust.   (II. iii. 129)

Lust and death are joined in ironic savagery as the murderers confront the new victim with the full scope of their intentions:

> we will enjoy
> That nice-preserved honesty of yours.   (II. iii. 134)

Lavinia's plea for pity, uttered in the name of nature, is answered by Tamora, who recalls the vengeance so brutally exacted on her own child, when she says: 'I know not what it means'; as the new victim puts it,

> The milk thou suck'st from her did turn to marble;
> Even at thy teat thou hadst thy tyranny.   (II. iii. 144)

The sons of Titus, in turn, find Bassianus' newly-slaughtered corpse in the 'unhallow'd blood-stained hole', the 'swallowing womb' of this 'detested, dark, blood-drinking pit'. The qualities of the wood have shifted yet again, or at least intensified their horror, to correspond to these new manifestations of human savagery.

Still in accordance with Aaron's plan, the sons of Titus are accused of

Bassianus' murder, and Marcus, still following the hunt, comes upon
Lavinia ravished, with her tongue cut out, like that of Philomel, and
her hands 'lopp'd and hew'd' as those of the Gothic prince had been at
the opening of the play. The episode finds its culmination in her
uncle's long and elaborate lament:

> Speak, gentle niece, what stern ungentle hands
> Have *lopp'd* and *hew'd* and made thy body bare
> Of her two branches, those sweet ornaments,
> Whose circling shadows kings have sought to sleep in,
> And might not gain so great a happiness
> As have thy love? Why dost not speak to me?
> Alas, a crimson river of warm blood,
> Like to a bubbling fountain stirr'd with wind,
> Doth rise and fall between thy rosed lips,
> Coming and going with thy honey breath.   (II. iv. 16)

Neither the elaborate expression nor the repugnant quality of the sentiment should conceal from us the continuity of purpose which links this
to the rest of the play. Lavinia's torture answers, as the wording of the
speech reminds us, to that formerly meted out by her brothers to their
defeated foe. The persistent use of images related to trees ('lopp'd and
hew'd', 'branches'), and the turning to blood of the crystalline streams
of pastoral fantasy, both serve to relate these horrors to the woods and
natural surroundings which have already been so variously evoked in
their relation to human passions and desires; and behind all this, of
course, there lies the sustained parallel with the revenge of Tereus which
Titus will in due course carry through to its culmination of savagery.

At the end of these crucial scenes the action returns to a simpler
pattern of horrors. Titus pleads in vain for his sons, who stand under
conviction for murder. The prevailing tone of his plea is, as ever,
typically elegiac, the overflow of

> My heart's deep languor and my soul's sad tears.   (III. i. 13)

It falls, however, upon totally unresponsive ears. As Lucius puts it, 'you
recount your sorrows to a stone', and Titus himself is left to conclude
that stones have in some sense more feeling than the Romans who
reject his prayers. 'A stone is soft as wax, tribunes more hard than
stones'. From now on, the far greater tragedy of fear is at times faintly
foreshadowed in Titus' reflections as he too turns towards madness;

> Why, foolish Lucius, dost thou not perceive
> That Rome is but a wilderness of tigers?[7]

> Tigers must prey, and Rome affords no prey
> But me and mine.   (III. i. 53)

As Lavinia, who has already had occasion to compare her enemies to
tigers,[8] is brought to her father, tongueless and ravished, Titus is forced
to recognize his isolation from humanity in terms which remind us of
Timon announcing his last refuge from the ferocity of mankind:

> For now I stand as one upon a rock,
> Environ'd with a wilderness of sea;[9]   (III. i. 94)

we may perhaps find something appropriate in this parallel between
two plays each conceived, though with great difference in dramatic and
poetic power, as it were at the verge, the extreme limit of possible
human attitudes.

As Titus recalls his condemned sons to his ravaged and mutilated
daughter, her speechless emotion conveys itself pathetically to his
words:

> When I did name her brothers, then fresh tears
> Stood on her cheeks, as doth the honey-dew
> Upon a gather'd lily almost wither'd.   (III. i. 112)

Sentiment, however, continues to be poised, in the manner of this play,
against a caustic irony. Whilst the father and his remaining children
unite in lamenting these cruelties, Aaron enters with news of the
emperor's last mockery of justice. Titus is to sever his own hand in the
hope of saving his offspring from their fate. Whilst the deceived father
expresses his gratitude for this crowning irony:

> O gracious emperor! O gentle Aaron!
> Did ever raven sing so like a lark?—   (III. i. 158)

and disputes with his sons the gruesome privilege of making the sacrifice,
Aaron comments with typical sarcasm:

> Nay, come, agree whose hand shall go along,
> For fear they die before their pardon come.   (III. i. 175)

This, in turn, has hardly been uttered, and the sacrifice made, before the
messenger returns, bearing two heads and the hand newly sacrificed. As
Lavinia kisses her father, Titus, with a last outburst of feeling, says

> that kiss is comfortless
> As frozen water to a starved snake,   (III. i. 250)

before bursting out into the frenzied 'Ha, ha, ha!' which marks both his final collapse into madness and the confirmation of his dedication to an inhuman revenge. As the scene ends, each brother takes up a severed head, and Lavinia follows with her father's hand grotesquely clenched between her teeth. They go in search of 'Revenge's cave', the abode of darkness and unnatural horror, whilst Lucius is sent, in an equally unnatural reversal of patriotic ties, to rouse the Gothic enemy to arms against Rome.

The episodes which follow, presenting Titus as finally mad, are heavy with artifice and sententiousness. His protest against his son's killing of 'an innocent fly' is warded off by Marcus when he compares the 'victim' to the 'empress' Moor'; we are reminded on the surface—but only on the surface—of Lear's greater madness.[10] Finally Lavinia, in an episode towards which one of the play's principal threads of reiterated imagery has been leading, exposes her murderers through the book which tells the story of Philomel, 'ravish'd and wrong'd', 'Forced in the ruthless, vast and gloomy woods',[11] in a spot

> By nature made for murders and for rapes. (IV. i. 58)

Nature herself appears to reflect the inhuman aberrations of man, and Titus, though he seems for a moment to turn aside from the vengeance which his sons propose, does so only because his mind is dedicated to a course which will soon reveal itself as still more ferocious and extreme.

At this point a measure of much-needed human relief is afforded, however grotesquely, by the birth (IV. ii) of Tamora's 'blackamoor child'. With a supreme turn of irony Aaron, defying the general consensus of outraged opinion, begins to celebrate his 'first-born son and heir' even as Demetrius threatens, in the play's characteristic idiom, to 'broach the tadpole on my rapier's point'. The birth in Aaron of a paternal instinct which he declares emphatically against the loathing of the world to which he has attached himself is one of the most effective strokes, poised between irony and grim farce, in the entire play. It leads through his grotesque expressions of endearment—

> Look, how the black slave smiles upon the father,
> As who should say 'Old lad, I am thine own'— (IV. ii. 121)

to the killing of the Nurse, equally grotesque in the ironic key—

> Weke, weke!
> So cries a pig prepared to the spit— (IV. ii. 147)

and to the final paternal caricature which accompanies his departure:

> Come on, you thick-lipp'd slave, I'll bear you hence;
> For it is you that puts us to our shifts.   (IV. ii. 177)

This new development in Aaron, not less unexpected for being entirely
in accord with the prevailing irony of his presentation, is one of this
tragedy's most effective devices.

Titus, meanwhile, dedicated to madness and engaged in shooting
arrows bearing messages for the avenging gods (IV. iii), searches for
'justice' on land and sea, but finds only its dreadful caricature, revenge;
as his nephew Publius puts it in the form of a reputed reply from the
other world,

> Pluto sends you word,
> If you will have Revenge from hell, you shall:
> Marry, for Justice, she is so employ'd,
> He thinks, with Jove in heaven, *or somewhere else*,
> So that perforce you needs must stay a time.   (IV. iii. 37)

Revenge, indeed, can only come from 'hell', from the reversal of all
ties of piety and natural feeling, and it is appropriately at this point that
news comes (IV. iv) of the return of Lucius, leading the Goths against
Saturninus, whilst Tamora prepares to placate Titus in order to stave off
the threat to their common rule.

The entry of Lucius with his Gothic allies (V. i) initiates, accordingly,
the last stage of the action. Aaron, brought before him, appeals for the
only grace that now truly concerns him, the life of his child: 'Touch
not the boy; he is of royal blood'. His appeal is made, in a typically
detached way, to the religion of the conqueror, which he does not
pretend to share:

> I know thou art religious,
> And hast a thing within thee called conscience,
> With twenty popish tricks and ceremonies.   (V. i. 74)

For himself, he admits to the possession of no such 'thing', contemplating in equal good spirit the crime against Lavinia—

> she was wash'd and cut and trimm'd, and 'twas
> Trim sport for them that had the doing of it—   (V. i. 95)

and the deception which led to Andronicus' loss of his hand:

> I play'd the cheater for thy father's hand;
> And, when I had it, drew myself apart,
> And almost broke my heart with extreme laughter.   (V. i. 111)

Aaron's departure from the play, as consistently unrepentant as when he entered it, is perhaps Shakespeare's most successful achievement in the ironic, 'Marlovian' manner. He was to do other things infinitely more worth the doing, but—within the limits he set himself—this is as finished a performance as any.

The approaching conclusion (V. ii) meanwhile brings Tamora, disguised as Revenge, to Titus with her sons. Mad as he is, he recognizes her, and adds Rape and Murder, in the persons of Chiron and Demetrius, to their mother's presence: 'Good Lord, how like the empress' sons they are!' This is admirable use of the personifications of the old drama which Shakespeare was even at this moment in the process of out-distancing. Already a deliberately sardonic note prevails over melodrama, as Titus rises to the bitterness of his denunciation:

> Look round about the wicked streets of Rome,
> And when thou findst a man that's like thyself,
> Good Murder, stab him; he's a murderer. (V. ii. 98)

Outmanœuvring Tamora at her own game, he is successful in getting 'Rape' and 'Murder' to remain with him till he cuts their throats. The way is clear for the final feast, in which the revenge of Philomel—so obsessively present in the preceding action—is finally re-enacted in a spirit of dreadful irony:

> The feast is ready, which the careful Titus
> Hath ordain'd to an honourable end,
> For peace, for love, for league and good to Rome. (V. iii. 21)

The dedication amounts by now to a savage parody of all the public spirit and decorum for which Titus himself stood in the play's opening scenes. With his purpose achieved, and after the general slaughter, it only remains for him to die at the hands of Saturninus, whom Lucius in turn immediately kills.

As the play ends, with its impulse to destruction exhausted in death, Marcus calls the Roman people to restore their unity:

> O, let me teach you how to knit again
> This scatter'd corn into one mutual sheaf,
> These broken limbs again into one body. (V. iii. 70)

With peace and unity thus invoked through the supreme 'natural' symbols of concord, which will rarely be far henceforth from Shakespeare's thought, the crimes of the past are exposed and Lucius hailed as lawful emperor. Marcus dedicates to his dead father an appropriate elegy—'Tear for tear and loving kiss for kiss'—and Titus' grandson is called upon, in the name of 'kind nature', to add his tears to the general lament:

> Bid him farewell; commit him to the grave;
> Do him that kindness, and take leave of him.   (V. iii. 170)

To the last, the pieties of the family stand out, if only by contrast, in this uniquely savage play. Only Aaron, of the survivors, is excluded from them, left 'breast-deep in earth' to famish in the sensualist's appropriate torture. To the end, however, he is consistent in his refusal to recognize the existence of good:

> If one good deed in all my life I did,
> I do repent it from my very soul;   (V. iii. 189)

only through consistency in ill-doing can the 'soul', in which—paradoxically—he has consistently declared that he does not believe, attain the expression of its malevolence. Tamora too remains beyond redemption. 'Heinous tiger' to her last breath, she is left without the grace of burial in answer to her own ferocity; for, as Lucius says,

> Her life was beastly and devoid of pity,
> And, being so, shall have like want of pity.   (V. iii. 199)

With the fall of the curtain, Lucius declares his intention so to 'order well the state' that 'like events may ne'er it ruinate'.

III

THE EARLY COMEDIES

1 The Comedy of Errors

LIKE NOT a few other great artists, Shakespeare's development at the outset of his dramatic career seems to have been relatively slow. Had he died at the early age of Christopher Marlowe, it is quite possible that we might to-day have found him the less striking, the less obviously original of the two writers. The judgement, however, would have been rash, even illusory. If we may concede that the impact of Marlowe's genius was at this stage more obviously emphatic, it is at least equally certain that the early plays of Shakespeare show a wider range, a closer adaptation to more varied dramatic ends. We have already traced in the early chronicle plays the growth of a remarkably forceful unifying conception which ended by producing, in *Richard III*, what is in effect a new kind of drama; and we have found even in the apparently unpromising material offered by *Titus Andronicus* anticipations of effects later to be vastly developed. At the same time, in another series of early plays, Shakespeare was engaged in exploring the possibilities of the comic convention, shaping it by a process resembling trial and error into an instrument for expressing the finished statements about life—and more especially about love and marriage as central realities in the pattern of living—that he was already, beneath the obvious desire to entertain, concerned to make. Since Shakespeare embarked upon his career as a comic writer and since he also finished it by writing comedies—albeit of a very different kind—it seems appropriate to give due consideration at each stage to his constantly developing conception of the comic forms.[1]

The first step in this life-long process may well have been *The Comedy of Errors*, which seems to have been acted for the first time in 1594 but which was possibly written as much as two years earlier. The play is basically a comedy of 'intrigue' conceived on well-established classical lines; the plot is derived from two plays by Plautus[2] and shows a considerable skill in weaving incidents from both these works into a coherent dramatic structure. The result is a formal construction of some intricacy. It is in fact through its pleasurable juggling with a plot continually expanding into new situations, repeatedly threatening to escape the demands of dramatic logic and yet always found to be under control, that the piece achieves its effect. On the strictly formal side it is worth noting that Shakespeare accepted the challenge implied in the added intricacy of his plot; the play offers us *two* Dromios against Plautus' one and places *two* women in significant contrast. Since the working out to harmonious conclusions of intricate sets of personal relationships is to be an essential part of Shakespeare's mature comic conception, which none of his greater comedies will fail to use to the full, we should not underestimate the importance of this initial exercise in elaborate plot-making for his developing art.

There is, however, a good deal more than this to *The Comedy of Errors*. That Shakespeare was concerned with an effect more complex than any which mere intrigue plotting could give is suggested by his setting of the comic action in a framework which answers to a different, a notably more serious mood. As the play opens, the Syracusan merchant Aegeon, searching for the wife and child he has lost at sea, finds himself condemned to die in the hostile city of Ephesus. He relates his adventures in verse which, although we may find it relatively crude, conveys a certain sense of solemnity, a suggestion of meanings beyond those immediately apparent. When a Shakespearean character can speak, at this early stage in the dramatist's career, of 'the always wind-obeying deep' and of his own ship as 'sinking-ripe': when he can answer the Duke's expression of helpless compassion—'For we may pity, though not pardon thee'—by referring to the action of supernatural powers:

> O, had the gods done so, I had not now
> Worthily term'd them merciless to us;   (I. i. 98)

when, finally, he can balance 'love' against 'loss' as he recalls the son from whom an adverse fate has separated him:

> Whom whilst I labour'd of a love to see,
> I hazarded the loss of whom I loved: (I. i. 130)

we must feel that we are moving in a world which, for all the obvious

difference in depth of feeling and mastery of expression, is not entirely
remote from that of the final romances. The antitheses and the solemnity, the balance of loss and gain, suggest a desire to set the main
intrigue against a more ample background, less immediately definable
in terms of comic incident, than itself.

The opening lines of the principal story (I. ii) serve, indeed, to connect it with what has gone before. Antipholus of Syracuse is shown on
his first appearance to be possessed by melancholy, in search of a content which he feels, albeit obscurely, that he needs to find beyond the
limitations of the self:

> He that commends me to mine own content
> Commends me to the thing I cannot get.
> I to the world am like a drop of water,
> That in the ocean seeks another drop;
> Who, falling there to find his fellow forth,
> Unseen, inquisitive, confounds himself:
> So I, to find a mother and a brother,
> In quest of them, unhappy, lose myself.   (I. ii. 33)

There is something more here than mere intrigue comedy. Whereas
this is habitually and exclusively concentrated upon confusion, upon
the entrance mistakenly sought to the wrong house and the blow given
and taken in error, Shakespeare's comic incidents normally suggest
something beyond themselves, point—on the further side of their surface impact, which we may enjoy for its own sake—to a deeper reflection of the human situation. The speaker of the words we have just
quoted is concerned to 'find himself'; and the point of the web of
errors into which he—and with him those around him—fall in the
course of undertaking this search lies in their irrational and finally even
sinister inversion of reality. As Antipholus goes on to say of Ephesus:

> They say this town is full of cozenage;
> As, nimble jugglers that deceive the eye,
> Dark-working sorcerers that change the mind,
> Soul-killing witches that deform the body,
> Disguised cheaters, prating mountebanks,
> And many such-like liberties of sin.   (I. ii. 97)

The essence of Shakespearean comedy lies in the undermining of the
common order of reality, in its temporary substitution by an unfamiliar
and more disturbing world from which the principal characters finally

return to that same order with their initial pre-conceptions shattered
and their natures correspondingly enriched. At the far end of this
exposure to the comic nightmare which is about to engulf him Antipholus, and the rest with him, will see life in something closer to its true
nature, will—always within the limits which comedy finally imposes—
find himself in his relation to others. The experience will be positively
rewarding; but during the course of it, in his in-between state of loss
and bewilderment, he will always be on the point of leaving Ephesus
and so of placing this happiness behind him, leaving his final reconciliation to the real world and to his own nature unachieved.

The comic nightmare initiated in this way is connected with human
relationships and, at their centre, with love and its fulfilment in marriage. It is for this reason that Shakespeare, extending the scope of his
classical sources, introduces *two* women into his action, contrasting and
humanizing them in a way that is entirely his own. Adriana, when she
first appears, is moved by jealousy to question the natural dependence
of marriage upon a reasonable acceptance of male authority. 'Why',
she asks, speaking of the men whose freedom she envies, 'should their
liberty than ours be more?' (II. i. 10). Her companion Luciana bases her
reply upon traditional views of the marriage relationship, asserting that
'Men more divine, the masters of all these' are, by virtue of their
superior endowment with 'intellectual sense and souls' 'masters to
their females', and concludes: 'Ere I learn love, I'll practise to obey'.
The argument is based in the last resort upon an acceptance of natural
order. As Luciana forcibly puts it,

> Why, headstrong liberty is lash'd with woe.
> There's nothing situate under heaven's eye
> But hath his bound, in earth, in sea, in sky;   (II. i. 15)

but, although this view is clearly intended to prevail, as it will prevail
even more emphatically in *The Taming of the Shrew*,[3] there is also some
force in Adriana's reply:

> They can be meek that have no other cause.
> A wretched soul, bruised with adversity,
> We bid be quiet when we hear it cry;
> But were we burden'd with like weight of pain,
> As much or more, we should ourselves complain.   (II. i. 33)

There is an element of debate here, a juxtaposition of contrasted points
of view, which will be very close to Shakespeare's mature genius; but
the possibility of holding the balance should not blind us to the fact that

Adriana's jealousy is, as Luciana truly sees, 'self-harming' (II. i), and that the comic situations of this play turn repeatedly on people who appear, as we have already seen in the case of Antipholus, to be thrown in upon themselves, humanly isolated in a way which finds its comic reflection in a kind of madness. Adriana echoes Antipholus' original comparison of himself to 'a drop of water' seeking its fellow in the ocean[4] when, even in her jealousy, she sets forth a true view of marriage—

> For know, my love, as easy mayst thou fall
> A drop of water in the breaking gulf,
> And take unmingled thence that drop again,
> Without addition or diminishing,
> As take from me thyself, and not me too—   (II. ii. 129)

although she drives it in her obsession to falsely possessive and violent conclusions:

> For if we two be one, and thou play false,
> I do digest the poison of thy flesh,
> Being strumpeted by thy contagion.   (II. ii. 146)

These relatively external parallels in word and situation initiate, however imperfectly, comic devices that Shakespeare will later turn to immeasurably greater effect.

The presentation of contrasted attitudes, leading to a truth greater than any single one of them can compass, is extended in the course of the play to other aspects of love. Antipholus of Syracuse expresses his love for Luciana in characteristically romantic terms:

> Sing, siren, for thyself, and I will *dote*:
>   Spread o'er the silver waves thy golden hairs,
> And as a bed I'll take them, and there lie;
>   And in that glorious supposition, think
> He gains by death that hath such means to die;   (III. ii. 48)

but his use of the word 'dote', which responds repeatedly, in Shakespearean comic terms, to the excesses of sentimental passion, is a sure pointer to the true nature of his 'glorious supposition', and Luciana has no hesitation in calling him 'mad' and in directing him firmly towards sanity through an acceptance of the sober truth of marriage: 'Gaze where you should, and that will clear your sight'. Only, of course, it is an essential part of the general comic alienation that it is the *wrong* Antipholus whom she is thus soundly advising. Obstinate in the illusion he has chosen to follow, the Syracusan calls her

> mine own self's better part,
> Mine eye's clear eye, my dear heart's dearer heart,
> My food, my fortune, and my sweet hope's aim,
> My sole earth's heaven, and my heaven's claim; (III. ii. 61)

but this, which converts the true language of married love into the excess of love's idolatry, is realistically balanced by his servant's description, in the same scene, of the pursuit to which he has been subjected by the kitchen-maid of Ephesus. For Dromio speaks of love in terms deliberately and exaggeratedly opposite to those used by his master; Luce, he says, makes upon him 'such claim as you would lay to your horse': and again: 'she would have me as a beast; not that, I being a beast she would have me; but that she, being a very beastly creature, lays claim to me', in order to transform him, as he also says, to 'a curtal dog' (III. ii. 152). The point here does not lie in the quality of the humour which is, as is often the case with Shakespeare's early clowns, at once coarse and rather tedious, but in the opposing of an element of realism, stressed even to the point of vulgarity, to the excesses of romantic love. In the end, at all events, Antipholus himself is ready to confess to the existence of a part of 'madness' in his love:

> She that doth call me husband, even my soul
> Doth for a wife abhor. But her fair sister,
> Possess'd with such a gentle sovereign grace,
> Of such enchanting presence and discourse,
> Hath almost made me *traitor to myself*:
> But lest myself be *guilty to self-wrong*,
> I'll stop mine ears against the mermaid's song.   (III. ii. 164)

By the end of the intrigue he will have been brought from this 'madness', this 'betrayal' of his own true nature, to 'sanity' in another, more positive and inclusive order of things.

Until that conclusion is revealed, however, contradiction prevails everywhere in Ephesus. Adriana's jealousy, and the conflict to which it gives rise, are portrayed with an effort at psychological plausibility that very notably surpasses the hard-boiled, finally pitiless attitudes that Shakespeare might, had he so desired, have taken over from his classical originals. In her resentment she describes her husband as

> deformed, crooked, old and sere,
> Ill-faced, worse bodied, shapeless everywhere;
> Vicious, ungentle, foolish, blunt, unkind;
> Stigmatical in making, worse in mind.   (IV. ii. 14)

The concentration upon physical deformity and inadequacy as an instrument of comic ridicule answers fully to the spirit of Shakespeare's Roman models; but it is noteworthy that, in the same breath, Adriana goes on to recognize the difference between what jealousy has made her say and what, in her heart, she knows to be the truth: 'I think him better than I say. . . . My heart prays for him, though my tongue do curse'. In this admission we are shown, if we care to read, the way out of madness and excess, the replacement of irrational possessiveness, and the contrary and self-consuming excesses to which it gives rise, by the natural order of married love.

Meanwhile, and until the moment has come for the truth to be revealed, the world of Ephesian madness prevails as Dromio enters with the news of his supposed master's arrest; as the other Antipholus puts it, only moments later,

> here we wander *in illusions*:
> Some *blessed power* deliver us from hence! (IV. iii. 42)

The Courtezan makes her brief appearance to the Syracusan Antipholus, who sees her as 'mistress Satan', whilst his twin of Ephesus is incomprehensibly arrested and subjected to the comic exorcism of Pinch (IV. iv). We can hardly be surprised that Antipholus of Syracuse, finding himself once more at the heart of the nightmare, determines yet again to seek safety in flight: 'I will not stay to-night for all the town' (IV. iv. 159).

But his departure, of course, would take him, against all appearances, away from sanity and the true resolution of his problems. It is at this point, accordingly, as master and servant seek refuge in the priory from the lunacy which everywhere surrounds them, that we return to the spirit of the 'serious' framework which contains the comic plot. The return, expressed in terms of Shakespearean comedy, is to reality and natural life. Adriana enters, in search of her 'poor distracted husband' and the Abbess, in whose hands the final resolution rests, reproves her gravely for the jealousy which has been her own form of insanity:

> And therefore came it that the man was mad.
> The venom clamours of a jealous woman
> Poisons more deadly than a mad dog's tooth. (V. i. 68)

Adriana, in turn, confirms her awakening to reality by taking the rebuke in good part: 'She did betray me to my own reproof'. The

Abbess, in return, agrees to restore her husband 'to his wits again', for this is, as she affirms with proper solemnity, 'A charitable duty of my order'. The pattern, however, is still far from complete. At this point, as Aegeon enters under arrest, we are reminded of the sombre framework in which this farce has deliberately been set, invited to contemplate

> the melancholy vale,
> The place of death and sorry execution.   (V. i. 120)

As Antipholus of Ephesus makes his entry, demanding 'justice' against his wife, the Duke, as though to emphasize the precarious and relative nature of our understanding of life, concludes that all alike have 'drunk of Circe's cup' and are accordingly alienated from their right minds. Aegeon, surprised by the failure of the wrong Antipholus to recognize him in the hour of his greatest need, speaks in rueful solemnity of time's betraying action:

> O, grief hath changed me since you saw me last,
> And careful hours with time's deformed hand
> Have written strange defeatures in my face.   (V. i. 298)[5]

But even as he exclaims in bitterness against 'time's extremity', the entry of the second twin enables the Abbess to bring sanity out of alienation, to clear up the intrigue in what will come to be the constant manner of Shakespearean comedy. The Abbess is recognized to be Aegeon's lost wife and, in the light of this discovery, asserts the restoration of sane harmony, the resolution of past sorrow into present joy:

> Thirty-three years have I but gone in travail
> Of you, my sons: and till this present hour
> My heavy burthen ne'er delivered.   (V. i. 403)

The long years of 'travail' have at last borne their natural and appropriate fruit. The masters embrace to celebrate their restoration to one another in the sane light of day; and their servants, having renounced all claim to invidious precedence, which their very twinship denies—

> We came into the world like brother and brother;
> And now let's go hand in hand, not one before another—   (V. i. 427)

go in to take part in the social consummation represented by what they call 'the gossiping'.

2 The Taming of The Shrew

For what may have been his second exercise in comedy, *The Taming of the Shrew*, Shakespeare took another plot of the 'intrigue' type, but developed it in ways which suggest that his experience with *The Comedy of Errors* had made him aware that this type of play would not easily adapt itself to the purposes he already had in mind. *The Comedy of Errors* set its comic action in the 'serious' framework provided by its opening and conclusion, thus establishing a contrast which served to point the play's deeper meanings. In *The Taming of the Shrew* the dramatist preferred to incorporate side by side two separate and distinct strands of plot, extracting his comic effects precisely from the constantly shifting interplay between them; but he also provided an Induction, which answers in some sense to the 'framework' of the previous play but differs notably from it by the absence of any return to it in the conclusion, the main action being left accordingly open in a way that separates the new play fundamentally from the effect sought and obtained in its predecessor.

The Taming of the Shrew turns, accordingly, upon three different elements of plot, two of which operate at a different level from the third. The first of these is the Induction which, in the course of the two opening scenes, sets the entire comic action in a framework provided by the transformation of the drunken tinker Christopher Sly into an 'aristocratic' spectator of the play which has been arranged for his benefit. Next to this, and answering to the main substance of the comedy, is the popular knockabout story of Katherine the shrew and her marriage to Petruchio, which Shakespeare uses to put forward in comic form certain ideas about marriage and about the natural relationship between the sexes. Finally, the story of Bianca and her suitors, which is derived ultimately from Ariosto's play *I Suppositi*,[6] introduces by way of deliberate contrast a relatively sophisticated element of Italianate comedy. No single one of these diverse threads is perhaps, taken in itself, of outstanding interest or comic value, though we should not underestimate the effect which they are capable of making on the stage; but, taken together, their significance lies, in what is already coming to be Shakespeare's characteristic comic manner, in the way in which they play upon one another to bring out the full intention of the play.

We begin, then, with the Induction, which aims at providing the principal comic story with a framework, a setting which at once isolates it from common reality and conveys, in some measure, an implicit comment upon it. Sly is a man taken out of himself, induced, in the words of the Lord who plans his transformation, to 'forget himself'; and then within this illusion, as though to provide an additional element of indirectness, a second deception is set up with the arrival of the players to perform their comedy. The result is an effect of considerable subtlety, which notably exceeds in its complexity anything in the previous play. Having been introduced on the stage to Sly, in his mixture of boorishness and ignorance, we are asked as spectators to stand aside *with him*, to step into the illusion and to watch a further action being carried out on what is, to all intents and purposes, a stage within a stage. The device should save us, among other things, from taking too seriously the story of the shrew and her taming, from reading into it too directly what is apt to strike us as an inhuman and primitive attitude towards women. Compared with Sly, all the characters of the main action appear as what they are, creatures of the stage, instruments of theatrical illusion. In this way, Shakespeare is already foreshadowing his characteristic comic balance between what *is* and what *seems*, between appearance and reality.

Sly, indeed, emerges, when considered in this context, as a figure of some potential subtlety. In the course of his brief occupation of the stage he is imaginatively translated, carried to a new world of the imagination, which he initially resists in the name of common sense but to which he finally succumbs. At first, the luxury to which he awakens from his drunken sleep is contrasted with the prose plainness of his reaction: 'Am not I Christopher Sly, old Sly's son of Burton heath, by birth a pedlar, by education a card-maker, by transmutation a bearherd, and now by present profession a tinker?' (*Induction*, ii. 18); but gradually his unbelief is overcome as he is absorbed into a dream which the reality around him seems to confirm:

> I do not sleep; I see, I hear, I speak;
> I smell sweet savours and I feel soft things:
> Upon my life, I am a lord indeed,
> And not a tinker, nor Cristophero Sly.   (*Induction*, ii. 72)

Finally it is the reality of his own waking state which becomes for him a 'dream', and the present illusion the truth from which he becomes anxious not to awaken; 'I would be loath', he says in his new, 'trans-formed' state, 'to fall into my dreams again: I will therefore tarry in despite of the flesh and the blood' (*Induction*, ii. 128). Although this device may seem crude in the manner of its development, some of its implications already answer, however dimly, to the nature of drama itself.

Within the framework thus provided, we are given two plots brought together in ways which the dramatist certainly intended to be mutually revealing. The first, and more important, is the 'tumbling-trick' or 'Christmas gambol'[7] of Katherine's 'taming'; the second, more urbane and sophisticated in its effect, is the story of Bianca and her lovers. Taken together, these two stories set a realistic against what purports to be an idealistic attitude towards marriage; but—and it is at this point that we approach the substance of Shakespeare's intention—it is in the end Katherine, the supposedly heartless and rejected shrew, who submits to the balanced, 'natural' view of marriage, and the idealized, idolized Bianca who is seen by her final attitude to reject it.

In responding to the impression of barbarism which the 'shrew' story may initially make upon us, we shall do well to take into account a number of qualifying factors. Katherine at the outset has good reason to protest against her father's demand that she should marry before her sister. To her reasonable protest against this treatment—

> I pray you, sir, is it your will
> To make a stale of me amongst these mates?—   (I. i. 57)

the brief and obstinate assertion of Baptista's bare determination—'Gentlemen, content you: I am resolved'—is less than an adequate answer. If Shakespeare here, as in later plays, is ready to argue in favour of a proper submission as natural, implicit in the order of things, this must emphatically *not* be taken to mean that submission has no limits, that the relationship between father and children, or between man and wife, is conceived by him in one-sided terms of domination and subservience.

Nor, if we care to remember that this is a play, a conventional reflec-tion of life—and one, moreover, which the dramatist has been careful, by setting it within a more 'realistic' framework, to remove from immediate reality—shall we find Petruchio as harsh and unreasonable as may appear. The contrast is throughout between his commonsense grasp of real life and the wildly romantic devotion which induces Lucentio to say of the worthless Bianca:

> Tranio, I saw her coral lips to move,
> And with her breath she did perfume the air:
> Sacred and sweet was all I saw in her;   (I. i. 178)

to which the servant, in a notably more realistic mood, replies by speaking of his master's infatuation as a 'trance' and by advising him to prove the worth of these high-flown assertions by acting in accordance with them:

> if you love the maid,
> Bend thoughts and wits to achieve her.   (I. i. 182)

For all its apparent crudity, Petruchio's attitude has a hard-headed actuality which that of Lucentio lacks. When the latter says,

> Tranio, I burn, I pine, I perish, Tranio,
> If I achieve not this young modest girl,   (I. i. 159)

an element of romantic excess, finally self-regarding and self-indulgent, colours his declaration: whereas, when Petruchio declares frankly that his motives are to make his fortune and to see the world:—

> I come to wive it wealthily in Padua;
> If wealthily, then happily in Padua—   (I. ii. 75)

we can still leave it to events to show whether the speaker is capable of understanding that there is more than this to marriage, or whether bluntness of this kind is compatible with true feeling.

The entire attitude of Petruchio, indeed, reflects an essential common-sense which stands in contrast to the behaviour of Bianca's various lovers in this play: to that of Gremio who, being old, is content to woo her with his wealth,[8] and of Lucentio, whose romanticism turns out, when put to the test, to be compatible with the readiness to deceive which leads him to use a personification of his father to gain his ends.[9] In contrast to so much artifice and deceit, it is revealing to set the terms in which the supposedly insensitive Petruchio describes Katherine to herself mingling burlesque with a forthright, natural strain of poetry:

> 'Twas told me you were rough and coy and sullen,
> And now I find report a very liar;
> For thou art pleasant, gamesome, passing courteous,
> But slow in speech, yet sweet as spring-time flowers:
> Thou canst not frown, thou canst not look askance,
> Nor bite the lip, as angry wenches will,
> Nor hast thou pleasure to be cross in talk,

> But thou with mildness entertain'st thy wooers,
> With gentle conference, soft and affable.
> Why does the world report that Kate doth limp?
> O slanderous world! Kate, like the hazel-twig,
> Is straight and slender, and as brown in hue
> As hazel nuts and sweeter than the kernels.   (II. i. 238)

We may feel that Petruchio is in effect revealing the *real* Kate to her-self, showing what is—though she does not yet know it and her behaviour has so far seemed to belie it—her true nature to a girl who has been systematically belittled by all around her, not excluding her own father. Petruchio is announcing his programme, describing Kate less as she is than as she is capable of becoming once he has, by his deliberate use of violence in a stage situation, succeeded in moulding her to what the play takes to be the natural, the reasonable attitude to marriage. Petruchio's statement of his positions is habitually extreme, as befits the kind of comedy with which we are here concerned, but the positions themselves are invariably a defence of nature—even when he insists, with a brutal directness which such as Lucentio would find intolerably gross, upon the child-bearing function of woman: 'Women were made to bear, and so are you' (II. i. 201). Petruchio's positions stand out by contrast to the facile and disembodied idealism exhibited in an obsessive concern with the dowry, the main chance, in a world finally steeped in self-interest, by Bianca's devoted servants. When Katherine's father and his own friends are horrified by the 'unreverent robes' in which he presents himself for his wedding, Petruchio can retort 'To me she's married, not unto my clothes', and go on to say, with striking and characteristic modesty:

> Could I repair what she will wear in me,
> As I can change these poor accoutrements,
> 'Twere well for Kate, and *better for myself*.   (III. ii. 121)

In this further contrast between *seeming* and *being*, between the external appearance a man can so easily put on and the reality of his nature, Petruchio shows a moral seriousness which, in our attention to the slapstick action, we can too easily neglect.

Accordingly, as the crude episodes of the 'taming' follow upon one another, we are brought to see that Petruchio's treatment of his shrew implies a process of education, that it is aimed, among other things and rather surprisingly, at teaching her to *feel*. This is apparent when he strikes his servants before her and gets her to protest against what seems to be his lack of human consideration. Katherine does in fact develop in the course of the play in the direction of the feeling and humanity which she seemed initially to lack:

> My tongue will tell the anger of my heart;
> Or else my heart, concealing it, will break.   (IV. iii. 77)

If she begins by beating her sister without mercy (II. i), she ends by protesting against her husband's treatment of the Tailor and the Haberdasher (IV. iii); and it is no doubt precisely his intention that she should react in this way. When this advance from the hoydenish invective of the early scenes has been confirmed by her behaviour under test, he is ready to respond with a statement of the 'natural' relationship between men and women and by an assumption of true marriage. This he does even whilst satirizing the excesses of love-sick romanticism by calling his spaniel Troilus (IV. i) and just at the moment when the third of Bianca's suitors, Hortensio, renounces her in favour of 'a wealthy widow' (IV. ii).

The contrast, indeed, to which the play leads us is one between Kate who, prepared by the rude process of education to which she is subjected, becomes the good wife she has always had it in her to be, and Bianca, the idealized *coquette* who ends by refusing to obey her husband's command. The play's 'philosophy', if so pretentious a word may be allowed, depends upon the assertion of nature which it has all along been Petruchio's function to defend:

> Thus the bowl should run,
> And not unluckily against the bias.   (IV. v. 24)

This is the foundation of his whole attitude; and the argument is that when things are so arranged, when the relationships of society run in accordance with and not against 'nature', subjection and strife, which are contrasted sides of the same coin, are replaced by free agreement and mutual harmony. Against what may appear to be the spirit of much of its story, the play thus emerges as a civilizing effort on Shakespeare's part, one not essentially out of line with the spirit of his later comedies, which tend always to enhance human relationships, to provide for them a foundation in tenderness and mutual respect.

As the play ends, the husband receives his due—'love, fair looks, and true obedience'—in return for the burden of responsibility he has taken upon himself, and Kate, in the play's most striking utterance, asserts her free conformity with the position he has defended:

> Such duty as the subject owes the prince
> Even such a woman oweth to her husband;
> And when she is froward, peevish, sullen, sour,
> And not obedient to his honest will,
> What is she but a foul contending rebel,
> And graceless traitor to her loving lord? . . .
> My mind hath been as big as one of yours,
> My heart as great, my reason haply more,
> To bandy word for word and frown for frown;
> But now I see our lances are but straws,
> Our strength as weak, our weakness past compare,
> That seeming to be most, which we indeed least are.
> Then vail your stomachs, for it is no boot,
> And place your hands below your husband's foot.   (V. ii. 156)

This is emphatically not an argument from subservience or cowed spirit. Kate's 'mind', her 'heart' and—not least—her 'reason' have been as great as those of the two women—Bianca and the Widow—whom the world has so short-sightedly preferred to her and who have just revealed themselves in their essential frivolity. She has had some motive in the course of the action to 'bandy word for word'; but it is in the nature of things, which society ignores or distorts at its peril, that the wife is bound to stand to her husband, deferring to his '*honest* will' (the adjective is important in so far as it amounts to the deliberate exclusion of arbitrary domination), as the true subject to his prince. The family requires the one relationship no less than the proper ordering of the state the other. The stress is laid, as it will be so often in Shakespeare's later and more developed plays, on the ordering of things according to 'nature', and what Kate has learnt in the course of her knockabout tribulations is precisely neither more nor less than to be 'natural'.

3 The Two Gentlemen of Verona

The Two Gentlemen of Verona, which may have been written after *The Comedy of Errors* and either before or after *The Taming of the Shrew*, has some claim to be considered Shakespeare's most tedious play. It is more profitable, however, to see it as standing somewhere between these early exercises in comic realism and *A Midsummer Night's Dream*. With *The Taming of the Shrew* Shakespeare seems to have exhausted, at least for the moment, the possibilities of intrigue comedy. Indeed, such a play as *The Comedy of Errors* already combines intrigue a little uneasily with less realistic matter; and now, in *The Two Gentlemen*, he turns away from realism itself to the conventions of courtly love and friendship which he was perhaps already using in the Sonnets and which were to be developed in various different forms through his subsequent comedies. The result is a play which foreshadows, although generally in a tentative and imperfect fashion, nearly all the devices he was to use in later and much finer plays.

The central theme of this comedy, which seems to derive from the Spanish author Jorge de Montemayor's *Diana*, written in 1542 and translated by Bartholomew Young, is—for what was to prove the first of many occasions—the difference between appearance and reality, between what *seems* and what *is*. Valentine, who begins by repudiating romantic love in the person of his friend Proteus—

> writers say, as the most forward bud
> Is eaten by the canker ere it blow,
> Even so by love the young and tender wit
> Is turn'd to folly—   (I. i. 45)

ends by falling a victim to it; Proteus, who declares himself as the play opens 'a votary to fond desire', whose heart is 'sick with thought', ends by deserting the object of his passion and by betraying his friend. So contrasted, each provides by implication a comment on the other. Thus, when Valentine has so far fallen a victim to the ill he once despised as to invite Proteus to join him in calling Silvia 'divine', his friend exclaims 'I will not flatter her', and when he falls into the idealistic excess of dignifying Proteus' own mistress Julia with

> this high honour—
> To bear my lady's train, lest the base earth
> Should from her vesture chance to steal a kiss,   (II. iv. 159)

his friend repudiates these high-flown words as so much 'braggartism'. Yet this same realism is in turn exposed when Proteus himself comes to covet Silvia and is ready for her sake to inflict the deepest of 'private wounds' upon his life-long friend.

The point thus made is developed through the entire course of the action, tediously indeed and at times inexpertly, but with some consistency. Valentine, once he has fallen a victim to the passion he formerly despised, expresses his new sentiments with typical excess:

> why, man, she is mine own;
> And I as rich in having such a jewel
> As twenty seas, if all their sand were pearl,
> The water nectar, and the rocks pure gold.   (II. iv. 169)

This suggests already the characteristic ambivalence which will so often, in the comedies, mark Shakespeare's evocations of romantic love; the 'jewel' of the lover's possession is a real one, represents a genuine enrichment of life, but the phrases which reflect this precious possession are often indicative of strain and exaggeration. Proteus, on the other hand, as he finds out that 'one nail by strength drives out another', shows the beginnings of psychological analysis. 'Love bade me swear, and love bids me forswear': 'Unheedful vows may heedfully be broken'; the speech, as it proceeds, develops into a certain meaningful complexity:

> I cannot leave to love, and yet I do;
> But there I leave to love where I should love.
> Julia I lose, and Valentine I lose:
> If I keep them, I needs must lose myself;
> If I lose them, thus find I by their loss
> For Valentine, myself, for Julia, Silvia.
> I to myself am dearer than a friend,
> For love is still most precious in itself.   (II. vi. 17)

The effort to make Proteus' abrupt transformation credible certainly makes itself felt at this point. Working through the artificiality of the literary conceit, the speech aims at pressing that artifice into the service of a rudimentary analysis. The intention is finally that of the exposure of egoism. Precisely because Proteus can regard it as axiomatic that 'I to myself am dearer than a friend'—this reads, indeed, like a transposition into the comic key of Richard III's 'Richard loves Richard; that is, I am I!'[10]—he can find in his kind of love an emotion 'most precious in itself' and be ready to seek self-gratification through betrayal and abasement. Proteus is disposed to talk easily of 'true love' which, he says, 'hath better deeds than words to grace it' (II. ii. 18); but, even as he speaks in this way, he is getting ready to betray this truth by his own behaviour. Knowing at heart his passion to be 'erring' and himself to be 'blind', he is nonetheless disposed to go to the depths of degradation to obtain the satisfaction he both abjectly and treacherously craves:

> If I can check my erring love, I will;
> If not, to compass her I'll use my skill.   (II. iv. 214)

In this readiness to set aside all natural ties and obligations in the following of what is finally an irrational and ignoble servitude we find, indicated almost for the first time, one of the constant themes of Shakespearean comedy.

It is significant, in this same connection, that Proteus, who is ready to carry egoism to the point of betrayal, has at his finger-tips the most far-fetched expressions of romantic idealism. These he uses to advance his cause with Silvia under the guise of advising the aged Thurio to make his own absurd claim:

> Say that upon the altar of her beauty
> You sacrifice your tears, your sighs, your heart:
> Write till your ink be dry, and with your tears
> Moist it again; and frame some feeling line
> That may discover such integrity;
> For Orpheus' lute was strung with poet's sinews;
> Whose golden touch could soften steel and stones,
> Make tigers tame, and huge leviathans
> Forsake unsounded deeps to dance on sands.
> After your dire-lamenting elegies,
> Visit by night your lady's chamber-window
> With some sweet consort; to their instruments
> Tune a deploring dump; the night's dead silence
> Will well become such sweet-complaining grievance.
> This, or else nothing, will inherit her.   (III. ii. 73)

It is typical of what will come to be Shakespeare's distinctive comic method that this, which can be read as one of the play's more distinguished expressions of emotion, is at the same time a revelation of the limitations of romantic love. Proteus, in recommending the writing of 'some feeling line' to produce an illusion of 'integrity', reveals by implication the artifice that underlies his 'dire-lamenting elegies', the 'deploring dumps' of his self-conscious melancholy. In much the same way, though to much greater poetic effect, Orsino in *Twelfth Night*[11] will at once feel and indulge feeling, combine in his own moody self-awareness the attractions and the short-comings of romantic love.

Other devices contribute to much the same effect. As in still earlier plays, the comic prose of the servants provides a realistic judgement on the irrational behaviour of their masters. Speed asserts the 'deformed' vision of Valentine in love:

—You never saw her since she was deformed.
—How long hath she been deformed?

—Ever since you loved her.

—I loved her ever since I saw her; and still I see her beautiful.

—If you love her, you cannot see her.

—Why?

—Because Love is blind.   (II. i. 70)

As usual we shall not confine the truth to either party to this dialogue: Valentine and Speed each affirm their 'truth' and the point of the exchange lies, not in the one-sided assertion of their respective points of view, but in the interplay of contrasted attitudes. A similar effect can be detected, on another level, in the comments of the women who come out of this comedy so much better than the men who respectively idealize or deceive them. When Julia speaks of Proteus' 'divine perfection' and of herself as 'a true-devoted pilgrim' in the name of love at the very moment when this paragon is engaged in betraying her, the waiting-woman Lucetta is perfectly aware that she is speaking 'above the bounds of reason' (II. vii. 23); and it is to reaffirm these bounds, to free valid human attachments from excess and 'fever', restoring them to their proper place in a sane and balanced conception of life, that Shakespeare's romantic comedy finally aims.

The Two Gentlemen of Verona sets out, in short, to use convention to attain a position from which excess, self-ignorance and self-indulgence have been eliminated. The depths to which these faults can lead are glimpsed, occasionally, in the later scenes. When Proteus sinks into the degradation which his unrequited passion implies, he tells us that Silvia

> bids me think how I have been foresworn
> In breaking faith with Julia whom I loved . . .
> Yet, spaniel-like, the more she spurns my love,
> The more it grows, and fawneth on her still.   (IV. ii. 10)

'Spaniel-like': 'fawneth': Proteus could have used no more characteristic Shakespearean images of abasement and self-disgust to express his predicament.[12]

It is left to Silvia and Julia, who anticipate in this the heroines of later comedies, to oppose to corrupt convention their own firm and clear-eyed view of reality. Silvia denounces Proteus as a 'subtle, perjured, false, disloyal man' (IV. ii. 98); and Julia, reading into his devotion to her rival's painted image a reflection of the confused values which have led to her own betrayal, turns her meditation into a repudiation of the 'idolatry' which love of this kind implies:

> O thou senseless form,
> Thou shalt be worshipp'd, kiss'd, lov'd, and adored
> And, were there sense in his idolatry,
> My substance should be statue in thy stead.   (IV. iv. 206)

For this reason the best-known lines in the play, though sung on behalf of the absurd Sir Thurio, in his attempt to seduce Silvia from her true devotion, answer to a truth which in some measure transcends their setting in convention and courtly intrigue:

> Who is Silvia? what is she,
>   That all our swains commend her?
> Holy, fair, and wise is she;
>   The heavens such grace did lend her,
> That she might admired be.   (IV. ii. 40)

'Holy, fair, and wise' are perhaps terms which surpass anything that this play has to offer. They belong to a kind of idealization which is of its essence literary, and partakes of the limitations of mere literature; but such significance as they have lies in the dramatist's effort to give them a foundation in flesh and blood, to show them as operative in terms of real humanity and normal behaviour. The assertion of feminine common-sense and good faith represents one of the points in which this pale comedy most closely anticipates the future.

The final restoration of sanity and order is preceded, as it will be in later comedies, by a temporary removal from the court to the simplicities of 'natural' life in the forest. The removal is brief, and its effect somewhat ridiculous, but this should not blind us to its connection with later and more impressive devices of a similar kind. In these new surroundings, truth is made apparent, prevails decisively over artifice and error. Valentine, struck to the quick by his friend's betrayal—

> I am sorry I must never trust thee more,
> But count the world a stranger for thy sake—   (V. iv. 69)

is yet capable of rousing Proteus to a confession of 'shame and guilt'; having done so, he shows himself magnanimous to the point—realistically absurd, but justified in terms of the comic convention—of making the gesture of renouncing his own love for the benefit of his betrayer:

> Who by repentance is not satisfied
> Is nor of heaven nor earth, for these are pleased;   (V. iv. 79)

to which gesture, Proteus with equal fittingness replies:

O heaven, were man
But constant, he were perfect! That one error
Fills him with faults; makes him run through all the sins.
(V. iv. 110)

Ridiculous though it is in terms of real life the incident can yet be
justified in terms of the comic conception. As the play ends, Valentine
is declared by the Duke, precisely because he has been constant and has
shown himself ready to risk all for Silvia, to be 'worthy of an empress'
love', and the bandits, to whom the civilized and courtly lovers have
been momentarily subjected in order that they may find themselves in
new and strange surroundings, are recognized to be 'civil, full of good'
and so fit to return with the rest to the world of civilized and social
humanity. Beyond the various absurdities of this conclusion we need to
see neither more nor less than a first essay in the more meaningful
patterns of later comedies. In these, conventions not altogether dissimilar, though immensely deepened and developed, are to become
instruments for the exploration of human relationships, more especially
in love, and for the expression of a true attitude to love itself: an attitude
in which poetry and realism, romance and comedy, are variously
combined. Although it would be dangerous to read too much into this
early and imperfect piece, it is worth noting that it ends already with a
reconciliation of conflicting opposites, the uniting of its lovers and the
return of its outlaws to civilized and social existence: a reconciliation
the unreality of which stresses indeed the distance still to be travelled,
but which has possibilities of development once the dramatic, poetic,
and human contents of the action have been simultaneously expanded.

4 Love's Labour's Lost

Love's Labour's Lost is at once the most obviously formal and the most
immediately impressive of Shakespeare's early comedies. Like much
else about the play, its date and the circumstances under which it was
written are open to question. The Quarto edition is dated as late as
1598, but is described on the title page as 'newly corrected and aug-
mented' The strong element of artificiality in the play has been thought
to favour the theory of an early dating; but, as we already have occasion

to know, an element of artifice is of the stuff of Shakespearean comedy, and the relative polish of a great deal of the writing could very easily point the other way. The use of type names for some of the characters in the Quarto text—Braggart for Armado, Pedant for Holofernes, and so on—suggest some connection with the Italian *commedia dell'arte*, and the use of doggerel rhyme and other varied verse forms indicate the presence of an element of deliberate experiment. Possible references to contemporary literary controversies—to the so-called 'School of Night', to Nashe, Raleigh, Gabriel Harvey, and others—have been suggested, but are too tenuous to lead to firm conclusions and too complicated to be discussed here.

What is certain is that the play opens with a flourish as Navarre and his companions declare their intention of withdrawing from the claims and distractions of normal society to become 'brave conquerors of the world's desires'. The artifice of the declaration, with its studied opening gesture to fame, 'that all hunt after in their lives', its carefully balanced phrasing—'grace us in the disgrace of death'—and its facile defiance of 'cormorant devouring Time' (I. i. 4), leaves us asking ourselves from the first moment whether the course of action upon which this little group is so light-heartedly embarking is either possible or desirable; and much the same impression is left by Navarre's statement that his associates have bound themselves to

> war against your own affections,
> And the huge army of the world's desires.   (I. i. 9)

In other words, can the 'little academe' which advances its pretensions with such airy confidence in fact maintain itself 'Still and contemplative in living art', or will real life break in, first to disturb its resolution and finally, in its own despite, to enrich its purposes?

Almost from the first moment, indeed, the criticism of artifice makes itself felt within the devoted circle. Its mouthpiece is Biron. Biron is the first of a long series of Shakespearean characters who express themselves with notable detachment on the direction taken by the life around them even as they share in its course; Falstaff is the last and greatest example of this type of comic character, but Biron stands on the early stages of the road which led to that immense achievement. It is Biron who almost at once calls the vows taken by his fellow-'academicians' devotion to so many 'barren tasks', the pursuit of 'things hid and barr'd from common-sense', and who defends his own scepticism by referring explicitly to 'nature':

> At Christmas I no more desire a rose,
> Than wish a snow in May's new-fangled shows;
> But like of each thing that in season grows.
> So you, to study now it is too late,
> Climb o'er the house to unlock the little gate. (I. i. 105)

What is proposed is, in fact, as Biron sees, an 'abortive birth'; and his attitude is at once confirmed by the approach of the daughter of the King of France, 'A maid of grace and complete majesty', representing in no uncertain terms the entry of the external world and recalling Navarre to those obligations which, most typically, it turns out by his own admission that he has 'quite forgot'.

As the action expands, the elements of artifice and unreality which have prompted Navarre's project are exposed and criticized from a variety of standpoints. The sum of these, indeed, might be said to be the essence of the play. Nearly all the subsidiary figures who surround the central court situation drop into it from time to time their grain of revealing comment, contribute to an impression in their 'betters' of vain and self-absorbed contrivance. Armado, the 'refined traveller of Spain', a man in love with his own 'fire-new words' (I. i. 177), is obviously himself an object of satire, a parody of certain current literary fashions; but he is none the less found to be susceptible to normal human attractions, in the shape of the charms of the country wench Jaquenetta. He may be absurd, himself the object of comic ridicule, but the very fact of his attachment implies an exposure of the pretentious make-believe of his masters. So also Costard, perhaps the most attractive and variously human of Shakespeare's subsidiary comic figures to be created up to this time. It is Costard who asserts with engaging diffidence 'the simplicity of man to hearken after the flesh' and who finds it no more than natural that Armado should admit to consorting, in spite of his master's decree, with 'a child of our grand-mother Eve' (I. i. 263). It is the function of Costard, in short, to call attention to those simple incontrovertible realities which those around him, exclusively concerned with their own notions and the image of themselves which they are concerned to project upon the world, are too busy to take into account. Faced by the incomprehensible fact of the King's life-denying edict, Costard confesses freely that he has paid little attention to it—'I do confess much of the hearing it, but little of the marking of it'—and concludes with typical, if disarmingly confused bluntness: 'I suffer for the truth, sir; for true it is, I was taken with Jaquenetta, and Jaquenetta is a true girl: and therefore welcome the sour cup of prosperity! Affliction may one day smile again; and till then, sit thee down, sorrow!' (I. i. 309). Such utterances contain much of the spirit of Shakespeare's later comedy, even look forward in their own slighter way to the tone of Pompey's defence of nature and the flesh in the sombre, 'realistic' scenes of *Measure for Measure*.[13]

No sooner, in fact, have the two worlds—that of reality and that of self-absorbed intellectual fantasy—been brought together by the entry of the Princess and her companions than the inadequacy of the positions taken up by the 'academe' stands apparent. The newcomers could be described, perhaps a little unkindly, as a band of blue-stockings; but their liveliness is apparent in their keen wit and they bring with them, together with their courtly sophistication, the appeal of life, a kind of fresh air of which this court is badly in need. Subjected to this test, indeed, the proclaimed self-sufficiency of Navarre and his friends very soon collapses. The Princess has hardly made her first entry (II. i) when she refers to Longaville's 'short-lived wits' and makes her appeal to what will later become, in *As You Like It*, the spirit of Arden. 'The roof of this court', she says to Navarre, speaking of the open air, 'is too high to be yours, and welcome to the wide fields too base to be mine' (II. i. 92). She points too, and in no uncertain terms, to the essential frivolity which has always been implied in Navarre's oath:

> I hear your Grace hath sworn out house-keeping:
> 'Tis deadly sin to keep that oath, my lord,
> And sin to break it.   (II. i. 104)

The emphatic terms of this reproof should suffice to tell us that beneath the wit and the artifice serious issues, closely affecting the fabric of human life, are being brought into play.

As we might expect from his attitude at the beginning, it is Biron who reacts most frankly to this exposure of the untenable positions which he and his companions have so light-heartedly assumed. In so doing he sees himself, with characteristic self-dramatization, as 'love's whip',

> A critic, nay a night-watch constable:
> A domineering pedant o'er the boy,   (III. i. 186)

one who is, by his own admission, falsely and even absurdly confident of his capacity to impose his own judgement upon life. In this respect, he at once stands with his fellows, whose vow he has after all, however sceptically, taken, and maintains himself at a distance. Ready to confess in the face of reality the inadequacy of the attitudes he has, not without frivolity, assumed, he recalls in the detached frankness of his self-criticism something of the spirit to be displayed, under very different circumstances, by Faulconbridge in *King John*.[14] Like Faulconbridge, Biron is an individualist, with the qualities and short-comings of the type, a man who can see his own behaviour from the outside for what it is but who finds it more difficult to propose to himself with conviction a truly adequate course of action: an anticipation, in short, of those later Shakespearean creations—Falstaff, as we have already said,[15] is the supreme example—who live at once inside and outside their dramatic actions, dominating by the force of their comments upon it the very world to which, when seen from another point of view, they are subject:

> What! I love! I sue! I seek a wife!
> A woman, that is like a German clock,
> Still a-repairing, ever out of frame,
> And never going aright, being a watch,
> But being watch'd that it may still go right!
> Nay, to be perjured, which is worst of all:
> And, among three, to love the worst of all;
> A whitely wanton with a velvet brow,
> With two pitch-balls stuck in her face for eyes;
> Ay, and by heaven, one that will do the deed,
> Though Argus were her eunuch and her guard.   (III. i. 199)

Such is the human condition, seen by one who feels the absurdity of his decisions even as, in the interests of a quiet and self-engrossed life, he accepts those which others have made in his name: a state of subjection to the 'plague' which Cupid imposes upon those who are rash enough to call into question 'his almighty dreadful little might'.

Very quickly, indeed, all the 'academicians' find themselves for-sworn and busily engaged, moreover, in seeking comfort for their wounded self-importance in the assurance that they are not, after all, alone in having deserted their ideals. The revelation of their inconstancy is, like everything else in the play, formal and gradual; each of the victims is placed in a position where, acutely conscious of his own weak-ness, he can observe that of the others without being himself observed. Biron can still satirize in his discomfiture the excesses of romantic-literary love as he finds them in Longaville:

> This is the liver-vein, which makes flesh a deity,
> A green goose a goddess: pure, pure idolatry—   (IV. iii. 74)

even as he goes on to admit, 'As true we are as flesh and blood can be'. From this position, it is natural for him to argue that the real 'academes', 'the true Promethean fire', lie, not where he and his master Navarre have perversely sought them, but in the eyes of woman. His argument, still founded upon literary concepts and elaborately artificial in expression, turns none the less into the affirmation of a reality that transcends sophistication, that is capable of gathering up 'learning' into a more living order, a more valid conception of human relationships. 'For where', so the detached and disillusioned courtier finds himself driven to ask,

> is any author in the world
> Teaches such beauty as a woman's eye?
> Learning is but an adjunct to ourself,
> And where we are our learning likewise is,
> Then when ourselves we see in ladies' eyes,
> Do we not likewise see our learning there?   (IV. iii. 312)

This Platonizing concept leads Biron to an apotheosis of love which is one of the outstanding utterances of the play:

> But love, first learned in a lady's eyes,
> Lives not alone immured in the brain;
> But, with the motion of all elements,
> Courses as swift as thought in every power,
> And gives to every power a double power,
> Above their functions and their offices.
> It adds a precious seeing to the eye;
> A lover's eyes will gaze an eagle blind;
> A lover's ear will hear the lowest sound,
> When the suspicious head of theft is stopp'd;
> Love's feeling is more soft and sensible
> Than are the tender horns of cockled snails;
> Love's tongue proves dainty Bacchus gross in taste:
> For valour, is not love a Hercules,
> Still climbing trees in the Hesperides?
> Subtle as Sphinx: as sweet and musical
> As bright Apollo's lute, strung with his hair;
> And when Love speaks, the voice of all the gods
> Makes heaven drowsy with the harmony.   (IV. iii. 327)

The splendour of this culmination, and the lines which follow, represent, always within the terms of artifice which the mode of the play imposes, an affirmation of love as a principal source of life, of enhanced

vitality; but the artifice acts also, and not less deliberately, to limit the
validity of the claim. We know enough of Biron from self-revelation
to realize that even this must not be taken too seriously. The deliberate
poetic elaboration of his thoughts serves to limit them, placing them as
products in some measure of ingenuity and sophistication; and yet the
conclusion:

> Let us once lose our oaths to find ourselves,
> Or else we lose ourselves to keep our oaths—   (IV. iii. 361)

is serious enough to outlive the spirit of jest implied in the King's
summons—'Saint Cupid, then! and, soldiers to the field' (IV. iii. 366)—
and to bear what is, in effect, a principal moral of the entire comedy.

The last Act of the play is an elaborate drawing together of the
separate threads of the action, long and slowly developed, in a manner
which will become increasingly typical of Shakespearean comedy, to
lead to a conclusion which stresses the relativity of the whole by setting
it finally against a background notably greater, more universal in its
implications, than itself. The Princess and her companions know well
enough that

> None are so surely caught, when they are catch'd,
> As wit turn'd fool;   (V. ii. 69)

and so, precisely with the object of teaching the now crest-fallen
'academicians' the error of their ways, the situation of the opening is
reversed and those who once refused to admit the ladies to their society
now approach them in absurd disguise, only to find themselves wittily
and heartlessly spurned. It now appears to the discomforted 'Muscovites' that Boyet speaks no more than the truth when he asserts that

> The tongues of mocking wenches are as keen
> As is the razor's edge invisible,
> Cutting a smaller hair than may be seen;
> Above the sense of sense: (V. ii. 257)

and this they learn to their cost when the Princess briefly and contemptuously dismisses them to the tune of 'Twenty adieus, my frozen
Muscovites'. When, moreover, they have accepted their defeat in the
hope of winning clemency, they are still further mocked as so many
'Muscovites, in shapeless gear'; and to this they can make no reply
which is not in effect a confession of ignominious defeat.

It is, as might be expected, Biron who first sees that he must yield
and, abjuring his beloved verbal dexterity—what Moth has ridiculed,

not long before, to Costard when he says: 'They have been at a great
feast of languages, and stolen the scraps' (V. i. 39)—confine himself to
the expression of true sentiment in natural and direct speech:

> Taffeta phrases, silken terms precise,
>   Three-piled hyperboles, spruce affectation,
> Figures pedantical; these summer flies
>   Have blown me full of maggot ostentation:
> I do forswear them; and I here protest,
>   By this white glove—how white the hand, God knows!—
> Henceforth my wooing mind shall be express'd
>   In russet yeas, and honest kersey noes;   (V. ii. 407)

for in such language alone, he concludes, the love which he now proposes can appear as it should, 'sound, sans crack, or flaw'. The reference
to 'summer flies' and 'maggot ostentation' is enough to communicate
to us that the lesson learnt by Biron is one that has more than merely
verbal or literary reverberations, that it has extended beyond these to
cover the field of what is socially and morally appropriate. The learning
of this lesson, which begins in the typical manner of this play as a
renunciation of literary affectation and ends as an affirmation of natural
propriety, is very close to the conception of this and the following
comedies.

Side by side with this just, if unceremonious treatment of Navarre
and his courtiers, the conclusion sets that of Armado and his followers
who are in turn exposed for their more simple pretensions in the burlesque pageant of the Nine Worthies. This serves, on its own level, as a
parallel to the 'Muscovite' masque which ended in the rout of their
'betters'. The treatment accorded to the lower orders, however, is
notably more gentle than that meted out to Biron and his associates.
When the King seeks to discourage them from presenting their show of
loyalty, which he expects to find it tedious to contemplate, the Princess
—rather like Theseus in his attitude towards the 'rude mechanicals' and
their entertainment in A Midsummer Night's Dream[16]—shows that she
can combine wit with humanity, as she pleads for the rights of ingenuous
simplicity: 'That sport best pleaseth that doth least know how' (V. ii.
517). Here again the stress is upon nature, upon good intention and
unfeigned spontaneity of gesture; and since it is precisely over-sophisti-
cation that has been the prevailing fault at the court of Navarre, the
plea for its opposite is very much to the point. The pageant itself, and
the behaviour of those who so naively take part in it, indicate very
much the same conclusion. Costard's anxious hope that he was 'per-

fect' in his role as Pompey the Great is set against his readiness to admit
to 'a little fault'; Sir Nathaniel, entrusted with the part of none less than
Alexander, reflects his character, to use Costard's words again, as 'a
foolish mild man'. The emphasis, indeed, is deliberately placed upon
mildness, unpretentious simplicity, rather than upon folly; for this is
'an *honest* man, look you' and, as such, 'soon dashed'. The last word is
spoken once more, and in inimitable fashion, by Costard: 'He is a
marvellous good neighbour, faith, and a very good bowler: but, for
Alisander—alas, you see how 'tis—a little o'erparted'. Even Holofernes
the pedant, whom we might reasonably expect to receive shorter shrift,
is allowed to utter his protest in terms not devoid of dignity against
Biron's too facile ridicule of his efforts—'This is not generous, not
gentle, not humble' (V. ii. 629)—and, though we shall recognize him
indeed for the absurd figure that he is, we are left with every reason to
believe that the Princess at least will be human enough to take his
meaning.

With the various threads of the action thus brought together, the last
stages of the comedy raise the entire artificial action to a different level
by announcing the death of the Princess' father, the King of France.
The news is delivered with a blunt directness that makes its own effect
in a play so largely devoted to artifice and sophistication:

> the news I bring
> Is heavy in my tongue. The king your father—
> —Dead, for my life!
> —Even so; my tale is told—   (V. ii. 724)

and as such it is received. 'Worthies, away!' says Biron, responding at
once to the change of mood, 'the scene begins to cloud'; and, indeed, it
is profoundly true to the spirit of Shakespearean comedy that the tragic
note should in this way be drawn into its moments of resolution. Under
the shadow of this assertion of mortality Biron confesses the nature, as
he has now come to see it, of love as a valid and enriching human
emotion. The confession is made in such a way as to throw a new light
upon the absurdity of his own previous attitudes, and those of his
companions:

> And what in us hath seem'd ridiculous,—
> As love is full of unbefitting strains;
> All wanton as a child, skipping and vain;
> Form'd by the eye, and therefore, like the eye,
> Full of strange shapes, of habits and of forms,
> Varying in subjects as the eye doth roll

> To every varied object in his glance:
> Which parti-coated presence of loose love
> Put on by us, if, in your heavenly eyes,
> Have misbecomed our oaths and gravities,
> Those heavenly eyes, that look into these faults,
> Suggested us to make. Therefore, ladies,
> Our love being yours, the error that love makes
> Is likewise yours: we to ourselves prove false,
> By being false for ever to be true
> To those that make us both—fair ladies, you:
> And even that falsehood, in itself a sin,
> Thus purifies itself, and turns to grace.   (V. ii. 767)

Once more Biron is left, as his speech ends, balanced between artifice and a deeper content. His speech is, on one level, an elegant dedication of his duties, and those of his friends, to the 'fair ladies' that now inspire them; but it is also, beneath its artificial terms, a comic apology for their own defeat. For this is the justification of love in terms of the comic sense of the incongruous, the bringing together of apparent opposites through which Biron now confirms, in his own way, his previous celebration of the lessons to be learnt from 'a lady's eyes'.

The practical consequences of the lesson so learnt are not, however, immediately or easily to come into their own. Biron's surrender to his own courtly, sophisticated version of love is a step in the direction of humanity and life; but it is by no means life itself. In the new mood introduced by the news of her father's last surrender to the action of 'the sudden hand of death' (V. ii. 823), the Princess refuses to enter too easily into the 'world without end' bargain of marriage which is now offered her and her companions by the reformed wits of whom we may say, perhaps, that we are not sure if they yet realize completely that it is for a 'bargain' of this nature and this solemnity that they are in fact asking. She prefers for the moment to give its proper due to the obligation of mourning for the dead, and in this her companions follow her. To Navarre she says, with a touch of deliberate and salutary asperity:

> Your oath I will not trust; but go with speed
> To some forlorn and naked hermitage,
> Remote from all the pleasures of the world;
> There stay until the twelve celestial signs
> Have brought about the annual reckoning.
> If this austere insociable life
> Change not your offer made in heat of blood;
> If frosts and fasts, hard lodging and thin weeds

> Nip not the gaudy blossoms of your love;
> But that it bear this trial, and last love;
> Then, at the expiration of the year,
> Come challenge me, challenge me by these deserts,
> And, by this virgin palm now kissing thine,
> I will be thine.   (V. ii. 802)

The 'forlorn and naked hermitage' to which Navarre is now directed is clearly in some sense the counterpart of the 'academe' into which he formerly planned to take refuge from the world; but the 'austere' and 'insociable' life which he is to embrace, though only for a time, to expose to 'trial' the 'gaudy blossoms' of his only too untried love, bear little resemblance to the comfortable and pedantic retreat of his original caprice. Life affirms itself in this way too, imposes some degree of renunciation upon those who would achieve its more lasting gifts. Biron, for his part, receives from Rosaline the same injunction to wait, and added to it the obligation, as penance for his former irresponsibility, to set his vaunted wit in competition with the realities of death and suffering so that only what can stand this severe testing may survive into his changed state:

> You shall this twelvemonth term from day to day
> Visit the speechless sick, and still converse
> With groaning wretches; and your task shall be,
> With all the fierce endeavour of your wit
> To enforce the pained impotent to smile.   (V. ii. 858)

'To more wild laughter in the throat of death' is, then, to be Biron's appropriate expiation for past presumption; whilst Armado, on his own more humble level, ends the action by announcing that he has vowed to Jacquenetta to hold the plough for her sweet love three years'. Finally, to his concluding words—'This side is Hiems, Winter, this Ver, the Spring; the one maintained by the owl, the other by the cuckoo'—the songs of Spring and Winter introduce themes older, more close to folk experience, than any touched upon elsewhere in the play. The effect is to set the entire comedy, decoratively indeed but in a spirit that goes beyond mere decoration, in the context of the pattern conferred upon life by the revolving seasons. The cuckoo and the owl, spring and winter, birth and death respectively, give their last words to a comedy which already conveys, beneath its surface polish and elaborate contrivance, no small measure of the Shakespearean intuition of life.

IV
THE SONNETS

CERTAIN ASPECTS of the transition between Shakespeare's earliest plays and the more complex modes realized in his later work are usefully approached through the Sonnets. Published for the first time as a collection late in the poet's career, in 1609, the Sonnets have been variously dated, often to fit in with highly problematic interpretations of unknown facts in his biography. The present tendency seems to favour, on purely scholarly grounds, a relatively early dating; even if we do not follow the theory that certain poems in the series contain references to events connected with the defeat of the Spanish Armada in 1588 and must therefore be ascribed to the very earliest stages in Shakespeare's career,[1] we shall probably find the evidence which points to most of the Sonnets as having been written well before the end of the sixteenth-century sufficiently convincing. Within the limits of this general conclusion, however, we may equally decide that the poems do not correspond entirely to any single inspiration, or reflect, beneath their variety of theme and treatment, any one stage in Shakespeare's development. It is clear, indeed, that certain common subjects can be detected in the Sonnets and are often dealt with in deliberate sequence; but beyond this, it seems possible to conclude that the collection as finally published unites poems originally written at different times and only at a later date brought together in an attempt to give them something like a logical argument and a degree of continuity. The answer to the problem raised by these poems is likely, in other words, to be neither single nor simple; and it may be doubted whether, from this standpoint, anything much more positive can safely be said.

A purely literary approach goes some way to confirm this impression. Although the general level of the poems is remarkably high, and the sense of personal commitment much more marked than in most sonnet series, not all of them are equal in merit. A certain proportion clearly consists of little more than literary exercises, addressed either to a patron of letters or, especially in the case of a few of the later numbers, to a more or less conventional mistress. All, however, conventional or otherwise, show in varying degrees signs of the way in which the sonnet form, by the very strictness of its formal limits, imposed upon language a distinctive economy and intensity; and the best of them develop these qualities to a degree which makes them, within their strictly observed limits, comparable to much in the mature plays. This infinity of variations, indeed, is a most valuable feature of the Sonnets, for in it we can trace, perhaps more clearly than elsewhere, some aspects of a process similar to that by which, in the plays we have already considered, conventional plots and versification became moulded to the more complex and individual purposes of the later dramas. I say more clearly because the sharply defined limits of the sonnet convention, and the brevity of the poems themselves, make it simpler for us to observe the modifications introduced into them by the author's constantly developing purposes.

The conventions of the sonnet, as already established by such predecessors as Sidney and Spenser, inevitably influenced Shakespeare's own use of the form. Indeed, Shakespeare's achievement might be defined as the playing off of his keen sense of actuality against a conventional basis which gave it both pointedness and enormous possibilities of varying the poetic mood. The relation of personal emotion to an established convention involves a contrast which may be used either to intensify feeling or to indicate the presence of irony by a suggestion of incompatibility with the original mode. This complexity, which is a characteristic feature of many of the best poems in the series, is reflected in distinct linguistic qualities. The sonnet, as Shakespeare found it and as he himself on occasion used it, encouraged great formal ingenuity, which was at times little more than an exercise in poetic sophistication. It affected even punctuation. There is one sonnet in Shakespeare's series (LXXXI) in which every possible pair of lines, if we make exception of the second, the third, and the eleventh, can be read so as to make a complete sentence. The device is, in itself, of little poetic value; but it suggests the degree of formal control behind the Sonnets, a control which needed only to be informed by urgency of feeling to produce the subtle intensity of the best of these poems.

The presence in any given sonnet of the characteristic Shakespearean immediacy can, as usual, be gauged by the appearance of a distinctive verbal quality. It makes itself felt in such lines as

> Against my love shall be, as I am now,
> With time's injurious hand crush'd and o'erworn   (LXIII)

and the famous

> Lilies that *fester* smell far worse than weeds.   (XCIV)

In the first instance, the impression of the passage of time and its action
upon the individual is conveyed with a fresh, concrete vividness that
produces, moreover, a pairing of words in cumulative effect that is one
of the poet's favourite ways of intensifying the emotional content of his
poetry[2]; in the second, the striking unexpectedness of 'fester' cuts
sharply across the conventional associations of 'lilies' in a manner that
recalls—to go no further—Angelo's tense, clipped utterances at critical
moments in *Measure for Measure*.[3] Under the stress of the feeling so
reflected, the fashionable weaving of word patterns at which the courtly
sonneteers aimed is transformed into a vivid use of the resources of
speech to develop a high degree of intensity in a relatively short space.
This same keen economy of language, when set in the plays against the
prevailing rhetorical structure of the blank verse period, soon produced
corresponding modifications in the field of stress. Taken together, these
two factors—verbal immediacy developed to an unusual degree and the
moulding of stress to the movement of living, changing, and developing emotion—account in very great measure for the unique impression
produced by Shakespeare's mature poetry. It is probable that the
linguistic discipline imposed by the sonnet form upon his natural
Elizabethan exuberance was a decisive factor in the formation of the
poet's mastery of expression. It made him associate compression with
depth of content and variety of emotional response to a degree un-
paralleled in English (though similar qualities distinguish the best work
of Donne and others of his contemporaries) and so give both point and
intensity to the development of personal feeling.

These considerations are so important in relation to the emergence of
Shakespeare's distinctive modes of expression that it is worth taking a
typical Sonnet to show how what might have been mere misplaced
ingenuity becomes a pregnant poetic device:

> When my love swears that she is made of truth,
> I do believe her, though I know she lies,
> That she might think me some untutor'd youth,
> Unlearned in the world's false subtleties.
> Thus vainly thinking that she thinks me young,
> Although she knows my days are past the best,
> Simply I credit her false-speaking tongue:
> On both sides thus is simple truth suppress'd.

> But wherefore says she not she is unjust?
> And wherefore say not I that I am old?
> O, love's best habit is in seeming trust,
> And age in love loves not to have years told:
>> Therefore I lie with her and she with me,
>> And in our faults by lies we flatter'd be. (CXXXVIII)

The situation announced in the first two lines is, at bottom, the conventional complaint of the lover against the faithlessness of the beloved; yet the development is a good deal more than merely conventional. The transition from convention is marked by fresh linguistic subtlety, seen most obviously in the varied meanings attached to the word 'lie'. The double sense beneath this word is most clearly conveyed in the final couplet; it implies not only conscious deception but also a lying together as man and mistress. The point, however, lies less in the ambiguity than in its justification, which is not in any way verbal or scholastic, but rather a question of the nature of the experience to be conveyed. The play upon 'lie', in fact, enabled Shakespeare to state two emotions contradictory yet simultaneous, both contained in one situation. The lying together, which is from one point of view the natural physical fulfilment of love, is none the less based in this case on mutual falsity, for reasons which are made clear in the rest of the Sonnet. These reasons are faithlessness, covered by concealment on the part of the mistress, and age and disillusionment on the side of the lover. Shakespeare's use of a deliberate ambiguity in this poem is justified by the precision of his thought, or, more exactly, of his analysis of experience. A line like 'I do believe her, though I know she lies' calls for an exactitude of thinking and feeling that a modern reader does not always associate with emotional intensity. It is a type of poetry which justifies ambiguity, because its complexity is balanced by its content, because it is able to gather the divergent possibilities of a single situation into the unifying framework of a realized convention.

These new tendencies in verse and rhythm were closely accompanied, in the most interesting of the Sonnets, by the repeated exploration of certain recurring themes. The most important of these look forward, like so much else in the parallel linguistic development, to the plays upon which Shakespeare was engaged between the time when we may suppose him to have written most of these poems and the beginning of what we may conveniently call his tragic period. The linguistic resourcefulness of these poems was occasioned by profoundly personal interests, though these were not necessarily or even probably of the kind favoured by the promoters of various biographical theories. The nature of these interests is to some extent indicated by the very choice of the sonnet form. The sonnet, as is well known, based its conventions originally on a highly intellectualized conception of the relations that were held to exist, in a society which we may call aristocratic, between the lover and his mistress, between, respectively, the servant and the source of love. It is true, of course, that in the use of them made by later poets, and very notably by Shakespeare himself, these conventions came to cover a variety of human relationships only very remotely, if at all, connected with this original situation. The majority of Shakespeare's Sonnets are not addressed to a woman, but to a man with whom his relations cover varying elements of patronage and friendship, dependence and intimacy; but in spite of this, the spirit of the poems continued to be affected by their origin, and it is true to say that many of Shakespeare's most successful exercises in the sonnet form are more closely related, in spirit and expression, to those of his plays which analyse the nature of human relationship in love than to any other aspect of his work. They represent, in fact, beneath the variety of their subjects and attitudes a first exploration of themes which were later realized, in either tragic or comic form, in the great series of plays dealing primarily with love which began with *Romeo and Juliet* and *A Midsummer Night's Dream* and ended, many years later, with *Antony and Cleopatra*.

The Sonnets, therefore, although they deal with situations that differ very widely from one another, make constant use of imagery connected with the traditional conception of the union between the lover and the object of his desire. This union, when consummated, should find expression in terms of natural increase; the opening sequence, composed of poems addressed to a friend and urging upon him the desirability of marriage, is notably full of references to planting and husbandry:

> For where is she so fair whose unear'd womb
> Disdains the tillage of thy husbandry?   (III)[4]

The necessity for true love to embark upon the adventure of giving, to seek fulfilment in an act of creation, is a theme constantly repeated in Shakespeare's comedies which turn indeed very largely upon just this kind of situation. The recipient of these early Sonnets is constantly being urged to consider the necessity of living, not for himself alone, but in relation to the world beyond himself. The very first poem in the series

reproaches him, in effect, for self-centredness, for refusing to make the
creative gesture which ensures the continuity of life and in the absence
of which life itself withers in sterile self-contemplation:

> But thou, contracted to thine own bright eyes,
> Feed'st thy light's flame with *self-substantial* fuel,
> Making a famine where abundance lies,
> *Thyself thy foe, to thy sweet self too cruel.* (I)

And again, a little later in the series:

> For having traffic with thyself alone,
> *Thou of thyself thy sweet self dost deceive.*
> Then how, when nature calls thee to be gone,
> What acceptable audit canst thou leave? (IV)

The conclusion to all these early Sonnets—that the recipient should
fulfil the duty of perpetuating himself through an heir—may be considered conventional in its expression, as is also much of the imagery of
usury and law—'audit' and 'executors'[5]—used to condemn the
'beauteous niggard' and urge him to 'bounteous largess'[6]; but the
intense concentration of the phrases which condemn self-centredness is
remarkable and points to the counter-assertion of generosity in giving
as a law of life which the comedies, in particular, will be concerned to
develop, equally through convention, as one of their principal themes.
When Bassanio, in *The Merchant of Venice*, chooses the casket which
urges him to 'give and hazard all he hath'[7] and makes himself thereby
worthy of Portia's answering self-dedication, he is in effect responding
to the same universal law of love by which the whole range of human
life in enriched and transformed.

It is interesting, indeed, that so many of the Sonnets should lay stress
upon this aspect of love; but even more significant, possibly, is the fact
that some of the most individual of them are less concerned with this
desirable consummation than with the thwarting of this natural and
beneficent relationship by shortcomings which seem to be inherent in
the very quality of passion. So much is implied even in the relatively
conventional numbers of the series, where issues are initially raised
which some of the most famous of the later poems will seem to raise to
the status of a universal and sombre law of life. Human love and friendship, according to the mood expressed in some of the most striking of
the Sonnets, are inevitably vitiated by inconstancy: not, however,
merely by the conventional inconstancy of the courtly sonneteers, the
theme of endless doleful and ultimately self-regarding complaints

(Shakespeare dealt faithfully with these in many of his comedies),[8] but by a flaw, or vice, felt to be inseparable from the nature of passion itself. The subject of a considerable proportion of the Sonnets that have a genuine claim to individuality is, in one form or another, this inescapable thwarting of the natural human desire for union and increase:

> Let me confess that we two must be twain,
> Although our undivided loves are one; (XXXVI)

the 'loves' which should be 'one', 'undivided', because it is in the nature of love to seek unity in the creative gift of self to its object, are in fact inexorably separate, rendered 'twain' by what amounts to a contrary and tragic fatality. This frustration, as we have said, is felt as a *necessary* flaw at the heart of passion; and this flaw tends to be identified, in the Sonnets with which we are concerned, with the action of impersonal and destructive time.

The sense of the hostility of time, indeed, is fundamental not only to the Sonnets but to many of the plays of this period in Shakespeare's career. The theme was a commonplace of the age, associated with the Platonizing philosophy of the court poets, which contrasted the ideal perfection of eternity with the corruptible realities of earthly existence, and with the religious 'pessimism' of mediaeval tradition. Both these elements are variously present in Shakespeare's work, but in the Sonnets it is the newer, the more 'modern' attitude which on the whole prevails:

> Time doth transfix the flourish set on youth
> And delves the parallels in beauty's brow. (LX)

> Ruin hath taught me thus to ruminate,
> That time will come and take my love away. (LXIV)

> O fearful meditation! where, alack,
> Shall Time's best jewel from Time's chest lie hid? (LXV)

Time is conceived in many of the most striking of these poems as a conditioning element in human experience, which it first brings into being and then, following inexorable laws of its own, proceeds to destroy. The apparent solidity and permanence of natural objects and human creations—'brass', 'stone', and 'gates of steel': 'earth', 'boundless sea', and 'rocks impregnable'[9]—are all equally destined to decay by a process against which human endeavour can only set its fragile and finally impermanent aspirations. Natural fear of the action of time, conceived now as an eternal process of attrition, neither beginning in a

definite act of creation nor directed towards a meaningful and redemp-
tive conclusion, is not balanced in these poems by any consistent residue
of traditional morality, still less by any sense of the possible significance
as well as of the inevitability of death. Renaissance feeling regarded
time as the enemy and solvent of personal experience, which it wears
remorselessly into insensibility. Shakespeare gave this feeling magnificent expression when he transformed the classical commonplace *Tempus
edax rerum*[10] into the sombre intensity of the opening of Sonnet XIX:

> Devouring time, blunt thou the lion's paws,

where the epithet 'devouring', which belongs naturally to the lion, is
transferred to 'time', thus creating a very intricate balance of emotions.
The lion naturally raises associations of splendid life and activity as well
as of a menacing terror; but the transfer of 'devouring' indicates that
the end of all this activity is a fatal consuming, a wearing down of life
into pure annihilation. The verb 'blunt' shows the typical sensing of the
intangible in terms of the immediate life of the finger-tips; it simply
makes more intense by contrast the energy which is so wastefully subdued to the consuming action of mutability.

The attitude expressed by the Sonnets towards the relationship of
time to individual experience, and especially to the personal ties of love
and friendship, is accordingly various and even contradictory. At times
the poet expresses his conviction, in harmony with the poetic conventions, of the permanence and unique validity of emotion in its
different forms; and then his attitude is that stated in one of the most
famous and eloquent of all the Sonnets:

> Love's not time's fool, though rosy lips and cheeks
> Within his bending sickle's compass come;
> Love alters not with his brief hours and weeks,
> But bears it out even to the edge of doom. (CXVI)

Splendidly as this conviction is expressed, however, there is about the
Sonnet, and more especially about its closing lines, a suggestion of the
rhetorical, of an effort to carry conviction by mere weight of affirmation:

> If this be error, and upon me proved,
> I never writ, nor no man ever loved.

The conclusion surely conveys an odd sense of weakness and insecurity
after the powerful development which has preceded it. The 'bending
sickle's compass' is, in terms of language and rhythmic vigour, superbly

real in comparison with the lame, unsupported weight of assertion in which the poem is supposed to culminate.[11] The poet is saying, in effect, that the experience with which he is dealing *must* have a timeless validity, because to accept the contrary would be to convert the experience itself into something tragically meaningless. It is precisely this situation, this sense of emotional conviction balanced by rational doubt that makes its contribution, with other elements, to the tragedy of *Romeo and Juliet*[12] and that was eventually more comprehensively dramatized in *Troilus and Cressida*.[13]

Under such circumstances it is not surprising that, in other moods, a contrary attitude prevails. Such is the case in the opening lines of the almost equally famous Sonnet CXXIX:

> The expense of spirit in a waste of shame
> Is lust in action.

The force of this opening answers to something more than a moralizing reflection on the nature and impermanence of passion. The familiar condemnation of 'lust' is extended, by the very force of its expression, to something like a judgement on the nature of love itself. Under the pressure of mutability our spiritual instincts appear, at times, baseless illusions which no logical reading of the facts appears to justify. 'Love', thus considered, becomes identified with 'lust', changes from the most intense and valuable of human experiences in time into an expenditure, of 'spirit' indeed—because some of our deepest aspirations are involved—but of spirit destined to sterility, destined to lose itself in a 'waste' (a desert which is at the same time a useless giving out of life) 'of shame'. This Sonnet and the one quoted above represent, in fact, the two contrasted sides of a single picture. Both are reactions to the facts implied in human subjection to the temporal process which governs our lives. Love and friendship, which is a reflection of love, are seen in these poems as a reaction against the process of temporal decay, an attempt to grasp through accepted experience an intuition of permanent spiritual value; but precisely because they are born in time, they are destined to destruction. What is rooted in time, and owes its nature to time, time itself destroys. If man, as a temporal unity of body and spirit, can only perceive spiritual values under the guise of time, it is equally true that his perceptions are, in time, fatally transient. Shakespeare's reaction as poet to this necessity underlies the bitterness which is to be found in many of his Sonnets and which inspires much in the plays most closely related to them.[14] Since love and friendship, though so desirable, appear to be dedicated to vanity, the poet's vision of them becomes at times vicious and repellent; the very value which is presumed to be in them only makes them, by a strange paradox, more potent to corrupt. 'Lilies that fester smell far worse than weeds'. The action of time becomes associated with the corrupt inconstancy of the flesh, as though one necessarily implied the other. A great part of Shakespeare's tragic experience can be described, from this point of view (there are, of course, many others), in terms of a reaction against his consciousness of the sombre implications of the temporal nature of man; of the quality of that reaction the most individual of the Sonnets, written as they presumably were still relatively near the outset of his career, provide an illuminating illustration.

We are now in a position to see that Shakespeare's use in many of the Sonnets of imagery compounded of contradiction is directly related to the nature of the experience he wished to convey. The final ambiguity with which these poems are concerned lies in the simultaneous fulfilment and destruction of the values of human life by time; it depends not upon a verbal interest, but upon an emotional situation of tragic depth and content. This situation will be carried on, absorbed into vaster constructions covering a far wider range of human experiences, in the dramatic works of Shakespeare's maturity. The great tragedies, though they are of course far from being confined to this single aspect, can be seen as forming a continuous process in the exploration and extension of it; and each stage in this exploration, this extension, involves a further organization of verse and language. The comedies too are engaged, from their own point of view, in illuminating other areas, not finally unrelated, of the same field. From *Romeo and Juliet* and *A Midsummer Night's Dream*, through *Troilus and Cressida* and *Twelfth Night* to *Antony and Cleopatra*, there is a continual development from original ambiguity, which expresses a clash within experience, to a fully organized verse which in turn implies a harmonious ordering of the elements of experience and with it the complete realization of the dramatist's art.

V

FROM
'ROMEO AND JULIET'
TO 'RICHARD II'

THE IMPRESSION left by a survey of Shakespeare's earliest work is, perhaps, of variety even more than of the not inconsiderable achievement. The young dramatist whose first series of plays on English history shows such considerable intellectual grasp in conceiving and following through a complex pattern of political behaviour was at the same time engaged in evolving, through successive experiments in dramatic structure, a type of comedy which might answer to the variety and balance of what he had to say. If none of these first plays, considered in its own right, gives at first sight quite that impression of dominating personal genius which we may derive from Marlowe's work at its best, it is at least equally certain that Shakespeare's production during these years, taken as a whole, already points to a scope and breadth of interest quite beyond the reach of his most brilliant contemporary.

At some time immediately after the writing of these first plays, and well before the turn of the century, Shakespeare built, upon the foundations thus securely laid, the first unquestioned masterpieces of his career. Within what was certainly a very brief period of time—not, we may assume, much more than two years—he produced successively his first great tragedy, *Romeo and Juliet*, a comedy of startling brilliance, *A Midsummer Night's Dream*, which views the same central theme of love in a completely different light, and—as if this were not enough—a historical play, *Richard II*, which gives the chronicle type of drama an entirely new dimension and lays the foundations for a whole series of still greater plays to follow. The ability to achieve so high a standard of excellence in so many different undertakings within so short a period of time, and at so early a stage in his development as a dramatist, is in itself a testimony to the unique nature of Shakespeare's genius.

1 Romeo and Juliet

Romeo and Juliet, Shakespeare's first youthful tragedy—if we exclude for the present purpose, *Titus Andronicus*—has a number of clear points of contact with the Sonnets. These are most obviously apparent in the style of the play, which here and there incorporates actual sonnets into the dramatic structure and makes at all times a considerable use of sonnet imagery; but the theme too turns, as in some of the sonnets we have just considered,[1] upon the relation of love to the action of time and adverse circumstance. At least one of the questions which the tragedy poses is, indeed, familiar from the Sonnets. To what degree can youthful love be regarded as its own justification—'bears it out even to the edge of doom',[2] as the Sonnet has it—or, alternatively, to what extent is the conviction shared by the lovers themselves that this is simply an empty, rhetorical affirmation? The answer which the play gives to this question lies not in any simple assertion, whether affirmative or otherwise, but rather in a balance of contrasted realities. The Prologue strikes a sinister note from the outset by telling us that we are about to witness 'the *fearful* passage of a *death-marked* love'; but it is necessary to add that the disaster to which this love will be brought is in great part a result of the hatred of the older generations, in which the young participate, if at all, as victims involved in a situation which is not of their choosing. Though the young lovers are indeed 'star-crossed', destined to die, their response to experience, and the contrast with those around them who only *believe* that they are reasonable and mature, gives the relationship to which they have pledged their generosity a proper measure of validity. Their love must indeed accept the reality of death, which its very origin and nature demand; but once this has been accepted, it remains true that a sense of incommensurate worth, of *true* value, survives to colour their tragedy.

The Prologue has no sooner been spoken when the circumstances which will lead fatally to the destruction of love are introduced in the shape of the irrational vanity of the Capulet–Montague feud. The serving-men who so touchily eye one another in the streets of Verona are at once lecherous and self-important, uneasily conscious of breaking what they know to be the law even as they insult their opposites. The masters, on this first showing, are little or no better than their men, combining touchiness and senility in a particularly distasteful way. Their wives know them better than themselves; when Capulet testily calls for his sword to join in the *melee*, his wife says ironically: 'A crutch, a crutch! why call you for a sword!' (I. i. 82), and Lady Montague is equally at pains to hold back her husband from 'seeking a foe'. On the more active side, reason is habitually overruled by brute instinct, Benvolio's sensible attitude—'I do but keep the peace'—balanced by Tybalt's irrational spoiling for a fight: 'I hate hell, all Montagues, and thee!' (I. i. 77). The fair comment on so much obstinate and 'canker'd hate' is left, here as it will be throughout the play, to Prince Escalus who shows himself conscious, as an impartial ruler, of the ruin to which these senseless attitudes will lead, and who does what he can to hold them in check. We may conclude by the end of this opening that, if this is a fair picture of 'experience', there is likely to be something to be said in favour of the romantic idealism of youth.

Romeo himself, however, is by no means romantically presented on his first appearance: not, at any rate, if 'romanticism' means an acceptance of him at his own estimate. Benvolio tells us of having seen him stealing furtively, almost as a man ashamed, 'into the covert of the wood', and Montague speaks of him locking out 'fair daylight', making 'himself an artificial night' (I. i. 145). Even in the conventional idiom of *The Two Gentlemen of Verona*, we should recognize these as unfavourable signs. They prepare us for a Romeo who is at this stage in love with himself as Rosaline's unrequited lover, a Romeo

> to himself so *secret* and so *close*, . . .
> As is the bud bit with *an envious worm*; (I. i. 154)

a creature, in other words, 'doting' rather than loving, perversely enamoured of his own self-centred and melancholy reflections. The distance he will cover in his progress through the play needs to be measured against the deliberate conventionality of this beginning.

All this is amply confirmed when Romeo himself appears, and utters his first elaborate 'complaints':

> O brawling love! O loving hate!
> O anything, of nothing first create!
> O heavy lightness! serious vanity!; (I. i. 181)

to which, shortly after, he adds further considerations on a more sententious level:

> Love is a smoke raised with the fume of sighs;
> Being purged, a fire sparkling in lovers' eyes;
> Being vex'd, a sea nourish'd with lovers' tears:

> What is it else? a madness most discreet,
> A choking gall and a preserving sweet.   (I. i. 196)

This is a Romeo who can indeed say of himself, a good deal more truly than he yet knows, 'This is not Romeo: he's some other where', even as he complains from a point of view still naively limited to the self, that his mistress has no share in love's generosity, that she will not *give* herself in fulfilment of its essential law. To Benvolio's question, 'Then she hath sworn that she will still live chaste?" Romeo replies:

> She hath, and in that sparing makes huge waste;
> For beauty, starved with her severity,
> Cuts beauty off from all posterity.   (I. i. 224)

This is, of course, an argument familiar from the Sonnets,[3] and one which this play will in due course turn to serious ends. Romeo is still speaking within the limits of convention, urging upon the object of his desire that generosity which he has not yet had occasion to show in himself. He is soon to find a love that is ready to give for what is, in the eyes of the world, folly; but, until this is so, his character cannot begin to develop to its true tragic stature.

At this point, and after some talk of Capulet's forthcoming feast, we turn from Romeo to Juliet, who is urged by her mother to think of marriage and who replies, in her still unawakened simplicity: 'It is an honour that I dream not of' (I. iii. 66). Juliet, indeed, is surrounded here, as she will be almost to the end of the play, by the 'experienced', by those who are always ready to give their advice on the proper conduct of her life. Such is the Nurse, with her combination of easy sentiment and deep-rooted cynicism, her belief, at once normal and senile in its discursive presentation, that love is a prompting of the flesh which is destined to find its social fulfilment in a suitably contrived marriage; such too is her own mother, who looks back complacently on the destiny which at some remote moment in the past gave her to Capulet and which she is ready to elevate, for her daughter's benefit, into a universal pattern:

> By my count,
> I was your mother much upon these years
> That you are now a maid.   (I. iii. 71)

As Lady Capulet goes on to refer to Paris' suit in language deliberately and appropriately contrived:—

> This precious book of love, this unbound lover,
> To beautify him, only lacks a cover—   (I. iii. 87)

Juliet, the moment of whose awakening is still to come, can only reply in the simple terms of filial obedience.

As Romeo moves towards the fatal meeting with Juliet, his attitude is set in contrast to that of Mercutio, who offers him advice in terms of an essentially worldly common-sense, which is not on that account less relevant to his state of sentiment. Mercutio is convinced that the supposed tribulations of love have an easy remedy which he and his friends propose to apply:

> we'll draw thee from the mire
> Of this sir-reverence love, wherein thou stick'st
> Up to the ears.   (I. iv. 41)

The famous 'Queen Mab' speech, to which these exchanges lead, is a brilliant exercise in poetic *bravura*, of the type to which Shakespeare, in the first flush of his creative powers, was especially attracted. It is, however, also more than that, in so much as it emphasizes, against Romeo's superficially settled attitudes, the inconstancy of human impulses in the state of love, the lively unpredictability of love itself:

> This is that very Mab
> That plats the manes of horses in the night,
> And bakes the elf-locks in foul, sluttish hairs,
> Which once untangled much misfortune bodes:
> This is the hag, when maids lie on their backs,
> That presses them and learns them first to bear.   (I. iv. 89)

The similarity between this and the habitual language of Puck, in *A Midsummer Night's Dream*, is surely not accidental; there is the same sense of the mischievous and the incongruous, even the same faintly sinister delight in the upsetting of fixed sentimental attitudes and unalterable moral categories. This is essentially a *comic* attitude to love, as different from Romeo's self-absorbed devotion to Rosaline as it will prove to be from his dedication to Juliet. Romeo moves at this point, as he will continue to do, in a sphere entirely remote from Mercutio's comic exhortations; but it is notable that he answers his friend's exuberance with a first obscure intimation of fear. When Mercutio has confessed that his talk has been of 'nothing but vain fantasy', 'thin of substance as the air', and 'more inconstant than the wind', he recognizes his foreboding in the face of the still unknown future:

> my mind misgives
> Some consequence, yet hanging in the stars,
> Shall bitterly begin his fearful date

> With this night's revels, and expire the term
> Of a despised life closed in my breast,
> By some vile forfeit of untimely death.   (I. iv. 107)

Romeo's concern for his 'despised life' still answers to his early sentimental state, which finds in pessimism an intimate, finally self-indulging
necessity; but it remains true that it is at this point that the play's
persistent association of love and death enters the hero's mind for the
first time.

In this way we are brought to the fatal ball in the house of the
Capulets. Old Capulet, most typically, plays his part as host to the
accompaniment of jests about 'corns' and memories of his lost youth:

> I have seen the day
> That I have worn a visor, and could tell
> A whispering tale in a fair lady's ear,   (I. v. 25)

and so forth for as long as his relations and friends will bear with him;
but, as he goes on to confess to his cousin, 'you and I are past our
dancing days', and the present lies with Romeo as he forms his fatal
question:

> What lady's that, which doth *enrich* the hand
> Of yonder knight?

It is typical of Romeo that his first reference to Juliet should speak of
her in terms of 'enrichment', the enhancing effect proper to beauty;
significant too that his first reaction to the sight of her should give him
the force to break through all former artifice, to rise to what, though
still romantic in inspiration, is in effect a new intensity:

> O, she doth teach the torches to burn bright!
> It seems she hangs upon the cheek of night
> Like a rich jewel in an Ethiop's ear;   (I. v. 48)

a beauty capable, indeed, of transforming life, but which he can also,
with what is already a sense of foreboding, hail immediately afterwards
as 'Beauty too rich for use, for earth too dear'. Already, moreover, the
world is ominously present at the birth of this new vision, and answers
to the lover's rapt confession of his transformed state—'I ne'er saw true
beauty till this night'—with Tybalt's harsh recognition—'This, by his
voice, should be a Montague'—even as he calls for his sword. The
sinister note has been struck once and for all, briefly but not at that
account less powerfully, in spite of Capulet's determination that his
feast shall not be interrupted, and in spite of the confrontation of

Romeo's unruly enemy with the old man's stubborn 'will'. Yet again, as will occur so often in this play, age and youth, authority and passion meet, as Capulet's angry assertion of his right to command—'Am I the master here? or you? go to'—meets the younger man's grudging aside:

> Patience perforce with wilful choler meeting,
> Makes my flesh tremble in their different greeting,   (I. v. 93)

and as this in turn leads to the threatening conclusion:

> this intrusion shall,
> Now seeming sweet, convert to bitterest gall.

The spare, tense economy of these exchanges is the sign of a dramatist working at the height of his newly-discovered and continually expanding powers.

The first exchange between Romeo and Juliet, which follows immediately on this clash of contrary and headstrong wills, is carried on, by a most effective contrast, in artificial sonnet form, which makes it a matter of 'saints' and 'pilgrims', the expression of a still strained and tense devotion. As the lovers exchange their first kiss, however, it is already to a play upon 'sin' which carries threatening overtones:

> —Thus from my lips by thine my sin is purg'd.
> —Then have my lips the sin that they have took.
> —Sin from my lips? O trespass sweetly urged!
> Give me my sin again.   (I. v. 111)

At this point, if ever, we may feel familiar poetic conventions in the process of being brought to what is finally a dangerous, a precarious life. Indeed, when Juliet, after Romeo has left her, says:

> If he be married,
> My grave is like to be my wedding-bed,   (I. v. 138)

the play's characteristic note of ominous splendour is being firmly struck; we may already sense, however obscurely, that this love is destined to end in death, but that death itself may be ennobled by the dedication which love can bring to its acceptance. For the immediate moment, moreover, we should note that the new situation is conveyed through a corresponding development in character; for Juliet, who has hitherto shown herself submissive to parental authority, being now newly born to love learns at once to disguise her true feelings. Already she has shown enough presence of mind to preface her question about Romeo's identity by enquiries about two other guests, whose identity

in no way concerns her; and when she has been betrayed by the
intensity of her own feeling into crying, incautiously,

> Prodigious birth of love it is to me,
> That I must love a loathed enemy,   (I. v. 144)

and is challenged by the Nurse to explain her outburst, she turns aside
the threatened revelation with a beautifully off-hand reference to

> A rhyme I learn'd even now
> Of one I danced withal.

By the end of this admirably contrived scene, a situation as tensely
actual, as ominously poised over contradiction, as any briefly conveyed
in the Sonnets, is being endowed with dramatic life.

In the episode which follows, after the Chorus has further underlined
the elements of foreboding which accompany the birth of this love,
Mercutio proceeds with his taunting of Romeo for his infatuated devotion to Rosaline. 'Speak but one rhyme, and I am satisfied', he urges,
continuing his comic attack upon the romantic excess to which he still
believes his friend is subject; but he fails, of course, to obtain the
response of his victim, whose heart and mind are fully engaged elsewhere. Romeo's true answer, indeed, is uttered before Juliet:

> But soft! what light through yonder window breaks?
> It is the east, and Juliet is the sun!   (II. ii. 2)

In the invocation which follows, the expression is, of course, still conventional in form, still a reflection of some of the most familiar motives
of the poetry of courtly love:

> her eyes in heaven
> Would through the airy region stream so bright
> That birds would sing and think it were not night.   (II. ii. 20)

Beyond this deliberate play with words and conceits, however, we can
respond also to a process by which true sentiment, not necessarily of a
mature or admirable kind, is engaged upon the task of filling out convention, endowing it with life. The young lover, as he contemplates the
object of his desire, projects his sensuous imagination into the celebration of her person:

> See, how she leans her cheek upon her hand!
> O, that I were a glove upon that hand,
> That I might touch that cheek!   (II. ii. 23)

The urgency of the expression in fact, though still extreme and pre-carious in its quality, is being made to answer to the reality of intense emotion: 'Call me but love, and I'll be new baptized': 'dear saint'. We are not being invited here to any easy identification with the lover's new states of feeling. The language which prevails in this speech, and through the greater part of the entire episode, is at once plainly exces-sive, even an indulgence of sentiment, and, in terms of romantic love, expressive of a true devotion, entirely different from the superficial, self-centred attitudes which have prevailed, almost up to this moment, in Romeo's declarations of his love for Rosaline. The new situation is far more complex, a far more intricate compound of conflicting realities. Because this new love bears within itself an element of excess, a neglect of all realities except those which its own consummation in-volves, it will end in death; but because it is also a true emotion (and true not least in relation to the aged experience that sets itself up so consistently to thwart it, to deny its truth), because its intensity answers, when all has been said, to love's *value*, it will be felt to achieve, even in its inevitable frustration, a certain measure of triumph over circum-stance.

The element of contradiction makes its presence felt throughout this famous scene. Juliet, here as nearly always a good deal more realistic than Romeo, knows from the first that their love is surrounded by a sinister reality which its material circumstances confirm:

> The orchard walls are high and hard to climb,
> And the place death, considering who thou art; (II. ii. 63)

to which his passionate reply is at once, when viewed in terms of worldly common-sense, a further expression of excess, and, in relation to the new vision which has taken possession of him, a sign of the nature of true love:

> With love's light wings did I o'erperch these walls,
> For stony limits cannot hold love out:
> And what love can do, that dares love attempt. (II. ii. 66)

The Romeo who speaks after this fashion, and who goes on to say:

> wert thou as far
> As that vast shore wash'd with the farthest sea,
> I would adventure for such merchandise. (II. ii. 82)

is clearly a new person in relation to the conventional lover whom Mercutio and his friends could justly ridicule in the opening scenes. His eyes have been opened to the reality of love as an 'adventure', involving the total commitment of self, the willingness to risk all to obtain the rich 'merchandise', the prize of great value which love—if in fact it is a central reality in human experience—implies. This gesture of the gift of self, however, is at once necessary and dangerous, balanced over a void. This is recognized again, and in a new way, by Juliet when she answers Romeo's entranced declarations with a direct simplicity of her own and calls for an answering directness and simplicity from her lover:

> O gentle Romeo,
> If thou dost love, pronounce it faithfully. (II. ii. 93)

Romeo's far-flung declarations of the value and intensity of love call, as their natural counterpart, for plainer, more naturally human decisions, and it is these which Juliet is here emphasizing. By so doing, she does not, of course, call in question the truth and validity of the emotions which have transported Romeo to what is in effect a new life; but she is saying that these transports call for translation into a more intimate key, demand incorporation into a more common, but not on that account a less precious or valid reality.

The following duet, as we may properly call it, carries on this balance of intensity and artifice, idealism and reality:

> —Lady, by yonder blessed moon I swear,
> That tips with silver all these fruit-tree tops,—
> —O, swear not by the moon, th'inconstant moon,
> That monthly changes in her circled orb,
> Lest that thy love prove likewise variable.
> —What shall I swear by?
> —   Do not swear at all;
> Or, if thou wilt, swear by thy gracious self,
> Which is the god of my idolatry,
> And I'll believe thee. (II. ii. 107)

Juliet prefers plain statement to Romeo's elaborate declarations of faith; declarations, moreover, made in the name of the 'inconstant' moon, and so ominously suggesting impermanence. 'Do not swear at all', she pleads, or swear, if at all, by the plain object of her love, his 'gracious self'; but she too strikes the note of impermanence in her confession of 'idolatry', which at once answers to a true intensity and places it in the expression whilst leading to her final confession of misgiving:

> I have no joy of this contract to-night:
> It is too rash, too unadvised, too sudden,

> Too like the lightning, which doth cease to be
> Ere one can say, 'it lightens'.   (II. ii. 117)[4]

Throughout this exchange, the imagery of night which provides the appropriate conditions for the romanticism that unites these lovers is also the background, finally embracing a sinister element, against which love shines out in real but precarious and transitory splendour. Having thus expressed the misgivings which already shadow her love, and which she is more ready at this stage to grasp than Romeo, Juliet counters them with her affirmation, equally splendid and more positive in its implications, of love's inherent generosity:

> My bounty is as boundless as the sea,
> My love as deep: the more I give to thee,
> The more I have, for both are infinite.   (II. ii. 133)

This is the central Shakespearean affirmation that love asserts itself through giving, and that its gift is of the kind which enriches and is an indication of value, of 'infinity'. In the light of this, her repeated returns to the casement to salute Romeo yet again are, dramatically speaking, profoundly true to life. They serve to rouse Romeo from the misgivings to which he has been subjected, and which in his case are associated with night and the illusion of dreams—

> I am *afeard*,
> Being in night, all this is but a dream,
> Too flattering-sweet to be substantial—   (II. ii. 139)

until his doubts are finally dispelled in the positive affirmation of his outburst: 'It is my soul that calls upon my name', and in the final blended dedication:

> —I have forgot why I did call thee back.
> —Let me stand here till thou remember it.
> —I shall forget, to have thee still stand there,
> Remembering how I love thy company.
> —And I'll still stay, to have thee still forget,
> Forgetting any other home but this.   (II. ii. 170)

Poised against a background of night and impermanence love asserts briefly, for the duration of this scene, its anticipation of life and permanence to come.

As this statement of dedication draws to a close, we are brought back once more in contrast to the world of experience, which returns this time in the shape of Friar Lawrence; he—unlike the other old men in this play—is aware that the young have feelings of their own, but, being himself old, is debarred from sharing the reality of their feelings. It is within the limits of his understanding of life that he should see birth and death as related processes of nature:

> The earth that's nature's mother is her tomb;
> What is her burying grave, that is her womb;   (II. iii. 9)

it is also within his capacity to make allowances, theoretically and as an observer, for the contradictory principles that he sees, not without a certain subtlety of vision, as exercising their dominating and opposite action upon human nature:

> Two such opposed kings encamp them still
> In man as well as herbs, grace and rude will.   (II. iii. 27)

Yet, whilst recognizing in the Friar this true moralizing vision, we must also feel that the entry at this point of Romeo, 'wounded' and seeking the remedy for ills which are beyond all abstract cure, represents in most vivid form the impact of real life upon theory and remote moralizing. The Friar contemplates the lover's predicament from his own point of view, which Romeo must find irrelevant; for him Juliet is one more 'young woman' among many, with whom a young man has fallen in love. The Friar, moreover, is interested in this love, not in itself but as an instrument for ending, as he hopes, the family feud by which Verona is so intolerably divided; to this worthy end he will set his own typically old man's contrivances into action, only to discover for himself the truth that so many others will experience, mainly to their own undoing, in this play, that life will always tend to move, beyond the attempted control of those who seek to direct it in accordance with ends of their own, to its own conclusions.

It is in this spirit that the Friar agrees, although with foreboding, to perform the marriage that Romeo demands of him. He accedes, in fact, whilst Romeo, again prophetically, brings together love and death as he asserts the *value* of his devotion:

> come what sorrow can,
> It cannot countervail the exchange of joy
> That one short minute gives me in her sight:
> Do thou but close our hands with holy words,
> Then *love-devouring death* do what he dare,
> It is enough I may but call her mine.   (II. vi. 3)

This, with its desire to crowd the unique intensity of love into 'one

short minute', and to set the achievement of this union against the
devouring action of time, is close in spirit to the great Sonnets on
mutability. It amounts to a renewed and intensified bringing together of
the contrary sensations which make up what we can properly call the
'metaphysical' heart of this play. The Friar, speaking as ever in terms of
experience, utters his contrasted warning against the perils which these
one-sided ecstasies imply: 'These violent delights have violent ends', he
says, and, going on to speak, in terms which again touch upon a central
contradiction of the tragedy, of immoderate 'appetite', he urges the
pair to 'love moderately'. This, of course, he is able to do precisely
because he is a spectator, separated by age and outlook from the
imperious claims of passion. His attempts to understand the situation of
the lovers are, indeed, rather conscientiously painstaking than successful.
'O, so light a foot', he says feelingly of Juliet,

> Will ne'er wear out the everlasting flint;

and this, if it is true, as seen from one point of view, is from another—
that of the lovers themselves—besides the point. It is a view spoken
from the standpoint of 'experience', knowledge of the ways of the
world, which ignores, however, the reality of that engagement in their
emotion which is, in this same scene, the substance of Juliet's reply to
Romeo:

> They are but beggars that can count their worth;
> But my true love is grown to such excess,
> I cannot sum up sum of half my wealth.   (II. vi. 32)

Here we have a familiar cluster of ideas associated with love and
indicating its essential value. The refusal to consider emotion in terms of
mere accountancy, to 'count their wealth', saves lovers, in the moment
of their mutual engagement, from being 'beggars', gives to their 'true'
emotion such 'excess'—and here the elements of truth and exaggeration
are deliberately balanced one against the other—that it escapes all
temporal estimates of value and asserts, however dangerously and precariously, its own valuation. In phrases such as these, which the estimate
of 'reason' represented by such as Friar Lawrence finds finally incomprehensible, but in which love's generosity imposes, whilst the mutual
commitment lasts, its own conviction, the conventional poetic idea of
'love's wealth' points beyond any limit of mere convention to the
heart of the tragedy which here concerns us.

The outside world, however, though the lovers can succeed at certain
moments in ignoring it, is still there, ready to strike; as Benvolio says,

immediately after Juliet has spoken in this way, 'The day is hot, the Capulets abroad' (III. i. 2). Mercutio, reasonable after his own fashion to the last, exposes in no uncertain terms to his friend the essential vanity of all the family quarrels by which Verona is divided. 'Thou wilt quarrel', he points out, 'with a man that hath a hair more, or a hair less, in his beard than thou hast'; but as soon as Tybalt appears, dangerously on the warpath, he is as obstinate in refusing to give way as any of the others:

> —By my head, here comes the Capulets.
> —By my heel, I care not;   (III. i. 38)

and again, still more stubbornly, 'I will not budge for no man's pleasure, I'. The double stress on 'I' is proof that, in despite of his qualities of human and reasonable detachment, Mercutio is as subject as any other man to the irrational folly which prevails in both parties, and therefore as incapable as any of the rest of escaping the doom that awaits them all. It is striking to note that, in the midst of so much unreason, it is only Romeo, in his new situation, who expresses himself with realism to the man who insists in regarding himself as his mortal enemy:

> I do protest, I never injured thee,
> But love thee better than thou canst devise.   (III. i. 73)

In view of these words there is supreme irony in the fact that when Romeo, immediately after, intervenes to separate Mercutio and Tybalt, the only result is that his enemy is able to stab his friend under his arm. Once again, death makes his entry, but this time not in words alone, but in its irreparable reality, to be saluted by the dying Mercutio in phrases which contrast to magnificent effect, by their very sobriety, with all the alternately exuberant and fevered poetry which has decorated its impact to such varying effect in the preceding course of the play. 'The hurt cannot be much', says Romeo, at once expressing a friend's irrational hope and, we may feel, seeking to hide from himself the appalling consequences of his well-meant gesture. Mercutio's reply transposes the whole incident to a new level of tragedy. 'No', he says, with a rueful gravity to which the survival of his old humorous tone lends a further dimension, "tis not so deep as a well, nor so wide as a church-door; but 'tis enough, 'twill serve'; and again: 'ask for me to-morrow, and you shall find me a grave man' (III. i. 101). In this way, and to the accompaniment of Mercutio's last pun, the whole emotional quality of the play undergoes, in effect, a transformation. Nothing even in romantic and youthful love will be the same after Mercutio's departure as it was before it. The dying man's last judgement upon the events which have led to his death is indeed clear and final. 'A plague o' both your houses'; in the light of the unanswerable truth which this represents, Romeo's hesitant plea—'I thought all for the best'—may strike us as a pathetic illusion, finally something less than adequate. Romeo, indeed, is driven to feel his own responsibility for what has happened, and to fall in reaction, when Tybalt returns, into something very like the revenger's base rant. 'Fire-eyed fury be my conduct now', are the words he utters, just after he has said of himself, dwelling upon his love:

> O sweet Juliet,
> Thy beauty hath made me effeminate.   (III. i. 120)

We need not necessarily feel that the new mood of 'fury' is more manly—though Romeo may wish, as he speaks, to believe it so—than the 'effeminacy' which inspired him to behave reasonably towards the man he is now about to kill. At all events, it is the facts, rather than his attempt to react to them, that seriously count at this stage. As Romeo, in his new desperate mood, despatches Tybalt and accepts Benvolio's advice to flee, the action has passed beyond human control to fall under the influence of the 'stars' as the Prince pronounces, in stern justice and for the public peace, the sentence of banishment upon the latest murderer.

It is significant that it is at this precise moment, when the course of events can clearly be seen passing beyond the lovers' possible control, that Juliet shows more clearly than ever before how far she has developed beyond the unawakened adolescent of the opening scenes. If she now calls upon 'love-performing night', it is in no mere prolongation of the earlier romantic exchanges—and, indeed, in this sense it has always been Romeo, rather than herself, who has felt so intensely the attractions of the extinction of light—but in search of the full physical consummation of her love. Her words are in this sense precise and firm:

> O, I have bought the mansion of a love,
> But not possess'd it, and, though I am sold,
> Not yet enjoy'd; so tedious is this day
> As is the night before some festival
> To an impatient child that hath new robes
> And may not wear them.   (III. ii. 26)

Her new intensity, however, is not unrelated to a note of hysteria, and there is indeed something surprising in the presence, in the passage just quoted, of imagery that actually carries a hint of the brothel ('possess'd ... sold ... enjoy'd'); we should not suggest that Juliet's love is affected, in its quality, by these undertones, but that they answer to a new complexity, a shift towards darkness in the moral tone, that is making itself felt elsewhere. Similarly, when the Nurse enters, bringing, as she fears, news of Romeo's death, it is indeed hysteria that plays a major part in the conceptual impression of her contrary emotions:

> Hath Romeo slain himself? say thou but 'I',
> And that bare vowel 'I' shall poison more
> Than the death-darting eye of cockatrice:
> I am not I, if there be such an 'I',
> Or those eyes shut, that make thee answer 'I'.
> If he be slain, say 'I'.... (III. ii. 45)

The expressions of contradiction are prolonged through this speech to remarkable effect:

> O serpent heart, hid with a flowering face!...
> O nature, what hadst thou to do in hell,
> When thou didst bower the spirit of a fiend
> In mortal paradise of such sweet flesh?
> Was ever book containing such vile matter
> So fairly bound? O, that deceit should dwell
> In such a gorgeous palace! (III. ii. 73)

The last phrase is, in its intensity of contradiction, almost worthy of *Othello*. There is about all this a new sense of tragic complexity, and with it a new depth of psychological penetration, which is the result of balancing against one another the splendours and the impossibilities of romantic love. Juliet, awakened from adolescence into maturity, is discovering that 'deceit' can dwell in the 'gorgeous palace' of her dedication, seeing beneath the 'mortal paradise', at once sublimated and subject to decay, of the 'sweet flesh' in which the perfections of her lover are dangerously 'bowered', a 'spirit' indeed but—disconcertingly, opposed to the original simplicity of her youthful idealism—one which reveals itself under the external manifestations of a 'fiend'. The contradictions which the knot of human passion bears within itself are affirming themselves to this young, but rapidly maturing imagination with almost intolerable intensity.

Meanwhile, and at her side in the moment of stress, the voice of 'experience' continues to assert itself in the observations of the Nurse. Hers, wrapt in kindly forms, is the voice of a universal cynicism about the possibilities of love itself:

> There's no trust,
> No faith, no honesty in men: all perjured,
> All forsworn, all naught, all dissemblers.   (III. ii. 85)

It is finally, beneath its appearance of wisdom and detachment, a self-centred, an impotent voice—'These griefs, these woes, these sorrows, make me old'—one concerned only with its own situation. To Juliet it can bring no comfort, and she surrenders to the unique, impossible reality of her love as she affirms, at once naturally and against all reason, that

> My husband lives, that Tybalt would have slain;
> And Tybalt's dead, that would have slain my husband:
> All this is comfort.   (III. ii. 105)

The stressing of the fact that Romeo is now not merely her lover, the object of her romantic devotion, but her married 'husband' is designed to give to this assertion of 'comfort' in disaster an element of the natural; but Juliet herself must know, even as she speaks, that her situation, and that of Romeo, are not so simple, and indeed she follows this expression of an impossible hope with a recognition of the opposite reality:

> 'Romeo is banished': to speak that word,
> Is father, mother, Tybalt, Romeo, Juliet,
> All slain, all dead.   (III. ii. 122)

The premonition of death, once uttered, inevitably affirms itself in her thought. The end of all this tragic excess lies, most typically, in her own prayer: 'death, not Romeo, take my maidenhead'. It is left to the Nurse to maintain, in her own way and against the direction of her young mistress' mood, the ends of life as she declares her readiness to seek out Romeo for Juliet's 'comfort'; and to this proposal Juliet—who has, in the last analysis, no alternative—at the end accedes.

It is appropriately left to the Friar to keep up the note of foreboding. Romeo, he says, is 'wedded to calamity', as he brings him the news that he has been banished. Romeo's reply, affirming the love-centredness of all his thought—

> There is no world without Verona walls,
> But purgatory, torture, hell itself—   (III. iii. 17)

is from his point of view, outside both the excesses and the transforming effect of love, nothing less than a blasphemy; for Romeo's reactions are based upon the exclusive element of obsession in his passion—

heaven is here,

Where Juliet lives—   (III. iii. 29)

and find issue in the fevered contradictions of his high-flown, conceited
utterance: 'This may flies do, but I from this must fly' (III. iii. 40).
Once more, the element of artifice in these words is deliberate, answers
to a distraught and finally—as far as it goes—a corrupting emotional
state; but though the Friar can reasonably urge 'philosophy' upon his
penitent, his words remain those of an observer, outside both the
splendour and the peril of the lover's state, and Romeo can tell him
with natural indignation:

Hang up philosophy!

Unless philosophy can make a Juliet,   (III. iii. 56)

and point out, with bitter truth, that his mentor is in no position to feel
the valid, the essential truth of his situation: 'Thou canst not speak of
that thou dost not feel'. As though to support the pressure of experience
upon him, the Nurse also enters, to report that Juliet is in like case; but
her reproach to Romeo for what she sees as his excessive despair—
'stand, an you be a man'—is, like the Friar's, at once objectively true
and, from the victim's point of view, an irrelevance.

The truth is that Friar Lawrence, representing a common-sense which
is second nature to him, speaks at this moment of what he does not
understand. An onlooker from the outside, he sees in Romeo's transports of frustration and grief only 'the unreasonable fury of a beast',
and finds it natural to reprove the young man for his betrayal of true
manliness:

Thy noble shape is but a form of wax,

Digressing from the valour of a man, . . .

And thou dismember'd with thine own defence.   (III. iii. 125)

It is important, at this point, to see that this judgement, which is the
type of many others made in the course of the play, is at once true,
needing to be said, and—as seen from the standpoint of the victim—
beside the point, uttered by one who cannot, by his very nature, understand what is really at stake. In the same way, the Friar's attempts to
console Romeo, combining encouragement with reproach—

thy Juliet is alive,

For whose dear sake thou wast but lately dead . . .

Happiness courts thee in her best array;

But, like a misbehaved and sullen wench,

> Thou pout'st upon thy fortune and thy love:
> Take heed, take heed, for such die miserable—   (III. iii. 134)

constitute at once a valid warning, which the final tragedy will terribly
confirm, and amount—seen from the standpoint of Romeo's absorbing
and consuming passion—to so much irrelevant and facile moralizing.
Before the play ends the Friar's faith in 'experience' as a guide in life
will lead him to conclude that everything has its remedy, is susceptible
to a little rational manipulation; and it is in this spirit, well-meaning but
short-sighted, finally complacent, that he plans the stratagem which
will only serve to hasten the concluding disaster. For he and the Nurse
who so admires him—'O, what learning is!'—are, in the last analysis,
essentially of the same kind.

'Experience', meanwhile, in the grosser and more insensitive form
represented by old Capulet, is busy about its own short-sighted plans.
'Well, we were born to die' is his characteristic comment on Tybalt's
death, and it is decided that Juliet, in order to shake her from her
supposed grief for the dead man, shall be bundled as quickly as possible
into marriage with Paris. Once again, facile good intentions serve only
to hasten disaster. It is against this ominous background that Romeo
and Juliet achieve (III. v) the brief consummation of their mutual love.
It is a consummation, as we now have reason to expect, which is at once
intense, contradictory, and finally poised over fear: fear, above all, for
the future, whilst life is being plucked, in intense and breathless haste,
from the insubstantial present. The nightingale sings, for Juliet, in 'the
fearful hollow' of her lover's ear, and Romeo, exultant as he is in the
moment of achievement—

> Night's candles are burnt out, and *jocund* day
> Stands tip-toe on the misty mountain tops—   (III. v. 9)[5]

can only precariously maintain his happiness. 'I must be gone and live,
or stay and die'. Life is, for him, with Juliet, and absence from her
means death; so that, when Juliet, as ever more realistic at heart, clings
desperately to what she knows to be an illusion—'thou needst not to be
gone'—he is ready to deny truth in the name of his love: 'I'll say yon
grey is not the morning's eye'. Once again, however, the end of love is
foreseen to lie in death: 'Come, death, and welcome! Juliet wills it so'.
Even, however, as Romeo accepts the illusion upon which his life now
rests, it is Juliet who returns to daily reality—'It is the lark that sings so
out of tune'—and who foresees that they must separate. Truth, in other
words, stands most delicately balanced against illusion; to decide which

is which, and to what end they are interwoven, could be described as precisely the *crux* of this tragedy. As Juliet admits that 'more light and light it grows', it is left to Romeo to make his comment of tragic foreboding: 'More light and light: more dark and dark our woes'.

At this point reality intervenes in yet another form, as the Nurse interrupts the lovers to bring news, with day-break, of the approach of Lady Capulet. There is once again an ominous note in Juliet's last question, 'thinkst thou we shall ever meet again?'; and though Romeo's reply seems to suggest confidence—

> I doubt it not; and all these woes shall serve
> For sweet discourses in our time to come—   (III. v. 52)

the sinister death note reaffirms itself in the last words which, in the event, Juliet will speak to her lover alive:

> O God! I have an ill-divining soul.
> Methinks I see thee, now thou art below,
> As one dead in the bottom of a tomb.   (III. v. 54)

At the last she is left to rely upon fortune—that deity 'fickle' in the eyes of the world, tending at all times to impose separation—to send Romeo back to her arms.

The world beyond the lovers proceeds, meanwhile, on its own paths of misunderstanding. Lady Capulet believes that her daughter weeps for Tybalt and offers, in typically 'experienced' terms, her moralizing consolation:

> some grief shows much of love,
> But much of grief shows still some want of wit.

As always, 'experience' seeks the solution to all problems in 'moderation': seeks it precisely where love, of its very nature, is unable to find it. It is noteworthy, however, as a sign of the way in which the complexities of maturity are imposing themselves, that when Romeo is mentioned, Juliet shows herself old enough to dissemble to her mother. 'Indeed', she says,

> I never shall be satisfied
> With Romeo, till I behold him—dead;   (III. v. 95)

what she does not know, and what constitutes, of course, the irony of this situation, is that this 'satisfaction' is very shortly to be granted her. Her mother, meanwhile, has come to bring her news of the 'wedding' which has been arranged by the elderly and the 'experienced' for what they have decided is her own good; and her more formidable father now enters to confirm his 'decree'. At this point, we are clearly shown the fundamental insensibility of those who claim to be versed in the ways of the world: shown it nowhere more obviously than in Capulet's unreasoning rage at Juliet's timid attempts to cross him—'My fingers itch!'—and scarcely less evidently in her own mother's callous remark: 'I would the fool were married to her grave'. And so, indeed, she shall be, sooner than Lady Capulet knows; but meanwhile the Nurse is allowed to utter her protest in the name of a certain human feeling—'You are to blame, my lord, to rate her so'—only to evoke the father's egoistic stressing of what he believes to be his own unrewarded care and toil:

> Day, night, hour, tide, time, work, play,
> Alone, in company, still my care hath been
> To have her match'd.   (III. v. 178)

It is, in fact, his own self-esteem which feels itself affronted by his daughter's obstinacy, and which prompts him to turn her away unless she is docile to his will. Juliet, indeed, faced by a situation slipping beyond all possible control, feels herself caught in a trap:

> Alack, alack, that heaven should practise stratagems
> Upon so soft a subject as myself;   (III. v. 211)

but when she seeks advice from the Nurse, who has so recently shown her some measure of understanding, it is only to be told that Romeo is a 'dishclout' in comparison with Paris; there is point indeed in her own final disenchanted comment: 'Well, thou hast comforted me marvellous much'.

Thus abandoned by those from whom she might have expected help, Juliet decides to turn to the Friar, only—by yet another ironic mischance—to find Paris, her discreet and honourable suitor, in advance of her at his cell. Even as she asks for counsel, she already sees her ultimate 'solution' in the death which is pressing itself upon her intimate reflections. Rather than be forced to marry Paris, she says,

> shut me nightly in a charnel-house,
> O'ercovered quite with dead men's rattling bones,
> With reeking shanks and yellow chapless skulls;
> Or bid me go into a new-made grave,
> And hide me with a dead man in his shroud;
> Things that to hear them told, have made me tremble.   (IV. i. 81)

Her thoughts are full of the charnel-house, the obsessive presence which will from now on live in her mind side by side with love. Precisely these things, which she now regards with horror, she is fated to do; but we should recognize too that these forebodings, excessive as they are, are spoken in the name of loving faith:

> I will do it without fear or doubt,
> To live an unstain'd wife to my sweet love.   (IV. i. 87)

Strong in the love which this determination reflects, Juliet is able at this crisis to dissemble beyond her years. Her deception of her father, in the very act of professing filial obedience (IV. ii), is no doubt a sin, but a sin conceived in the name of natural love and in the face of an egoistic and unimaginative opposition; once more, we find ourselves faced with the play's central tragic contradiction. To affirm the rights of love, Juliet finds herself driven to dissemble; her situation is one which can, of its nature, have no happy solution, but we cannot—unless we are ready to share the egoism and incomprehension of her parents—simply leave her condemned of deception.

Alone with her resolution, Juliet is not surprisingly given over to fear. She confesses to feeling 'a faint cold fear' which 'thrills through' her 'veins' (IV. iii. 15) as she, who has found her elders so lacking in understanding, contemplates the possibility that even the Friar may be ready to betray her. The thought drives her back upon her increasing obsession with mortal decay, as she contemplates in her imagination the tomb

> Where bloody Tybalt, yet but green in earth,
> Lies festering in his shroud,

and thinks of the dreadful possibility of her awakening by his side:

> Alack, alack, is it not like that I
> So early waking, what with loathsome smells
> And shrieks like mandrakes torn out of the earth,
> That living mortals hearing them run mad:
> Of, if I wake, shall I not be distraught,
> Environed with all these hideous fears?   (IV. iii. 46)

Meanwhile, in the scene which at once follows these sombre premonitions (IV. iv), the preparations for life and festivity are afoot, and the Nurse, foreseeing an imminent marriage, is in her element; just before she discovers Juliet's 'death', and in the presence of her 'body', she jests broadly over the coming consummation of her wedding:

> Sleep for a week; for the next night, I warrant,
> The County Paris will set up his rest
> That you shall rest but little.   (IV. v. 5)

Gross and insensitive as they no doubt are, these are after all words of life; and it answers to the play's intention that they are the prelude to the Nurse's own discovery of what she thinks to be, not life, but the image of death, its opposite. Capulet too, in his lament, equally joins love and death as he reveals the 'truth' to Paris:

> O son, the night before thy wedding-day,
> Hath death lain with thy wife; see, where she lies,
> Flower as she was, deflowered by him. (IV. v. 35)

The Friar, for his part, adds his appropriate note to the whole by stressing another kind of life:

> confusion's cure lives not
> In these confusions. Heaven and yourself
> Had part in this fair maid: now heaven hath all . . .
> Your part in her you could not keep from death,
> But heaven keeps his part in eternal life. (IV. v. 65)

We need neither reject this simply as so much abstract moralizing, nor accept it as the last word on the tragedy which is now approaching its final stages. It represents the voice of 'experience', which belongs to but does not exhaust the total impact of life. 'She's best married that dies married young': 'Nature's tears are reason's merriment'; it is hard not to feel, as we hear these hard things so easily said, that from this sententious 'wisdom' something—which is, perhaps, finally life itself—has been excluded.

The illusion of life, indeed,—if illusion it be—is precisely what Romeo expresses in the very next scene:

> My bosom's lord sits lightly in his throne,
> And all this day an unaccustom'd spirit
> Lifts me above the ground with cheerful thoughts. (V. i. 3)

It affirms itself even against the contrary sensations which have taken possession of his sleep:

> I dreamt my lady came and found me dead—
> Strange dream, that gives a dead man leave to think!—
> And breathed such life with kisses in my lips,
> That I revived and was an emperor.
> Ah me! how sweet is love itself possess'd,
> When but love's shadows are so rich in joy! (V. i. 6)

Here the central contrast which we have followed through the whole course of the play presents itself from yet another standpoint. The force of love affirms itself, momentarily, in and through an illusion that yet partakes of life; but Romeo has no sooner spoken than Baltasar enters with news of Juliet's 'death', and her lover's answer corresponds to yet another change of mood: 'Is it e'en so? then I defy you, stars!' (V. i. 24). Where Juliet visited the Friar in search of advice and consolation, Romeo in the madness of his desperate resolve now seeks out the sinister apothecary—sinister by his own account (V. i)—to obtain poison for the ending of his life. Meanwhile, to emphasize the operations of a malignant fortune beyond human control, Friar John's mission has gone astray, undoing all Lawrence's previsions, and Juliet is left, in his own words, as 'Poor living corse, closed in a dead man's tomb!' (V. ii. 29).

The last scene of the tragedy opens with Paris at the monument, uttering over Juliet's 'tomb' his own decent lament in sonneteering terms. He is interrupted by Romeo in his new mood of desperate, essentially death-directed resolution:

> I will tear thee joint by joint
> And strew this hungry churchyard with thy limbs:
> The time and my intents are savage-wild,
> More fierce and inexorable by far
> Than empty tigers or the roaring sea.   (V. iii. 35)

The lover's thoughts revolve characteristically in his mad excess of grief—a fitting pendant to the almost equally mad excess which formerly marked one extreme of his love—round the obsession of the charnel—'Thou detestable maw, thou womb of death'—but it is worth noting that, even as he declares himself to Paris as 'a desperate man', he can still address his rival as 'Good gentle youth'. As he goes on to say, still to Paris, and with profound truth: 'By heaven, I love thee better than myself'; the mood is one which, as has often been pointed out, reminds us of Hamlet, whom he also now resembles in being driven unwillingly to kill. Awakening almost at once to the desperate reality of his deed, he sees his victim as joined obscurely to himself in a common adverse fate—'one writ with me in sour misfortune's book'—in an attitude which combines a measure of true nobility with a touch of self-compassion.

These events lead to their culmination in the moment at which Romeo looks on Juliet as she lies on her 'tomb' as on a marriage-bed, and sees in his grim surroundings, which the radiance of her presence in his imagination transforms, 'a feasting presence full of light'. We may

legitimately ask ourselves whether this represents reality, of an imaginative kind, or illusion in the eyes of common-sense; and the answer is
surely both. There follows Romeo's noble hymn to death, or rather to
beauty as transfigured by love and thereby rendered triumphant over
circumstance and the grave:

> Thou art not conquer'd; beauty's ensign yet
> Is crimson in thy lips and in thy cheeks,
> And death's pale flag is not advanced there;   (V. iii. 94)

but, of course, in reacting to and accepting the beauty of this, we shall
not forget that the point lies, though Romeo is unaware of it, in the
fact that Juliet is *alive*. Meanwhile, love and the desire to die are
romantically (or shall we say, pathetically? or even self-indulgently? or,
possibly, both?) fused in Romeo's words:

> shall I believe
> That unsubstantial death is amorous,
> And that the lean abhorred monster keeps
> Thee here in dark to be his paramour?   (V. iii. 102)

The truth is that 'the palace of dim night' exercises upon Romeo here,
as it has done to less extreme effect earlier in the play, a profound
attraction, which persuades him to seek his repose, 'here, here', 'with
worms that are thy chamber-maids'; the slightly sententious tone is
surely part, though we may agree that it is not all, of the complete
effect. Romeo's final nostalgia is, at all events, for 'everlasting rest', for
the opportunity to

> shake the yoke of inauspicious stars
> From this world-wearied flesh;   (V. iii. 111)

and we should perhaps be chary of either accepting this mood at its
declared value or of exclusively condemning it. Whilst giving its full
worth to the romantic power which inspires Romeo's words, we need
not take him at this moment entirely at his own self-estimate; for the
speaker is moved, on his own confession, by a 'desperate pilot', the end
of whose guidance will be to lead him to run on 'the dashing rocks' his
'sea-sick weary bark'. Never in Shakespeare, surely, is suicide accepted
quite simply at its own essentially self-dramatizing estimate; though we
must add, to do justice to the complete effect, that here it is given its full
value, in terms of the poetry, as an element in romantic love. Romeo's

final words before he kills himself sum up precisely this vital contrast, as they join life and death in a reflection of the play's complex mood: 'Thy drugs are quick' (*quick* in the double sense of *rapid* and *alive*), 'Thus with a *kiss* I die'. There could be no more fitting conclusion than this 'metaphysical' balance of contrasted emotions for a play which has turned from the first upon the twin realities, at once separate and identical, of love and death.

Immediately after this last gesture the world returns, in the shape of a Friar Lawrence now moved, most significantly, by fear. The limitations of 'experienced' detachment, even when joined to recognized virtue and good intention, have by now been thoroughly exposed. As Juliet, too late, awakens, he can only call her from

> that nest
> Of death, contagion, and unnatural sleep: (V. iii. 151)

only confess at the last his own human limitations:

> A greater power than we can contradict
> Hath thwarted our intents.

In a last effort to remedy what is in fact beyond mending, the Friar proposes to direct Juliet to a monastery, but here once more his measure of understanding and his desire to contrive for the best are powerless before the unanswerable vehemence of her retort: 'Go, get thee hence, for *I will not away*' (V. iii. 160). For her imagination, centred on love as the source of life to the exclusion of all other realities, the 'poison' on Romeo's lips may yet be a 'restorative'. None other, indeed, is logically available to her; for she is ready to die where she has been awakened to life, to seek in death the only remedy for her tragic situation.

To the aged survivors, now belatedly chastened by the tragedy that they have helped to bring about, the spectacle before them of the youthful dead comes as a reminder of their own approaching end; as Lady Capulet puts it,

> this sight of death is as a bell
> That warns my old age to a sepulchre. (V. iii. 206)

The Prince, as representative of law and civilization in a city where both have been set aside to tragic effect, is left to denounce a feud that has been the cause of so much death and loss, where life and unity might have resulted from the consummation of love in marriage:

> See, what a scourge is laid upon your hate,
> That heaven finds means to kill your joys with love,   (V. iii. 292)

Or, as he puts it in the act of winding up this tragic action, 'A glooming peace this morning with it brings'.

2 A Midsummer Night's Dream

Good reasons exist for supposing that *A Midsummer Night's Dream* must have been written at a date not very distant from that of *Romeo and Juliet*. There are moments, indeed, when the play may strike us as a comic counterpoise to the 'romantic' tragedy, exploring through the comic conventions other aspects of that irrational, but vital impulse, in the name of which the young lovers of Verona chose death as an alternative to the extinction of their mutual relationship. Through convention, in fact, Shakespeare works out in this play a pattern of contrasted attitudes to the love which seems to elude reason and, at times, to convert human beings into its slaves; a pattern, moreover, which is set finally in the framework of a rational and social attitude to marriage.

This attitude is given its expression, also in poetic terms, through the relationship of Theseus and Hippolyta, whose 'nuptial hour', we are told as the action opens, 'draws on apace'. Theirs is presented as a love compatible with experience, conscious of its true nature and of the dangers inherent in passion, but confident also of the ability of civilized human beings to turn passion to positive and beneficent ends. Theseus speaks of his past 'desires' as lingering on into the present, and makes a frank confession to his future bride of the part once played by violence in the beginnings of their own relationship:

> Hippolyta, I woo'd thee with my sword,
> And won thy love, doing thee injuries.   (I. i. 16)

This amounts to a recognition that love is compatible with the cruel and the irrational, as indeed much in the coming action will confirm. Side by side with this, however, and representing not the past but the present and the anticipated fulfilments of the future, Theseus asserts the ability of rational maturity to incorporate this vital impulse into the social and essentially civilizing dance of life, which this play will aim at reflecting in dramatic form; as he at once goes on to say, still to Hippolyta,

> I will wed thee in another key,
> With pomp, with triumph, and with revelling.   (I. i. 18)

The 'wooing' of the past, based on the immediate and even dangerous impulses of individual passion, is now to find its consummation in the social celebration of marriage; but before it does so, before the conclusion here anticipated is turned into the final reality, we shall have occasion to observe the operations of passion to less social ends, in a variety of contrasted situations and in surroundings which imply a deliberate withdrawal from the world of human and social living.

Scarcely, indeed, has Theseus stated these intentions with regard to his marriage than he is interrupted by the entry of Egeus, 'full of vexation', inspired by bitter resentment against his own child. Once again, as in *Romeo and Juliet*, although to different ends, we are made aware of the shortsighted confidence of 'experience' in its ability to assert its own designs at the expense of others. The father, in his determination to *impose* his own view upon his daughter, dismisses Hermia's declared preference for Lysander as a mere question of deceitful 'feigning' and unnatural 'love-tokens', finally as a manifestation of her perverse and unnatural 'cunning'; against this, he clings obstinately to the father's right to filial 'obedience', only to rouse against himself the irrational reality of a love which he can neither understand nor allow for, in 'stubborn harshness'.

Theseus, required to assert his authority in this dispute, does so in the name of an acceptance of natural dependence as the indispensable foundation of truly ordered and social living. The choice he places before Hermia is one between submission and death: death or, alternatively, an unnatural, life-long renunciation of love itself. In so doing, he acts as a ruler, as the voice of reason and natural law whose concern it is to direct the impulses of passion into their established and indispensable social channels. Hermia, however, protests against his decision, claiming the privilege, upon which true love must rest and which is equally a part of life, of seeing with her own eyes. 'I would', she says, 'my father look'd but with *my* eyes', rather than with those of the experienced 'judgement' to which he lays claim and which Theseus, as the voice of authority, is properly concerned to defend. Her plea is one uttered in exclusive attention to the satisfaction of her own impulses, and as such we shall not be tempted to accept it as it stands; but neither, on the other hand, shall we follow Egeus in his short-sighted and obstinate refusal to allow it any consideration at all. In point of fact, the action of the play will turn out to depend, to no small extent, precisely upon what different 'eyes' see in love, and it will be the harmonizing of these visions, rather than any arbitrary choice between them, that will finally constitute its substance. Already, Theseus' own position shows itself more understanding than a mere affirmation of authority would require. As Hermia clings to her decision with an obstinacy equal to that of her father, Theseus warns her that the consequences of her refusal to listen to reason will be the denial of natural life, a sterile obligation

> To live a *barren* sister all your life,
> Chanting *faint* hymns to the *cold fruitless* moon.   (I. i. 72)

He shows himself in this aware of the difference which separates such as Hermia, whose natural end is fulfilment in marriage, from those whose renunciation of the world is firmly founded, who in full knowledge *choose* the spiritual life. 'Thrice-blessed', indeed, he warns her, are those

> that master so their blood
> To undergo such maiden pilgrimage: (I. i. 74)

but, for the rest, for those who are called to live naturally in the world, the position is otherwise:

> *earthlier* happy is the rose distill'd,
> Than that which, *withering* on the *virgin thorn*,
> Grows, lives, and dies in single blessedness.   (I. i. 76)

It is a feature of Theseus' maturity, of the grasp of reality that makes him fit to rule, that he is capable of balancing these two attitudes, the spiritually dedicated and the naturally human, giving to each its appropriate value and demanding the one-sided rejection of neither.[6]

This truth, however, can only be finally affirmed at the end of an action which will be mainly concerned, until its conclusion, with the inter-play between various partial attitudes to love. Hermia and Lysander, as lovers, live in their own world, which has its own laws, but which is not in any event that of mature and reasonable experience. Their confidence is placed fully in that world and the vision which it imposes. As Lysander, appealing to reason from *his* own standpoint, says to his rival:

> You have her father's love, Demetrius;
> Let me have Hermia's: do you marry him: (I. i. 93)

an argument based on exclusive concern with his own compulsions, which Egeus is able to take up by asserting in turn his essentially *proprietary* view of his paternal rights:

> true, he hath my love,
> And what is *mine* my love shall render him.   (I. i. 95)

Lysander's reply to this is a claim to social equality with his rival and, more important, an assertion of the rights which, in his view, and Hermia's, the fact of love reciprocated in itself confers; but it is important to note that, whilst speaking thus in the defence of his own interest, he is ready to dismiss the love of others, as in the case of Helena, as so much irrational excess:

> she, sweet lady, *dotes*,
> Devoutly *dotes*, dotes in *idolatry*;[7]   (I. i. 108)

from which we are left to conclude that love, blind to its own partiality, is characteristically clear-sighted in relation to that of others.

Left alone after Theseus has declared his judgement, Lysander and Hermia consider the nature of love more closely. It is, they are aware, essentially ill-starred—'The course of true love never did run smooth'— but equally they know by personal experience that it is 'hell to choose love by another's eyes'. Its wilfulness is, in fact, at once its strength and its weakness, and its background is impermanence, an inescapable subjection to time and circumstance. As Lysander says:

> if there were a sympathy in choice,
> War, death, or sickness did lay siege to it,
> Making it momentary as a sound,
> Swift as a shadow, short as any dream;
> Brief as the lightning in the collied night,
> That, in a spleen, unfolds both heaven and earth,
> And ere a man hath power to say 'Behold!'
> The jaws of darkness do devour it up:
> So quick bright things come to confusion.   (I. i. 141)[8]

Here, clearly, we have an echo of the characteristic mood of Romeo, not less poignant or charged with feeling for being translated from a tragic to a comic action. Hermia is ready to accept the truth of her lover's comment, which she regards as the description of 'a customary cross'; but it is worth noting that she does so in the name of 'fancy' and therefore, up to a point, of illusion. In this spirit, which amounts to a decision to evade reality by attempted flight, Lysander persuades her to leave Athens with him; and she, as she accepts his proposal, swears to keep faith by Cupid, who is however notoriously fickle, by 'the simplicity of Venus' doves', who represent in fact anything but simplicity, and—most significantly of all—'By all the vows that ever men

10—A.T.S. I

have broke'. The essentially dual nature of passion, compounded of simplicity and deception, could hardly be more strongly affirmed.

The 'simplicity' of love, indeed, is immediately shown in a new light by the entry upon the scene of Helena, in whom the same exclusive devotion evokes no response from its declared object. In the exchange between herself and Hermia the cross-complexities of love are given their full value. Hermia, resting upon her own recent experience, stresses its transforming and essentially irrational power:

> Before the time I did Lysander see,
> Seem'd Athens as a paradise to me:
> O, then, what graces in my love do dwell,
> That he hath turn'd a heaven into a hell;   (I. i. 204)

whilst Lysander, equally concentrated on the satisfaction which his own position seems to afford him, touches somewhat patronizingly on the same theme in his final good wishes for Helena: 'As you on him, Demetrius *dote* on you.' To this Helena, in turn, can only answer that it is precisely Demetrius, whom she vainly loves, who 'dotes' not on her, but on her rival. Both love's strength and its weakness, accordingly, are seen to lie in its compelling power to act transformingly upon the real; as Helena goes on to say:

> Things base and vile, holding no quantity,
> Love can transpose to form and dignity;
> Love looks not with the eyes, but with the mind;
> And therefore is wing'd Cupid painted blind:
> Nor hath love's mind of any judgement taste;
> Wings, and no eyes, figure unheedy haste:
> And therefore is love said to be a child,
> Because in choice he is so oft beguiled.   (I. i. 232)

This is the sentence which sums up the meaning of what we have seen and are to see. The lovers themselves confirm it by their uncertain and unreasoning choices, as well as by the obstinacy with which they maintain them against all contrary considerations; and now Helena herself, having just admitted all this, is immediately inspired to betray the confidence of her friend in the hope of obtaining love's reward at her expense.

The entry of Bottom and his friends (I. ii) introduces a further contrast, another plane of the complete action. The play which they are preparing to perform before Theseus is in effect something very like a parody of Romeo's tragedy; it is 'the most lamentable comedy, and most cruel death of Pyramus and Thisby'. The time, however, has hardly come for this part of the action to be developed, and so the actors are soon replaced by the fairies (II. i), as life in its social and civilized forms gives way to the mysteriousness of the woods, where the irrational but potent impulses which it normally covers will be released and where its capacity to master these by gathering them into a more comprehensive humanity will be in some sense tested. As we are introduced to this new facet of the action, it is clear that even in the fairy realm passion has introduced its all too human disorder. Oberon, according to Puck's report, is 'passing fell and wroth', consumed with jealousy for his queen and with desire for the boy attendant whom she has enticed from his service; and Titania, on her side, clings to her conquest, 'perforce witholds the loved boy',

> Crowns him with flowers, and makes him all her joy: (II. i. 27)

treats the page, in short, exactly as she is shortly to treat the grotesquely transformed person of Bottom the weaver. As a result of this tense situation, the entire fairy realm is plunged into disorder. As Puck again reports:

> all their elves for fear
> Creep into acorn cups and hide them there; (II. i. 30)

and it is precisely this disorder which Puck in turn, as the very spirit of irresponsibility, makes particularly his own.[9]

Oberon and Titania, when they finally meet from opposite sides, accuse one another mutually and with considerable heat. Oberon is said to be 'amorous', in all the human sense of that word, and Titania is reminded of her former passion for Theseus in words which, spoken as they are in the woods, the home of the dark and irrational forces in life, are not devoid of a sense of menace:

> Didst thou not lead him through the glimmering night
> From Perigenia, whom he ravished? (II. i. 78)

There is indeed a sinister element in this fairy realm, one associated with the action of 'blood' and the darker side of the passions, not in any way less real than that of lyrical fancy and poetic decoration to which we can all respond. Titania speaks with feeling of 'the forgeries of jealousy', and nature itself is seen as subject to profound disturbance; the winds, 'as in revenge', have sucked up 'contagious fogs' from the sea, and 'the seasons alter', are subjected to an unnatural process of change:

> the spring, the summer,
> The childing autumn, angry winter change

> Their wonted liveries; and the mazed world,
> By their increase, now knows not which is which:
> And this same progeny of evil comes
> From our debate, from our dissension.   (II. i. 111)

In the face of this situation, Oberon sticks obstinately to the demand that his caprice be satisfied, denying all responsibility—'Do you amend it, then; it lies in you'— whilst Titania defies him in the name of her infatuation: 'The fairy land buys not the child of me'. Their final parting is, inevitably on terms of mutual defiance, with Oberon declaring that he will use the services of Puck to subject his queen to 'torment'; and it is in this mood that he at once sends the spirit to seek the flower called, not without meaning, 'love-in-idleness', the properties of which are such that they will make

> man or woman *madly dote*
> Upon the next live creature that it sees.   (II. i. 171)

By the action of this plant, Titania will be induced to confound her sense of reality, to pursue 'with the soul of love', which is thereby reduced to the absurd and the sinister, 'lion, bear, or wolf, or bull', and, perhaps even more ignominiously than these, 'meddling monkey' or 'busy ape'. The only reason which Oberon has for exposing her to this treatment is the hope that she may thereby be induced to 'render up her page to me'.

It is precisely at this point, when all the irrational and potentially destructive qualities of love seem to have been confirmed in the fairy order, that Helena enters 'doting', in vain pursuit of the same Demetrius who declares himself ready to 'slay' his rival Lysander even in the act of confessing that Hermia, the object of his passion, in turn 'slays' him by her failure to respond to his love. What better example could we find than this of love's excess, of the reflection of fairy perversity in human dedication to madness? In this spirit, Demetrius goes on to berate Helena soundly, whilst she in turn confesses to her abject state with a comparison of supreme indignity:

> I am your spaniel; and, Demetrius,
> The more you beat me, I will fawn on you,   (II. i. 203)[10]

only to receive his heartless reply: 'I am sick when I do look on thee', and to be threatened, at least by implication, with the loss, in addition to all else, of 'the rich worth of your virginity'. Helena, thoroughly caught in the trap of her unrequited love, can only answer with the abject recognition of her abasement: 'you in my respect are all the world'. Love, translated from its original courtly setting to the woods, has become a force that operates by reversing the normal order of things, that can hint at a sinister note when Helena says 'Apollo flies, and Daphne holds the chase', and find it amply confirmed when Demetrius, in the obsession of his own passion, utters his final threat to her: 'I shall do thee mischief in the wood'. Even after this, however, her irrational subjection to passion is such that she can say:

> I'll follow thee, and make a heaven of hell,
> To die upon the hand I love so well;   (II. i. 243)

whilst Oberon, on his return, declares that he is ready to make Titania full of just those 'hateful fantasies' that we have heard uttered in the human order.

In the scene which follows (II. ii), Oberon's purpose is at last fulfilled as Titania sleeps to the insistent evocation of beasts and insects shadowing her slumber, and as Oberon himself utters his culminating malevolence: 'Wake when some *vile* thing is near'. No sooner has this been accomplished than the connection with the human action is drawn still closer, as Lysander and Hermia enter, devoted to one another but exhausted by their prolonged wanderings in the woods. Lysander is still able to speak, poetically, of their being united as 'one heart', whilst Hermia shows herself more realistically aware of the dangers that encompass human relationships in the forest when she urges him to 'lie further off'. No sooner have they succumbed to sleep, and after Puck, following his fairy master's instructions, has thrown his charm in the wrong man's eyes, than Helena enters, still 'doting' upon the uncourteous Demetrius. When Lysander awakes, the web of unreason is drawn even tighter as he succumbs to his new love for Helena and makes his appeal—not, precisely at this moment, without irony—to what he is pleased to think of as reason:

> The will of man is by his reason sway'd,
> And reason says you are the worthier maid.   (II. ii. 115)

There could hardly be a more inauspicious moment for asserting the supremacy of 'reason' in the affairs of passion. The entire action in the woods, on the fairy and human levels alike, indicates that the will of man is moved in these matters by irrational factors, and indeed to Helena the sudden change in Lysander appears as one 'mockery' more, even as Lysander himself renounces, in most unreasonable terms, the love he formerly professed for Hermia:

> For as a surfeit of the sweetest things
> The deepest loathing to the stomach brings,
> Or as the heresies that men do leave
> Are hated most of those they did deceive,
> So thou, *my surfeit and my heresy*,
> Of all be hated, but the most of me!   (II. ii. 137)

Where, we may well ask after this, does 'doting' end and true love begin? The scene is brought to its appropriate conclusion when the abandoned Helena awakes, dreaming of a 'crawling serpent' at her breast, only to find Lysander gone and herself alone and subjected to terror in the woods.

This is the appropriate moment to extend the comic pattern further by bringing Bottom and his group to the heart of the action. Bottom and Titania are now to provide the supreme example, central to the whole play, of love's incongruity; and on the verge of this revelation the weaver's mixture of simplicity and basic common-sense is appropriately stressed. Puck intervenes to place the asses' head on Bottom, whilst his friends flee from him in fear, but whilst he himself retains his self-confidence and fundamental *aplomb*: 'this is to make an ass of me; to fright me if they could. But I will not stir from this place'. This is the same confidence which will enable Bottom to fall easily into his new role as Titania's consort, treating the attendant fairies with deference and even a certain dignity: the same which, more importantly, renders him immune to the fantasies that surround him in the forest, although insensible at the same time to its magic. Therein lies the essence of his attitude to love, and of his situation at this moment. Titania, on the other hand, is fully subjected to the follies and excesses that accompany unreasonable love. She, as she awakes, 'dotes' on her grotesque companion, whom her imagination entirely transforms from his reality. 'Mine ear', she says,

> is much enamour'd of thy note;
> So is mine eye enthralled to thy shape;   (III. i. 145)

for 'doting' enters through the senses, and true love, as distinct from enslavement to passion, calls for the confirmation of the mind.[11] Bottom's realistic comment upon this—'you should have little reason for that; and yet, to say the truth, reason and love keep little company together now-a-days' (III. i. 149)—has serious meaning, uttered though it is in an absurd situation, appropriate to the spirit of comedy; and as much can be said of his retort to Titania's further excess, 'Thou art as wise as thou art beautiful': 'Not so, neither; but if I had wit enough to get out of this wood, I have enough to serve mine own turn' (III. i. 155).[12] The wood, indeed, is in no sense a substitute for daily living in the workaday world. The appropriate home of a fairy, it can provide no permanent habitat for the human beings who will in due course return, with their minds and hearts suitably chastened and enriched, to normal social living; and, in so far as Bottom holds on to this truth in the midst of his grotesque translation, he is affirming a reality central to the entire conception.

The full meaning of this episode is, indeed, considerably more various and complex than any mere response to the obvious comic situation can suggest. Titania, duped as she is by Oberon's plot, is still 'a spirit of no common rate'. As such, she is able to respond, even in a situation calculated to make her words palpably absurd, to the vision of love as a purifying and essentially ennobling force. She can tell Bottom, in words which convey more than the obvious absurdity which her situation imposes:

> I will purge thy mortal grossness so,
> That thou shalt like an airy spirit go;   (III. i. 167)

and before the web of confusions in which they are both involved is ended, Bottom will have assimilated at least something of this point of view. The marriage of incongruities, indeed, as reflected in love and now supremely embodied in the inversion of normal human qualities and attitudes in the woods, is the essence of Shakespeare's comedy in this play.

In the episodes which follow this grotesque confrontation of 'spirit' and 'flesh', the fairy and the mortal worlds, irrationality and subjection to the forces in nature which evade reasonable control everywhere prevail. Oberon, in his confirmed malice, is ready to see Titania 'dote', and Puck finds pleasure in being able to bring him the news that she is so far alienated from her true self as to be in love with a 'monster'. Nature, indeed, is in the process of becoming more than a little sinister as the instrument of Puck's malicious devices:

> Their sense thus weak, lost with their fears thus strong,
> Made senseless things begin to do them wrong. . . .
> I led them on in this distracted fear,

> And left sweet Pyramus translated there:
> When in that moment, so it came to pass,
> Titania waked, and straightway loved an ass. (III. ii. 27)

Against this background, with all the normal attributes of reason suspended as each character pursues his exclusive, irrational desire, Demetrius enters, rebuked by Hermia for having, as she believes, killed Lysander; and of the supposed victim, Demetrius can only say, with significant brutality, 'I had rather give his carcass to my hounds'. For Puck, such excesses are no more than a pleasurable confirmation of his own conviction of human folly. As he says, contemplating the results of his own handiwork and with visible satisfaction, 'Lord, what fools these mortals be!'; for it is, as he himself declares, his nature to be 'best pleased' by those things that 'fall preposterously'. The situation is next still further complicated by the appearance of Lysander, who swears to his love for Helena, who in turn is determined to reject him. Once more the elements of reason and illusion are subject to significant inversion. Lysander, justifying his change of devotion, argues that he now has the 'judgement' which he formerly lacked; Helena replies by asserting that he is essentially unchanged, that he is without 'judgement' now, as in the past.

Further to complicate the intrigue Demetrius, at this point awakened, addresses himself to Helena in terms which are, always within the prevailing convention, frankly and undisguisedly sensual:

> O, let me kiss
> This princess of pure white, this seal of bliss; (III. ii. 143)

but the object of this address sees in it, in her own state of puzzled resentment, only 'spite', 'hell', and mockery, and is led by this to make her own counter appeal for a properly civilized behaviour:

> If you were *civil* and knew *courtesy*,
> You would not do me thus much injury. (III. ii. 147)

These are values, however, which do not belong to the woods, which will have in due course to be sought by a suitably chastened and enlightened return to social reality. Meanwhile, and until this can take place, all are alike involved in the bonds of confusion to which their own one-sided attitudes have brought them. Hermia, conscious of being plunged in 'dark night', trusts to her hearing, not to the plain evidence of her eyes, which has deserted her; but Lysander has been vouchsafed the visible manifestation of his new love—

> Fair Helena, who more engilds the night
> Than all yon fiery oes and eyes of light—   (III. ii. 187)

even as he declares that his former love for Hermia has turned to 'hate'.
Helena, however, far from accepting this shift in the direction of her
own former desire, can only see in all this a 'confederacy' against herself on the part of all the rest: this is what has resulted from seeking to
follow the love of the eyes in the wood, where its operations are subject
to irrational fairy powers. Under the pressure of these powers, the
friendship which formerly united the two girls in the civilized, human
world and which Helena now recalls—

> So we grew together,
> Like to a double cherry, seeming parted,
> But yet an union in partition—   (III. ii. 208)

is also on the point of breaking. As she asks,

> will you rent our ancient love asunder,
> To join with men in scorning your poor friend?   (III. ii. 215)

The plea, however, is made against a background of gathering confusion. Lysander turns on Hermia in abuse—'Hang off, thou cat, thou
burr! vile thing'—even as she pleads: 'Since night you loved me; yet
since night you left me'; and when Helena in turn asks to be forgiven
for having betrayed her to Demetrius and to be allowed to 'bear her
folly', forgiven, back to Athens, all the reply she gets is: 'Why, get you
gone; who is't that hinders you?'. All this 'jangling', meanwhile, in
which human beings are seen to be caught inextricably in the consequences of following exclusively their own passions, is esteemed by
Puck a 'sport', even as Lysander, vainly chasing Demetrius through the
forest in search of vengeance, confesses himself fallen 'in dark uneven
way'. By the time this web of intensified cross-purposes has been completely woven all the lovers, having followed their fanciful and unreal
purposes to this sorry end, are ready to express themselves as thoroughly
chastened. Helena is concerned only to seek relief 'from those that my
poor company detest', and Hermia confesses that her legs 'can keep no
pace with my desires'.[13] As both pairs, overcome by exhaustion, at last
address themselves to rest, all await the break of day and the moment to
seek rescue from this maze of madness in a return to normal life in
Athens.

Until, however, Titania has been released from her spell, there can be
no question of the lovers—and ourselves with them—finding themselves out of the wood. Pending her deliverance, and plunged in her

own parody of a falsely romantic vision of love, she still sees in the grotesque person of the translated Bottom her 'gentle joy', whom she addresses in terms which we have by now learnt to find typical: 'O, how I love thee! how I *dote* on thee' (IV. i. 51). In these terms Antipholus of Syracuse, also subjected to 'madness' in *The Comedy of Errors*, expressed his impossible love for Luciana[14]; so too, the pale lovers of *The Two Gentlemen of Verona* addressed themselves to the objects of their sentimental 'idolatry'.[15] Oberon, exercising the privilege of an observer, confirms this 'dotage' in his queen, whom however he is now ready to release from what he calls 'This hateful imperfection of her eyes' (IV. i. 69). He declares that everything that has happened in the woods as the result of his own devices shall be remembered only as the shadow of deformed passion, as 'the fierce vexation of a dream', once the dreamers have been recalled to their true selves, awakened from the following of desire in the night of error to the light of day and the truth of reason.

On the heels of these declarations, Titania accordingly at last awakes. She confesses that she has indeed seen 'visions', but of herself as 'enamoured of an ass'; as Oberon puts it, not without a certain stressed cruelty: 'There lies your love'. With the return of reason thus confirmed on the fairy level, it is time for Theseus and Hippolyta to enter in 'the vaward of the day', as the sound of hunting horns greets the morning to awaken the human sleepers at Theseus' command. The stress is laid now upon harmony, the bringing together of 'discord' into music, the uniting of the sounds of nature to those of human sociability in 'one mutual cry'. Lysander, restored to normal life, acknowledges his disobedience and Demetrius confesses that his recent behaviour has reflected an unreasonable fury; now, however, 'in health', he finds himself in a position to recognize his 'natural taste' for Helena and its power to replace his former unreasoning desire for Hermia. Theseus, with the ground thus prepared, 'overbears' Egeus' continued demand for punishment, and calls for reason and concord to be cemented in the social and civilizing bonds of marriage to which religion will lend its appropriate sanction:

> in the temple, by and by, with us
> These couples shall eternally be knit.   (IV. i. 186)

The lovers on their side, thus prompted, awaken to a dialogue which carries its own answering note of solemnity as they balance the insignificance of the past against the noble and mutually enriching prospects of the present:

> DEM: These things seem small and undistinguishable,
>   Like far-off mountains turned into clouds.
> HER: Methinks I see these things with parted eye,
>   When every thing seems double.
> HEL: So methinks;
>   And I have found Demetrius *like a jewel*,
>   Mine own, and not mine own.   (IV. i. 193)

The awakening is one which, in characteristic terms of Shakespearean comedy, hovers on the intuition of a new life.[16] To complete it with the inclusion of the comic incongruous, Bottom, too, in the very act of standing finally confirmed as an object of ridicule, asserts in terms which seems to go beyond the obvious reality of his situation, the vision by which he too is possessed:

> I have had a most rare vision. I have had a dream, past the wit
> of man to say what dream it was.   (IV. i. 211)

The substance of his dream, indeed, turns out to be nothing less than an echo, comically confused, but none the less compacted of reality, of St. Paul's vision of love as a transforming and unique power[17]:

> The eye of man hath not heard, the ear of man hath not seen,
> man's hand is not able to taste, his tongue to conceive, nor his
> heart to report, what my dream was.   (IV. i. 200)

From these words, we may gather that Bottom has his own contribution to make, from the standpoint of comedy, to the play's variations upon its central theme. For love, as this comedy conceives it, is seen to be at once a folly and to carry within itself, obscured indeed and even subject to absurdity, but none the less real, a glimpse of the divine element in human life; and at this point the ridiculous and the sublime meet in what is perhaps the play's deepest, most profound moment.

Vision and illusion are, indeed, explicitly blended in the opening of the final scene (V. i), where the various elements of the action are drawn together, mutually reinforcing one another in Shakespeare's characteristic comic manner. Theseus, speaking with the voice of reason, finds an element of excess in the respective visions of 'the lunatic, the lover, and the poet', but even in his words the divine faculty of 'imagination' is granted its transforming power side by side with the delusions born of mere 'frenzy'. In the light of the action we have just witnessed, the

contrary judgements which the contemplation of human behaviour
invites when inspired by passion are held in a delicate balance. The
imagination, romantically conceived, truly sees 'visions', of the kind
which inspired Romeo and Juliet in their mutual affirmations of love's
truth and validity, but equally from the realistic point of view, as we
have had ample occasion to see in the forest, the possibilities for misunderstanding and deception are great indeed:

> in the night, imagining some fear,
> How easy is a bush supposed a bear!   (V. i. 21)

But, even as Theseus thus judiciously holds the balance, Hippolyta in
her reply lays the stress finally on something more than mere deluded
fancy. In her eyes at least,

> all the story of the night told over,
> And all their minds transfigured so together,
> More witnesseth than fancy's images,
> And grows to something of *great constancy*;
> But, howsoever, strange and admirable.   (V. i. 23)

In the long run the imaginative vision imposes itself upon the images of
mere 'fancy', confirming the realities we have glimpsed beneath the
distracted behaviour of the human lovers in the wood and asserting
itself even beneath the obvious comedy of Bottom's 'translation'.

As the lovers enter against the background which this opening
exchange provides, the social and civilizing vision of love begins to
impose itself. They are 'full of joy and mirth' in contrast to their past
trials, and Theseus greets them as 'gentle friends', with the wish that
'joy and fresh days of love' may reign in their hearts. Lysander, in turn,
speaks for them all as he makes the appropriate reply. 'More' joy and
love than that which has been desired for themselves, he desires to
Theseus and Hippolyta,

> Wait in your royal walks, your board, your bed!   (V. i. 31)

This is the vision of the marriage union as life-giving in its effects,
joining body and soul, reason and feeling, imagination and fancy in its
essential 'truth'. Against it, however, Theseus, as he looks forward to
the entry of Bottom and his companions with the Pyramus play, can
still speak of 'the anguish of a torturing hour'. In easement of this
'anguish' the lovers, whom we have watched in the woods during their
action of passion, are now themselves to witness another action in which
romantic love is exposed to ridicule: and their reaction to what they see

enacted—their charity, or lack of it, in the light of their own recent experiences—will throw light upon what kind of men and women they are. As Theseus says in his conclusion, defending in advance the good faith which will render acceptable even the absurdities of these self-appointed actors,

> never anything can be amiss,
> When simpleness and duty tender it. (V. i. 82)

The lesson is once again that prompted by the masque of the Nine Worthies at the end of *Love's Labour's Lost*[18]: the lesson which Theseus again sums up when he says:

> Love, therefore, and tongue-tied simplicity,
> In least speak most, to my capacity: (V. i. 104)

the lesson which the loyalty of the simple-hearted in itself conveys and which the arrogant and the sophisticated ignore at their own peril.

The Prologue to the play confirms precisely this lesson with its initial words: 'If we offend, it is with our good will'. As Lysander comments, going rather beyond the surface mockery in search of the deeper meaning to which Theseus has just pointed: 'A good moral, my lord; it is not enough to speak, but to speak true'. The play itself, after this beginning, goes on to a sufficiently close parody of the Romeo attitudes to love and death; 'the cranny, right and sinister' through which Pyramus and Thisbe speak, 'the grim-look'd night', the 'night with hue so black' that envelops their meeting, are all familiar elements, transposed into another key, from the tragedy. Hippolyta, rather rashly, is inclined to dismiss all this as 'the silliest stuff that ever I heard', but Theseus in his reply penetrates more deeply to the spirit of this comedy when he says: 'The best in this kind are but shadows; and the worst are no worse, if imagination amend them' (V. i. 215); and Bottom, in a kind of parody of deeper intuitions of reconciliation and life, says of the lovers with his habitual touch of unconscious poetry: 'the wall is down that parted their fathers'.

The last word of the play, however, is not allowed to rest here. It is left principally, and in the first place, to Oberon as he delivers his celebration of married fruitfulness:

> Now, until the break of day,
> Through this house each fairy stray.
> To the best bride-bed will we,
> Which by us shall blessed be;

> And the issue there create
> Ever shall be fortunate.   (V. i. V. ii. 31.O.U.P. edition)

There is good reason to suppose that these lines, and indeed the play as a whole, were written with a definite marriage celebration in view; but Shakespeare was always capable of wedding such particular ends to his own more universal purposes, and these words in fact amount to an appropriate rounding off of the entire action.[19] In spite of this, however, they are not quite the end. To Puck, left alone on the stage, words are given which convey, if only in passing, a note somewhat more sinister in its effect. He speaks as 'The *iron tongue* of midnight hath told twelve', under the influence of 'the *heavy* gait of night', when the world of spirits emerges to come into its own, and his conclusion has a distinctive quality which has been present as an element in the play from the first and which now seems to come forward to affirm itself alone:

> Now the wasted brands do glow.
>   Whilst the screech-owl, screeching loud,
> Puts the wretch that lies in woe
>   In remembrance of a shroud.
> Now it is the time of night,
>   That the graves, all gaping wide,
> Every one lets forth his sprite,
>   In the church-way paths to glide:
> And we fairies that do run
>   By the triple Hecate's team,
> From the presence of the sun,
>   Following darkness like a dream,
> Now are frolic. . . .   (V. i. V. ii. 5 O.U.P. edition)

In these final references to Hecate and the grave-yard, to dreams and night, we may perhaps see something rather more than mere surface decoration, find a reminder of the life of which we have recently caught disturbing glimpses in the woods: a life now set indeed in the civilized Athenian framework which opens and closes the action, but felt none the less to be disturbingly endowed with a reality of its own. Love, though the bringer of light and life, has also its places of darkness, as we have had occasion to see from time to time in the recent alienations from reason, and though we must believe that the civilizing and rational order of marriage finally prevails in *A Midsummer Night's Dream*, it is not against a vacuum or in the absence of contrary realities that its triumph in this great comedy must be set.

3 Richard II

It is a remarkable sign of Shakespeare's creative energy at this early stage in his career that, at much the same time as he conceived the two great plays we have just considered, he must have embarked, with *Richard II*, on a venture of a very different kind. The play is one which, on a superficial view, it may be easy to underestimate. The style in which it is written is highly formal and elaborate: so much so that it may seem at first sight to be lacking in the vigour of real life. The formality and the elaboration, however, correspond to an acute and already highly personal reading of historical events. In Shakespeare's very selective treatment of this royal tragedy, careful study can detect a consistent concern to distinguish between fiction and truth, or—to put the matter in another way—to show the downfall of a traditional conception of royalty and its replacement by a political force at once more competent, more truly self-aware, and more precariously built on the foundations of its own desire for power. The problems, moral and political alike, posed by this development will provide the starting-point, a few years later, for a series of plays that represent one of the highest points in the dramatist's earlier career.[20]

In accordance with this general purpose the action of *Richard II* opens on a note of high formality, as the feudal lords Bolingbroke and Mowbray are uneasily confronted under the eyes of their King. Both these courtly rivals, presented in the initial act of replacing unity by strife, allegiance by passionate self-assertion, are still grouped in a pattern of loyalties dependent upon the crown; but, although they are at first careful to maintain the appearances of loyal respect, their formal statements of allegiance are soon replaced by blunt expressions of mutual defiance.

> *Now*, Thomas Mowbray, do I turn to thee,
> And mark my greeting well;   (I. i. 35)

and as Bolingbroke goes on to deliver his bitter challenge, and receives the tense, strained rhetoric of his rival's reply, we are made aware that the formality of the original exchanges is being replaced by something else, by a mood which includes, among other things, a notable sense of artifice and strain.

The change of tone is explained at least in part by the nature of the grievances which separate these rival lords; for these, and their final relation to the King himself, are something less than transparent. The main charges in Bolingbroke's indictment are solid enough. They include the embezzlement of royal revenues for 'lewd employments', persistent intrigue, and, above all, a part in the plotting of the Duke of Gloucester's death; the last accusation, most ominously of all, involves the King himself, the centre of the feudal structure of loyalty to which lip-service is still being paid, in ambiguity and a suggestion of guilt. Mowbray's reply, though rhetorically impressive, is notably evasive in the realm of fact. *Part* of the money received from the royal treasury was, he admits, held back, but—so it seems—to repay a debt contracted on another occasion; and whilst denying that Gloucester's death lies to his charge, he admits to neglect of his 'sworn duty' in that case and confesses, though with affirmations of subsequent repentance and reconciliation, to a plot against the life of Richard's uncle, John of Gaunt. Whatever the precise facts may be—and they are left deliberately vague—this is clearly a world more complex than that of rhetorical defiance and knightly conflict: and in it the King himself, though maintaining an attitude of royal impartiality, is more deeply involved than he cares to admit.

Richard's increasing evasiveness, indeed, is a notable feature of these early scenes. His first interventions in the quarrel are proper statements of detachment:

> Mowbray, impartial are our eyes and ears . . .
> He is our subject, Mowbray; so art thou:
> Free speech and fearless I to thee allow.   (I. i. 115)

So indeed should a King speak and act in the following of his vocation; but as the accusations implicitly approach his person, there is an increasing sense that this *fracas* is touching dangerous ground. Almost imperceptibly, this possibility affects the firmness of the royal stand. As Mowbray persists in answering defiance with defiance, Richard's initial gesture of peace-making takes on a cynical, almost a bored expression:

> Let's purge this choler without letting blood . . .
> Forget, forgive: conclude and be agreed;
> Our doctors say this is no month to bleed.   (I. i. 153)

Is this to be ascribed to intelligence or to indifference, to superior understanding or to a tendency in the speaker to evade the decisions and responsibilities to which his office calls him? Perhaps the answer lies finally in the spirit which seems to prevail throughout these early episodes of feudal rivalry. Perhaps the very elaboration of the conflicting expressions of defiance points to an underlying void which is filled, on the plane of action, by less respectable motives; and perhaps it is significant that Richard's own regality, which he knows so well how to present in impressive gestures and declarations, can easily turn into a kind of bored indifference which reflects his sense of insecurity. Possibly, indeed, neither the honour which these contending lords so glibly affirm that they value above life, nor Richard's own poses of royal impartiality, are altogether what they seem to be. In the world of lyrical rhetoric which surrounds the initial court action they are no doubt appropriate, but in the sphere of personal and political responsibility the reality is more obscure, less graciously defined. Richard himself seems to recognize this when, at the end of this first scene, he follows his final assertion of authority—'We were not born to sue, but to command'— with a rueful admission of helplessness: 'Which since we cannot do', and only partially covers the lapse by the concluding statement of his purposes: 'to make you friends' (I. i. 197).

It is not until after this scene, and the following interrupted tournament, that we see Richard in the company of his favourites, and the presentation of the man begins to prevail over that of the feudal monarch. With Bolingbroke banished and out of mind—as Green puts it: 'Well, he is gone; and with him go these thoughts' (I. iv. 37)—a new tone of thriftless cynicism makes itself apparent in the royal comments. The most damaging expression of this is the tone in which he greets the news of John of Gaunt's sickness:

> Now put it, God, in the physician's mind
> To help him to his grave immediately.   (I. iv. 59)

The wish is particularly meaningful because Gaunt, besides being Richard's uncle, represents on his death-bed the traditional spirit of an England associated, for this play, with Edward III and his blood: when Richard desires his death so as to be able to plunder 'the lining of his coffers' to provide him with soldiers for the Irish wars, it is in effect his own vocation that he is setting aside. This becomes clear when Richard and Gaunt are directly confronted. Gaunt's famous speech on England (II. i), so easily reduced to a set piece of poetic virtuosity, has a place of its own in the main development. Stylistically, its heightened lyricism is linked to the early court scenes, belongs—like them—to a past which is already succumbing to the inner hollowness that undermines it:

> The setting sun, and music at the close,
> As the last taste of sweets, is sweetest last;   (II. i. 12)

the elegiac note so powerful in Gaunt's words anticipates, beyond his own death, the passing of an order which Richard's authority can no longer effectively maintain.

Gaunt's poignant references to the past indicate, indeed, death and loss in the present. His speech is marked further by a Christian tone which both contrasts with his nephew's present cynicism and anticipates the religious note which Richard's later utterances will associate with the spectacle of royalty overthrown. As Gaunt's words rise to their highest intensity in the contemplation of sacred majesty, England becomes

> this teeming womb of royal kings,
> Fear'd by their breed and famous by their birth,
> Renowned by their deeds as far from home,
> For Christian service and true chivalry,
> As is the sepulchre in stubborn Jewry
> Of the world's ransom, blessed Mary's son.   (II. i. 51)

England, in its state of ideal unity, is an anticipation of perfection—'This precious stone set in the silver sea': 'This other Eden, demi-paradise'—and the substance of this blessed state is conveyed through a sublimation of the chivalry which survives, as a shadow blemished with strife and egoism, in Richard's own court. The presence of a Christian aspiration will be balanced, in the King's own later tragic utterances, by a sense of betrayal, the shadow of the gesture of Judas which will accompany him through his decline. Meanwhile, we have 'This land of such *dear souls*, this *dear*, *dear* land' (II. i. 57): beneath this poignant assertion of patriotism there lies the expression of a tragedy, reflected in Gaunt's own death, which seeks in the religious reference a universal expression.

Seen against this background, Gaunt's denunciation of Richard acquires a deeper meaning. The exchange between them is nicely balanced between feeling and artifice:

> —I mock my name, great king, to flatter thee;
> —Should dying men flatter with those that live?
> —No, no, men living flatter those that die.
> —Thou, now a-dying, say'st thou flatterest me.
> —O no! thou diest, though I the sicker be.   (II. i. 87)

The ideas of flattery and truth, health and sickness, life and death, are interwoven in a way which has relation to the complete conception. Gaunt is dying indeed, and his world with him: but Richard too is set on the path to decline, and his sickness, moreover, is that of his country. Against these realities, the final denunciation put into Gaunt's mouth— 'Landlord of England art thou now, not king' (II. i. 113)—is seen in its full meaning. England is described, by contrast with the preceding lyricism, as in a state of sickness; for it has been Richard's crowning irresponsibility to commit his 'anointed body', the health of which so closely figures that of his realm, to 'those physicians that first wounded thee'. The consequences of this betrayal still lie hidden in the future. Meanwhile, Richard's reaction to his uncle's rebuke confirms the moody, contradictory facets of his nature:

> let them die that age and sullens have;
> For both hast thou, and both become the grave. (II. i. 139)

Immediately afterwards, however, this bitterness is seen to imply an awareness of his own state and of the baseless fictions of loyalty which surround him. When York tries to turn his anger by affirming that Gaunt speaks out of love for him, and compares that love, with un-conscious irony, to that which Bolingbroke still professes, Richard's reply penetrates for a moment to the reality of events to come:

> Right, you say true: as Hereford's love, so his;
> As theirs, so mine; and all be as it is. (II. i. 145)

This mood of disillusioned fatalism, mingling insight with a touch of self-indulgence, is very close to Richard's nature. To set this incipient tone of tragic bitterness side by side with the childish callousness which prompts him, in the very shadow of his uncle's death, to seize his revenues, is to respond to a character and a situation which are growing in close relationship towards the revelation of their full reality.

These intimations of growing instability in Richard are followed by a notable change in the attitude of those who have so far professed allegiance to him. In York's defence of Bolingbroke's rights, tradi-tional feudal ideas merge into the defence of selfish interests. On the one hand, the claim of lineage, the rights of normal inheritance, are being properly defended by 'the last of noble Edward's sons'; on the other, a world of covetousness and mutual distrust is already feeling its way towards the overthrow of legitimate authority. What is in York in-decision, a clash of loyalties, is soon seen to involve in others a more direct awareness of threatened interests. After Richard has left, North-umberland adopts a tone which will be associated with his name in the following plays; the King is 'not himself', and the envious counsels of his flatterers will translate themselves into acts ''Gainst us, our lives, our children, and our heirs' (II. i. 246). The true implications of the rivalries with which the play opened are now emerging in their double nature. If the disintegration of loyalty proceeds from the unworthiness of its royal fountainhead, it is none the less in the form of unwarrantable resentment, the maintenance of selfish positions, that it extends itself.

Disintegration, indeed, is the final impression left by this scene with which the first stage of the play draws to a close. In the mounting indignation of the nobility, balanced between patriotic concern and self-interest, we see reflected the breaking unity of the English state. The episode ends, significantly, after Northumberland's remarkable phrase—

> even through the hollow eyes of death
> I spy life peering,—   (II. i. 271)

with the announcement of Bolingbroke's return. The action is now embarked upon the course which it will follow to the end of the play. The return of Lancaster, as he will from now on call himself, is simultaneously a necessity, if the foundations of order are to be restored upon the firm, conscious exercise of authority, and an expression of rebellious selfishness, defeating its own purposes by the perverse nature of its claim. The contradiction thus indicated between means and ends, between Lancaster's desires and the manner in which he usurps the crown, will dominate the following history.

From this moment up to the encounter between Richard and his rival the scope of the action narrows to present a clash of personalities. The tragic impotence of the King is balanced by his rival's purposeful advance towards the ends he has proposed to himself. From the moment of his setting foot again in England, Bolingbroke's advance is as cautious as it is sure. Potentially useful allies, like the young Harry Percy, he greets with effusive thanks and a tactful indication of recompense to come:

> And as my fortune ripens with thy love,
> It shall be still thy true love's recompense;   (II. iii. 48)

but to those of his enemies who, like the royal favourites Bushy and Green, fall into his hands, justice is inflexibly administered. In his separation, at such moments, of spiritual and political responsibilities:—

> Bushy and Green, I will not vex your souls,
> Since presently your souls must part your bodies—   (III. i. 2)

Bolingbroke shows himself already the father of the future Henry V[21]; solicitude in the spiritual order can exist side by side with the firm execution of justice, but the one must not interfere with the practical necessities of the other. It is always expedient, moreover, that the sentence should be publicly justified before it is carried out, and so—

> to wash your blood
> From off my hands, here *in the view of men*
> I will unfold some causes of your deaths.   (III. i. 5)

That in this particular case Henry is an instrument of justice is not to be doubted; but the anxiety to seek public justification for his necessary ruthlessness will be passed on by him to his son and may, on future occasions, find less impeccable causes on which to exercise itself. For the moment, the firm command—'My lord Northumberland, see them dispatch'd'—is significantly followed by an expedient gesture of courtesy to Richard's Queen ('Take special care my greetings be deliver'd') and by the practical aphorism which brings this episode to a close: 'Awhile to work, and after holiday' (III. i. 44).

It is no accident that the presentation of this firm dedication to the job in hand should be followed by Richard's return to the scene. He too has been away, spending in Ireland the resources plundered from Gaunt, and his return is the occasion for a typical display of sentiment, marks the reunion of 'a long-parted mother' with the child who 'plays fondly with her tears and smiles in meeting'. Richard as he returns to face his formidable rival, at once expresses tragic sentiments and plays with his emotions, 'weeping, smiling', as he greets the earth which both inspires him to genuine love and is used by him as the occasion for a self-conscious display of emotion. As he goes on, in the course of the same speech, to compare his enemies to 'spiders' and 'heavy-gaited toads', to 'stinging nettles' and 'lurking adders', Richard in effect reduces tragedy to melodrama. Beneath the artifice and the pathos which are so closely interwoven in what he says, we may feel the presence of that distraught and essentially morbid, febrile imagination, which is as much part of his nature as the capacity to respond with an impressive show of tragic dignity to his situation as a King betrayed. His emotions, indeed, have throughout an unconscious as well as a conscious content; and this gives the character, beyond its convention-ality and its public significance, a depth and complexity possibly greater than any so far attained by Shakespeare in his dramatic development.

These qualities soon reveal themselves in terms of his incapacity to

face practical necessity. Confronted by immediate danger, Richard is
ready enough to take up the conception of the divine vocation which
justifies his kingship, to assert that

> Not all the water in the rough rude sea
> Can wash the balm from an anointed king;   (III. ii. 54)

but it is not long before we are brought to see that this rhetorical confidence is balanced in him only by personal weakness and an intimate
disposition to give way to despair. Within five minutes of having thus
placed his confidence in God, he is considering, not without a kind of
complacency, a certain self-regarding pleasure in the contemplation of
disaster, the possible loss of his realm:

> Say, is my kingdom lost? why, 'twas my care;
> And what loss is it to be rid of care? ...
> Cry woe, destruction, ruin and decay;
> The worst is death, and death will have his day.   (III. ii. 95)

The fact is that, personally and politically, Richard is not equipped to
cope with his enemies. His best, his most nearly profound utterances,
reveal incapacity to act consistently, even a marked tendency to hysterical evasion of the truth. A tragic sentimentalist by nature, though one
capable from time to time of rousing himself moodily and dangerously
to resentful action, he uses his moments of misfortune to elaborate his
woes poetically, even to take a kind of perverse pleasure—actor-like—
in expressing his unhappy state.

These outbursts lead finally, in the culminating speech of the scene, to
a full expression of despair. As always, a certain conventionality persists
in the tone of Richard's lament, but can be felt in the process of giving
way to a stronger current of emotion:

> For God's sake, let us sit upon the ground
> And tell sad stories of the death of kings—
> How some have been deposed, some slain in war,
> Some haunted by the ghosts they have deposed,
> Some poisoned by their wives; some sleeping kill'd,
> All murder'd.   (III. ii. 155)

Basically, of course, this famous speech rests on a series of mediaeval
commonplaces, presents a traditional catalogue of the misfortunes that,
by the compensating action of Fortune's wheel, accompany the dangerous exaltation of the King. The examples are familiar; but in the flow of
the expression, the rise of the voice to the longer period in 'Some

haunted by the ghosts they have deposed', and the fall to 'All murder'd', we find conveyed, side by side with a true tragic sense, a notion of the insignificance which haunts the pomp of royalty, this particular speaker's capacity for dwelling on his own tragedy, exacting from his plight a sad refinement of sensation. Richard, true to character, at once expresses his tragedy in terms which genuinely move us—for it is a true tragedy, and it is an anointed King whom his subjects, sworn to loyalty, are about to betray—and finds a certain self-regarding pleasure in the consideration of his unhappy condition; so that it is not surprising that the speech, after the grave beauty to which it has risen in the contemplation of the vicissitudes of royalty, falls away into hysteria and self-pity:

> Cover your heads and mock not flesh and blood
> With solemn reverence. Throw away respect,
> Tradition, form, and ceremonious duty,
> For you have but mistook me all this while.
> I live with bread like you, feel want,
> Taste grief, need friends. Subjected thus,
> How can you say to me I am a king?   (III. ii. 171)

There is still an appeal here to the traditional sanctions that accompany the royal office, to the 'reverence', 'form', and 'ceremony' that surround a legitimate King; but it is at the same time an appeal theatrically conceived, a turning of tragedy to self-exhibition which at once attains, in the broken rhythm of the final lines, a real pathos and covers a weak man's resentment against what he prefers to regard as the incomprehensible turns of fate.

Such a man can be no rival for the clear-sighted and ruthless politician who is determined to replace him on the throne. The 'brazen trumpet' of Bolingbroke's messenger conveys 'the breath of parley' into the 'ruined ears' of Richard, pitifully sheltered behind the 'rude ribs' of his ancient castle. The forms of loyal service, which the newcomer is at first careful to maintain, conceal the realities of domination, the 'tender show' of 'stooping duty' is stressed almost subserviently to cover the bare grasping of power that underlies it. Northumberland, bringing what is in effect his new master's ultimatum, and disposed to respond to the new situation with a courtier's eye firmly fixed upon the main chance, covers it with a wealth of stylistic affectation. Richard, on his side, is perfectly aware of his situation. It has never been intelligence he has lacked, but something else, less easily definable but not, for a man placed as he is, less important. We may, if we will, call this something

consistency of character; and its lack expresses itself, even as he replies
with an assumption of weakness, in the awareness that a stern reality is
undermining the content of his words:

> We do debase ourselves, cousin, do we not,
> To look so poorly, and to speak so fair.   (III. iii. 127)

Already, indeed, Richard looks forward to the march of events which,
derived in great part from his own weakness, is leading inexorably to a
tragic conclusion:

> Oh God, oh God, that e'er this tongue of mine,
> That laid the sentence of dread banishment
> On yon proud man, should take it off again
> With words of sooth! O, that I were as great
> As is my grief, or lesser than my name!
> Or that I could forget what I have been,
> Or not remember what I must be now!   (III. iii. 133)

Here, at least, the utterance is simple, direct enough to pass beyond
artifice and pretence to penetrate to the true extent of a royal tragedy.

More often, however, Richard's sense that the reversal of his original
judgement will undo him expresses itself in what he knows to be, even
as he speaks, 'idle talk'. This is apparent in the elaborate self-exhibition
of 'What must the king do now? must he submit?' and the lines which
follow:

> I'll give my jewels for a set of beads,
> My gorgeous palace for a hermitage,
> My gay apparel for an almsman's gown,
> My figured goblets for a dish of wood,
> My sceptre for a palmer's walking staff,
> My subjects for a pair of carved saints,
> And my large kingdom for a little grave,
> A little, little grave, an obscure grave;
> Or I'll be buried in the king's highway,
> Some way of common trade, where subject's feet
> May hourly trample on their sovereign's head;
> For on my heart they tread now whilst I live;
> And buried once, why not upon my head?   (III. iii. 147)

In these words, and in the rest of the speech, artifice, weakness, and
pathos are variously interwoven. It is interesting to compare this utterance to that, partially similar, which expressed Henry VI's nostalgia for
the simple life when faced with the horrors of civil war.[22] The artificial

construction is parallel, but is put to ends substantially different; for in Richard, far more than in Henry, it is a kind of pathetic self-pity, as much the exhibition of sorrow as grief itself, that prevails. Sensing that he is doomed, Richard exploits his condition self-consciously; but his artifice, besides being moving as related to a royal tragedy, is sufficiently realized in terms of character to evoke that compassion which only the emotions of a person can give. For Richard, even as he 'plays the wanton' with his woes, is aware that just this is what he is doing:

> Would not this ill do well? Well, well, I see
> I talk but idly, and you laugh at me. (III. iii. 170)

The speaker's feeling, precisely by being aware of its artificial expression, becomes more real than that of Henry VI, less confined to the literary order and more capable of arousing pity.

The end of this confrontation confirms the situation of its central figures by giving them external projection. Brought back to reality by Northumberland's blunt request, 'may it please you to come down', Richard takes up once more the image of the sun of royalty which his rival has applied to him: 'Down, down I come, like glistering Phaeton'. The image, besides answering to the speaker's characteristically aesthetic self-awareness, leads directly to the meeting with Bolingbroke, in which power, still cloaked in the forms of loyalty, is brought face to face with helplessness, with what Northumberland, typically cruel to the fallen, brushes aside as 'the fondness of a frantic man'. Henry, kneeling in the external show of deference, calls upon his followers to 'show fair duty to his majesty'; but Richard, not content to respond to these empty shows, penetrates more directly to the bare facts of his situation when he says, calling upon his rival to rise:

> Up, cousin, up; your heart is up, I know,
> Thus high at least, although your knee be low. (III. iii. 194)

To the newcomer's sober statement, 'I come but for mine own', he replies, with a still more penetrating realism, 'Your own is yours, and I am yours, and all', and follows this, most realistically of all, with his rejoinder to Bolingbroke's empty offer of service:

> Well you deserve; they well deserve to have,
> That know the strong'st and surest way to get. (III. iii. 200)

The distance travelled by Richard since the early scenes of courtly pageantry is never more apparent than at this moment, in which his

personal tragedy is seen as the foundation for a long political development to follow after his death.

From the moment of his spectacular descent 'into the base court',
Richard's fate is to all intents and purposes sealed. The latter part of the
play confirms his fall and consummates the process of his rival's rise to
power. The proclamation of Bolingbroke as King is followed by the
demand, pitilessly pressed, that his predecessor should publicly renounce
his office: 'Are you contented to resign the crown?' (IV. i. 200). In
Richard's reply, complex and contradictory by comparison with this
ruthless challenge, the germ of many later Shakespearean developments
can be discerned. His thoughts turn, not merely on natural grief, but on
a sense of vanity—*nothingness*—which the very artificiality of the
expression paradoxically deepens:

> Ay, no; no, ay; for I must nothing be; ...
> Make me, that *nothing* have, with *nothing* grieved,
> And thou with all pleased, that hast all achieved!
> Long mayst thou live in Richard's seat to sit,
> And soon lie Richard in an earthy pit!   (IV. i. 201)

We must feel at this moment that the word nearest to the speaker's
heart is, after all his elaborations, *nothing*, and that his mood issues in an
intense craving for the release from effort and choice which only death
can bring. But the *nothingness*, it must be added, is also reflected in
Bolingbroke's absorbing pursuit of power. Richard's attitude to his
political responsibilities is of course extreme, one more example of his
essential self-indulgence; but his comment at this decisive moment in
his fortunes is also relevant for the usurper who is now, with little but
devices of policy in his mind, preparing to replace him on the throne.
Nothing, nothing: in the long run any relevant conception of political
power will have to come to terms with the challenge which that word
implies and which so much of the public behaviour shown in this play
amply confirms.

Meanwhile, however, the case against Richard is bitterly pressed
home. To his final, exhausted question, 'What more remains?', there
corresponds, not any expression of human compassion on the part of his
enemies, but the prosecution of the accusations prepared against him:

> No more, but that you read
> These accusations and these grievous crimes,   (IV. i. 222)

followed by an admission that the real purpose of this proceeding is to
justify the usurper in the eyes of the world. Surrounded by so much

ruthless calculation, Richard's very real weaknesses become increasingly subsidiary to the pathos of his tragedy as King deposed. His reply to Northumberland raises to a fresh level of poignancy the Christian parallel which runs as a principal thread of feeling through the tragedy:

> Nay, all of you that stand and look upon,
> Whilst that my wretchedness doth bait myself,
> Though some of you with Pilate wash your hands
> Showing an outward pity; yet you Pilates
> Have here deliver'd me to my sour cross,
> And water cannot wash away your sin.   (IV. i. 237)

Our reaction to this is necessarily double. Richard is engaged to the last in exhibiting his emotions, playing with feelings the seriousness of which we cannot, in the light of his known failings and consequent responsibility for his state, fully accept; and yet the betrayal, based on the calculation that everywhere surrounds him, implies a setting aside of every normal human obligation and its effect is deepened by the fact that it is a King whom his subjects, sworn to loyalty, are engaged in deserting. It is the tragedy of betrayal, as well as that of fallen royalty, that is being enacted round Richard's isolated and unhappy person; and the treachery, moreover, is doubly personal, in so much as Richard has, by his own past behaviour and dubious choices, betrayed himself before he was in turn betrayed:

> Nay, if I turn mine eyes upon myself,
> I find myself a traitor with the rest.   (IV. i. 247)

Richard has betrayed the office which he has held unworthily, and the betrayal has bred a corresponding treachery which leads to his destruction. Bolingbroke, in a way not finally dissimilar, will prove in due course to be divided between the political virtues that are undoubtedly his and a desire for power which is ominously reflected in the court of time-serving and ambitious lords who seek their own convenience by accompanying his rise to authority.

Beneath the conventionality of Richard's expression lies, indeed, an effort to define his relation to the tragic course of events. This culminates in his request for a mirror, in which once more artificiality, conscious self-exhibition, and a measure of true self-exploration are variously blended. Henry, now secure master of the situation, contemptuously accedes to the latest emotional trick of his victim, whilst Northumberland, ruthless as ever, presses the charges against him—

Read o'er this paper while the glass doth come—

and stresses yet again the political motive beneath his disapproval of his master's careless concession:

The commons will not then be satisfied.   (IV. i. 272)

When the mirror is at last brought, Richard contemplates his features in it with a kind of tragic self-analysis. This opens, as he breaks the glass, with a typically artificial statement: 'How soon my sorrow hath destroy'd my face'; but the comment offered by Bolingbroke points to a deeper contrast between shadow and reality, which is not without tragic content:

The shadow of your sorrow hath destroy'd
The shadow of your face.   (IV. i. 292)

Bolingbroke perhaps speaks here more deeply than he knows; but the observation produces from Richard, as he takes up the related concepts of 'shadow', 'sun', and 'substance', an indication of the deeper roots of his tragedy:

Say that again.
The shadow of my sorrow! ha! let's see!
'Tis very true, my grief lies all within;
And these external manners of laments
Are merely shadows to the unseen grief
That swells with silence in the tortured soul;
There lies the substance.   (IV. i. 293)

One can trace in Shakespeare's work the various stages of a process by which literary artifice, expanding in complexity and psychological correspondence, becomes an instrument of self-analysis. We have already found ample traces of this development in *Romeo and Juliet*[23]; and now the person of Richard, as revealed here, represents a further important stage in the same process. For Richard, as will later be the case for Hamlet, the outer forms of grief are mere 'shadows' of the 'substance' within[24]; between the tragic content of the two characters there is, of course, no comparison, but a process could be traced by which the artifice of the one is transformed into the greater complexity of the other. Once more, the later plays in the series will throw light on the nature of this transformation.[25] For the moment, Richard's sense of his tragedy leads to the final breakdown, which accompanies his request for 'leave to go'

Whither you will, so I were from your sights,   (IV. i. 315) in which the measureless bitterness of his situation is amply expressed.

By the last scenes of the play, Richard has been awakened in no uncertain terms from his former 'dream' of worldly felicity to 'the truth of what we are':

> A king of beasts indeed; if aught but beasts,
> I had been still a happy king of men: (V. i. 35)

though we may doubt even now whether, beneath the pathos and the horror, the speaker has understood how far he is himself connected with the world which he has found such good reason to despise. Everything in the action at this stage—Richard's increasingly severe imprisonment, the fear which prompts York servilely to accuse his own son of treason to his new master (V. ii. iii)—confirms this bitter estimate. Richard's last speech, the immediate prelude to his murder, opens against this sombre background of fear and treachery, with what seems at first sight an academic exercise in poetic pessimism:

> I have been studying how I may compare
> This prison where I live unto the world. (V. v. 1)

An oddly remote occupation, we may be tempted to conclude, for a King plunged into darkness and solitude, and moreover about to die; but, apart from the fact that a certain measure of artifice is in character, still answers to this particular King's nature as revealed throughout, the development of his thoughts moves beyond mere artifice to achieve a more valid tragic effect. As his meditations move to their climax a deeper effect is attained, a more felt reference to the human situation touched upon, when Richard returns to the idea of *nothing* which has been so persistently present as a background, expressed and implied, to his thoughts:

> whate'er I be,
> Nor I nor any man that but man is
> With *nothing* shall be pleased, till he be eased
> With being *nothing*. (V. v. 39)

Here, at least, beneath the carefully balanced expression, is a serious attempt to make words respond to feeling, in something like a tragic statement about life. Richard feels that what he is about to say is valid not only for himself, but 'for any man that but man is', who shares the essential limitations of the human state. It is worth noting, moreover, that this increase in depth is at once followed, most improbably in terms of realism, by the playing of 'music', in what we may consider a first dim foreshadowing of one of the mature Shakespearean symbols. The harmony, suitably contradictory in its effects to match the speaker's thoughts—

> how sour sweet music is,
> When time is broke and no proportion kept!—   (V. v. 42)

resolves itself into an attempt at more subtle analysis:

> here have I the daintiness of ear
> To check time broke in a disorder'd string;
> But for the concord of my state and time
> Had not an ear to hear my true time broke.   (V. v. 45)

Beneath the artificial balance of the phrasing, the speaker is attempting a valid statement on his condition and the errors which have brought him to it, and in the observation which follows—'I wasted time, and now doth time waste me'—he almost succeeds. Even the elaborate expression has a certain justification in terms of character, as the utterance of one who has habitually *acted* on his royal stage, observed, as it were, his attitudes with an eye to public effect and personal gratification:

> Thus play I in one person many people,
> And none contented.   (V. v. 31)

The devices of this speech, to convince fully, would need to be filled out with a sense of personal commitment to a degree here never quite attained; but, imperfect though it may be, the meditation does foreshadow later developments in the presentation of the tragic hero. Certainly the murder which follows is, by comparison, a pedestrian piece of melodrama. Perhaps Richard's last individual word is spoken in his bitter comment to the Groom on the value of human titles and honours: 'The cheapest of us is ten groats too dear' (V. v. 68). This is at once legitimate comment and the confirmation of a character, the evaluation of an inhuman situation and the expression of a King who has always tended to find in an effective show of cynicism a refuge from the collapse of his self-indulgent sentiments.

After the murder, the play ends with a brief and sinister indication of the triumph of the new order. Already, it is becoming clear that Bolingbroke's crime, tacitly admitted as such, will bring neither personal nor political peace. The 'latest news' is that the 'rebels'—not now his own supporters, but those who have in turn risen against his usurped power— have 'consumed with fire' the town of Cicester. On all sides, executions respond to a renewal of civil strife; the heads of numerous 'traitors'—

so called by he who has just ceased to be such—are on their way to
London, and the spiritual power, henceforth to be increasingly involved
in political intrigues, is curtailed by the death of the Abbot of Westminster and the banishment of the loyal and plain-spoken Carlisle. Upon
this catalogue of mischance and cross-purposes, the murderers of
Richard enter with his body, not to be commended for their 'deed of
slander', but yet to pin firmly on the real assassin the guilt to which he
himself admits. To Exton's unanswerable 'From your own mouth, my
lord, did I this deed', Henry can only correspond with a statement of
moral contradiction, the first of those that will be almost habitual in his
mouth:

> They love not poison that do poison need,
> Nor do I thee: though I did wish him dead,
> I hate the murderer, love him murdered.   (V. vi. 38)

Here is the politician, typically engaged in shuffling off the responsibility for his decisions upon others; but beneath the careful balance of
the phrasing, the 'guilt of conscience' is firmly placed where it belongs,
and the new King's last words announce the intention, which will
accompany him to his death as an unfulfilled aspiration, to redeem his
'guilt' by a spiritual enterprise in the Holy Land. This aspiration, the
failure to fulfil it, and its transformation into a more limited national
purpose under his son, are the themes of the later, and greater plays to
follow.[26]

VI

'KING JOHN' AND
'THE MERCHANT
OF VENICE'

1 King John

AFTER THE achievement represented by the three great plays considered in the last chapter, Shakespeare seems to have produced two
pieces comparatively tentative, even in some respects unsatisfactory in
quality. The first of these, *King John*, must have been written between
his two series of plays on English history and occupies something like
an intermediate position between them. It is, indeed, one of his most
curious and uneven efforts. Much of the writing is strikingly disjointed,
either over-rhetorical or simply excessively contrived in relation to the
meanings conveyed: but these factors, which go together with a
dramatic structure that seems in some ways oddly primitive, a survival
from cruder conceptions of what constitutes a chronicle play, now and
then give way to a more profound effect, answer to an unmistakably
personal reading of history. These more successful moments are almost
invariably associated with the figure of Philip Faulconbridge, the
Bastard.

The play opens with a set-piece disputation over rival claims to the
English throne between King John and an ambassador from France.
John is clearly the subject of approval in so far as he affirms his rights
against the foreign claimant: but the justice of his position in relation to
his nephew Prince Arthur soon becomes the subject of doubt in the
comment made, for his ears alone, by Elinor the Queen-mother;
strength rather than right—'Your strong possession much more than
your right' (I. i. 40)—must be, she says, the foundation of her son's
confidence in his cause. No sooner has this been said, and after John has
announced his intention of pursuing the war with funds to be derived

from the properties of the Church, than a 'strange controversy' between Robert Faulconbridge and his bastard brother, Philip, comes before him for judgement. In a world where the principles of legitimacy and order are evidently in peril, the Bastard, as the illegitimate son of Richard Coeur de Lion, is ready to rely upon his own wits and strength, and to give up whatever claim he may have to the Faulconbridge inheritance to pursue an adventure which, though less certain in its results, may bring him far greater rewards:

> Brother, take you my land, I'll take my chance.
> Your face hath got five hundred pound a year,
> Yet sell your face for fivepence and 'tis dear. (I. i. 151)

The expression of his decision, made before his royal origins are finally confirmed, is typical in its easy confidence and contemptuous dismissal of safe, respectable motives as a guide in life. When Queen Elinor finally discloses that he is indeed her grandson, his reception of this support is as characteristic in its easy aphoristic style, as it is frankly amoral in essential content:

> Madam, by chance but not by truth? what though?
> Something about, a little from the right,
>   In at the window, or else o'er the hatch;
> Who dares not stir by day must walk by night,
>   And have is have, however men do catch:
> Near or far off, well won is still well shot,
>   And *I am I*, howe'er I was begot. (I. i. 169)

The phrase 'I am I' is, of course, an echo from Richard Crookback,[1] and much in the Bastard's attitude to life at once reminds us of that previous incarnation of political energy and carries us, in certain respects, as far forward as the Edmund of *King Lear*, whose attitude towards 'legitimacy'[2] Faulconbridge would certainly have understood. For the moment, perhaps, it is enough to say that when the Bastard thus defines himself in his relation to the world, he is at once pointing to the virtues which will distinguish him, always *within this world*, from the alternately corrupt and pusillanimous dignitaries who surround him, and suggesting what will prove to be, on a longer view, his essential limitations as a human being.

For the moment, it is the virtues that most clearly stand out. The Bastard goes on to declare himself careless of hereditary distinctions, which he is inclined to think of as having little or no substance—'For

new-made honour doth forget men's names'—and to parody the
artifices of court life to considerable effect:

> And when my knightly stomach is sufficed,
> Why then I suck my teeth and catechize
> My picked man of countries: 'My dear sir',
> Thus, leaning on my elbow, I begin,
> 'I shall beseech you'—that is question now;
> And then comes answer like an Absey book;
> 'O sir', says answer, 'at your best command;
> At your employment: at your service, sir';
> 'No sir', says question, 'I, sweet sir, at yours',   (I. i. 191)

until at the last he is able to gratify himself with the detached irony of
his conclusion:

> this is worshipful society,
> And fits the mounting spirit like myself;
> For he is but a bastard to the time
> That doth not smack of observation.   (I. i. 205)

'Observation', indeed, the dispassionate weighing of men and situations as they are in a world in which neither hereditary pretensions nor
excess of moral scruples appear conducive to advancement, or indeed,
even to survival, is the peculiar and appropriate gift of the 'mounting
spirit'. It is a gift which this particular student of life exercises with a
frankly confessed eye to his own advantage: an eye which falls short of
deliberate dishonesty—for, as he himself goes on to say, 'I will not
practise to deceive'—but which remains confident of its owner's
ability to outdo the deceiver, if need be, at his own game: 'Yet, to
avoid deceit, I mean to learn.[3] This, indeed, is very much the spirit in
which Faulconbridge considers his own origins. When his mother
confesses, at the end of this first scene, that he was born in sin, his reply
is a notably cheerful, 'Madam, I would not wish a better father',
which he follows up with a still more cheerful defiance:

> Who lives and dares but say thou didst not well
> When I was got, I'll send his soul to hell.   (I. i. 271)

The combination of easy confidence and rhetorical bravado, firm self-
reliance and a careless attitude towards most merely external forms and
prejudices answers very exactly to the tone of many of the most
interesting parts of the play.

It is not long before Faulconbridge is able to apply this outlook to the
necessities of foreign war. The episode which presents the rival armies

of England and France before the uncommitted walls of Angiers (II. i)
is no doubt long and clumsily developed; but it serves to show the
prevailing political attitudes and to present the Bastard in action against
a typically 'politic' background. Lewis the Dauphin declares himself
for Arthur, whilst his follower Austria adds a typically sanctimonious
comment, upon which the action to follow will cast an odd light:

> The peace of heaven is theirs that lift their swords
> In such a just and charitable war: (II. i. 35)

to all of which the French King at once adds his more realistic observation for the benefit of all concerned:

> We'll lay before this town our royal bones,
> Wade to the market-place in Frenchmen's blood.   (II. i. 41)

He goes on to accuse John of being a usurper, after which, to the accompaniment of mutual scolding from the womenfolk, the two Kings
compete ruthlessly for the support of Arthur, who is in the unhappy
position of wishing to choose neither: 'I am not worth this coil that's
made for me'.[4]

After these preliminaries have been disposed of, both monarchs in turn
state their claims formally to the beleaguered citizens who cautiously
prefer to await the issue of battle before giving access to either. Faulconbridge, assuming the typical role of an impartial bystander, belittles
both claimants by referring caustically to the presence of 'bastards' on
either side; though he is himself dedicated to the English cause, and will
in due course show himself capable of patriotism, his service is offered
in a spirit of detachment from rhetorical excess and pretension of all
kinds. When the battle is finally joined, he rejoices, but still after his
own fashion, without illusion or excessive commitment, at the prospect
of action:

> Ha, majesty! how high thy glory towers,
> When the rich blood of kings is set on fire!
> O, now doth Death line his dead chaps with steel;
> The swords of soldiers are his teeth, his fangs;
> And now he feasts, mousing the flesh of men,
> In undetermined differences of kings.
> Why stand these royal fronts amazed thus?
> Cry 'havoc!', kings; back to the stained field,
> You equal potents, fiery kindled spirits!
> Then let confusion of one part confirm
> The other's peace: till then, blows, blood, and death!   (II. i. 350)

This is rhetoric of a peculiar kind, drawn to the prospect of chaos and death even whilst it reacts against both by asserting the attraction of action as an end in itself: rhetoric ultimately poised, like so many of Faulconbridge's utterances beneath their patriotic surface, on the borderline of satire. In a logical extension of his essential common-sense, and in a situation which offers little incitement to look beyond it, he goes on to propose that John and Philip should sink their differences in common action against the defiant citizens, taking up their quarrel again only after this obstacle has been overcome. The terms of his advice amount to a mockery of both parties for their common inadequacy:

> these scroyles of Angiers flout you, kings,
> And stand securely on their battlements,
> As in a theatre, whence they gape and point
> At your industrious scenes and acts of death. (II. i. 373)[5]

After they have got themselves by concerted action out of this ridiculous position in which their self-esteem inevitably suffers, he suggests that they leave the arbitration of their quarrel to the fickle resolution of Fortune. This is 'counsel', 'policy', of a finally disillusioned kind in which the Bastard delights, seeing in it the only acceptable proof of man's capacity to dominate the course of events in what is, he suspects, in the last resort a meaningless world; though it should be noted that, for all his talk of 'Fortune' as the ultimate arbiter, he is careful to weight his advice cannily in favour of his own side by ensuring that, in the battle to come,

> From north to south,
> Austria and France shoot in each other's mouth, (II. i. 413)

thus advancing their mutual destruction.

The consequences of this strange argument are not far removed from the farcical. Seeing the danger which threatens from the acceptance by the rival monarchs of Faulconbridge's proposal, the citizens hastily seek safety in proposing a political marriage, of the kind which Shakespeare uses more than once in his historical plays.[6] Let Lewis the Dauphin, they suggest, seek the hand of John's niece, Blanch of Spain. The politicians take up this idea with alacrity, and though Blanch is something less than enthusiastic about her future husband—

> Further I will not flatter you, my lord,
> That all I see in you is worthy love— (II. i. 516)

Lewis' interested acceptance carries the day. Once again the Bastard is
left to make his sardonic comment, this time in the sonnet form appropriate to a parody of love. 'This is pity now', he says of the prospective
bridegroom,

> That, hang'd and drawn and quarter'd, there should be
> In such a love so vile a lout as he.   (II. i. 508)

We are not to forget, of course, as we follow these proceedings, that
agreement between these recently embattled rivals is being reached at
the expense of Constance and Arthur, whom the French have pledged
themselves, with repeated invocations of morality, both religious and
political, to support in a just cause. The last word remains yet again with
Faulconbridge as he utters, in words marked by even more than usual
of his typical linguistic vigour and by the comparative complexity of
life which distinguishes it from most of the play, his disenchanted
comment upon the operations of 'commodity' as the ultimate, if
unconfessed arbiter of public conduct:

> John, to stop Arthur's title in the whole,
> Hath willingly departed with a part:
> And France, whose armour conscience buckled on,
> Whom zeal and charity brought to the field
> As God's own soldier, rounded in the ear
> With that same purpose-changer, that sly devil,
> That broker, that still breaks the pate of faith,
> That daily break-vow, he that wins of all,
> Of kings, of beggars, old men, young men, maids,
> Who, having no external thing to lose
> But the word 'maid', cheats the poor maid of that,
> That smooth-faced gentleman, tickling Commodity.   (II. i. 562)

In a speech of this kind we can sense something of the process by which
the natural exuberance of Elizabethan speech was moulded into Shakespeare's own charged and sensitive expression. The hurried, almost
chaotic unfolding of the Bastard's thought is typical of much contemporary writing, but more personal to Shakespeare is the vivacity of
illustration and the ready recourse to familiar, even popular personifications. The speed with which the abstraction 'Commodity' is
visualized as a plausible, 'smooth-faced gentleman' by a series of
graphic illustrations—'purpose-changer', 'sly devil', 'broker' that
'breaks the pate of faith': the very confusion which causes us to hesitate
between ascribing the relative in the last lines to the 'maids' or to
'Commodity' itself: all these show, if we will, a certain incoherence,

but are redeemed by the powerful vigour which indicates the impact of a personal utterance.

This impact is, of course, a reflection of the Bastard's own personality, of the extent to which he is not subdued, like those around him, to the quality of the action in which he moves. He stands out in a world in which the rival factions, though always ready to ascribe to 'conscience', to the highest motives, the buckling on of their armour, are moved in fact by self-interest and political design. His attitude towards surrounding events is one which we are invited at once to share and to feel as a problem. He appears, on the one hand, to stand out as honest judge and bluff commentator in a play which he dominates by his level-headed impartiality; on the other, although this is not entirely clear in *King John*, the very amorality which his attitudes imply will turn, in the long run, into the problem of the man of drive and intelligence whose motives are entirely limited to immediate political ends.[7] Although Faulconbridge succeeds in imposing his dispassionate and detached view of the world around him, we should note that at the last he recognizes that he too belongs to the world of 'commodity', even though—unlike the rest—he makes no attempt to disguise its true nature either from himself or from those who associate with him.

As he asks himself, assessing his motives with his usual honesty:

> why rail I on this Commodity?
> But for because he hath not woo'd me yet:
> Not that I have the power to clutch my hand,
> When his fair angels would salute my palm;
> But for my hand, as unattempted yet,
> Like a poor beggar, raileth on the rich.
> Well, whiles I am a beggar I will rail
> And say there is no sin but to be rich;
> And being rich, my virtue then shall be,
> To say there is no vice but beggary.   (II. i. 587)

The Bastard justifies himself finally in relation to the standards upheld by those around him. Not a few of his attitudes will be found again, considerably developed and transformed, in later plays, notably in some parts of *Henry IV* and, as we have already suggested, in certain aspects of the character of Edmund in *King Lear*. It is only in these later works that the virtues which he represents are seen to be founded, paradoxically, upon his limitations, and so to raise the problem of the relation of what we may call, in the widest sense, 'politic' behaviour to a moral conception of life.

In the scene (III. i) which follows this central speech, the unhappy Constance is left to rail against Fortune, whilst the politicians on either side, having completed their betrayal of her cause by mutual consent, go through the motions of comforting her. Once again, as she turns indignantly on Austria, the last word is left with the Bastard in exposure of his enemy's mixture of sanctimonious 'virtue' and cunning; and, as the victim of these taunts utters his braggart assertions of outraged vanity—'O, that a man should speak these words to me!'—and calls upon his rival to make his mockery good, the latter echoes Constance's denunciation in his own ironic refrain: 'And hang a calf-skin on those recreant limbs'. At this point the scope of the action is further extended by the intervention of Pandulph, 'of fair Milan cardinal', a typical political cleric who denounces John in the interest of Holy Church and is denounced by him in terms which seem to echo the original Protestant 'morality' which preceded Shakespeare's play.[8] Philip, also challenged by the churchman for deserting the cause he has sworn to uphold, utters his plea for peace and honest dealing with a certain eloquence. 'Shall these hands', he asks,

> so lately purg'd of blood,
> So newly join'd in love, so strong in both,
> Unyoke this seizure and this kind regreet?
> Play fast and loose with faith? so jest with heaven,
> Make such unconstant children of ourselves,
> As now again to snatch our palm from palm,
> Unswear faith sworn, and on the marriage-bed
> Of smiling peace to march a bloody host,
> And make a riot on the gentle brow
> Of true sincerity? (III. i. 239)

The question falls on deaf ears. For the Cardinal only hatred of England, which has threatened the material interests of the Church, counts, and, instigated by him, both sides return to arms. In the battle which follows the Bastard soon has the satisfaction of killing Austria (III. ii), whilst John, with typical duplicity, urges Hubert to dispose in secret of the life of Arthur. In much of this part of the play, as in Constance's melodramatic speech craving death—

> O amiable lovely death!
> Thou odoriferous stench! sound rottenness!— (III. iv. 25)

we may feel the expression balanced between irony and horror, realism and rhetoric, and moving towards new complexities of feeling. Philip comments significantly on these excesses when he tells Constance that she is 'as fond of grief as of your child' (III. iv. 92), and Pandulph insinuates that, with the murder of Arthur, which he foresees and approves, Lewis' chance to seize the English crown will come, and with it the opportunity to advance the interests of the Church:

> How green you are and fresh in this old world!
> John lays you plots; the times conspire with you! (III. iv. 145)

This is the voice of the ecclesiastical politician, secure—or so he believes —in his understanding of an ageing world and of public motives for what they are.

In contrast with so much ruthless calculation Hubert refrains, in a scene which plays deliberately and with some elaboration upon sentiment (IV. i), from carrying out John's command to blind the helpless Arthur. The assembled English lords have by now reason to suspect their King's intentions and, when Hubert falsely announces the Prince's death, accuse him bitterly of foul play. From now to the play's desolate conclusion they are left torn between treason and righteous indignation, whilst retribution is announced in the extreme form of a foreign invasion of England and the ear of the unhappy Queen-mother is reported to be 'stopp'd with dust' (IV. ii. 120). Finally, after Peter of Pomfret has uttered his prophecies of foreboding against the King, Hubert announces that 'Young Arthur is alive', thus making unnecessary John's hysterical efforts, which later Shakespearean murderers will echo, to shift the blame for his intended crime from his own shoulders.

Here, however, the tragic irony which is so heavily laboured throughout assumes control of the course of events. Arthur kills himself in despair (IV. iii), thereby carrying out his uncle's unnatural purpose, but at a time when John for reasons of cowardice and policy has decided to desist from it. The King fails, accordingly, to get any undeserved credit for his change of plan, and the incensed nobles press for revenge. They turn first upon Hubert, but are put off in characteristic terms by Faulconbridge who treats Salisbury with a display of his usual aplomb:

> Put up thy sword betime;
> Or I'll so maul you and your toasting-iron,
> That you shall think the devil is come from hell; (IV. iii. 98)

he fails, however, to prevent the English nobility from seeking help traitorously in the French camp. As a result of this failure the Bastard is left, in a typically sudden shift of mood, to utter what are possibly the

most profound words of the whole play. He, who has always presented
himself to the world with a show of self-confidence, now declares
himself, in this moment of abandoned loyalties, as a man lost, bewildered by the situation in which he finds himself:

> I am amazed, methinks, and lose my way
> Among the thorns and dangers of this world.   (IV. iii. 140)

The confession strikes a fresh note in the strange compound of incongruities that makes up his character; and, basing himself upon it, he
goes on, in the mood which the contemplation of so much cowardice
and unworthy motivation imposes, to utter more clearly than elsewhere his personal vision, disillusioned and sombre in its clear-sightedness, of the state of the nation which he has sincerely, on his own terms,
desired to serve:

> From forth this morsel of dead royalty,
> The life, the right and truth of all this realm
> Is fled to heaven; and England now is left
> To tug and scramble and to part by the teeth
> The unowed interests of proud-swelling state.   (IV. iii. 143)

All that remains, according to this same vision, is a bare prospect of
anarchy and civil ruin:

> Now for *the bare-picked bone of majesty*
> Doth dogged war bristle his angry crest
> And snarleth in *the gentle eyes of peace*:   (IV. iii. 148)

or again, perhaps even more forcibly, more vivid in its presentation of a
seemingly irreversible process of social decay:

> Now powers from home and discontents at home
> Meet in one line; and *vast confusion* waits,
> As doth a raven on a sick-fallen beast,
> The imminent *decay* of wrested pomp.   (IV. iii. 151)

Against this denuded vision of disaster, Faulconbridge can only continue to assert, as he has consistently done, his own virtues of disillusioned self-reliance, affirming a kind of tough loyalty to himself—and
to the England with which, in spite of all, he has chosen to identify his
fortunes—in the face of a hostile, broken, and ignoble world:

> Now happy he whose cloak and cincture can
> Hold out this tempest.   (IV. iii. 155)

To survive without committing an act of essential self-betrayal, without surrendering to a degradation which can only end in anarchy and ruin, is as much as the self-reliant man, drawing about himself such defences as he can muster in his own bleakly isolated person, can hope at this inauspicious moment to achieve.

The Bastard, however, is alone in England in showing this reaction to the blows of an adverse fate. John is revealed by contrast as a man terrified, ready to cling to any hope, however ignoble, which may save for him the crown, and with it his skin. All around him is shifting and baseless. The Cardinal, once he has achieved his political ends, is ready to invoke peace in terms which join arrogance to calculation. 'It was my breath', he tells the cowering English King, 'that blew this tempest up' to punish John for his 'stubborn usage' of the Pope; but now that the erstwhile rebel is showing himself 'a gentle convertite'—the phrase, addressed to whom it is, covers a wealth of irony—he is ready to act as peace-maker: 'My tongue shall hush again this storm of war' (V. i. 20).

Scarcely have these arrogant and shameless words been spoken than Faulconbridge returns to confirm the death of Arthur—responsibility for which John seeks to pin on Hubert—and to announce that the French are in London. He makes a characteristic effort to rouse the King to put a brave face upon adversity, as he is himself ready to do:

> Grow great by your example and put on
> The dauntless spirit of resolution; (V. i. 52)

but John, deliberately turning his back upon this appeal, prefers to rest his illusions upon the 'happy peace' which he hopes the papal legate will secure for him. Amid so much base calculation and intimate betrayal, the Bastard's call to arms leaves him, in replacement of his cowardly and shameless King, the immediate arbiter of events.

The mastery of Faulconbridge remains limited, however, as he at heart knows, by the nature of the corrupt cause to which he stands committed. A sense of unworthiness and divided loyalty dominates the last stages of the action as Salisbury, bound in spite of himself to the support of a foreign invader, laments the part which circumstances force him to play in civil war and his own country's ruin:

> is't not pity, O my grieved friends,
> That we, the sons and children of this isle,
> Were born to see so sad an hour as this;
> Wherein we step after a stranger, march
> Upon her gentle bosom, and fill up
> Her enemy's ranks,—I must withdraw and weep

Upon the spot of this enforced cause,—
To grace the gentry of a land remote,
And follow unacquainted colours here?   (V. ii. 24)

The spirit of this lament, which the contrast with the Bastard's loyalty suggests is too easily uttered, will be echoed, in more poignant terms, by Henry Bolingbroke from his throne at the opening of *Henry IV, Part I*.[9] Lewis, as an interested party, seeks to persuade Salisbury that this unnatural action will end in benefits for all concerned; but, even as he brings his argument to a close by saying 'even there, methinks, an angel spoke' (and there is a pun here upon the 'angel' coin, the price of treachery) the 'holy legate' enters—he, of all men, most committed to political manœuvring—to urge the reconciliation which the interest of his Church now demands. The course of events, however, has moved beyond the control of clerical intrigue, and Lewis can have no further use for offers of reconciliation. In the terms of his own blunt retort: 'What is that peace to me?' (V. ii. 92). The Bastard, who sees his self-reliance, thus justified, is left to welcome the refusal of the enemy to treat and to utter, in typically heightened, rhetorical terms, as befits the finally dubious cause he has been obliged to espouse, the English defiance.

The final battle is accordingly joined (V. iii), with John already stricken by mortal sickness. The wounded French noble, Melun, brings news to the English of the ruthless design which now inspires their unnatural ally: 'Fly, noble English, you are bought and sold!' (V. iv. 10). The adjective is, perhaps, excessively kind to these unwilling traitors but the news comes, at all events, as a comment upon John's illusion that peace can be bought for his own advantage. The English, indeed, are at last in the process of learning their bitter lesson. They declare their return to their natural allegiance:

We will untread the steps of damned flight,
And like a bated and retired flood,
Leaving our rankness and irregular course,
Stoop low within these bounds we have o'erlook'd,
And calmly run on in obedience
Even to our ocean, to our great King John;   (V. iv. 52)

once again we seem to anticipate *Henry IV*, this time in his final exhortation to the rebels on the eve of Shrewsbury.[10] For John's tainted cause, however, this reversal comes too late. Hubert brings news of his poisoning (V. vi)—at the hands, appropriately, of a treacherous monk—

and Faulconbridge confesses that his own power has been scattered in the Wash. John makes his last entry, feeling the poison within him as the 'hell' he has amply deserved (V. vii), whilst the Dauphin, answering to the Legate's persuasions, makes his offer of peace after the English King has died. The Bastard, facing a still uncertain future, continues to pin his faith to self-reliance. The blessings of peace, he says, will the more readily be consolidated if based upon preparedness for continued war; and, to further this end, he offers his 'faithful services' to the new occupant of the throne. His last exhortation to England—

> Nothing shall make us rue,
> If England to itself do rest but true—   (V. vii. 117)

may be said to wring a practical and patriotic moral out of the sorry series of events we have been called upon to contemplate.

2 The Merchant of Venice

By comparison with Shakespeare's earlier exercises in the comic form, *The Merchant of Venice*, which may have been written in 1596, seems— together with *A Midsummer Night's Dream*—to announce the transition to a more elaborate conception of comedy. The play is in certain respects a little tentative, not altogether assimilated to a single dominating conception. The contrast between Belmont and the Rialto, romantic love and the pursuit of wealth through merchant endeavour, is perhaps incompletely worked out, and the allegory of the caskets can scarcely bear the burden of moral significance which seems to be thrust a little half-heartedly upon it. Above all, the disturbing presence of Shylock threatens to load the comedy with a sombre sense of reality that leaves it by contrast, and in his absence, strangely deprived of solidity and meaning. Originally conceived as an object of repudiation, even of ridicule, Shylock almost ends by shattering the framework of comic artifice by introducing a dark and twisted strain from real life; but, although we may think that his presence in a certain sense unbalances the play, *The Merchant of Venice* excels Shakespeare's earliest comedies in the skilful blending of its various elements and indicates, in its greater complexity and more varied reflection of reality, an approach to some of the more permanent features of his mature comic creations.

The action opens, as will often be the case in later comedies, and notably in *Twelfth Night*,[11] upon characters whose reflections are tinged with melancholy, an indefinable discontent with their present state of life. The wealthy merchant Antonio, who appears to lack nothing that riches can provide, is none the less possessed, as his first words indicate, by a kind of boredom, dissatisfied, beneath all the opulent references to the world of merchant adventure which surrounds him, with the kind of existence to which he feels himself obscurely condemned:

> In sooth, I know not why I am so sad:
> It wearies me; you say it wearies you;
> But how I caught it, found it, or came by it,
> What stuff 'tis made of, whereof it is born,
> I am to learn.   (I. i. 1)

Much the same is true, though in a different way, of Portia. Committed as a rich heiress in the golden seclusion of Belmont to her father's choice, which she respects as in natural duty bound but cannot fail to find constraining, she confesses that 'my little body is aweary of this great world' (I. ii. 2). Each feels confined to an existence which seems to exclude the decisive act of self-surrender, of free dedication to the claims and opportunities which life offers and which finally justify it. Before the play ends Antonio will have found, and taken, his chance to escape this limitation in the opportunity, which is also the risk, of dedicating his wealth, and with it his life, to the happiness of his friend Bassanio; and Portia, in turn, already senses in the gift of herself in marriage a means of release from the golden cage in which she must otherwise decoratively and uselessly dwell.

Seen from this point of view, the long drawn out symbolism of the casket episodes acquires a new significance. Portia's first two suitors are found, each in his own appropriate way, to be wanting. Morocco chooses gold, 'which many men desire' (II. vii. 5), only to find that his choice brings him, not life, but its opposite: in the words of the inscription in his casket 'Gilded tombs do worms infold'. Arragon, in turn, chooses silver in the name of self-esteem and receives, not the award he has rashly assumed to be his due, but the 'fool's head' that this self-regarding choice brings with it:

> Some there be that shadows kiss,
> Such have but a shadow's bliss.   (II. ix. 66)

Each of these weighty personages in effect chooses self and is subjected to the mockery which his choice invites. The attitude of Bassanio, for whom Portia has been instinctively waiting, is different. His first words on the subject of his love reveal him as the typical romantic lover in his most positive aspect:

> her sunny locks
> Hang on her temples like a golden fleece;
> Which makes her seat of Belmont Colchos' strand,
> And many Jasons come in quest of her.   (I. i. 170)

That Bassanio may strike us in realistic terms as a thin character, even as one suspiciously ready to rest his hopes upon the sacrifice of his friend, is neither here nor there. He is to be judged in terms of the romantic comedy to which he belongs; and it is as such, as a 'Jason' dedicated to love's adventure and disposed—unlike his rivals—to risk for it, that he shows himself ready in the moment of his trial to give in order to receive, to choose inner reality rather than the deception of outward show. Taking the risk which the injunction on his casket conveys, and which is in these comedies a law of life—'who chooseth me must give and hazard all he hath' (II. vii. 9)—he receives his appropriate reward in the graceful simplicity of Portia's answering self-surrender:

> You see me, Lord Bassanio, where I stand,
> Such as I am; though for myself alone
> I would not be ambitious in my wish,
> To wish myself much better; yet for you
> I would be trebled twenty times myself;
> A thousand times more fair, ten thousand times
> More rich;
> That only to stand high in your account,
> I might in virtue, beauties, livings, friends,
> Exceed account: but the full sum of me
> Is sum of something which, to term in gross,
> Is an unlesson'd girl, unschool'd, unpractised;
> Happy in this, she is not yet so old
> But she may learn; happier than this,
> She is not bred so dull but she can learn;
> Happiest of all in that her gentle spirit
> Commits itself to yours to be directed,
> As from her lord, her governor, her king.
> Myself and what is mine to you and yours
> Is now converted: but now I was the lord
> Of this fair mansion, master of my servants,

> Queen o'er myself; and even now, but now,
> This house, these servants, and this same myself
> Are yours, my lord: I give them with this ring. (III. ii. 149)

Once again, as in the case of Bassanio, it is easy to misinterpret this, to find Portia's self-presentation as an 'unlesson'd girl' disingenuous, even artful, in view of her own later mastery of the complexities of the trial scene. This, however, is once more to ignore the comic terms on the basis of which she was created. What is in question here is not psychological realism but the familiar accountancy of love, which rests on giving rather than on seeking to take, and which finds its fulfilment in generous and free self-dedication as opposed to the vanity of self-assertion. In Portia's lines we may properly feel that the content of Katherine's final speech on the marriage relationship in *The Taming of the Shrew*[12] has been taken up and given a new depth of personal tenderness and a greater humanity of content.

The ideals and satisfactions of romantic love, however, are not allowed to stand alone in this play. In choosing to help Bassanio, Antonio has accepted the risk which the leaden casket enjoined. By so doing, he has taken upon himself the rule of friendship, and opened to himself the possibility of obtaining its true wealth, which is not to be assessed in terms of temporal merchandise; but his choice exposes him to the hazards of the world and through them to the real possibility of tragedy. The real world, which shadows the colourful and self-absorbed society of the Rialto, is represented not merely by the brightly coloured talk of argosies and swelling sails, of merchandise and far-flung affairs—topics in which this society delights—but by the sombre reality of Shylock.

The interpretation of Shylock's part in the play calls in any event for considerable firmness in discrimination. It may even be that Shakespeare, when he embarked upon his comedy, was not in every respect fully conscious of what he was in fact bringing into being. It is essential, of course, to avoid the modern temptation to sentimentalize Shylock, or to read his character in terms of our own preoccupation with racial realities. The melodramatic villain, the heartless usurer, and the enemy of Christianity all belong to the conception, and an Elizabethan audience would certainly have found nothing unusual or unseemly in the final downfall of all three. This downfall is amply accomplished before the end of the play and is certainly essential to its intended effect; but even before Shakespeare Marlowe had gone a considerable way, in the early scenes of his *Jew of Malta*,[13] to apportion blame between the races, and what Shakespeare has done in *The Merchant* is to follow his instinct for powerful dramatic effect to the extent of conferring upon his Jew, at the moments when that effect requires them, a consistency and human solidity which, reflecting disquieting aspects of the real world, threatens at times to break through the elaborate poetic fabric of his Venetian romance.

An unprejudiced reading of the play, indeed, can leave us in no doubt concerning the scope of this achievement. The contemptuous treatment afforded to Shylock by the Christians, not excluding Antonio, is, of course, to be seen primarily through Elizabethan eyes. It is justified, in these terms, by the generally accepted need to repudiate the position of one who sins by taking 'A breed for barren metal of his friend' (I. iii. 135), who seeks, in other words, to make inanimate gold 'breed' and so assume a function properly confined to living creatures. The rejection and final punishment which this aberration brings upon the sinner is both in itself appropriate and necessary, by contrast, to bring out the truth implied both in Antonio's generosity and Portia's essential plea for 'the quality of mercy' (IV. i. 184). Shylock, in fact, is brought to ruin because these positives are beyond his comprehension; but Shakespeare's instinct for a dramatic situation was not thereby prevented from giving due force, when the situation called for it, to his response to the contempt of his enemies and even to the appeal to racial tradition implied in his quoting of the Old Testament story of Laban (I. iii) and elsewhere. Similarly, the betrayal of the Jew by his own daughter is clearly to be regarded as justified both as an act of religious conversion and as an escape from what are finally inhuman attitudes; but though Shylock is evidently at once comic and ignoble when presented, in Salanio's description (II. viii), as confounding the loss of Jessica with that of his 'ducats' there are moments when his deprivation of both is invested with a degree of passion that, while it cannot justify him, does add a note at least akin to tragedy to the initial effect. When Tubal reports that one of Antonio's creditors has been seen abroad with 'a ring that he had of your daughter for a monkey', Shylock's reaction—

> Thou torturest me, Tubal: it was my turquoise; I had it of Leah when I was a bachelor: I would not have given it for a wilderness of monkeys—
>
> (III. i. 128)

is sufficiently steeped in emotion, personal and, as it were, racial, to produce an effect that finally evades the merely comic. Incidents of this kind are common in Shakespeare's presentation of Shylock; they are used, beyond the evident intention of condemning the usurious unbeliever, beyond even that of showing an incompletely human being entrapped in the insufficiency of his own attitudes, to lend depth and dramatic verisimilitude to the Jew's passion, to what is seen at certain culminating moments to be his intense desire to *survive* by clinging to his own separate standards. This is the desire which makes him, on his first appearance, declare himself ready to 'buy with you, sell with you, talk with you, walk with you', but not, on the other hand, to 'eat with you, drink with you, nor pray with you' (I. iii. 36); to cling, in other words, by every means in his power—including, notably, his command over money—to his separate identity in a world implacably, if reasonably hostile to everything for which he stands.

It is his understanding of these deeper issues behind Shylock's admitted 'villainy', even his rejection of the human law of compassion, that enables Shakespeare to present the Jew's reactions to Christian society with a force that makes it impossible for us simply to pass them by. It is not in any sense that Shylock is to be regarded as being in the right. On the contrary, his attitudes are based on what all the comedies agree in regarding as basic human limitations, blind spots which, when persisted in, make a balanced and fully human life unattainable. Shylock is finally condemned by his persistence in his own perverse choices, by the warped attitudes which prompt him to reject life when it is offered him upon the only terms on which, according to these comedies, it is available; but the rejection itself is rendered dramatically understandable, takes possession of our minds as a dark and twisted strain that threatens at times to affect our attitude to the play as a whole. His retort to Antonio's initial request for a loan, so spare and tense with passion against the brilliant but relatively trivial decoration that surrounds it, is charged, on any interpretation, with the unmistakable accents of reality:

> Go to, then: you come to me, and you say
> 'Shylock, we would have moneys': you say so;
> You, that did void your rheum upon my beard,
> And foot me as you spurn a stranger cur
> Over your threshold: moneys is your suit.
> What should I say to you? Should I not say
> 'Hath a dog money? Is it possible
> A cur can lend three thousand ducats?' or
> Shall I bend low and in a bondman's key,

> With bated breath and whispering humbleness,
> Say this:—
> 'Fair sir, you spit on me on Wednesday last;
> You spurn'd me such a day; another time
> You call'd me dog; and for these courtesies
> I'll lend you thus much moneys?'   (I. iii. 116)

Here, if anywhere, the compulsive dramatic instinct is at work conferring life upon a character beyond all possible abstract limits or
overall necessities. The development of the rhythm, with its repetition
of key words ('moneys', 'dog', 'cur'), the calculated pauses, the breaks
in the flow of the argument after the accumulation of indignant irony
(the short 'Say this' following the broad sweep of the preceding line)
all this shows verse no longer dominated by the rigid pattern of sound
but reaching out in the movement of thought and emotion to convey
the true springs of the speaker's emotion.

   All this does not mean, as we have said, that we need be tempted to
simplify the reading of the character so presented. The conventional
Elizabethan view of the Jew and the usurer continues to be, at this
point as always, the foundation of Shakespeare's conception of Shylock
as, indeed the entire comic conception requires it; but, whilst he has
taken this view as his starting-point, and is on the way to accepting it
for his conclusion, his sense of dramatic contrast is clearly at work
humanizing it, balancing it—even at some risk to the effect made by his
play as a whole—against other factors that, if they do not contradict, at
least profoundly modify it. The modification sometimes even threatens
to colour our view of Shylock's Christian opponents, those whom the
general line of the comedy would have us see as uniformly benign and
superior. It produces, in reply to the explosion of resentment just
quoted, Antonio's ruthlessly complacent expression of superiority:

> I am as like to call thee so again,
> To spit on thee again, to spurn thee too;   (I. iii. 131)

so that we may even feel that, when he explicitly tells Shylock:

> If thou wilt lend this money, lend it not
> As to thy friends; ...
> But lend it rather to thine enemy;
> Who, if he break, thou mayest with better face
> Exact the penalty,   (I. iii. 133)

he is in effect inviting the fate which will in due course threaten to undo

him. The appropriate reversal of this episode comes, indeed, when
Antonio is driven to throw himself upon the Jew's mercy, only to
receive what is, always within its own terms, the unanswerable logic of
his reply:

> I am a Jew. Hath not a Jew eyes? hath not a Jew hands, organs, dimensions,
> senses, affections, passions? . . . . If a Jew wrong a Christian, what is his
> humility? Revenge. If a Christian wrong a Jew, what should his sufferance be
> by Christian example? Why, revenge. The villainy you teach me, I will
> execute; and it shall go hard but I will better the instruction.   (III. i. 62)

We have already stressed that the temptation to whitewash Shylock in
the light of our own notions in these matters must be avoided. To
'better instruction' in this way is by no means to escape the charge of
'villainy' which remains firmly fixed; but recognition of this evident
reality need not lead us to ignore the plain evidence of the text which
gives this same 'villainy' a real, if perverse motivation or to discount
the full balance which his sense of a dramatic situation imposed at this
and other points on Shakespeare's conception.

It is in the light of these considerations that we may best approach
the famous trial scene (IV. i) where the two worlds of romance and
reality which divide the play so uneasily between them are finally
brought together. The presence of elements of artifice and make-
believe derived from traditional story-telling, and not on that account
less effective on the stage, should not blind us to the serious nature of
the conflict here presented. Shylock, whose attitude to Antonio we
have seen to be more complex, even in its admitted perversity, than a
simple Gentile view would be ready to recognize, has recourse to a
justice which he feels to be, for once, on his side. Antonio himself
recognizes the strength of the Jew's position in terms of law:

> The Duke cannot deny the course of law:
> For the commodity that strangers have
> With us in Venice, if it be denied,
> Will much impeach the justice of his state;
> Since that the trade and profit of the city
> Consisteth of all nations;   (III. iii. 26)

for reasons characteristically mercantile, and in themselves entirely
respectable, the powers that rule Venice are obliged to reject humanity
in the name of the law upon which their credit is founded. This obligation gives Shylock the opportunity which turns eventually into the
occasion of his downfall. By the opening of this scene we shall certainly

have learnt not to underestimate Shylock, or to give his outbursts of
dark and twisted emotion less than their share of human value; but we
must add that his own appeal to justice is seen at the crucial moment to
be limited by this same resentment, to remain bound up in self and
blind to the higher human reality of compassion. It is for this reason,
now seen in its relation to the preceding symbolism of the casket scenes,
that Portia, transformed from the object of Bassanio's romantic love
into the mouthpiece of a more universal law, intervenes in the proceedings. She does so to a double end. In the first place, and throughout
the earlier part of the long scene, she grants the Jew, in the name of
justice, all that in justice is his right. By so doing, she underlines the
reality of Antonio's 'hazard', by which he is finally to be redeemed;
but, having done this, she goes on to raise her plea beyond 'justice' to
invoke a 'mercy' which is beyond all covenant of law, and which is
the gratuitous gift of 'heaven': a 'mercy' of which all men, just and
unjust, Christian and Jew alike, stand in need. Unless we grasp its
place in the complete conception we shall not respond fully to Portia's
most famous utterance:

> The quality of mercy is not strain'd,
> It droppeth as the gentle rain from heaven
> Upon the place beneath: it is twice blest;
> *It blesseth him that gives, and him that takes:* . . .
> It is an attribute to God himself,
> And earthly power doth then show likest God's
> When mercy seasons justice. *Therefore, Jew,*
> *Though justice be thy plea, consider this,*
> *That, in the course of justice, none of us*
> *Should see salvation: we do pray for mercy;*
> *And that same prayer doth teach us all to render*
> *The deeds of mercy.* (IV. i. 184)

It would be wrong indeed to read as a mere set-piece a speech the
leading ideas of which will be echoed in later plays, from *Henry V* to
Hamlet and *Measure for Measure*,[14] which threatens indeed to burst the
bonds of comedy and to anticipate a more profound and complex
vision of life. Meanwhile the last lines, more especially, constitute the
deepest, the most permanent 'meaning' of Shakespeare's play, and
provide—among other things—the foundation of an outlook from
which Shylock, who has himself so passionately invoked 'justice', may
fittingly be judged. For Shylock, in the very moment of seeming to
obtain the judgement which is recognized to be his due, is condemned

by his failure to temper 'justice' with 'mercy', recognizing thereby his share in the universal human situation. He too needs 'mercy', and is called upon to 'give' as well as to exact; and because this lesson of the caskets, translated from allegory to a situation tense with human drama, fails to move him, the very 'justice' he has invoked finally breaks in his hands and he is judged in the light of the narrow and implacable standards upon which he has chosen to take his stand.

With the departure of Shylock we return, a little uneasily, to the world of poetry and artifice which has generally prevailed whenever he has been absent from the stage. As the various pairs of lovers finally come together, in the appropriate comic manner, romance and music are united in a poetic effect which is sometimes principally decorative (as in the famous duet 'In such a night' (V. i. 1) between Lorenzo and Jessica, where the beauty of the verse cannot quite lead us to forget the element of deception and heartlessness by which their love has been shadowed), but which occasionally rises, as in Lorenzo's most eloquent utterance, to a more profound 'Platonic' statement of spiritual harmonies:

> How sweet the moonlight sleeps upon this bank!
> Here will we sit, and let the sounds of music
> Creep in our ears: soft stillness and the night
> Become the touches of sweet harmony.
> Sit, Jessica. Look how the floor of heaven
> Is thick inlaid with patines of bright gold;
> There's not the smallest orb which thou behold'st
> But in his motion like an angel sings,
> Still quiring to the young-eyed cherubins;
> Such harmony is in immortal souls;
> But whilst this muddy vesture of decay
> Doth grossly close it in, we cannot hear it.   (V. i. 54)

The enchanted harmonies of music become here the reflection of something more profound, a deeper intuition, glimpsed if not retained, of universal fitness. The absorbing beauty of life which everywhere surrounds man and his inability to maintain other than fugitively his hold upon it becomes at such moments the pervasive background of Shakespeare's comic devices.

It only remains to mention in conclusion the episode of the lovers' gift to Portia and her maid of their rings and of their final return to their respective owners. Drawn in all probability from a story by Boccaccio, the incident parallels in a broadly comic key the central moral of love as consisting of accepted risk, of the spontaneous and irrevocable gift of self. The rings were originally conferred as pledges of mutual fidelity. Portia now confiscates them in the name of 'justice'— to remind us that, in 'justice', 'all men are frail'—and returns them, on the plea precisely of Antonio who has already shown under sterner circumstances his readiness to make the life-giving gift of self for his friend. As he now says:

> I did once lend my body for his wealth;
> Which, but for him that had your husband's ring
> Had quite miscarried: I dare be bound again,
> *My soul upon the forfeit*, that your lord
> Will never more break faith advisedly;   (V. i. 249)

and Portia makes the return, in answer to Antonio's renewed, but this time spiritual guarantee, in a comic reflection of 'mercy', of that capacity for tolerant and compassionate understanding upon which alone any durable human relationship can be founded. Thus expressed, it may seem that the device can hardly bear the burden of meaning placed upon it, and this is indeed an impression which a good deal of this play is likely to give us. The entire action is dominated, possibly even beyond the author's initial intention, by the human and dramatic stature of Shylock; but, for all the imperfect co-ordination—as we may feel it—of the various elements which compose it, *The Merchant of Venice* not only lives as the dramatic re-telling of more than one ancient and familiar story, but suggests themes which elsewhere—in the relation of reality and make-believe which Shakespeare used so triumphantly in his later and greater comedies—were to be more profoundly and coherently developed.[15]

VII
'HENRY IV'—
PARTS I AND II, AND
'HENRY V'

THE SERIES OF plays initiated with *Richard II* and developed, some three years later, through the two Parts of *Henry IV* and *Henry V*,[1] represents without doubt one of the peaks of Shakespeare's achievement during the earlier period of his dramatic career. Its starting-point is, in accordance with the inherited conception, an adaptation to the exigencies of Tudor political thought of traditional conceptions of monarchy.[2] The royal office is assumed to be divinely instituted, the indispensable guarantee of order in a state nationally and patriotically conceived; the political thought expressed in these plays combined the fervent nationalism of the day with sacramental notions of monarchy more venerable than itself. In the period covered by this series, however, the emphasis rests on the interruption of the relationship which should naturally exist, according to the traditional view, between King and subject, on the disastrous consequences of that interruption, and on the restoration of ordered rule, after the uneasy interim of Henry IV's reign, on a more secure, if more limited, basis under the authority of his son.

Shakespeare, however, who shared with Machiavelli—the real Machiavelli, not the conventional 'Machiavel' of the Elizabethan imagination, whose relevance to the dramatist's thought has been greatly exaggerated—a keen awareness of the political realities of his age, used this story to develop insights of his own into the questions raised by the attainment and exercise of power. The story he inherited presented an appropriate motive in the portrayal of Prince Hal, whose progress from dissolute heir apparent to responsible monarch gives a main thread of continuity to the series. Hal's career, of course, can properly be seen in traditional terms as a manifestation of Christian kingship. This, indeed, is the foundation upon which Shakespeare's design unequivocally rests; but, although this reading of his hero's character is never irrelevant, or less than properly impressive, it comes increasingly to be seen in relation to unanswered, and perhaps unanswerable, questions which are implicit in the very attainment of his necessary and patriotic ends. What, to put the matter in slightly different terms, are the personal as distinct from the political qualities that go to the making of a King? The answer emerges in several stages, each of which is at once based on inherited notions of the political character and vastly extends the implications of these notions, passing from an affirmation of the necessity of kingship to a searching consideration of the qualities and limitations of the public personality.[3]

1 Henry IV—Part I

The expository scene which opens the First Part of *Henry IV* shows Bolingbroke weighed down, as the concluding scenes of *Richard II* have anticipated,[4] by thoughts of anarchy and civil war. Its background is the bitter memory of 'civil butchery', of strife between rivals 'All of one nature, of one substance bred', clashes within the body politic that can only serve to wound and destroy it. To counter the threatened renewal of this condition, the new King calls upon his barons to unite, under the sign of the Cross, for the liberation of the Holy Sepulchre:

> Therefore, friends,
> As far as to the sepulchre of Christ,
> Whose soldier now, under whose blessed cross
> We are impressed and engaged to fight,
> Forthwith a power of English shall we levy;
> Whose arms were moulded in their mothers' womb
> To chase these pagans in those holy fields
> Over whose acres walk'd those blessed feet
> Which fourteen hundred years ago were nail'd
> For our advantage on the bitter cross.   (I. i. 19)

The tone of this appeal, at once eloquent and nostalgic, is one of emotional compensation, of the casting off of a personal burden of sin. Henry already knows at heart that his desire to play properly his royal role is flawed past mending by the way in which he has so recently come to the throne. His murder of Richard fatally engenders the strife

which he now aims at ending. No sooner has he affirmed his purpose
than 'heavy news' comes 'all athwart' from Wales to force a postpone-
ment of the crusading project. The reign which opens with the summons to a holy enterprise will end, after years of weary disillusionment,
in a room 'called Jerusalem'[5] which will be his nearest approach to the
Holy Land; and in between it will have seen little but plot and counter-
plot, battles in which victory serves only to sow the seeds of further
civil strife.

Already, indeed, Henry feels himself obscurely punished for his sins
not only as King in the weariness which his opening words betray, but
in his son's notorious dedication to the 'riot and dishonour' visibly
incarnate in the person of Falstaff.[6] To the tavern, accordingly, and to
Falstaff in it, the action logically turns. Falstaff's opening question to
Hal—'What time of day is it, lad?'—is at once a challenge to the basic
assumptions of the serious action and an indication of his own limitation. Falstaff, as the Prince brings out in his elaborate reply, lives by
repudiating time. Time is at this stage no concern of his, as it is of the
politicians who will become—as we shall see[7]—in ever increasing
measure its victims, but the very fact that he ignores its call to the
exercise of responsible choice implies that he will himself have to be
repudiated before the Prince can take up a vocation in which he will be
at once conscious of time and, in some measure, its victim. The process
of repudiation is foreshadowed from the very outset of their relationship. As Falstaff's imaginative energy asserts itself through the flaunting
of his irresponsibility, his refusal to be bound by common human
limitations, so does the Prince withdraw into detachment, into a
refusal to be committed, that is equally typical of his own nature.
Falstaff's specious references to thieves as 'squires of the night's body',
'Diana's foresters . . . governed, as the sea is, by our noble and chaste
mistress the moon' are balanced by Hal's more realistic estimate of the
ultimate prospects of robbery:

> . . . the fortune of us that are the moon's men doth ebb and flow like the sea,
> being governed, as the sea is, by the moon. As for proof, now: a purse of gold
> most resolutely snatched on Monday night and most dissolutely spent on
> Tuesday morning; got with swearing 'Lay by' and spent with crying 'Bring
> in'; now in as low an ebb as the foot of the ladder, and by and by in as high a
> flow as the ridge of the gallows.   (I. ii. 35)

From the imaginative fancy of the devotees of thievery as 'the moon's
men', governed by the varying tides of fortune, to the stark reality of

the gallows a single logically defined sequence imposes itself. The bringing back of Falstaff's irresponsible exuberance to dispassionate reality and implied condemnation is typical of the Prince. From the first he is presented in ultimate detachment from Falstaff. There is in his future development no real conversion, because the moral estimate of his temporary companion is from the beginning firmly present in his mind. The divergence of spirit thus indicated belongs to the central conception of the play.

For it is necessary, in considering the effect of the scenes of low life, which so abound in this play, and which constitute so splendid a manifestation of its comic inspiration, to arrive at a balanced estimate of the part played in them by both the leading actors. In the case of Falstaff, we shall no doubt need to take not a few traditional elements into account.[8] He bears about him elements of the buffoon, the Vice of the mediaeval stage, and incarnates the temptations against morality and duty which the young king-in-the-making will be required to abjure. He is not, however, entirely bound by limitations of this kind. The Falstaff of *Henry IV, Part I*, besides representing the vices which Hal must put aside in the following of his vocation, increasingly stands out from the political action in which he moves, serves as a connecting link between two contrasted worlds, the tavern world of comic incident in which he is at home and the world of court rhetoric and political decision to which he also has access. So situated in two worlds and confined entirely to neither, his is a voice that lies outside the prevailing spirit of the play, that draws its cogency—though of a limited kind, condemned even as it is expressed for being partial, for the sin of mistaking the part for the whole—from the author's own insight expressing itself in a flow of comic energy. From this standpoint, and without ignoring the other, the very real darker side of the picture, we may say that Falstaff represents certain valid aspects of the humanity which it seems that the public man must necessarily exclude. That humanity is full of gross imperfections, which must end by destroying the life they seem to affirm; but the Falstaff of this play, whilst he shares these imperfections and is indeed their supreme incarnation, is not altogether limited to his role of scapegoat and instigator of corruption. The comic spirit which went to his creation has other facets, less morally austere but not on that account less relevant to a balanced view of life. His keen intelligence, his real understanding, his refusal to be fobbed off by empty or hypocritical phrases—these are characteristics that enable him, in his most successful moments, to

transcend his world and to become the expression of a great and completely serious conception. Nothing Shakespeare had so far done in the
comic spirit—or even, perhaps, was subsequently to do—can over-
shadow this achievement.

Against it, equally a necessary part of the complete effect, we need to
set the detachment and self-awareness of Falstaff's princely associate.
Both are shown, at the end of this first 'comic' scene, in Hal's soliloquy.
This touches on a theme always close to his father's heart[9] and stressed
throughout as a constant feature of the family character: the tendency
to live for public effect, to grade behaviour to the reaction that it is
desired to produce in the world. The impression made by the soliloquy
is explained in part by the nature of the material inherited by the
dramatist. The Prince, as he appeared in the popular account, was an
outstanding example of the dissolute young man who, when faced by
grave responsibilities, underwent a kind of moral conversion and
finally made good in the sphere to which he was called. The story, thus
conceived, was too familiar, too powerful in its evident appeal, to be
ignored; on the other hand, its conception of character and motive was
too naive to appeal to a Shakespeare already moving towards the mood
in which he was shortly to produce *Hamlet*. Faced with this dilemma
the dramatist chose to accept the very improbability of the story and
turn it to account. The Prince, from his first appearance, has substantially made his choice; he looks forward to a reformation which,
precisely because it has never really been in question, is partly moved
by a political calculation which reflects his father's character. In this
way what no doubt began as a simple self-revelation, an explanation
uttered with an eye to the future, ended as something rather different.
If it is Hal's destiny, as the story demands, to change, or rather to *be seen*
to change, it is at least in part because he is aware that a transformation
of this kind will attract popularity; for it is a fact of public life that
'nothing pleaseth but rare accidents' (I. ii. 229) and these the political
realist will be careful to supply. The whole process of 'reformation', as
Hal describes it in these initial reflections, has a surface quality, glitters
with a kind of metallic speciousness over previous faults 'like bright
metal on a sullen ground'; and its purpose is to '*show* more goodly' and
'attract more eyes'. The 'conversion', thus partially transformed from
an edifying example to a deliberate instrument of policy, enters into the
permanent characteristics of the House of Lancaster. The future Henry
V, destined to become an incarnation of the political virtues (which are
in no sense to be despised), begins by conditioning intimate conviction

to the public display of moral qualities; for behind Shakespeare's acceptance of a traditional story lies the sense, which grows as the action develops, that success in politics implies some measure of moral loss, the sacrifice of more immediately attractive qualities in the distinctively personal order.

The scene which follows (I. iii) returns, following the play's characteristic construction, to the 'serious' action to show the split between the King and the rebels in the process of coming into being. If Henry's kingship is in danger of being rendered sterile in its higher aspirations by the circumstances which led to his seizure of the crown, a similar frustration accompanies those who, having helped him to the throne to further selfish ends of their own, now wish to curb his power. Worcester refers meaningfully to

> that same greatness to which our own hands
> Have holp to make so portly,   (I. iii. 12)

and Hotspur, a little later, puts the relationship in less flattering terms when he describes his associates as the 'base second means', 'the cords, the ladder, or the hangman' involved in the late King's murder. Desire for power prompted the rebel leaders to give their assent to the crime of regicide, and now fear prompted by a mutual awareness of guilt makes inevitable the clash between the usurper and those who formerly served his ends. The result is an endless distrust, the consequences of which finally conclude, in this play, at Shrewsbury.

Against this background, and after the demonstration, just witnessed, of Hal's political detachment, yet another contrast—that between himself and Hotspur—begins to take shape. Hotspur's first speech, describing the courtier who brought the King's request for his prisoners after Holmedon, is finely conceived in the comic spirit; this is the man of action at his best, still sure of the validity of his values, direct, incisive, impatient of artifice and intrigue. What takes place after the King's angry departure, however, shows the subjection of this impulsive warrior to the labyrinth of politic behaviour. His first response to Henry's final demand is stated with an emphasis that betrays the tendency, always innate in him, to develop his emotions in excess of their cause:

> An if the devil come and roar for them,
> I will not send them: I will after straight
> And tell him so;   (I. iii. 125)

but Northumberland's immediate interruption counsels 'pause' and heralds, with the entry of Worcester, the change from emotional conflict to statecraft and the devices of 'policy'. Worcester is subtle enough to play upon this same impulsiveness by stressing the 'matter deep and dangerous' 'full of peril and adventurous spirit' (I. iii. 190) of the plot he is about to unfold. Hotspur's reaction to the prospect of hazard introduces for the first time the abstract 'honour' which represents at once the weakness and the strength of his position:

> Send danger from the east unto the west,
> So honour cross it from the north to south,
> And let them grapple. (I. iii. 195)

'Honour', thus followed, is in the process of converting itself for Hotspur into an emotional stimulus which, as it is mentioned, rouses an infallible response in high-sounding rhetoric. It is not difficult to see, in these outbursts, a comic anticipation of qualities which will find later expression in the subtle blend of 'nobility' and failure which characterizes so many of Shakespeare's tragic heroes. Othello, Antony, and Coriolanus, each in his own distinct way, reflect in their rhetoric a tendency to justify themselves, or to conform to an idealized presentation of their own behaviour in the very moment of failure; and if Hotspur is less subtly and, for the most part, less tragically conceived, the balance of true emotion and emptiness, the reliance on a noble conception barely developed beyond its verbal value reflects the moral adolescence which, to some degree and maintaining all the necessary differences, he shares with them. It would be hard to imagine a better foil to the dedicated and self-reliant competence which we have already seen taking shape beneath Hal's apparent dissolution.

Before the scene has ended Worcester, with all the politician's contempt for the simple values of the man of war, has involved his nephew in a web of intrigue. He persuades him first of all to give up his prisoners, retaining only the son of Douglas; and having done this, he turns from Hotspur to plot the more devious intricacies of 'policy' with Northumberland:

> Your son in Scotland being thus employ'd,
> Shall *secretly into the bosom creep*
> Of that same noble prelate, well beloved,
> The archbishop. (I. iii. 265)

The ambiguity which balances the idea of a serpent creeping into a prelate's bosom against the implications of 'noble' and 'well-beloved' is typical of Worcester's world. Hotspur, out of his depth, salutes his uncle's contrivance as 'a *noble* plot', whilst Worcester more accurately reveals its foundations in guilt and expediency:

> 'Tis no little reason bids us speed,
> To save our heads by raising of a head;
> For, bear ourselves as even as we can,
> The king will always think him in our debt,
> And think we think ourselves unsatisfied,
> Till he hath found a time to pay us home.   (I. iii. 284)

Fear, in this world, breeds fear, and produces the very rebellion which fear itself, working through a conscience of guilt, would desire to avoid. The end of the scene shows us Worcester about to '*steal* to Glendower and Lord Mortimer', seeking in dubious unity the remedy to 'much uncertainty'. Northumberland it leaves, not less typically, unsure of himself and of the future ('we shall thrive, I trust'), and Hotspur, a stranger in this world of intrigue with which he is none the less ready to compromise his 'nobility', clings to the supposed certainties of action with a rhetorical gesture which is really an evasion of the choices in which he finds himself involved:

> Uncle, adieu: O, let the hours be short
> Till fields and blows and groans applaud our sport.   (I. iii. 302)

These are, indeed, Hotspur's only constants to guide him through a world of shifting uncertainties; how inadequate they are, how opposed in their simplicity to the controlled self-awareness of the Prince, time will show.

After these opening scenes, which have mainly presented the contrasted facets of the political action, the interest shifts to embrace a comic parallel to the central theme. This change of vision has a double purpose: it extends the social range covered by the play, presenting a popular reflection of the prevailing crisis of authority, and further develops Hal's relation to Falstaff. The robbery itself is an active manifestation of disorder; it is no accident that the object of a theft in which the heir to the throne plays an ambiguous part is money on its way to the royal exchequer. The essence of the adventure (II. ii) lies in the contrast between Falstaff's participation, shameless, corrupt, and ridiculous by turn, and the Prince's blend of diversion and detachment. Falstaff appears more than ever the incarnation of 'misrule', distinguished—always within his dedication to dissolution—by the capacity to confer upon his own monstrosity an unexpected, paradoxical

normality. His triumphs, such as they are, depend on the evasion of
facts, whereas the superiority of the Prince rests on the dispassionate
observation of them. The ability to detach himself from his surroundings is at once Hal's virtue and in some sense his human limitation. After the trick played upon Falstaff, he says of his companion that
he '*lards* the lean earth as he walks upon'. The image is, of course,
appropriate to the incarnation of 'riot', open debauchery, and exorbi-
tant 'misrule'. The Prince, with his habitual clear-sightedness, imposes
his vision of things; but this peculiar type of physical imagery, the
product of a certain calculated and superior vulgarity, will be echoed at
various stages of the later action. Its relation to Falstaff's 'fleshly' inver-
sions of the spirit of Puritan morality is very close to the central
conception.

The scene at Eastcheap (II. iv) which follows the robbery is, besides
being the longest, one of the most important in the play. During its
course, the various aspects of the complete action, thus far separately
presented, are drawn together in their mutual relationship. The Gadshill
adventure, recently worked out in reality to Falstaff's discomfiture, is
gone over in retrospect and modified, in the process, by the comic
imagination of the victim. The Prince carries on his jest at the expense
of his companion, who simultaneously admits his defeat and evades it,
transforms it into something different; and finally, in the incident to
which the whole scene leads, both combine to enact in comic anticipation the crucial meeting between father and son, at which the latter will
accept the responsibilities imposed upon him by birth and the former
find some compensation for the disappointment which his own past
actions have inflicted upon him.

Falstaff's account of the robbery, and his subsequent exposure, bring
into play what are in effect two worlds, two contrasted attitudes to life.
His comic imagination plays upon the incident, transforming it at will
and making of it a satire of the exaggerations of heroic warfare. 'Eight
times thrust through the doublet, four through the hose ... I never
dealt better since I was a man': so might one of the warriors in the
serious action glorify his own prowess. The same expansive comic
energy, using the properties of the popular stage to superb effect, has
just produced a picture of the fat knight, in his own words, as beating
the future King out of his kingdom 'with a dagger of lath' (II. iv. 154)
and driving his subjects before him 'like a flock of wild geese'. Here, as
always, until he is curbed by the imposition of fact, Falstaff represents
life, the refusal to be bound by moral categories which, necessary in

themselves, are so often limited, even selfish in their particular applica-
tion. His imagination habitually transcends his situation, escapes its
immediate cause to rise to a generality of statement that is, in his
mouth, at once grotesque and variously true. So is it with his denunciation of the 'cowardice' of his fellows. To discuss whether Falstaff is
or is not a coward is finally irrelevant, because the character is not, at
these moments, conceived in terms of realistic motive at all; it is rather
that the categories of cowardice and valour have become, while he
speaks, momentarily irrelevant. So much is this so that social necessity,
which demands the acceptance of responsibility, the subjection of
individual impulse to the general good, leads finally to his elimination,
but will run the risk in eliminating him of killing the vitality it also
needs. To put the matter in another way, we may feel at these moments
an affinity with Falstaff as he rejects the common categories of virtue;
but—we must add—by these categories, in spite of him, life must
finally be lived, and only in the light of their necessity is the protest
against them comprehensible.

For this reason, the Prince is there to correct the balance. As Falstaff's
imagination moves away from the original sordidness of the Gadshill
incident, so does Hal's dry precision take pleasure in exposing the facts
of the case; and the exposure, again most typically, leads to that insistence upon sweat and grossness—'thou clay-brained guts, . . . thou
whoreson, obscene, greasy tallow-catch'—which is at once the true
reverse of Falstaff's exuberant fleshliness and a sign of the compensating
vulgarity which, in these comic scenes, so persistently shadows the
speaker's cold-blooded, efficient habits of thought. The clash of personalities ends, as usual, in a deliberate exaggeration on either side of
the contrasted physical qualities which incarnate their respective
natures. On the side of Falstaff, as seen by the Prince, we have 'this
sanguine coward', 'this huge hill of flesh', images which expand, affirm
themselves, as they convey the speaker's disapproval; on the side of
Hal, as pictured by his disreputable associate, we have 'you starveling,
you elf-skin, you dried neat's tongue, you bull's pizzle, you stock-fish'
and the rest. Both are exaggerations, exaggerations respectively of
warm corruption and cold efficiency, each revealed through its physical
qualities; but it is certain that, on this level, Falstaff will have the best of
the argument, and so the Prince, to reassert himself, returns to his own
realm of sobre fact and reason: 'when thou hast tired thyself in base
comparisons, hear me speak but this'. Hal's dominion is, in the long
run, that of the 'plain tale', the unvarnished fact; Falstaff's is that of the

comic fantasy playing upon reality, transforming it to ends in which truth and falsehood, life and illusion are blended. Both act in accordance with their own natures. The Prince, devoted to the concrete, the practical, will eventually become the representative of a morality dedicated primarily to necessary political ends; Falstaff, in whose phrases life thrusts insistently through all barriers and confinements, will be at once intensely alive and impatient of necessary order. The one will achieve his just purposes at the expense of some aspects of humanity; the other, whilst remaining human to the last, will end by distorting humanity to his own monstrous image, making it necessary for the moral judgement to disown him to escape the threat of complete anarchy.

Not, however, until the parody of the interview between Henry IV and his son is the connection between the 'serious' action and its 'comic' reflection made finally clear. The episode, of course, anticipates the real confrontation to follow; it is moreover an anticipation critical in kind, bringing out certain flaws in the situation which it exposes to comic scrutiny:

FALSTAFF: ... this chair shall be my state, this dagger my sceptre, and this cushion my crown.

PRINCE: Thy state is taken for a joined-stool, thy golden sceptre for a leaden dagger, and thy precious rich crown for a pitiful bald crown! (II. iv. 420)

The juxtaposition of the two speeches is not without meaning. Falstaff starts from the humble objects around him and subjects them in parody to a certain imaginative transformation. The chair becomes 'my state', the false dagger a 'sceptre', and the cushion a 'crown'; whilst for the Prince, who follows the inverse process in his concentration upon the real, the same state is restored to its true nature as a 'joined-stool', the 'golden sceptre' becomes once more a dagger of 'lead' and the 'rich crown' the pitiful 'bald crown' of advancing years. The process on either side is not without relation to the main conception.

As much can be said of Falstaff's behaviour after ascending his mock throne. This is, as we have said, a parody of the scene to follow between father and son; it is also a mock enthronement of 'misrule' in the spirit of carnival which leads finally to its necessary exposure. His description of the Prince, using the supposed words of his father, contains an element of sardonic caricature: 'That thou art my son, I have partly thy mother's word, partly my own opinion, but chiefly a villainous trick of thine eye, and a foolish hanging of thy nether lip, that doth warrant me' (II. iv. 448). It is not thus, of course, that Henry will actually speak to his son; but the disillusioned clarity, even the coarseness of the description, corresponds to something really present in the family nature, that makes itself felt repeatedly in the Prince's attitude towards his tavern life—especially in his moments of association with Poins—and is related to the detachment which is one ingredient of his political sense. For, in the light of what we have just seen, there is more than a little relevance in the question put by Falstaff into Henry's mouth: 'Shall the son of England prove a thief and take purses?' (II. iv. 456).

If this were Falstaff's last word he would be something less than the great comic creation he is. When he goes on to point to himself as the 'virtuous man' whom the Prince should keep by him, he is clearly saying the opposite of what Henry *must* say; and yet the following description carries enough life with it for us to realize that the circumstances which demand Falstaff's banishment also involve a loss which no necessity, political or moral, can make altogether irrelevant. For Falstaff, as he presents himself for this particular purpose (and his imagination can compass many presentations for many, even contradictory ends) is

A goodly portly man, i' faith, and a corpulent; of a cheerful look, a pleasing eye, and a most noble carriage. (II. iv. 470)

For all its admitted comic quality, there is no mistaking the positive, life-reflecting tone of that description. The speaker is imaginatively identified with his words even as he laughs at himself through them. When he makes the King say he sees 'virtue' in his eye, he is clearly mocking himself, and the image of the tree which is known by its fruit reaffirms the specific religious undertone, which is at once an object of ridicule in its Puritan implications, and a measure or standard; and yet when he stresses age in himself, 'inclining to threescore', it is a real pathos that he is reducing to absurdity, and humour of this kind can only proceed from a certain honest candour of approach. 'Goodly' and 'cheerful' in his portliness, we can neither accept Falstaff as representing a sufficient view of life nor follow the Prince in his dismissal of him. He is there at the heart of the play, and his comments, though never all the truth and often indeed a deliberate reversal of it, are always relevant to its complete definition.

This emerges clearly enough when it becomes the Prince's turn to parody his father. Falstaff becomes the butt of a grossness that is surely relevant to the character; in this parody of the relationship between father and son, the Prince heaps upon him such epithets as 'bolting-hutch of beastliness', 'swollen parcel of dropsies', 'huge bombard of sack', and 'stuffed cloak-bag of guts'. It is noteworthy, in an episode so variously related to popular traditions, that the King's supposed denunciation should turn largely on familiar conventions. If the 'roasted Manningtree ox with the pudding in his belly' derives explicitly from a popular feast, the further evocations of the 'reverend vice', 'grey iniquity' and 'vanity in years' clearly require for their appreciation a backward glance to the 'morality' tradition. This variety in his traditional and popular derivations largely accounts for the unique fascination exercised by Falstaff; it is as though many anonymous figures, consecrated by established custom and related to living popular traditions, were brought together, at once united and transformed, in this figure of swelling, if unregulated, vitality and comic vigour.

From participation in this wealth of disordered life the Prince is by the very responsibilities of his position, largely excluded. We have only to compare the spirit of his denunciation with Falstaff's equally material, but more human exuberance to see that a deliberate contrast is being pointed. The tone adopted by the Prince is no doubt a necessary corrective; it certainly brings out a true aspect of Falstaff's 'three score years of ageing villainy', and the repudiation is undoubtedly necessary if Hal is to fulfil his vocation. The truth, however, is so stated as to bring out certain less attractive qualities in the speaker, which may assist him in gaining his political ends but are not thereby made more humanly acceptable. It is as though Hal, whose every action tends to calculation, felt for his companion the repulsion inspired in the practical intellect by something which it can neither understand, ignore, nor, in the last resort, use. The Prince, in echoing Falstaff's idiom, brings to it a cold, efficient intensity that points to an underlying aversion. The flesh, with which the finished politician needs to reckon, is nevertheless an object of repulsion to him. Beneath the burlesque and the rowdiness we may already look forward to the final rejection.

Falstaff, indeed, in a plea not less pathetic for being a parody based on monstrous presumption, finally justifies himself in terms of human normality:

If sack and sugar be a fault, God help the wicked! if to be old and merry be a sin, then many an old host that I know is damned: if to be fat be to be hated, then Pharaoh's lean kine are to be loved. (II. iv. 524)

The plea is steeped in sentiment, even in the exploitation of feeling; and to that extent it cannot be admitted; but, as an expression of human qualities that Hal may be the poorer for having to exclude, it is supported by a religious reference that attains, through and in despite of parody, a force of its own. This morality justifies, at least as part of the complete effect, Falstaff's final appeal against dismissal: 'banish plump Jack, and banish all the world'. Banish Falstaff, in other words, and banish everything that cannot be reduced to an instrument of policy in the quest for a success that is, in its absence, haunted by a sense of emptiness. It is true to the Prince's nature, and to the exigencies of his vocation, that he can already reply without hesitation, speaking in anticipation of his own future action as much as in parody of his father's present attitude: 'I do, I will' (II. iv. 536). The long scene ends with Hal's statement that 'we must all to the wars', pointing to the change of spirit that will from now on overtake the action. Henceforth neither he nor Falstaff will be devoted entirely to the life of comic freedom, and their actions, like those of everyone else in the play, will look forward to the resolution at Shrewsbury.

By the end of the great tavern scene, the two main threads of the early action—the serious and the comic, the aristocratic and the popular—have been brought together, presented as mutually and variously illuminating. Thus united, they lead to a scene (III. ii) of central importance to the whole design, in which the King and his son are at last confronted and the choice between public vocation and private dissolution, ordered royalty and the chaos of 'misrule', finally made. Upon this choice depends the health of the English polity, already presented in its various elements as subjected to the disorder which emanates from the suspect origins of Henry's kingship. This decisive meeting is placed between two episodes which indicate between them the point of balance reached by the action as a whole. The first (III. i) stresses the growth of mutual recrimination in the rebel camp, and in the second (III. iii), the Prince and Falstaff meet in their tavern surroundings for the last time (in this play) and the subjection of the comic action to warlike events is finally confirmed.

The first scene turns initially on a clash between Hotspur and Glendower, in which neither is seen to advantage. If Glendower is a mixture of superstition, vanity, and incompetence whose self-regard prompts him to see insults at every turn, Hotspur, the admired soul of

'honour', is not only ready to carve his own country into the spoils of
war but to quarrel over the division; and when at last he has forced
Glendower to agree to his proposal, he admits in effect that his obstinacy
has been the product of ill-tempered spleen:

> I do not care; I'll give thrice so much land
> To any well-deserving friend;
> But in the way of bargain, mark ye me,
> I'll cavil on the ninth part of a hair.   (III. i. 136)

Here, at least, the reverse side of Hotspur's 'generosity' is apparent.
Having risked the unity of the enterprise to which he is committed, he
is able, having got his way, to thrust aside his anger with an off-hand
'I do not care' and a specious show of magnanimity; but the stubborn
obstinacy of his final words, and the pursuit of his feud with Glendower to a point at which it places the common interest in jeopardy, are
revelations of an unstable and immature outlook.

It is left, as usual, to Worcester to provide a 'politic' comment on
these developments. Hotspur is rebuked for

> Defect of manners, want of government,
> Pride, haughtiness, opinion and disdain;   (III. i. 183)

and, at the end of the scene, the comic contrast between Mortimer's
'romantic' interlude with his wife, in which Glendower's 'magic'
devices seek to bridge the gap of language between them, and the
ironic comments of Hotspur and Lady Percy continues to indicate
flaws in character with economy and relevance. Hotspur's concealment
of tenderness, of which he is made ashamed by the excessively facile
emotions before him, once more suggests an incomplete attitude to
personal relationships:

> Swear me, Kate, like a lady as thou art,
> A good mouth-filling oath, and leave 'in sooth',
> And such protest of pepper-gingerbread,
> To velvet-guards and Sunday-citizens.   (III. i. 257)

The comment contains both a true criticism of the false conventions
which surround Mortimer's 'romance' and an implied exposure of the
speaker's own limitation to a set of prejudices imposed upon him by
character and class alike. The traditional aristocrat's pride in his own
plain-speaking and his contempt for the pretensions to breeding so
absurdly assumed by the lower orders are here combined in an admirable

portrait from which neither detachment nor a certain affection are absent. In its modest way, this piece of 'popular' comedy already reflects the mature Shakespearean capacity for extracting a variety of meanings from the dramatic presentation of human relationships.

With the movement of the scene to the King's private counsels (III. ii) the relation of the play's 'personal' to its 'political' theme is at last directly explored. The confronting of Henry with his son has, of course, a 'public', rhetorical value which the traditional story imposed. Henry's opening words, however, modify this conception to include a more intimate concern. Prince Hal, destined to become the incarnation of political virtue, is in his unregenerate state a 'scourge' in the hands of God, a reminder to his father of the 'displeasing service' performed by him in the past:

> I know not whether God will have it so,
> For some displeasing service I have done,
> That, in his secret doom, out of my blood
> He'll breed revengement and a scourge for me;
> But thou dost in thy passages of life
> Make me believe that thou art only marked
> For the hot vengeance and the rod of heaven
> To punish my mistreadings.   (III. ii. 4)

The stressing of the theme of retribution corresponds already to an intimate sense of tragic fatality.[10] The 'doom' is 'secret', the 'revengement' obscurely bred out of the sinner's own blood to chastise him; and yet the sense of guilt which burdens the speech is presented in relation to an overmastering sense of expediency. What Henry condemns in his son is finally a public, a political blemish. His preoccupation is with the 'low' and 'inordinate' nature of desires that do not correspond to the princely standing of his heir; Hal's 'attempts' are 'poor', 'bare', 'lewd' and 'mean', his pleasures 'barren', and the essence of his faults a surrender to 'rude society' which prejudices his 'greatness' and is incompatible with the obligations of his 'princely heart'. From the very first the tragic quality of Henry's intimate meditations is associated with the public, visible nature of the vocation he has dubiously assumed and which is turning into the consuming burden of his life.

As Henry's long reflections develop we suspect indeed, not for the first time, that the only true *moral* criterion of this King has been, from the beginning, *political* effectiveness. His thoughts as he contemplates his past career, turn with preference on an estimate of the public effect of a show of 'virtuous' discretion:

> By being seldom seen, I could not stir
> But like a comet I was wonder'd at;
> That men would tell their children 'This is he';
> Others would say 'Where, which is Bolingbroke?'. (III. ii. 46)

The use of modesty to arrive at a position of pride, of concealment to attract universal attention, is deeply implanted in this essentially, exclusively public personality. Bolingbroke, in his own words, '*stole all courtesy from heaven*', '*dress'd*' himself in a humility which is clearly less a moral virtue than a device of policy. For Henry the criterion of morality has always tended to be success; and, that being so, it is not surprising that his son should have learnt, when necessary, to separate feeling from the necessities of political behaviour and that filial tenderness, real as it is in him in his moments of deeper sincerity, should exist side by side with a readiness to subject personal considerations to public achievement. In the realization, born of bitter experience, that the quest for this achievement can also be an illusion, lies the secret of the tragic note which dominates the King's later years.

His father's reproaches lead at length to the Prince's reaction in which, for the first of many occasions, denigration of his character exacts the response of a fixed, firm intensity of purpose. 'I will redeem all this on Percy's head', he replies, and goes on to paint a picture of himself as a ruthless warrior which will be repeated in due course, and in terms not altogether dissimilar, by Henry V at the gates of Harfleur[11]:

> I will wear a garment all of blood,
> And stain my favours in a bloody mask
> Which, wash'd away, shall scour my shame with it. . . .
> Percy is but my factor, good my lord,
> To engross up glorious deeds on my behalf;
> And I will call him to so strict account,
> That he shall render every glory up,
> Yea, even the slightest worship of his time,
> Or I will tear the reckoning from his heart,
> This, in the name of God, I promise here. (III. ii. 135)

The total effect of this speech is not easily to be described. The reformation of the private dissolute into the public figure is, without doubt, essential to it; the Prince is vowing himself to duty, and his behaviour will never again be what it was in the irresponsible early scenes. Yet there are other aspects of this dedication which need equally to be considered. Among them is the emphasis on 'I',[12] a cold determination which the speech also shows and which is, at least in part, a reaction against the galling superiority attributed to his rival; for behind the phrase 'your unthought-of Harry' bitter resentment exists side by side with filial concern. It is the birth of a rigid war-machine as well as a prince finding his true nature that is being evoked here, and the culminating dedication to 'God' needs to be seen simultaneously under both aspects if the full value of the scene is to be realized. 'I will tear the reckoning from his heart': from this moment, an iron fatality has been set in motion which will assert itself on the field at Shrewsbury and—finally—at Harfleur and at Agincourt.

The following scene (III. iii), carrying on the device by which the 'serious' action and its comic reflection are alternately developed, shows a parallel shift in spirit. Falstaff's first words take us back to the 'action' on Gadshill, but in a changed and chastened mood: 'Bardolph, am I not fallen away vilely since this last action? do I not bate? do I not dwindle?'. Falstaff can still look upon himself with comic detachment, as when he says that 'my skin hangs about me like an old lady's loose gown', or compares his 'withered' state to that of an 'old apple-john'; but the emphasis on age and exhaustion is new, and the elements of the following comedy equally indicate a change of attitude. Immediately after these first indications, the comic phrases turn upon conceptions of repentance and amendment, already used by Falstaff when, in the first tavern scene (I. ii), he had spoken of 'giving over this life'; but whereas repentance had there been made light of, the new utterance is perceptibly more sombre in tone:

Well, I'll repent, and that suddenly, while I am in some liking; I shall be out of heart shortly, and then I shall have no strength to repent. (III. iii. 5)

No doubt the element of religious parody is still present here, but Shakespeare has a way of combining various purposes in a single phrase, and the change of spirit at this point, confirmed as it is by what follows, is a clear sign that the discomfiture of 'misrule' is acting as a limiting factor on the free expansion of the comic spirit.

The dialogue which follows relates this shift of feeling to other facets of the character. When Bardolph comically falls in with this feigned spirit of repentance by saying 'you cannot live long', Falstaff replies by taking up the other, the 'fleshly' and disorderly side of his nature: 'Come, sing me a bawdy song; make me merry'. This continual capacity to move from one aspect of his presentation to another is of the essence of the complete conception. At this point it turns into a satire upon gentility. 'I was as virtuously given as a gentleman need to be', Falstaff begins, weighing comedy with a certain mock nostalgia implied in his backward glance to a lost past. As a 'gentleman' Falstaff was 'virtuous', but mildly so, 'virtuous *enough*'; and the following phrases balance virtue with its opposite in humorous antithesis:

> swore *little*; diced not above *seven times a week*; went to a bawdy-house *not above once in a quarter—of an hour*; paid money that I borrowed, *three or four times*. (III. iii. 18)

The whole is a satire on the life lived 'in good compass'. At the end of it, Falstaff falls back on yet another of his traditional aspects, that which he drives from the Vice, the incarnation of disorder and the refusal to accept 'rule'; for, in his own words, which characteristically combine his moral with his physical qualities, 'now I live out of all order, out of all compass'. Bardolph, in taking up this last phrase, stresses the purely physical aspect of thus living 'out of compass'; but the physical is, of course, a reflection of the moral reality, and Falstaff, in asserting his freedom, is in fact limiting it, relating it to a spiritual tradition which the play in its moments of greatest depth at once accepts and balances against a profound if anarchic vitality.

This last consideration is important. Falstaff's utterances are habitually steeped in tradition, religious and theatrical, and upon the variety of his reaction to tradition depends a good deal of the force of his presentation. He shares with his audience a whole world of imagery, a common inheritance which gives him reality more especially by contrast with the orators and politicians of the 'serious' action. The ease with which the theatrical passes into the religious reference is clearly seen in his comment on Bardolph's nose, to which he refers as 'a death's head or a memento mori'—'I never see thy face but I think upon hell fire and Dives that lived in purple' (III. iii. 35). In such phrases we feel what the strength of a still living popular tradition could offer to the dramatist. Assimilated into Falstaff's utterances as their natural background, it enables him to bring to his criticism of his political 'betters' a realism that is, in its profounder moments, neither self-regarding nor altogether cynical, but derived from a balanced view, still accessible to the author for dramatic purposes, of man's nature and destiny.

The reverse side of the picture is stressed, almost at once, with the entry of the Hostess. This brings out the predatory Falstaff, ready to exploit human weakness, to borrow mercilessly, and to accuse his companions of having stolen his possessions. His attitude to the Hostess

is marked by a persistent emphasis upon the flesh: an emphasis unredeemed by the spirit of comedy and intended to stress the sordid
manifestations of appetite in an ageing cynic:

> There's no more faith in thee than in a stewed prune; nor no more truth in
> thee than in a drawn fox; and for womanhood, Maid Marian may be the
> deputy's wife of the ward to thee.   (III. iii. 126)

Even at this point, however, the more serious aspects of the conception
impose themselves. Faced by the unanswerable truth of the Prince's
denunciation—'there's no room for faith, truth, nor honesty in this
bosom of thine'—and the relation of it to his physical enormity—'it is
all filled up with guts and midriff'—Falstaff can still balance this
evocation of the life lived 'out of all compass' with a deeper, more
tragic intuition which makes itself felt not less on account of the comic
use to which it is put. At his most serious moments—for in him comedy
repeatedly touches the serious—Falstaff gives his comic utterances a
taste of universality by relating them to the familiar drama of mankind
worked out in the individual between birth and death, and in the race
between the Creation and the Last Judgement: 'Thou knowest in the
state of innocency Adam fell; and what should poor Jack Falstaff do
in the days of villainy? Thou seest I have more flesh than another man,
and therefore more frailty' (III. iii. 184). To take this too seriously
would be as misleading as to deny it all seriousness. Falstaff's tone is in
part comic, mocking religious phraseology for ends of his own; but the
reference to the flesh includes the meaning sanctioned by Christian
tradition, and it is in his sense of the relationship between the two
realities that Falstaff acquires his full stature. We need not, should not
say, that he simply accepts the Christian tradition. A great part of him
clearly does not, and will be finally repudiated in consequence by a
Prince whose indispensable vocation rests precisely upon that tradition;
but the tradition is present, alive even in the utterances that express his
refusal to submit to it, and giving him, even in this refusal, a complexity
that enables him at his best to dominate an action whose internal logic
drives it increasingly away from him. This, however, is an anticipation
of things to come. For the moment, the spirit of comic independence
reasserts itself in Falstaff's remark on rebellion: 'Well, God be thanked
for these rebels, they offend none but the virtuous', which at once
confirms disorder and repudiates, in the act of inverting its own
phraseology, the 'virtue' which will increasingly wear a political garb
in the development of the series.

In the last stages of *Henry IV, Part I*, the various threads of the action are drawn together to meet at Shrewsbury. As the moment of decision approaches, Northumberland's 'politic' infirmity shows the remaining rebel leaders seeking to evade the bitter truths which at heart they recognize. Hotspur and Douglas, as men of action, meet the news with a specious show of confidence, based on the readiness to see things as they are not:

> DOUG.: A comfort of retirement lives in this.
> HOT.:   A rendezvous, a home to fly unto,
>   If that the devil and mischance look big
>   Upon the maidenhead of our affairs.   (IV. i. 56)

Worcester, as the 'politician' of the conspiracy, knows better. Persuasiveness and 'reason', born of cunning and experience, are his gods; but for all this he is a rebel, and as such driven to exclude the operations of true reason as fatal to his own projects. He admits this flaw when he tells his associates:

> For well you know we of the offering side
> Must keep aloof from strict arbitrement,
> And stop all sight-holes, every loop from whence
> The eye of reason may pry in upon us.   (IV. i. 69)

The fruits of rebellion are, like its origins, disunity and chaos; this truth illustrates a fatality of which Worcester is dimly aware, which he strives to exclude, but which is seen at this moment in the process of overtaking the enterprise to which greed and the desire for power originally committed him.

The end of the scene, with the intervention of Vernon, introduces in contrast a conception of chivalry which is, by any standard, superior in strength and consistency:

> I saw young Harry, with his beaver on,
> His cuisses on his thighs, gallantly arm'd,
> Rise from the ground like feather'd Mercury,
> And vaulted with such ease into his seat,
> As if an angel dropp'd down from the clouds,
> To turn and wind a fiery Pegasus,
> And witch the world with noble horsemanship.   (IV. i. 104)

A reader used to the complexities of Shakespeare's mature judgements—and this play already reveals a considerable degree of maturity —will not give to this description either more or less value than can properly be attached to it. Already we have been presented with enough material to form a realistic, and in some respects a limiting judgement of the type of humanity which Hal has inherited and which he will shortly elevate to a supreme political virtue. These limitations, however, belong to the human rather than to the political order, and are compatible with supreme value in action. This value is here caught in its first public revelation. Henry is here embarked on the process of development which will finally lead him to the triumph of Agincourt, a triumph which his very shortcomings will enable him to attain more securely by excluding all the complexities which might have undermined the self-confidence necessary to his patriotic function.

Certainly by the side of this resplendent martial confidence, Hotspur's rhetoric strikes us as hollow, in a relevant sense as *dated*:

> No more, no more: worse than the sun in March,
> This praise doth nourish agues. Let them come;
> They come like sacrifices in their trim,
> And to the fire-eyed god of smoky war
> All hot and bleeding will we offer them:
> The mailed Mars shall on his altar sit
> Up to the ears in blood.   (IV. i. 111)

The emphasis on 'blood', the adolescent insensibility turned into verbal ruthlessness points, by contrast with the preceding picture of Hal's martial regeneration, to an essential emptiness. The Hotspur here revealed is connected with the object of the Prince's previous satire on his rival's domestic behaviour.[13] He appears as a man who has failed to mature, whose 'honour'—overtaken by the changing times—is in the last analysis an empty rhetorical device, and who will shortly be eliminated from a world in which he has resolved to play a part without understanding the true nature of the issues in which his fate, and the manœuvres of the politicians around him, have involved him.

These manœuvres are seen in operation in the episodes which lead, through a varied compound of deception and misunderstanding, to the final resolution. The King makes Worcester and Vernon a generous offer of peace in which he sees the hope of a restoration of natural order based on the free recognition of just authority. His action in so doing is proper to a king; but the origins of his power, which he would now prefer to forget, make their endless consequences felt to frustrate his intentions. Worcester, on his side, is driven first to shut out reason and then to conceal the fact that peace has been offered. His reasons amount to a denial of the rebel's ability to choose responsibly:

> It is not possible, it cannot be,
> The king should keep his word in loving us;
> He will suspect us still and find a time
> To punish this offence in other faults.   (V. ii. 4)

Worcester's distrust, like Henry's tragedy, has its origins in the past. It owes its existence to the initial crime by which the seeds of disorder and suspicion were sown to work themselves out on either side in conflict. Both parties in this action are as much victims of 'fortune' as conscious agents of their respective purposes. Both evoke 'honour' and other lofty sanctions to confer dignity upon their cause; but, though their culpability can never be equal, it remains true that crime born on either side of self-interest is bearing fruit in unnecessary bloodshed.

Against this background the rivalry between Hal and Hotspur is marked by the chivalrous modesty of the challenger. Vernon's emphasis on the Prince's transformation needs to be set against the play's various attitudes to Hotspur, in whom we should not, like the cynical Worcester, see simply what is implied by the caustic phrase: 'A *harebrain'd* Hotspur, governed by a spleen' (V. ii. 19). This is certainly part of the truth about Hal's rival; but another view would discover in him a manifestation, inadequate but sincere, of honourable chivalry. This type of chivalry can achieve the romantic quality of

> I will embrace him with a soldier's arm,
> That he shall shrink under my courtesy,   (V. ii. 73)

lines which might have been uttered, later in Shakespeare's career, by Coriolanus or his rival Aufidius.[14] As in the case of the Roman heroes, it combines an attractiveness of its own with an insufficiency which will be finally demonstrated in the warrior's own field of action. Most significant, perhaps, in this respect is Hotspur's assertion, as the scene ends, of the helplessness of human values against the action of time:

> O gentlemen, the time of life is short!
> To spend that shortness basely were too long,
> If life did ride upon a dial's point,
> Still ending at the arrival of an hour.
> An if we live, we live to tread on kings;
> If die, brave death, when princes die with us!   (V. ii. 81)

In this speech, Hotspur touches on something relevant not only to an understanding of his own nature but to the history as a whole. The rhetorical flourish of his conclusion cannot conceal the fact that, as in so many of the Sonnets, which deal with similar themes, it is a sense of

the precarious, the transitory quality of the emotional impulses that
appear to constitute life that dominates the speech. It makes Hotspur's
affirmations of 'honour', if not empty, pathetic and ultimately invalid;
and the sense of their inadequacy is shortly confirmed by his death at
the hands of a more controlled and mature conception of duty associated
with the growth of the ideal King.

The battle episodes to which these preliminaries lead turn upon a nice
opposition between traditional concepts of 'honour' and a critical
presentation of the heroism of war. Sir Walter Blunt, who dies for his
King (V. iii), is seen as something less than a master of his fate. For
Hotspur, to whom the simple idea of 'honour' has always been a sufficient guide, he was a 'gallant knight'; but his slayer Douglas, a character
less committed to the heroic idea and indeed drawn on lines altogether
more barbarous, utters his epitaph in savage terms in which frustrated
impatience and a certain rough contempt both play their part:

> A fool go with thy soul, whither it goes!
> A borrowed title hast thou bought too dear.   (V. iii. 22)

As usual, something like the last word is left with Falstaff, whose part in
the battle is not circumscribed to the mixture of self-interest and heroic
values by which the main political actors are at once moved and
limited. 'Sir Walter Blunt: here's honour for you! here's no vanity!'
To appreciate the comment we need to sense the touch of mortality
which underlies it. 'Vanity', of course, offers a double sense, that of
pride (which ends in the traditional fall) and that of nothingness,
futility, itself related to death and to the sense of empty 'honour' that
has brought it upon the victim.

Falstaff's exchange with the Prince, which concludes this scene,
answers to a similar intention. Hal, as befits his regenerated state, is
concerned with the death of the 'noblemen' who lie

> stark and stiff
> Under the hoofs of vaunting enemies;   (V. iii. 42)

we need not call the phrase insincere, but there is something limiting
about its rhetorical quality which Falstaff is perfectly fitted to take up.
He does so, first in his own parody of warlike boasting—'Turk
Gregory never did such deeds in arms as I have done this day'—and
then by giving Hal his 'pistol', which turns out to be a bottle of sack.
What is at stake here is not cowardice or its opposite, but rather the
assertion of an independence that refuses to accept verbal values at their

own estimate, but plays upon them by converting humour and farce
into a distinctive irony. Such is the spirit of his famous comment on
Blunt's sacrifice: 'I like not such grinning honour as Sir Walter hath:
give me life: which if I can save, so; if not, honour comes unlooked for,
and there's an end' (V. iii. 61). In the phrase 'give me life' may be
found the key to this judgement in which we may detect, if we will, a
foundation of fear, but in which this 'cowardice', if it exists, is transformed by self-awareness into something very different; for this is a
comment on the waste implied (among other things: the judgement is
relevant, not final) in a battle so many of whose causes have been shown
to be suspect. Falstaff is, let us say, a coward who can contemplate his
own cowardice with detachment; and, by so doing, he offers an
estimate of the heroic values which are themselves related to a positive
interpretation of life, but which need the operation of this objective
check to prevent them from degenerating into a verbose pose.

The Prince, meanwhile, follows his own path, which leads him,
through the rescue of his father from death at the hands of Douglas
(V. iv), to the final confrontation with Hotspur. With this, the central
duel between rival conceptions of 'honour' and their relation to the
'destiny' which overshadows them is at last brought to a head. These
conceptions are, indeed, mutually exclusive; this is implied in the
Prince's words 'Two stars keep not their motion in one sphere', and
the type of 'glory' with which both are here concerned is not of the
kind that can be shared in life. The clash between them follows, and
ends in Hotspur's death. His last speech is important in its suggestion of
a relationship between the speaker's conception of 'honour' and certain
themes growing to mature expression in Shakespeare's work at this
time. Hotspur, dying, affirms the value of the 'proud titles' of glory
above those of 'brittle life'; but in the adjective there is a sense of
hollowness which contrasts with the content of the vaguely conceived
'titles' themselves and suggests that sense of tragic emptiness which
Shakespeare comes increasingly to set in pathetic contrast to the heroic
ideal. The whole of Hotspur's response to his rival's final words is
wrapped in a characteristic pessimism:

> They wound my thoughts worse than thy sword my flesh:
> But thought's the slave of life, and life time's fool;
> And time, that takes survey of all the world,
> Must have a stop.   (V. iv. 80)

To interpret this adequately is to be aware of a conflict more subtle than may immediately appear. It is at once an attempted excuse for inner emptiness, for chivalrous values seen at the decisive moment to be void of true significance, and a pathetic affirmation of the tragedy which the recognition of this reality implies. The sense of the passage of time, unredeemed by a corresponding conception of 'value', is typical of many of the Sonnets[15] and of much of Shakespeare's work at this period. Originally relatively abstract in expression, we see it now gaining a personal and pathetic quality which will eventually affect the dramatist's attitude to his tragic heroes.

At this point, indeed, Hotspur is at once expressing disillusionment and, in expressing it, seeking a last emotional compensation. At Shrewsbury he has fallen before a conception of honour deeper and, as the future will confirm, more effective than his own; but he has fallen also on behalf of the policies incarnated in Worcester, policies which his emotion has too readily accepted but which are less creditable than those which his own nature should have been able to assimilate. His death leaves us with an impression poised between the tragic and the ironic, adequately summed up in the self-conscious pathos of his reference to the 'earthy and cold hand of death' and in the contrast of attitudes contained in his conqueror's brief completion of his final 'food for —': 'For *worms*, *brave* Percy'. This is simply one aspect of the fatality that overshadows a battle in which the rebels fail to attain their end and in which it is foreseen that the King will equally be prevented from achieving the unity for which he is *now*, but too late, genuinely striving.

The Prince's oration over his dead rival is, as far as it goes, fitting and impressive, one more sign of his growing stature; but it belongs, like so much in his nature, to the *public* rather than to the truly personal order. In calling Hotspur 'great heart' and 'so stout a gentleman' he affirms the values of courtesy which are to be a part of his own royal virtues; but, even in so doing, in the lending of his 'favours' to cover his enemy's 'mangled face' with 'rites of tenderness', we may feel a weight correspondingly laid on vanity:

> When that this body did contain a spirit,
> A kingdom for it was too small a bound;
> But now two paces of the vilest earth
> Is room enough.   (V. iv. 89)

Beneath the formal quality of this epitaph lies a preoccupation with the 'vanity' upon which Falstaff has already touched in irony; the modifica-

tion of the chivalrous note by a qualifying sense of tragedy is full of
meaning for the interpretation of later plays.

It is no accident that Falstaff has been a spectator of this duel of
contrasted incarnations of 'honour'. Before the battle, his contact with
the popular sphere implied a parallel, at once cynical and humorous, to
the serious action, and now his mock death carries this parallel to a
logical culmination; whilst the Prince, having delivered his chivalrous
epitaph over Hotspur, turns to a comic shadow of it in his reflections
over Falstaff's body:

> O, I should have a heavy miss of thee,
> If I were much in love with vanity!
> Death hath not struck so fat a deer to-day,
> Though many dearer, in this bloody fray.   (V. iv. 105)

The easy flow of rhyme offers a clear contrast to the preceding heroic
seriousness, and even the reference to 'vanity' rouses echoes from the
past action. The Prince's humour, with its somewhat self-conscious
disclaimer, 'If I were much in love with vanity', is indeed in character,
as is the pun on 'deer' and 'dearer' which is of a kind that can be
paralleled elsewhere in his utterances. Comic as the speech is in intention, its spirit is that of a commentary offered in character, a placing of
what has gone before; nor is this mock death, and the Prince's equally
mock farewell, at this moment in which he has decisively confirmed
himself in his 'serious' political function, entirely without significance
for their future relationship.

Falstaff's comment after his 'resurrection' contains as usual an assertion of simple vitality against the claims of verbal obligation: 'To die,
is to be a counterfeit; for he is but the counterfeit of a man who hath
not the life of a man: but to counterfeit dying, when a man thereby
liveth, is to be no counterfeit, but the true and perfect image of life
indeed' (V. iv. 117). The stress laid upon 'life', in its 'true and perfect
image', illuminates the function of Falstaff in this play without, however, exhausting it. In the light of this assertion, the speaker's 'cowardice' is seen to include a positive comic value, and even the final
stabbing of Hotspur's dead body and the taking of the grotesque burden
on his back, though no doubt it is the final manifestation of the braggart
soldier of theatrical convention, contains also an ironic reference to the
serious, 'chivalrous' combat we have just witnessed. At this point, the
last word of the play has really been spoken. The final scene (V. v)
simply winds up the political action, justifies Henry against the

treachery of Worcester, and allows the Prince to express himself with proper generosity towards Douglas. The King's concluding reference to the future campaigns against his remaining enemies places us on the threshold of the play to follow.

2 Henry IV—Part II

Henry IV, Part II, although carrying on the design initiated in the preceding play,[16] differs in certain respects from its predecessor. Henry IV, whose struggle to assert his kingship had provided a principal thread of action in Part I, has ceased in the sequel to exercise any positive influence over the course of events. As a result, the state of England—more extensively and realistically portrayed than before—is shown as given over to anarchy and corruption. Aged and cynical rebels share a sense of adverse fatality with the King whom they originally backed in his crime of usurpation, whilst in the popular sphere, a predatory and decaying Falstaff exercises his wits in drawing from misery, corruption, and impotence an uneasy and parasitic sustenance. The consequences of the crisis in authority initiated by Bolingbroke's murder of Richard cover the entire realm and threaten its vital unity with extinction. It would hardly be possible to stress more forcibly the urgency, the indispensable need, of Henry V's approaching affirmation of authority.

The earlier political action is concentrated, as though to emphasize the prevalence of disorder, upon the counsels of the rebel leaders. These are developed with an elaboration which is perhaps best studied in the words spoken by Northumberland when the news of defeat at Shrewsbury is finally brought home to him:

> In poison there is physic; and these news,
> Having been well, that would have made me sick,
> Being sick, have in some measure made me well:
> And as the wretch, whose fever-weaken'd joints,
> Like strengthless hinges, buckle under life,
> Impatient of his fit, breaks like a fire
> Out of his keeper's arms, even so my limbs,
> Weaken'd with grief, being now enraged with grief,
> Are thrice themselves.   (I. i. 137)

The verse is, in ancestry, clearly that of the early Shakespeare. The machinery is prominent to a degree that would never be tolerated in the greater plays; but there is a feeling, too, that the poet is reaching out through these devices to new elaborations of experience. The speech aims, however obscurely, at a new effect, an attempt to carry the shifts and tensions of consciousness in the strain of self-definition. In Northumberland's mind health and sickness, action and renunciation, are chaotically intertwined. 'Poison' comes to him, or so he would like to think in the form of 'physic'; the bad news that, in a state of health, would have reduced him to sickness, has now, precisely because he is 'sick', created in him an illusion of health. The intention, moreover, is not simply to contrast age and weakness with the need for decisive action. It is to convey in the motion of the verse the tragic disharmony that exists in the old man and unites him to a history not less tragically conceived. The words 'well' and 'sick', as he uses them, shift in their context, refer at different moments to his own condition and to the news he has received. It is the effect of perversity in rebellion to produce a state of moral 'sickness' which the external action confirms and which, in the last analysis, Northumberland shares with the King he is striving to overthrow.

Northumberland, to put the matter in another way, is not simply a figure to be observed and analysed in terms of motivation. From the beginning, his helplessness is related to an overriding sense of tragic circumstance. His first words, spoken to Lord Bardolph,

> The times are wild; contention, like a horse,
> Full of high feeding, madly hath broke loose
> And bears down all before him,   (I. i. 9)

have already conveyed a sense of impending disaster which, superbly embodied in the blind sensual energy of the horse, looms over the petty drama of senile indecision enacted, as it were, beneath its menacing shadow. Now, as defeat is confirmed, the threat extends itself, is concentrated upon a vision of universal chaos:

> Let heaven kiss earth; now let not Nature's hand
> Keep the wild flood confined! *let order die!*
> And let this world no longer be a stage
> To feed contention in a lingering act;
> But let one spirit of the first-born Cain
> Reign in all bosoms, that, each heart being set

> On bloody courses, the rude scene may end
> And darkness be the burier of the dead!   (I. i. 153)

Here, if anywhere, rhetoric touches, through the broken and hysterical reaction of a defeated old man, upon the universal implications of sedition. The rebels of this play are no longer primarily crafty politicians, realistically presented. The emphasis now is hardly upon responsibility at all. The dim figures who have survived the disaster at Shrewsbury are no longer, like Hotspur and Douglas, active and impetuous leaders; nor are they even particularly crafty, as Worcester had been, or, like Glendower, opinionated and obstinately vain. Their personal qualities, such as they are, have been relegated to the background; like Northumberland himself, though in varying degrees, they have become old and disillusioned shadows, no longer in control of the events which they have set in motion and which now push them on to conclusions only foreseen as disastrous.

The lengthy ratiocinations of Lord Bardolph and his fellow conspirators in the next political episode (I. iii) show them wrapped in the foreboding,

> Conjecture, expectation, and surmise
> Of aids uncertain,   (I. iii. 23)

which their arguments strive to conjure. They are built on an elaboration of concepts which finally, somewhat like that of the Greek leaders in *Troilus and Cressida*, excludes true purpose.[17] The initial emphasis on the need for decision—the answer of '*instant* action' to the challenge offered by 'the *present* quality of war'—fades into a contrary stagnation. This development answers to a natural process; for, as Lord Bardolph recognizes,

> a cause on foot
> Lives so in hope, as in an early spring
> We see the appearing buds; which to prove fruit,
> Hope gives not so much warrant as despair
> That frosts will bite them.   (I. iii. 37)[18]

The imagery, like so much in the Sonnets and plays of this period, rests upon convention, but the contrast between 'spring' growth and the lack of final fulfilment, between deceptive 'hope' and harsh reality, is very close to the sense of frustration which dogs the rebel leaders in these scenes. This is already, in an elementary form, the problem with which Agamemnon and the Greek leaders will so long and vainly wrestle under the walls of Troy.[19]

The last of these early political scenes (II. iii) confirms the death of virtue and its replacement by senile indecision in an age of self-seeking policy. Northumberland is striving to maintain against his wife and Percy's widow the outward appearance of self-respect. It is his 'honour', he argues, which is 'at pawn', imposing upon him a course of action which he tacitly admits to be irrational. The word, so closely associated with her husband's memory, prompts Lady Percy to affirm the passing, in his person, of an order that died finally, as at once inadequate and incompatible with the spirit of the successful politicians of these plays, at Shrewsbury. Her answer to Northumberland's wavering appeal to 'honour' is clear and decisive; for when 'honour' was alive, incarnate in Hotspur, he deserted it, leaving 'two honours lost, yours and your son's' (II. iii. 16). Her outburst culminates in the celebration of a chivalrous ideal at once compelling, endowed with a magnetism of its own, and irretrievably lost. Hotspur is remembered as the norm of aristocratic conduct, the inspiration by whose light

> Did all the chivalry of England move
> To do brave acts.   (II. iii. 20)

The inspiration, however, led only to public disaster and personal loss. Hotspur is dead, 'food for worms'.[20] Those who have survived him—and not on the rebel side alone—share between them a world of calculation, to which Northumberland has already accommodated himself. The adjustment, dishonourable as it is, will not bring with it the safety for which he craves. He admits that, if he is to fight, it will be as a victim caught in a web of circumstances from which there is no final escape:

> I must go and meet with danger there,
> Or it will seek me in another place
> And find me worse provided.   (II. iii. 48)

In the end, however, the instinct to temporize prevails, and the aged politician's last words confirm the uncertainty which derives from subjection to a temporal process which he knows to be beyond his control:

> 'Tis with my mind
> As with the tide swell'd up unto his height,
> That makes a still-stand, running neither way.   (II. iii. 62)

'Time and vantage' are in charge of events, and no decision grasped at by Northumberland's tortuous and infirm mind can turn aside the approaching execution of his fate.

The presentation of a Falstaff in some respects notably changed from his previous image provides a parallel to the 'serious' episodes we have just considered. His words and actions still contain a commentary on public events, but the spirit of that commentary has undergone a certain transformation. No longer felt to stand in some measure apart from the events in which he participates, he has become subdued to the tone of the life around him. If he feels his years as a burden, so do the politicians who have accompanied, with approval or dissent, Henry's rise to power; and, if he is diseased, we have seen that disease is both the counterpart of rebellion and a sign of the disorder which it will be Hal's stern duty to extirpate from the imperilled body of his realm.

In the light of this general statement, it is worth noting that Falstaff's first words in this play refer to his need to consult a physician. His 'water', according to the doctor, is 'a good healthy water', but 'for the party that owed it, he might have more diseases than he knew for' (I. ii. 3). The statement links the ageing Falstaff to the infirm plottings of the rebel leaders and, beyond these, to the state of the English kingdom infected—as the action will progressively show—by the dubious origins of its King's authority. It is true that Falstaff can still turn his circumstances to laughter, be 'the cause that wit is in other men'; but his jokes under the new circumstances deviate significantly from the best of those in Part I, are attuned to the changed world in which he finds himself. In his grotesque picture of himself as 'a sow that hath overwhelmed all her litter but one' the self-consuming consequences of anarchy are emphasized in the act of reducing them to laughter; and this gives way, in his following reference to the Prince—'He may keep his own grace, but he's almost out of mine, I can assure him' (I. ii. 30)— to a first comic inversion of what will eventually be his own rejection. The physical embodiment of 'riot' announces himself, in his growing presumption, as able to reject the master who will finally reject him.

These opening manifestations are preliminary to the main purpose of the scene: the clash between Falstaff, in whom the spirit of anarchic self-assertion is embodied in the flesh, and the claims of control incarnated in the figure of the Lord Chief Justice. The exchange between them culminates in due course in a statement of irreconcilable positions:

—Well, the truth is, Sir John, you live in great infamy.
—He that buckles him in my belt cannot live in less.

—Your means are very slender, and your waste is great.

—I would it were otherwise; I would my means were greater, and my waist slenderer.

—You have misled the youthful prince.

—The young prince hath misled me; I am the fellow with the great belly, and he my dog. (I. ii. 157)

Beneath the play of verbal opposites lies a contrast close to the central conception. To the Chief Justice's moral accusation Falstaff replies with an assertion of physical expansiveness, but, in accordance with the mood that increasingly prevails, physical freedom corresponds to profligacy, expansion becomes 'waste', and finally Falstaff turns his physical bulk to an evocation of penury and the Prince whom he is accused of leading astray into the 'dog' who leads the beggar in his helplessness. Falstaff's wit still imposes itself but its end is now, not the expression of a criticism of life, but an evasion of the claims of restraint, which will none the less prove inescapable for serious and comic, virtuous and profligate alike.

The final exchanges answer to the same spirit. The Lord Chief Justice counters Falstaff's insolent reference to 'the capacities of us that are young' with a bitterly realistic catalogue of decay:

Have you not a moist eye? a dry hand? a yellow cheek? a white beard? a decreasing leg? an increasing belly? is not your voice broken? your wind short? your chin double? your wit single? and every part about you blasted with antiquity? (I. ii. 206)

The Falstaff of *Part I* would never have been subjected to so merciless an exposure and would never have accepted it if he had[21]; but now his fictitious affirmation of perennial youth—'I was born about three of the clock with a white head and something a round belly'—and his satire on Puritan piety—'For my voice, I have lost it with halloing and singing of anthems'—affect us chiefly as echoes of earlier, more carefree felicities. These are indeed 'costermonger times', corresponding to an ageing world in which 'virtue' is neglected and the figure of 'valour' has become that of the soldier returning broken from the wars and reduced, as Falstaff also puts it, to the miserable occupation of 'bear-herd'. In Falstaff himself, impecuniosity has similarly become 'consumption of the purse', an 'incurable malady', whilst 'age' and 'covetousness' are no less intimately connected than 'young limbs' and 'lechery'; but—as he goes on to say—'the gout galls the one, and the pox pinches the other' (I. ii. 262), so that the final effect is one in which

comedy seems well on the way to the sardonic cynicism affected by
Thersites in *Troilus and Cressida*. Falstaff, with the 'gout' or the 'pox'
and affected by the 'incurable' disease of poverty which borrowing
'only lingers out', ends by seeing in the circumstances of war no more
than a means of putting off his inevitable exposure: 'A good wit will
make use of anything: I will turn diseases to commodity' (I. ii. 281).
That the Prince will be amply justified in rejecting a Falstaff so conceived is not open to question; but the fact that the companion of his
former tavern exploits so expresses himself is a sign, not only of his own
decline in years and comic energy, but of that of the world in which he
and the Prince both move.

Lest we should fail to relate this change in Falstaff to the surrounding
action, the scenes which follow introduce a Prince almost equally
subdued to the general disenchantment. Hal's attempt to convey to
Poins, in whom—as he well knows—the world's reactions are reflected,
the sorrow which his father's illness inspires in him is met with complete incredulity. Poins' scepticism, which confirms his own intimate
mood, is met by an appeal to the future development already foreseen:
'let the end try the man'. The end will bring triumph, self-mastery,
and self-affirmation; but even these desirable ends have their price, as is
implied in the melancholy which peers through self-exculpation in the
following phrase:

> I tell thee, my heart bleeds inwardly that my father is so sick: and keeping
> such vile company as thou art hath in reason taken from me all ostentation of
> sorrow. (II. ii. 53)

The 'vile company' which, in his first soliloquy,[22] Hal accepted as a
means to his political education, confident that he could discard it at
will, has become a constraining factor in his life. Poins, no longer
merely the companion of his leisure hours, now appears as an epitome
of what the world thinks about him—'never a man's thought in the
world keeps the road-way better than thine'—and if the element of
condescension, the belief that company can be assumed and discarded
like an old coat, is still present, there is also a new sense of confinement,
of being caught in circumstances formerly accepted in levity which
oblige the speaker to keep his deepest emotions to himself, making
them lie as an undivulged burden at his heart. For one brief moment,
we see Hal as the victim of his own past choice, oppressed with
emotions which he cannot, having chosen his own peculiar path to
public success, allow himself freely to express.

The great tavern scene (II. iv) in which this part of the action culminates is designed to recall the Prince's former adventures at Eastcheap.[23] Once more Hal, subjected to Falstaff's ironic comments, discovers his identity; and once again Falstaff, asserting himself in the spirit of 'riot', parodies the serious claims to valour of his aristocratic betters. The difference in mood, however, is more significant than these parallels. Falstaff, whose influence over the Prince is to all intents and purposes dead, continues to be presented in decline. His victory over Pistol is a poor shadow of the exuberance which had once triumphed, in imaginative retrospect, over the 'men in buckram'[24] and which is now reduced to mere evasion, to an effort to escape the imposition of fact. The spirit of comedy, modified to meet the approaching vindication of moral order, is blended with pathos, burdened with a sense of the corruption of human values by time and ill-living.

Behind these intimations of decay the scene stresses, through the relationship between Falstaff and Doll Tearsheet, the presence of a compensating humanity. This is accomplished with no undue concession to sentiment, no disguise of the corrupting effects of senile appetite: 'If the cook help to make the gluttony, you help to make the diseases, Doll; we catch of you, Doll, we catch of you; grant that, my poor virtue, grant that'. The combination of realism and decayed sentiment, ironic resignation and an echo of compassion ('my poor virtue') reflects a situation already charged with human complexity; and to it Doll, destined by the weakness of her sex to bear the 'huge full hogshead', the monstrous weight of Falstaff's carnality, responds by clinging to his faded physical exuberance as to the shadow of life:

> Come, I'll be friends with thee, Jack: thou art going to the wars; and whether I shall ever see thee again or no, there is nobody cares.   (II. iv. 69)

To her flushed imagination, his 'victory' over Pistol presents itself as a heroic episode, to be celebrated in a grotesque parody of the bombastic rhetoric so prominent in the Ancient's own utterances:

> Ah, rogue! i' faith, I love thee: thou art as valorous as Hector of Troy, worth five of Agamemnon, and ten times better than the Nine Worthies.
>
> (II. iv. 234)

The effect here is purely comic; and in Falstaff's complacent appreciation of his own worth it is a similar absurdity, the contrast between his claim and its miserable object, that counts. This incongruity, however, bears with it an intimation of decline that ends by attaching itself to Doll's fuddled emotions. Thus moved, she takes up the image of the 'martlemas', the boar destined for slaughter at the outset of winter, and invests it, beneath the obvious comedy, with a characteristic pathos:

> Thou whoreson little tidy Bartholomew boar-pig, when wilt thou leave fighting o' days and foining o' nights, and begin to patch up thine old body for heaven? (II. iv. 249)

At this point, the grotesque endearments of the prostitute, presented without abuse of sentiment, touch upon the scene's distinctive undertone of moral tragedy. If a sense of age and impotence now surrounds Falstaff, and if his behaviour, no longer fresh and freely personal, is concentrated on the sordid realities of brawling by day and lechery by night, the change carries with it an awareness of impending dissolution. A note of moral reflection colours, albeit unwillingly, the twilight of his relationship with Doll, and makes it the occasion for some of the deepest sentiments of the play.

Doll's expressions of affection, indeed, finally inspire the most unequivocal of all Falstaff's intimations of decline: 'Peace, good Doll! do not speak like a death's-head: do not bid me remember mine end'. The phrase, in cutting right across the simplified effects of realistic comedy, connects Falstaff with the dark feeling of the political action, a connection made still more explicit, a moment later, in Poins' ironic comment on his relations with Doll: 'Is it not strange that desire should so many years outlive performance?'.[25] Once more, as in *Part I*— though towards ends notably transformed—the 'low' episodes echo their aristocratic counterpart and Falstaff's burden of disease and concupiscence is presented as a reflection of the malady and disharmony shared by the senile rivals who, prior to the Prince's affirmation of his royal vocation, divide between them the public life of England.

It is on a return to this blend of sentiment and tragedy that the exchange with Doll ends. 'I am old, I am old', Falstaff repeats, receiving in return another of those answers in which calculation and gross sentiment shade into an intimation of deeper feeling: 'I love thee better than I love e'er a scurvy young boy of them all'. This declaration in turn inspires the reply, 'Thou'lt forget me when I am gone', in which the recognition by age of its own impotence is touched, at least for a moment, by the shadow of true emotion. The effect of these sombre reflections is greatly enhanced by their setting in the surrounding comedy, which leads finally to the renewed exposure of Falstaff. When the Prince and Poins reveal their identity, he still has presence of mind to recover, to return to an echo of his former attacking mood; for the exclamation 'Ha! a bastard son of the king's? And art thou not Poins his brother?' shows him stressing the community between Hal and his associate to which these scenes more than once revert. His gift for evasion, however, is now exercised under unfavourable conditions. The presence of moral reality which colours, however unwillingly, his thought makes itself felt when he crowns Doll's question to the Prince, 'What says your grace?' with the embittered pun: 'His grace says that which his flesh rebels against'. The echoes which derive from this wry evocation of the conflict between body and spirit are manifold. To link it with the reference, which immediately precedes it, to Lenten abstinence and the illegal eating of flesh, is to approach very closely the intimate spirit of this scene; and to see its further relation to the contrast between law and its evasion, moral rigour and unregulated appetite, setting the choice thus postulated against the background of burning in hell-fire, is to respond to some of the sombre undercurrents which, associated with age, decay, and approaching retribution, amount to a profound transformation of the entire comic effect.

By the end of the Second Act the internal strife and decay which threaten Henry IV's England with dissolution have been extensively portrayed. Both in the rebel counsels and in the tavern world from which Hal is detaching himself, the shadow of age and impotence lies heavily over the action. The presentation of the King, from whose false position—false at least in its origins—this disorder springs, now marks a turning-point in the entire history. Henry's old age is dominated by disappointment and by an obsessive preoccupation with infirmity:

> Then you perceive the body of our kingdom
> How foul it is; what rank diseases grow,
> And with what danger, near the heart of it. (III. i. 38)

The enterprises planned in the earlier part of the reign have all remained without fulfilment. Accepting this frustration as part of the nature of things, Henry's strongest emotion has become a nostalgia for peace and sleep. This nostalgia is born less of immediate experience than of a sense of the meaningless procession of events beyond human control:

> O God! that one might read the book of fate,
> And see the revolution of the times,
> Make mountains level, and the continent,
> Weary of solid firmness, melt itself
> Into the sea! (III. i. 45)

This stressed subjection to mutability derives ultimately from the King's

contemplation of his past career, in which he now sees nothing but
division proceeding (in great part by his own act) out of original
concord:

> 'Tis not ten years gone
> Since Richard and Northumberland, great friends,
> Did feast together, and in two years after
> Were they at wars: it is but eight years since
> This Percy was the man nearest my soul,
> Who like a brother toil'd in my affairs,
> And laid his love and life under my foot.   (III. i. 57)

The lesson of the past comes home to him at the end of his career with
the force of a universal law. Recalling Richard's original prophecy—

> The time will come that foul sin, gathering head,
> Shall break into corruption—   (III. i. 76)[26]

the King has come to read into the subsequent history of his reign a
confirmation of the operations of fate; but it is his tragedy that, having
accepted the reality of his condition, he is no longer in a position to
derive benefit from any practical lesson to be drawn from it:

> O, if this were seen,
> The happiest youth, viewing his progress through,
> What perils past, what crosses to ensue,
> Would shut the book, and sit him down and die.   (III. i. 53)

A sense of the weight of necessity, of an obscure fatality born of human
error and bearing down upon individual helplessness, is the only lesson
derived by Henry from the long chain of events which has brought him
to exhaustion and his kingdom to the verge of dissolution.

The transfer of the action to Falstaff's exploits in Gloucester (III. ii)
further underlines this impression of 'necessity'. In his relations with
Shallow and Silence, he is brought into touch with the very embodi-
ments of powerless senility. 'Mad Shallow', 'lusty Shallow', shifting
from the contemplation of mortality—'death, as the Psalmist saith, is
certain to all; all shall die'—and the memory of his youth at the Inns of
Court to matters of hard calculation—'How a good yoke of bullocks at
Stamford fair?'—is thoroughly in keeping with the spirit of the play.
The switch from tragic impotence to the shrewd bargaining of the
market place is various in its implications. It stresses the speaker's lack of
sensibility, his senile tendency to turn, without any sense of incongruity, from universal tragedy to the petty routine of avarice; but

equally the emphasis on the market place points in its own way to the continued processes of life which individual decline cannot altogether obscure. Life goes on even under the shadow of death; its manifestations, grasping, absurd, and inadequate though they may be, are variously interwoven with the sense of mortality which the action at this stage so strongly conveys.

Falstaff himself has no illusions about the world around him, or about his own place in it. He sees to the 'bottom' of Shallow—'Lord, Lord, how subject we old men are to this vice of lying'—in his mixture of present helplessness and remembered, or coveted, lechery; he can do so because he knows that the cynical observer and his victim are alike in being 'time's subjects'. 'We have heard the chimes at midnight, Master Shallow' (III. ii. 232), and the echoes which these chimes evoke touch life at many points. Falstaff's own vision is, like so much else in this play, the product of experience coloured by age. His previous repudiation of 'honour' bears fruit in his changed attitude to the human victims of civil strife. The 'food for powder'[27] which he had led to battle at Shrewsbury now speaks to him through Feeble, who has also been pressed into a cause which has no meaning for him and who resigns himself to his probable fate in words which recall those once spoken by the Prince to Falstaff himself at Shrewsbury, 'a man can die but once: we owe God a death'.[28] The words are similar, but the attitude of Falstaff, confronted with all that they imply, has changed. Whereas his reply to the Prince had been tinged, beneath its evident disrepute, with irony and wit, had implied an affirmation of the rights of life beyond the selfish calculations of politicians, the Falstaff of *Part II*, after allowing Mouldy and Bullcalf to buy their freedom, is content to accept his victim's submission to his fate; for such, and no other, is the nature of things, and in Gloucestershire, as in the counsels of kings and courtiers, *necessity* justifies all: 'if the young dace be a bait for the old pike, I see no reason, *in the law of nature*, but I may snap at him. *Let time shape*, and there an end' (III. ii. 359).

The scenes which follow lead to the final resolution of the political crisis. To rebels aware of participating in a state of organic failing and sickness which embraces the entire state—as York puts it, echoing his King,

> we are all diseased,
> And with our surfeiting and wanton hours
> Have brought ourselves into a burning fever,
> And we must bleed for it— (IV. i. 54)[29]

the action of time opposes, on the loyalist side, the representatives of a
new generation. The responsibilities abdicated, to all intents and purposes, by Henry are now momentarily concentrated upon John of
Lancaster. What has been in Henry IV a tragic sense of adverse fatality
becomes in his sons a practical grasp of human limitation. Having
played no part in the crime which brought their father to the throne, the
Prince and his brother are free to attain all that he can no longer hope to
achieve. Yet—since the past after all lives on in their present circumstances—the achievement itself, positive and necessary as it is, loses
some of its savour. The cool competence of Lancaster's handling of the
rebels, his impeccable appeal to all the correct doctrines, lead up to the
hollow victory at Gaultree, adequately summed up in his parsimonious
ascription of it to divine collaboration: 'God, and not we, hath *safely*
fought to-day' (IV. ii. 122). The voice that speaks throughout this
scene is the voice of political sufficiency, condemning its enemies—
justly—for their shallowness, in perfect mastery of the course of events.
It is a voice that we shall hear again in *Henry V*, deepened indeed by
reference to other, less merely political values, but present as a factor
determining the new King's decisions and contributing to his success.

As usual, the final comment is left to Falstaff who, though in some
ways the shadow of his former self, can still assert himself on occasions
against the prevailing tone of the action. The taking of Colevile after
the rebel surrender reflects upon the spirit of the political exchange we
have just witnessed. Colevile speaks bitterly of the 'betters' who have
led him to his fate; and both he and Falstaff are in turn commented
upon, flatly and coldly, by the presiding genius of this unsavoury
action. For Falstaff, Lancaster has a level-toned rebuke, the theme of
which has often been anticipated by Hal in the tavern:

> These tardy tricks of yours will, on my life,
> One time or other break some gallows' back;   (IV. iii. 31)

and for Colevile, 'famous rebel', he decrees 'present execution'. In the
political sphere the triumph of loyal efficiency is as complete as it is
salutary; yet even here we are allowed, before the scene ends, a glimpse
of Falstaff's judgement on Lancaster and, through him, on so much in
this play. He describes Prince John as 'a young, sober-blooded boy',
one of those who 'when they marry, get wenches' (IV. iii. 101). The
rich flexibility of the prose, as it flows on in a succession of phrases like
'apprehensive, quick, forgetive, full of nimble, fiery and delectable
shapes', emphasizes by contrast the coldness which has inspired the

successful princes and leaders in their vindication of the principle of authority. The phrasing, indeed, is a product of 'inflammation', and Falstaff has no illusions about his own pretensions to heroism. 'Some of us', he comments, would also be 'fools and cowards', were it not for the artificial heightening of the emotions; but emotion of any kind comes as a natural relief after the action we have just witnessed.

The two scenes (IV. iv, v) which follow take us back to the infirm King, now about to die with the weight of his past acts lying heavily upon his conscience. His comment on his son, whom Warwick attempts to defend, is one in which scepticism and bitterness prevail:

> 'Tis seldom when the bee doth leave her comb
> In the dead carrion;   (IV. iv. 79)

and, a little later, he receives the news of the defeat of the rebels in a mood that recalls the contradictions of the aged Northumberland:

> And wherefore should these good news make me sick?
> Will Fortune never come with both hands full,
> And write her fair words still in foulest letters?
> She either gives a stomach and no food;
> Such are the poor, in health; or else a feast
> And takes away the stomach; such are the rich,
> That have abundance and enjoy it not.   (IV. iv. 102)[30]

It is—as we have seen—no accident that the King and his former accomplice, now his defeated enemy, are thus bound together by subjection to age and the sense of a lack of solid achievement. Both belong to a world in which sickness and decline prevail, and are mirrors of inner tragedy. Both are victims rather than agents, once their respective selfish choices have been made; and both stand, without the prospect of entering it, upon the threshold of a world in which the criterion of effective success will be married to a simple and positive set of moral judgements.

The birth of this world is confirmed in the next scene (IV. v), as the Prince is reconciled to his father on his death-bed and assumes, in all its glory and burden, the vocation which his birth has imposed upon him. The fatal decision, to which the whole action has been tending, is now expressed in two speeches. In the first, the King, conscious of the approach of death, gathers up his sense of vanity in one complete evocation of the rule of 'riot' which, as he foresees, will fall upon England when his son is crowned. Beyond the vanity of death, he sees another, still more bitter vanity, the dissolution of everything for which he has striven into the chaos of 'misrule':

> For the fifth Harry from curb'd license plucks
> The muzzle of restraint, and the wild dog
> Shall flesh his tooth on every innocent.
> O my poor kingdom, sick with civil blows!
> When that my care could not withhold thy riots,
> What wilt thou do when riot is thy care?
> O, thou wilt be a wilderness again,
> Peopled with wolves, thy old inhabitants! (IV. v. 129)

In this speech Henry is affected personally, tragically if we will, by the foreseen ruin of the structure to which he has so painfully devoted his life; for his son's assumption of the crown will, he anticipates, lead to the destitution of his officers and the abandonment of his decrees. In the culminating part of the speech, the whole 'public' significance of the Falstaff scenes is summed up in a bitter apprehension of chaos. 'Form', by which alone the fragile political structure can be maintained through allegiance to its royal key-stone, will be mocked and 'vanity' rule to the dissolution of civilized customs. The gold which is, in the crown, the emblem of kingship will 'gild' the shame of misrule, and the result will be an endless disorder in which 'riot', deprived of its mask of conviviality, will assume its true visage of predatory ruthlessness, to the dissolution of the national community and of all civilized life.

To this bitter reproach the Prince replies with an expression of filial reverence which at last reconciles him to his father. His kneeling is an exterior expression of obedience, the sign of a 'most inward true and duteous spirit'; and it leads to an affirmation of the conversion which has been from the first anticipated and is now at least a reality:

> If I do feign,
> O, let me in my present wildness die,
> And never live to show the incredulous world
> The noble change that I have purposed! (IV. v. 150)

It is noteworthy, however, that this 'conversion' is still essentially a *public* matter, a question of showing the 'incredulous world' to what extent it has misjudged the future King. We need not, should not, affirm that this makes the Prince insincere: for he is a public figure and his emotions are necessarily publicly, politically conceived. If this play contains deep personal feeling, this lies precisely in the gap which is felt at certain moments to separate public from private emotion; where the one is triumphant in the necessary assertion of authority, the other sees in the exercise of the royal power a burden of responsibility almost intolerable to be borne, a constricting framework enclosing life and making the King's office barely human in its implications. This latter sense the Prince expresses as he sums up the content of his meditations on the crown:

> thou, most fine, most honour'd, most renown'd,
> Hast eat thy bearer up. (IV. v. 162)

The incidence here of intense private sentiment is communicated in words which point to the presence of inherited, traditional feeling. For this play shows emotion of a tragic kind making itself felt, in its attitude to the royal office, partly through traditional conceptions and partly in contrast to them; and in the shifting relationship between these two strains lies the explanation of some of the deepest effects which it is capable of producing.

At the end of his speech, the Prince asserts his own attitude to the crown in a spirit which combines sober resolution with a touch of pessimism:

> Thus, my most royal liege,
> Accusing it, I put it on my head,
> To try with it, as with an enemy
> That had before my face murder'd my father,
> The quarrel of a true inheritor.
> But if it did infect my blood with joy,
> Or swell my thoughts to any strain of pride;
> If any rebel or vain spirit of mine
> Did with the least affection of a welcome
> Give entertainment to the might of it,
> Let God for ever keep it from my head,
> And make me as the poorest vassal is,
> That doth with awe and terror kneel to it! (IV. v. 163)

The sense of the crown as an 'enemy' is close to the deeper feeling of much of the play, and cuts across the confidence required by the 'public' action in a way that we can only call tragic. As a public figure, Hal has justly asserted his determination to maintain the power which God has conferred upon him; but here, in the face of his father's disillusionment, he speaks of the crown as a 'murderer' and abjures the very 'strain of pride' which other words of his, not so very long before, seem to have reflected. His vocation is a severe and sombre one, and to rejoice in it at this moment, in the presence of a father who has, indeed, been 'murdered' by the weight of it, would be to show a 'rebel spirit', an 'infection' of the blood. On the threshold of his assumption of the power he is vowing to maintain, the Prince shows himself aware of the need to keep in check the temptations which accompany the exercise of authority; in this sense of a tension between control and the assertion of self-will lies, as we shall see,[31] the key to certain elements in the nature of Henry V.

The father's reply is poised to the last between contradictory emotions. He is happy to hear this rehabilitation of his son's 'public' character and filial devotion; but in his 'latest counsel' his thoughts turn back to the 'by-paths and indirect crook'd ways' by which he achieved the crown. As he looks back upon his reign, he sees it as showing the response of anarchy to the anarchy which his own actions first set loose:

> For all my reign hath been but as a scene
> Acting that argument;   (IV. v. 196)

and even though his death 'changes the mode', so that what in him was vile 'purchase' is translated 'in a more fairer sort', it is worth noting that his last advice is still pessimistically conceived:

> all my friends, which thou must make thy friends,
> Have but their stings and teeth newly ta'en out.   (IV. v. 203)

Surely in this use of the word 'friends' we may detect the presence of a deep tragic irony. It confers upon the dying King, as he takes his leave of life, a sense of ironic fatality against which even his son's determined practical affirmation seems strangely limited:

> My gracious liege,
> You won it, wore it, kept it, gave it me;
> Then plain and right must my possession be:
> Which I with more than with a common pain
> 'Gainst all the world will rightfully maintain.   (IV. v. 219)

The words 'right' and 'rightfully', 'plain' as their sense is to the speaker, show already the virtues and the limitations of the future Henry V. It is no part of the Prince's nature to look too closely into the origins of his power, with which his father has been so closely concerned. By refraining from so doing, by regarding his inheritance of the crown as a sufficient reason for affirming the justice of his holding of it, he lays the foundations for his future success and for the precious unity of his kingdom; but, amply justified though he is in the political order, and though confidence in his own right is a proper attribute of kingship, we cannot but sense that 'public' necessity has triumphed over the personal theme, and that from now on individual feeling will have no primary part to play in what is becoming, more than ever before, an essentially political action. Its exclusion, together with that of anarchy, 'riot', and indulgence, will be confirmed in the last meeting with Falstaff.

First, however, the new King has to be reconciled to the personal embodiment of the justice upon which his power will rest. The Lord Chief Justice stresses his position as the 'image' of the royal power, and insists upon the dependence of rule itself on a proper respect for the sanctions embodied in his office:

> Behold yourself so by a son disdain'd;
> And then imagine me taking your part,
> And in your power soft silencing your son:
> After this cold consideration, sentence me. (V. ii. 95)

Henry, in his reply, assumes the impersonal function required of him. Publicly, he announces his determination to 'stoop and humble' his intents to 'your well-practised wise directions', to what is, in effect, less a moral conception than one of policy and practical wisdom; though in saying this one does not assert the presence of deceit, but rather of a necessary Machiavellism, an understanding of what political effectiveness *really* implies, as essential to his conception. The gesture of acceptance having been made, as befits a King who is renouncing not only his unruly past, but in some sense the free impulses of his own youth, the speech rises to a firm affirmation of self-control, as impressive as it is curiously strained, emptied of normal feeling:

> The tide of blood in me
> Hath proudly flow'd in vanity till now:
> Now doth it turn and ebb back to the sea,
> Where it shall mingle with the state of floods
> And flow henceforth in formal majesty. (V. ii. 129)

This is an assertion of moral power rather than of human understanding. Behind the image of the tide so impressively evoked, there is a sense of the various resources of man turned, harnessed to an end, which is that gravely subsumed under the title of 'formal majesty'. The tone of this powerful declaration of intent prepares us, once Falstaff has been finally rejected, for the spirit in which Henry V will exercise his authority.

Falstaff, meanwhile, receives the news of the old King's death by vowing himself, and his companions in Gloucestershire, to the last and most presumptuous adventure of 'appetite';

> Away, Bardolph! saddle my horse. Master Robert Shallow, choose what office thou wilt in the land, 'tis thine. . . . I know the young king is sick for me. Let us take any man's horses; the laws of England are at my command-ment. Blessed are they that have been my friends; and woe to my lord chief justice. (V. iii. 125)

In the light of vain assertion on this scale, any sentimental approbation of Falstaff is placed firmly out of court. This is the voice of 'appetite' approaching its prey in the prospect of anarchy: rapacious, cruel—as in Pistol's echoing comment on the Chief Justice: 'Let vultures vile seize on his lungs also!'—and blown out, no longer merely with good living, but with the arrogant self-confidence that anticipates in reality nothing but its own ruin. The 'pleasant days' of Pistol's dream will be confronted with reality in the icy wind of righteous authority that blows from Westminster; but, inhuman as the wind may seem and to some extent be, the reality of the corruption it blows away will amply justify it.

These preliminaries, and the sombre little episode of Doll Tearsheet's arrest which follows them,[32] throw light upon the famous crux which rounds off the play—the rejection of Falstaff by Henry as he assumes his responsibilities. Falstaff comes to Westminster full of his new and sinister confidence. He will 'leer' upon the King to attract his favour, he will assume 'earnestness of affection', 'devotion', associating feelings which may once have possessed a certain sincerity with his new spirit of conscious calculation. The crowning moment is reached when Pistol, having recalled Doll's imprisonment, prompts the pretentious confidence of his reply—'I will deliver her'—and utters the final phrase, 'There roar'd the sea, and trumpet-clangour sounds' (V. v. 42), in which poetry and base rhetoric are so richly combined. The moment for settling accounts has at last come and it will show, among other things, that Doll is far beyond Falstaff's power to save.

The encounter, indeed, balances the contrasted themes of the play to remarkable effect. The breaking of the wave of Falstaff's enthusiasm against the fixity of the royal purpose is admirably conveyed in dramatic terms. 'God save thy grace, king Hal! my royal Hal!' Falstaff cries, transported by the prospect of his coming prosperity, and after Pistol has echoed him—'The heavens thee guard and keep, most royal imp of fame!'—he further adds 'God save thee, my sweet boy!' only to find these transports checked by the cold austerity of Henry's indirect rejoinder: 'My lord chief justice, speak to that vain man'. This in turn leads Falstaff to express—this time in terms which reflect, exploiting it if we will, genuine personal pathos—his inability to believe what he has heard: 'I speak to thee, my heart', deliberately ignoring the Lord Chief Justice's reproof: 'Have you your wits? know you what 'tis you speak?', before he receives finally, from the King's own mouth, the decisive, unanswerable rejoinder: 'I know thee not, old man'. The whole exchange is, in its brevity, marvellously varied, charged with the contrasted emotions that go to make up the play. From this moment, the full content of the scene is, to a discerning attention, apparent.

Shakespeare, indeed, not only accepted the artistic difficulty involved in the rejection, which the nature of his material and his own earlier presentation of Falstaff imposed upon him, but wove it into his own conception. There is no doubt that the change noted in the presentation of Falstaff in this play aims, among other things, at making the rejection both feasible and necessary. The Falstaff of *Part I* would never have allowed himself to be turned off without visible reaction, an aged, broken shadow, beneath his cynicism, of his former self. It is not accidental that he has been given a new burden of age, lechery, and disease, which fits the changed spirit of the play even as it justifies, and not only in political terms, his treatment at the hands of his former friend. When Henry denounces Falstaff as

> So surfeit-swell'd, so old, and so profane,

he is responding to the traditional content of his theme, which called for the young King to reject 'riot' on the threshold of his new responsibilities. He makes, in other words, a true criticism, which an Elizabethan audience would not have found excessive; and the criticism is backed up with the austerity of a great religious tradition when he adds:

> Make less thy body hence, and more thy grace.

From the *public* standpoint, which also carried with it in this case a moral and religious implication, this judgement represents a culminating point in the entire history. Henry, as King, cannot but make it, and by making it he lays the foundations of political and moral salvation for his kingdom.

Yet there is, equally, another side to the picture. Though the King's words must be given their proper value, the same applies to Falstaff's repeated criticisms of the royal family, which have run as an accompaniment through the preceding action and are no less part of the truth. This balancing of the issues, which should not be confused with indifference and unwillingness to assert judgement, is profoundly Shakespearean in its effect. The contrasted personalities of Falstaff and Prince Hal are seen as occupying no more than a part of the whole field of reality which conditions their dramatic being; they are complementary aspects of a creation whose principal of unity lies not solely in the vision of either but in the integration of the various standpoints which constitute the dramatic material as a whole. Henry's judgements, valid and inevitable as they are, suffer—like those of other Shakespearean characters—from being too easily made. Never is this more so than at this moment, in which he assumes the dignity and impersonality of his vocation. The denial of past friendship involved in 'I know thee not, old man', the tight-lipped implication of disgust in his advice to 'leave gormandizing', the studied gesture to the gallery, so appropriate in one whose life is to be lived from now on as a public function: 'Presume not that I am the thing I was'—all these are as revealing as the afterthought by which Falstaff, banished scarcely five minutes before, is arrested and thrown into prison. This final stroke has been variously interpreted by those who wish it to fit in with their conception of the new King's character; but surely, however we may choose to connect it with Henry's transformed nature, its final meaning is related also to the blow it strikes at Falstaff's halfhearted attempt to revive his confidence—'I shall be sent for soon at night'—and to the dissipation of the hopes, themselves connected with the exploitation of Shallow, to which he clings. We can feel for Falstaff at this moment without accepting his point of view, just as we can applaud the new King for his resolve without ceasing to count the human cost, not least for himself, of his decisions. This interplay of intimate motives, all relevant and none final, we should by now have learnt to see as a characteristic manifestation of Shakespeare's genius.

The final condemnation is accompanied, typically, by Lancaster's flat and unpleasing comment:

> I like this fair proceeding of the king's:
> He hath intent his wonted followers
> Shall all be very well provided for. (V. v. 103)

The concluding provision for Falstaff, though it clearly corresponds to an effort to justify the royal action in public terms, is only on the public plane satisfactory:

> For competence of life I will allow you,
> That lack of means enforce you not to evil:
> And, as we hear you do reform yourselves,
> We will, according to your strengths and qualities,
> Give you advancement. (V. v. 71)

Though perhaps a sufficient justification of the King, it does not help us to form a kinder estimate of the man. The comment surely needs to be read in the light of Falstaff's death as announced in *Henry V*. Far from being an afterthought, or—as some have held—a practical device to dispose of a character whom Shakespeare himself, having created him, could neither repeat indefinitely nor allow to dominate his historical conception, Falstaff's death is surely the logical conclusion of this action. Death and mortality are woven into the fabric of this great series of plays, and if the political development is dominated by these realities, so that only the frigid imposition of the will to govern, exercised in the common good, can obtain some measure of triumph over it, it is logical that the humanity which that will cannot compass, having undergone a corruption of its own, should finally die. Fair provision by the grace of the new order is no destiny for the creature that Falstaff has been. Even in his old age, his spirit is nearer to the related decay and tenderness of the exchanges with Doll Tearsheet[33]: and since neither tenderness nor decay have henceforth any real part in the new King's character, his death, and not merely his exposure as a symbol of 'riot', is inevitable.

There is no need, in the last analysis, to be sentimental on behalf of either the Prince or Falstaff. The 'unpleasantness' in their relationship is a necessary part of the play. It springs from all that is most personal in its conception; it translates yet again into dramatic terms the 'disease' which we have found hanging over the English state, and it relates all the divisions between age and youth, action and inaction, anarchic folly and cold calculation which embody that disease to a developing split in the dramatist's conception of the world as his plays reveal it. The precise meaning of this bitter contrast between aged dissolution and the controlled frigidity so unnaturally ascribed to youth needs to be defined in relation to certain of the Sonnets,[34] to *Troilus and Cressida*, and to *Measure for Measure*.[35] *Henry IV, Part II*, provides, in a word, through the presentation of a society in which the normal attributes of life are subjected to a peculiar and disquieting inversion, a fruitful approach to the issues more completely handled by Shakespeare in the first plays of his full maturity.

3 Henry V

The political success aimed at by Henry IV is finally achieved, in the last play of the series, by his son. The general theme of *Henry V* is the establishment in England of an order based on consecrated authority and crowned by action against France. The conditions of this order are, again in accordance with the main conception, moral as well as political. The crime of regicide which had stood between Bolingbroke and the attainment of peace no longer hangs over Henry V—unless as a disturbing memory—and the crusading purpose which had run as an unfulfilled aspiration through the father's life is replaced by the reality, at once brilliant and ruthless, of the son's victorious campaign.

This, as critics have not always realized, is less a conclusion than a point of departure for the understanding of *Henry V*. It was the conditions of kingship, at least as much as its results, that interested Shakespeare in these plays: and these conditions are viewed, by the time the last of them came to be conceived, in a light definitely akin to the tragic. The problem of political unity and that of personal order have been brought in the course of these historical studies into the closest relationship. The former has been achieved, in the preceding plays, by the development of a political capacity that recalls, in various of its aspects, the Machiavellian conception of the Prince; but success of this kind increasingly poses for Shakespeare, whose thought was at once more traditional and less limited to the political than that of the great Florentine, wider problems more definitely moral, even religious, in kind. Just as the state, already in *Henry IV*, *Part II*, is regarded in its divisions as a diseased body ravaged by a consuming fever, so is the individual seen increasingly as torn between the violence of his passions and the direction of reason; and just as the remedy to political anarchy lies in unquestioned allegiance to an authority divinely constituted, so does personal coherence depend upon the submission to reason of our uncontrolled desires. The link between the two states, political and personal, is provided in these plays by concentration upon the figure of the King. The problem of the state becomes that of the individual at its head. The King, who properly demands unquestioning allegiance from his subjects, is first called upon to show, through the perfection of his dedication, a complete and selfless devotion to his office. The personal implications, as well as the patriotic triumphs, which that devotion brings with it are considered in *Henry V*.

It demands, in the first place, an absolute measure of self-domination. Called upon to exercise justice and shape policies for the common good, the King can allow no trace of selfishness or frailty to affect his decisions. He must continually examine his motives, confirm them in the light of reason; and this means that he is engaged in a continual struggle against his share of human weakness. As the play proceeds, we become increasingly aware that there is in Henry an uneasy balance between violent passion, in certain of its forms, and firm self-control. The control is, indeed, an essential part of his political capacity and of his personal stature. Without it, Henry would not be a true King at all; but, precisely because he is a man and not a crowned puppet, there are times when an unmistakable sense of constraint makes itself felt, as for instance in his greeting to the French ambassador:

> We are no tyrant, but a Christian king;
> Unto whose grace our passion is as subject
> As are our wretches fettered in our prisons. (I. ii. 241)

The harshness of the comparison is, to say the least, remarkable. Such control, though admirable, and doubly so in a King, is necessarily precarious. The passions, 'fettered', treated with a disdain similar to that which, as Prince Hal, he has already displayed to the considerations of normal feeling when the fulfilment of his vocation imposed the renunciation of his past, may be expected to break out in forms not immediately attractive.

Almost at once, in fact, they do so. The French envoys, in fulfilling their mission by presenting him with the Dauphin's tennis balls, touch upon a raw spot in Henry's sensibility; they expose him to ridicule and, worst of all, they refer—by the observation that 'You cannot revel into dukedoms here'—to the abjured, but not forgotten past. Henry's reaction, in spite of the opening affirmation of self-control, takes the form of one of those outbursts which are habitual with him whenever his will is crossed. As when France was to be 'bent' or 'broken',[36] his rhetoric, measured and even cold on the surface, is full of accumulated passion:

> When we have match'd our rackets to these balls,
> We will, in France, by God's grace, play a set
> Shall strike his father's crown into the hazard. (I. ii. 261)

The reference to 'God's grace', rarely omitted from Henry's official utterances, clearly befits a Christian king, and we need not deny its propriety; but from the personal point of view, which the play is also concerned to stress, the note of resentment which rises through the speech is equally significant. It rankles at this point until the real motive, or an important part of it, becomes at last explicit:

> we understand him well,
> How he comes o'er us with our wilder days,
> Not measuring what use we made of them.   (I. ii. 266)

The personal offence once mentioned, the considerations of conscience are swept aside, at least for so long as the new emotion is in command. The horrors of war, the slaughter and misery attendant upon it, are once again mentioned, but only that he may disclaim responsibility for them. The tone of his words, following the swell of emotion, rises to one of ruthless and triumphant egoism:

> But *I* will rise there with so full a glory
> That *I* will dazzle all the eyes of France,
> Yea, strike the Dauphin blind to look on us.
> And tell the pleasant prince this mock of his
> Hath turn'd his balls to gun-stones; and his soul
> Shall stand sore charged for the wasteful vengeance
> That shall fly with them: for many a thousand widows
> Shall this his mock mock out of their dear husbands;
> Mock mothers from their sons, mock castles down;
> And some are yet ungotten and unborn
> That shall have cause to curse the Dauphin's scorn.   (I. ii. 278)

'*I* will rise there': '*I* will dazzle all the eyes of France'. The Dauphin's gibe has set free Henry's 'fettered' passions and these express themselves in a cumulative vision of destruction. The tone of the utterance—the impact of 'strike', the harsh reference to the balls which have been turned to 'gun-*stones*', the sense of irresistible, ruinous force behind 'mock castles down'—reflects the new feeling and anticipates the later, more masterly picture of Coriolanus in action.[37] This is not to say that we are to regard Henry as a monster at this point, or to deny that a proper sense of royal responsibility underlies his words. He is uttering a warning, condemning the real irresponsibility of others; but the speech has, beyond this, an intimate content which is also part of the complete effect. The sense of power, inhuman and destructive beneath the surface of righteous anger, has been unleashed in the King. The responsibility for coming events, already assumed by the Archbishop of Canterbury earlier in the same scene, has now been further fastened upon the Dauphin, and Henry is in a position to announce his coming descent

upon France with a phrase that incorporates into his new vehemence
the convenient certainty of righteousness:

> But all this lies within the will of God,
> To whom I do appeal.   (I. ii. 289)

No doubt the conviction is sincere: but the fact remains that the will of
God and the will of Henry, now fused in the passion released by the
Dauphin's jest, have become identical.

It is not until the opening of the French campaign that Henry's
utterances are translated into action. The poetry of war in this play
deserves careful attention. Much of it, corresponding to the spirit of the
patriotic chronicle, is full of life and vigour; such is the elaborate
description in the Prologue to this same Act of the 'fleet majestical'
which bears the English forces to Harfleur. The King 'embarks his
royalty' on a 'brave fleet', adorned and lighted by the dawn:

> behold the threaden sails,
> Borne with the invisible and creeping wind,
> Draw the huge bottoms through the furrow'd sea,
> Breasting the lofty surge: O, do but think
> You stand upon the rivage and behold
> A city on the inconstant billows dancing;
> For so appears this fleet majestical.   (III Prologue 10)

Such imagery, splendidly and consciously laden for its effect, is a contribution to the spirit of the play. It may be that some of its deeper notes
are not included in it, but the effect of a pageant, of the confident
display of might in beauty, is undoubtedly part of Shakespeare's debt to
his theme which, whilst balancing it against other elements, it was no
part of his intention to forgo. If, in much of this play, he qualifies the
note of majesty with more sombre and reflective tones, the effect of these
tones is in part gained by the contrast with the appeal of majesty itself.

Yet when, immediately after, Henry himself appears, much of his
first utterance, as he incites his followers to battle, has about it a strong
flavour of artificiality and strain:

> Then imitate the action of the tiger;
> Stiffen the sinews, summon up the blood,
> Disguise fair nature with hard-favour'd rage;
> Then lend the eye a terrible aspect;
> Let it pry through the portage of the head
> Like the brass cannon; let the brow o'erwhelm it
> As fearfully as doth a galled rock

> O'erhang and jutty his confounded base,
> Swill'd with the wild and wasteful ocean.
> Now set the teeth and stretch the nostril wide,
> Hold hard the breath and bend up every spirit
> To his full height.   (III. i. 6)

There is about this incitation something forced, incongruous, even (if we may risk taking the point a little too far) slightly absurd. The action of the warrior is an imitation, and an imitation of a wild beast at that, carried out by a deliberate exclusion of 'fair nature'. The blood is to be summoned up, the sinews stiffened to the necessary degree of artificial savagery, while the involved rhetorical comparisons which follow the references to the 'brass cannon' and the 'galled rock' strengthen the impression of something very like unreality. In stressing this note of inhumanity, the speech does not intend to deny the poetry of war which, as we have just seen, Shakespeare expresses most fully in certain passages from the various prologues of this play; but, as later in *Coriolanus*, he balances the conception of the warrior in his triumphant energy as 'a greyhound straining at the leash' against that, not less forcible, of a ruthless and inhuman engine of destruction. Both ruthlessness and splendour are inseparable aspects of the complete picture.

Henry's treatment of the governor and citizens of Harfleur relates this conception of the warrior to tensions already apparent in his own character. Not for the first time, two scenes are placed together to point a contrast. The way in which he presents his ultimatum is full of that sense of conflict between control and passion that was so prominent in his early utterances. The grotesque inhumanity implicit in his words is balanced by a suggestion of tragic destiny. Beneath his callousness is a sense that the horrors of war, once unleashed, freed from the sternest control, are irresistible. His soldiers, he warns the governor, are still held uneasily in check. 'The cool and temperate wind of grace', whose control over passion is the mark of a Christian soldier, still exercises its authority; but 'licentious wickedness' and 'the filthy and contagious clouds' of '*heady* murder' threaten to break out at any moment. In his catalogue of the horrors of war stress is laid upon rape and the crimes of 'blood'. The 'fresh-fair' virgins of Harfleur will become the victims of the soldiery, whose destructive atrocities are significantly referred to in terms of 'liberty':

> What rein can hold licentious wickedness
> When down the hill he holds his fierce career?   (III. iii. 22)

The process of evil, once unleashed, follows courses fatally determined;

but Henry, having described them in words which emphasize his awareness of their horror, ends by disclaiming all responsibility for them, just as he had once disclaimed all responsibility for the outbreak of the war. The whole matter, thus taken out of his hands, becomes indifferent to him:

> What is't to me, *when you yourselves are cause,*
> If your pure maidens fall into the hand
> Of hot and forcing violation?   (III. iii. 19)

Yet this very assertion of indifference carries with it, at bottom, a sense of the tragedy of the royal position. Only this denial of responsibility, it would seem, only the exclusion of humanity and the acceptance of a complete dualism between controlling 'grace' and the promptings of irresponsible passion, make possible that success in war which is, for the purposes of this play, the crown of kingship.

For it would certainly be wrong to suppose that Shakespeare, in portraying Henry, intends to stress a note of hypocrisy. His purpose is rather to bring out the burden of royalty, to point to certain contradictions, human and moral, which seem to be inherent in the notion of a successful King. As the play proceeds, Henry seems at times to be, at least in a moral sense, almost the victim of his position. The treasonable activities of Cambridge, Grey, and Scroop are indications of the duplicity with which monarchs are fated by their position to deal. Somewhere at the heart of this court there is a fundamental flaw which must constantly be allowed for by a successful ruler. It appears to Henry, in his dealings with the conspirators, as something deep-rooted enough to be associated with the original fall of man:

> seem they religious?
> Why, so didst thou: or are they spare in diet,
> Free from gross passion or of mirth or anger,
> Constant in spirit, not swerving with the blood,
> Garnish'd and deck'd in modest complement,
> Not working with the eye without the ear,
> And but in purged judgement trusting neither?
> Such and so finely bolted didst thou seem:
> And thus thy fall hath left a kind of blot,
> To mark the full-fraught man and best indued
> With some suspicion. I will weep for thee;
> For this revolt of thine, methinks, is like
> Another fall of man.   (II. ii. 130)

It is remarkable that Henry, in meditating upon this betrayal, should return once more to that theme of control, of freedom from passion, which is so prominent in his own nature. By concentrating on the functioning of the body, and on the sense of mutual divergence between eye, ear, and judgement in the difficult balance of the personality, the speech sets spiritual control in contrast with a sense of anarchy that proceeds, most typically, from the contemplation of physical processes. '*Gross* passion'—the adjective is significant—is associated with the irrational 'swerving of the blood', and the judgement which controls it needs to be 'purged' by fasting ('spare in diet') before it can attain a scarcely human freedom from 'mirth or anger'. By thus emphasizing the difficult and even unnatural nature of such control, the speech casts a shadow, at least by implication, over that of Henry himself; but it is also seen to be necessary, inseparable from his office. The administration of justice, upon which depends order within the kingdom and success in its foreign wars, demands in the monarch a detachment which borders on the inhuman. The state must be purged of 'treason lurking in its way' before it can be led, with that single-mindedness of purpose which is both Henry's strength and perhaps, in the long run, his limitation, to the victorious enterprise in France.

It is clear, indeed, that *Henry V* represents, however tentatively, a step in the realization of themes fully developed in the tragedies. Inheriting from his sources the conception of a victorious King, perfectly aware of his responsibilities and religiously devoted to the idea of duty, Shakespeare seems, in the most individual scenes of his play, to emphasize the difficulties of the conception, the obstacles, both personal and political, which lie between it and fulfilment. These difficulties, however, never amount to a questioning of the royal judgement. Even in the disguised Henry's debate with Williams and Bates on the morning of Agincourt (IV. i), where the implications of his power are most searchingly discussed, the King's right to command obedience is never in question. For Bates the duty of a subject lies in loyal execution of the royal will, and the responsibility for wrong action rests beyond the simple soldier with the King: 'we know enough, if we know we are the king's subjects'. Nor does Williams, though more sceptical in his attitude, question the postulate that the subject is bound to obey; for to disobey, as he put it, 'were against all property of subjection', and the emphasis is still upon the 'proportion' to be observed between King and subject, directing head and executing body, and upon the proper submission which the successful prosecution of the military effort requires.

Henry, of course, accepts this view of his position; but although the

questionings of his followers do not—and cannot—lead him to doubt
his own authority, they do force him to reflect deeply upon the weaknesses which even kings cannot overcome. 'The king is but a man as I
am; the violet smells to him as it doth to me; . . . all his senses have but
human conditions; his ceremonies laid by, in his nakedness he appears
but a man; and though his affections are higher mounted than ours, yet
when they stoop they stoop with the like wing' (IV. i. 106). There is
about the argument a universality which transcends the royal situation.
Men, differentiated by vain 'ceremony', are united in their common
'nakedness', and the most notable feature of human behaviour seems to
the speaker to be its domination by impulse, its helplessness before the
stooping of the affections.[38] In this respect the King is one with his men;
and just because he is so like them, because his senses too 'have but
human conditions' and are constantly liable to break through the guard
of rigid self-control imposed upon him by his vocation, there is something precarious, potentially disproportionate in his absolute claim upon
the allegiance of his followers.

The royal isolation is further underlined by Williams when he points
out the spiritual consequences of a conflict for which the King has
accepted full responsibility: 'For how can they [Henry's soldiers]
charitably dispose of anything when blood is their argument? Now, if
these men do not die well, it will be a black matter for the king that led
them to it' (IV. i. 150). These words repeat once more, but with a
greater urgency, a preoccupation with the horrors of war which Henry
has already expressed, even if he succeeded in shaking off responsibility
for them, to the French envoys and the governor of Harfleur. They
imply, beyond the sense of responsibility which derives from the
traditional conception of monarchy, a contrast—already familiar—
between the Christian law of 'charity' and the impulse to destruction
that threatens it in the necessary acts of war with the consequences of
unlimited brutality. The connection between this conflict of flesh and
spirit and the tendency of human societies, states and families alike, to
dissolve by the questioning of 'degree' into anarchy is not established
in this play as it is in the tragedies which followed. But Hamlet himself
might have reflected like Henry on the precarious basis of human
pretensions, and Angelo defined in similar terms the catastrophic
realization of it brought about by his encounter with Isabella. Had
Henry once followed his line of speculation far enough to doubt the
validity of his motives for action, or—on the other hand—had he given
free play to the sinister impulses dimly recognized in himself, he would

of course have been the protagonist of another and quite different play;
but the possibilities are there as a premonition, a first indication of issues
brought fully to light in later actions.

For the moment, Henry counters the implications of this argument
by pointing out that soldiers 'purpose not their death, when they
purpose their services'. Williams' sombre reflections, however, impose
themselves upon him, attach themselves to his own meditations, and
are profoundly echoed in his own words. Connecting war with sin, he
repeats the tone of earlier statements: 'Besides, there is no king, be his
cause never so spotless, if it come to the arbitrement of swords, can try
it out with all unspotted soldiers: some peradventure have on them the
guilt of premeditated and contrived murder; some, of beguiling
virgins with the broken seals of perjury' (IV. i. 169). The result is, in
part, a fresh emphasis on meticulous self-examination as a means of
conserving spiritual health—'Therefore should every soldier in the
wars do as every sick man in his bed, wash every mote out of his
conscience'—and, in the verse soliloquy which closes the scene, one of
those outbursts of nostalgic craving for release which have appeared
already, in his father's mouth, in *Henry IV, Part II*, and which will be
reflected with a new, more *physical* apprehension of existence, in
Hamlet's soliloquies and in the Duke's incitations to Claudio in *Measure
for Measure*:

> what infinite heart's ease
> Must kings neglect, that private men enjoy!   (IV. i. 256)

The craving for 'heart's ease' in this long speech is still, generally
speaking, what it is in *Henry IV*: a desire to be freed from the burden of
an office in which human purposes seem fatally divorced from human
achievement. The development of the verse is still painstaking, leisurely
in the expansion of its long periods, and a little rhetorical; but there are
moments which foreshadow the association in *Hamlet* of this nostalgia
with a desire to be free from the encumbrances, the 'fardels',[39] the
'things rank and gross in nature'[40] by which the flesh persistently seems
to obstruct the workings of the spirit. 'Greatness' is a 'fiery fever'
which consumes its royal victim like a bodily disease, and the contrasted peace of the humble subject is described with a curious ambiguity of tone:

> Not all these, laid in bed majestical,
> Can sleep so soundly as the wretched slave,
> Who with a body fill'd and vacant mind
> Gets him to rest, cramm'd with distressful bread.   (IV. i. 287)

In the association of peace with bodily fulness and vacancy of mind, in the impression, harshly and directly physical, behind 'fill'd' and 'cramm'd', there is a distinct suggestion of certain descriptions of satiated, idle contentment in plays as far apart as *Troilus and Cressida* and *Coriolanus*. Here already such imagery represents a kind of residue, intractable and irreducible, in direct contrast to the King's increasing emphasis on the need for spiritual discipline. It is no more than a suggestion, unabsorbed as yet into the main imaginative design of a play conceived on different, simpler lines; but, tentative as it is, it stands in a certain relationship to the clash of flesh and spirit—'passion' and 'grace'—which exacts continual vigilance from Henry and which is slowly moving through these developments of imagery to more open realization.

A similar potential cleavage can be detected in the treatment of the two sides drawn up for battle at Agincourt. Shakespeare differentiates between the French and English forces in a way which sometimes seems to foreshadow the balance held in *Troilus and Cressida* between Greeks and Trojans, though it is true that the unfavourable estimate of the English, which is scarcely compatible with the spirit of the play, is expressed only in the words of their enemies. The English are morally worthy of their victory, but the French account does go a little way to anticipate the possibility of criticism. The French, combining a touch of the unsubstantial chivalry of Troilus with a more than Trojan emptiness, are, like the Trojans, and more justly, defeated; the English, whom they represent as gross and dull-witted, are as undeniably successful as the Greeks. Shakespeare's handling of the battle carries on this conception. The French, trusting in a thin and rhetorical belief in their own aristocracy, rush hastily and incompetently to their deaths; the English, deriving their spirit from their King, win the day by their perseverance and self-control. Self-control, however, which is—as in Henry himself—not without some suggestion of harshness and inhumanity. Henry's righteousness does not prevent him from inflicting merciless reprisals on his prisoners, and, though these matters need to be looked at in the spirit of the times, and the play is careful to emphasize the base act of treachery which rouses Henry to righteous anger, there is something finally sardonic about Gower's comment that 'the king, *most worthily*, hath caused every soldier to cut his prisoner's throat. O, 'tis *a gallant king*' (IV. vii. 9). By such excellence, Shakespeare would seem to say, must even the most just and patriotic of wars be won.

There is, indeed, a good deal of throat-cutting in this play. The

King's ruthlessness, a logical consequence of his efficiency, needs to be seen against the human background which Shakespeare provided for it, most noticeably in the comic scenes which turn on the behaviour of the common soldiery. There is little room in *Henry V* for the more expansive notes of comedy. Shakespeare's delineation of character is, indeed, as clear-cut as ever, and his dialogue abundantly if discreetly flavoured with the sense of humanity; but there is about the humour of these scenes a certain desiccated flatness that contrasts sharply with the exuberance of earlier plays. Bardolph, Pistol, and the others, no longer enlivened by contact with Falstaff, quarrel like curs and—where occasion presents itself—steal like the creatures of rapine that they are; and their jokes turn largely upon the bawdy houses which will swallow them up on their return to England, and upon the cutting of throats. 'Men may sleep and they may have their throats about them at that time; and some say knives have edges' (II. i. 23). Nym's remark, itself dark and enigmatic, is prefaced by a sombre, fatalistic 'things must be as they may', which modifies the comic sententiousness of the speaker and implies a certain resigned acceptance of the ordering of life.

The humorous conception of the characters, in short, is toned down to fit in with a spirit no longer essentially humorous; and this applies not only to Nym but to his companions in arms. Fluellen and Gower, Williams and Bates are distinguished, not by comic vitality or by the penetration of their comments on men and events, but by their qualities of common-sense and by an attitude of tough loyalty and dedication to the work in hand; and it is by their devotion to the strictly practical virtues and by their definition of their various national idiosyncrasies that they live. The best of these comic episodes is contained in Fluellen's expression of devotion to his King after the great victory has been won: 'I will confess it to all the 'orld: I need not to be ashamed of your majesty, praised be God, *so long as your majesty is an honest man*' (IV. vii. 118). Should we need a word to describe the best positive values of this play, that which distinguishes it from mere patriotic rhetoric on the one side and sardonic pessimism on the other (and both moods are constituent parts of it), it would be the word 'honest' as here used; honesty which can offer loyalty whilst maintaining independence of judgement, and which is brought out, as much as the cruelty which balances it, by the sombre circumstances of war which no merely patriotic show of rhetoric or romantic comradeship in death can conceal. These soldiers, revering the necessary form of monarchy, can yet see in it the reflection of their common humanity. It is this reflection,

by which they are ennobled, which has brought them to victory over
enemies for whom 'common' humanity is no object of reverence or
understanding. If this understanding points eventually to an intuition
increasingly tragic in its implications, it is also related to the patriotic
purposes which equally prevail in this play.

It is by his possession to an eminent degree of precisely this kind of
virtue that Henry finally affirms himself as a King. His essentially
'political' wooing of Katherine of France at the end of the play most
nearly approaches true emotion when, in his characteristic, direct prose,
he contrasts the passing nature of man's decorative virtues with the
constancy of a 'good heart':

> a speaker is but a prater; a rhyme is but a ballad. A good leg will fall; a
> straight back will stoop; a black beard will turn white; a curled pate will
> grow bald; a fair face will wither; a full eye will wax hollow; but a good
> heart, Kate, is the sun and the moon; or rather the sun and not the moon; for
> it shines bright and never changes, but keeps his course truly. (V. ii. 165)

This, at least, belongs rather to Henry's virtues than to the political
arrangements being proposed. The same virtues enabled him, in the
morning of Agincourt, to unite his followers in the true fellowship of
'a band of brothers'. They are, indeed, no mean virtues, but they are
necessarily dedicated in this play to the public, the political sphere, and
in a world which is no longer—for better or worse—that of *Henry IV,
Part I*. Falstaff himself, out of place in this world, is remembered in his
death, serving as a kind of measure by contrast with which Shakespeare
emphasizes what seems to be a changing vision of humanity. This
death—it is worth noting—is ascribed directly to the King, who has
'killed his heart'; and Nym, repeating that phrase of resignation which
conveys so much more than he realizes of the spirit of this new world,
relates Henry's treatment of him to an obscure, inherent fatality: 'The
king is a good king; but *it must be as it may*; he passes some humours and
careers' (II. i. 131). His companions who remain must now accommodate themselves to the times. They do so by abandoning domestic
crime to follow their King to France. War and its prospects of plunder
are for them no more and no less than a means of livelihood and an
alternative to preying upon one another. As Bardolph puts it: 'We
must to France together; why the devil should we keep knives to cut
one another's throats?' (II. i. 94). The end of their adventure—after the
stern episode of Bardolph's hanging for sacrilege—is contained in
Pistol's final speech, revealing the death of Nell, 'of malady of France'
(V. i), and his own anticipation of his future:

> Old do I wax; and from my weary limbs
> Honour is cudgelled. Well, bawd I'll turn,
> And something lean to cutpurse of quick hand.
> To England will I steal, and there I'll steal:
> And patches will I get unto these cudgell'd scars,
> And swear I got them in the Gallia wars.   (V. i. 89)

For Pistol is the last and least worthy survivor of another world, and his anticipated future and the King's plain and dispassionate honesty each looks forward, in its own way, to a very different one to come.

It is indeed significant, in making a final estimate of this play, that the account in it of the death of Falstaff is, by common consent, the most human and deeply felt thing in the entire story. In an action where the touchstone of conduct is success, and in which humanity has to accommodate itself to the claims of expediency, there is no place for Falstaff. Shakespeare had already recognized this, and prepared us for the necessary changes, when he accepted the logic of the 'rejection' scene and of the events leading up to it; and now his end affects us tragically as the last glimpse of another and, in part, a less sombre world. No doubt there is a patriotic purpose, not irrelevant to the play, and no doubt Shakespeare conceived his successful monarch with that purpose in mind. One aim does not, in Shakespeare, necessarily exclude another; and the fact remains that as we consider the uncompromising study of achieved and just success which rounds off this trilogy, a certain coldness takes possession of us as it took possession, step by step, of the limbs of the dying Falstaff. We too, in reaching the end of this sobre, balanced presentation of public virtue, find ourselves in our own way 'babbling of green fields'.[41]

4 The Merry Wives of Windsor

It will hardly be necessary to deal at any length with *The Merry Wives of Windsor*. To say this is not to deny the piece its characteristic virtues. The comic intrigue, leading to the exposure of a jealous husband and frustrating the short-sighted matchmaking of a pair of parents, is skilfully handled and conveys a lively sense of the middle-class scene; the action works out effectively enough on the stage and there is no reason why we should belittle or deny the achievement which this represents. The previous series of historical plays, however, having introduced us to Falstaff, makes it inevitable that we should look first to him in any play in which he appears; and the fact is, quite simply, that the Falstaff of *The Merry Wives* strikes us as making what we can only call a posthumous appearance, seems to represent no more than the half-hearted revival of a character originally conceived in a very different spirit.

It might seem sufficient to leave the matter thus, were it not that certain incidents—and more particularly the conclusion of the play— are there to leave an impression which is, in the last analysis, rather different. Falstaff bundled into the basket of dirty clothes and thrown into the Thames, or Falstaff dressed up to evade discovery as Mrs. Ford's 'maid's aunt, the fat woman of Brentford' (IV. i) and soundly beaten in his disguise, we can accept as a creation which, although it has little or nothing to do with the Sir John we have known, exists farci- cally in its own right; but Falstaff in the guise of a 'woodman', making his appeal to the 'hot-blooded gods' of antiquity and excusing himself in the name of the frailties committed by these same gods—'When gods have hot backs, what shall poor men do?'—is, to some extent at least, another matter. The scene under the oak in Windsor Park seems to answer, beneath its obvious farcical content, to an exorcizing process, represents the final projection of 'riot' and 'misrule' into a form of monstrous and presumptuous fleshliness which is to be cast out, expelled through the words of incantation uttered over his supine form by the 'fairies' in disguise:

> Fie on sinful fantasy!
> Fie on lust and luxury!
> Lust is but a bloody fire,
> Kindled with unchaste desire,
> Fed in heart, whose flames aspire
> As thoughts do blow them, higher and higher.   (V. v. 99)

The song is uttered over a Falstaff stripped of all his attributes of comic energy, left with only the monstrosity of his fleshly appetites, and, as such, ready for expulsion from the life of society; and it concludes, significantly, in what are, still beneath their obvious farcical connota- tion, in effect ritual words of expulsion:

> Pinch him, fairies, mutually:
> Pinch him for his villainy:
> Pinch him, and burn him, and turn him about,
> Till candles and starlight and moonshine be out.   (V. v. 105)

The words, in their mixture of nonsense and incantation, read very like the confused memories of a rite of purification. As such they link Falstaff, even in his new fallen state and in the exclusion which is decreed over him 'mutually', in the name of society, to a kind of life deeper, more profoundly related to immemorial instincts and ancestral memories, than any to which the main comic action would seem to lead us: a life which may make the play itself more adequate, as the last appearance of this great comic creation, than the general tone of the rest of the action would in itself justify.

VIII
THE GREAT COMEDIES

RELATIVELY LITTLE that really illuminates has been written upon Shakespeare's comedies. This is perhaps due in part to the presence in them of an important element of convention, which has to be mastered before the human content of the plays, their relation to normal experience, can begin to make itself felt. A similar element no doubt exists also in the tragedies and the historical plays, but in these the universal significance of the dramatic action asserts itself more obviously and directly. Othello, Lear—and, we might add, Henry V—are recognizable human beings, facing predicaments and challenges which may be on a different scale from those familiar in ordinary life but to which, none the less, we can readily respond. In Shakespeare's comedies, however, a content not finally dissimilar in kind is canalized into conventional forms. Artificial situations, contrived marriages, elaborate happy endings, all set in countries of the imagination, frequently act, even while they exercise their magic upon us, as impediments to full and direct participation in the dramatist's intention: impediments which, without doubt, it is well worth overcoming, but which call for a special effort, a particular kind of attention, before the necessary fullness of response can be achieved.

That the effort *is* worth making is not seriously open to question. At approximately the same time as he embarked, in his second great series of plays on English history, on an extended exploration of the implications, personal and public alike, of political behaviour, Shakespeare chose to develop his own concept of comedy, already approached in earlier plays, to reflect other aspects, not finally less serious or compelling, of human behaviour. In *Much Ado about Nothing*, he allowed his mind and imagination to play, with unique wit and brilliance, upon the validity and the limitations of love in a brittle and scintillating society. In *As You Like It*, he followed this remarkable success by a greater, involving the creation of an entire comic world which reflected, beneath the deliberate conventionality and artifice of its forms, some of his deepest and most personal intuitions concerning the nature of human life; and finally, in *Twelfth Night*, these same intuitions found projection in one of the most consistent, as well as the most intangibly elusive, of all his creations. Nothing that he was later to write—not even *Hamlet*, *King Lear*, or *Antony and Cleopatra*—can diminish the value of these successive triumphs, or prevent us from seeing them as what they are, the most individual—in some sense the most harmoniously finished—of all his earlier achievements.

1 Much Ado about Nothing

Much Ado about Nothing is not, perhaps, one of the most immediately attractive or satisfying of Shakespeare's comedies. None, indeed, contains more moments of striking verbal brilliance, or carries on with greater assurance the game of polished and slightly heartless repartee which often seems to constitute the main business of life in Messina. To pass, however, from an appreciation of these epigrammatic felicities to more direct consideration of the persons who utter them and the situations which inspire them may be to risk a certain disenchantment. It is easy enough to respond to the vivacity of some of the characters and situations and one can be tempted to concentrate on the exchanges of wit between Beatrice and Benedick to the exclusion of practically everything else in the play, finding Hero by comparison the most colourless of heroines and Claudio positively unattractive. To lay emphasis in this way upon the obvious brilliance of certain parts is, however, to do less than justice to a play which its author undoubtedly conceived as a coherent and indivisible whole. *Much Ado* is, above all, a highly formal comedy working through strict conventions and a progressive interplay of situations which are revealed in their true nature through mutual contrast and which, in the process of this revelation, illuminate various facets of truth and illusion in the central reality of love.

The starting point of the action is the return of a group of courtiers from the wars. In these, 'a young Florentine called Claudio' has—we are told—borne himself 'beyond the promise of his age' to 'better expectation' (I. i. 14). The play, however, sets out to show Claudio under a different aspect as he declares his love for Hero, the daughter of the governor of Messina, a girl whom he confesses that he has scarcely had occasion to see but whose outward appearance strikes him—to use his own words—as a 'jewel' of great price to force the idea of marriage upon him. The nature of this love, however, is expressed rather by omission than through any sign of positive emotion. Hero must be the least articulate of all Shakespeare's heroines; and Claudio, when he is left alone with Don Pedro, declares himself in a way which suggests that his newly discovered feeling for her rests on a very slender foundation of knowledge. 'I looked upon her', he says, referring back to his recent past,

> with a soldier's eye,
> That liked, but had a rougher task in hand
> Than to drive liking to the name of love:
> But now I am return'd and that war-thoughts
> Have left their places vacant, in their rooms
> Come thronging soft and delicate desires,
> All prompting me how fair young Hero is,
> Saying, I liked her ere I went to wars.   (I. i. 308)

The tone of this is lukewarm enough to suggest that Claudio's newly found 'soft and delicate desires', the conclusion that he formerly 'liked' Hero but has only now had time to give the matter serious thought, are signs of his unpreparedness to offer the object of these 'desires' anything like the deliberate and conscious gift of self in which true love consists. That he himself feels a lack of confidence in his own capacity to love is indicated, indeed, by the fact that he has just begged Don Pedro, in an oddly tentative manner—'My liege, your highness now may do me good'—to take up his cause with Hero; and his diffidence is matched in turn by the older and more experienced man's perhaps over-confident readiness to serve his turn.

Side by side with this gauche and diffident pair, she almost entirely tongue-tied, he alternately diffident and inclined to set too high a worth upon his own feelings, the opening of the play offers us two other characters—Beatrice and Benedick—who seem to be only agreed in believing that they are indifferent to one another and have seen through love itself as an illusion. It is in this conviction that Benedick comments, with partial truth, on Claudio's new feelings towards Hero. When Claudio, seeking support for his own precarious decision, asks him 'Can the world buy such a jewel?', Benedick replies: 'Yea, and a case to put it into'; and when he goes on to say: 'In mine eye she is the sweetest lady that ever I looked on', Benedick's retort is a confident assertion of his own realism: 'I can see yet without spectacles, and I see no such matter' (I. i. 198). This deliberate deflation of the excesses of romantic love is, of course, amply familiar to us from earlier plays, and there is no reason why we should not allow it a due measure of validity in this case. We should, however, also by now know enough of the spirit of Shakespearean comedy to refrain from taking Benedick's confident attitude simply at its face value. Once more we are being offered different views of the same reality as seen through the deceptive medium of individual eyes; views which we might call respectively romantic and realistic, in whose clash and interrelation lies a great part of the substance of the play. Even without foreseeing the eventual outcome we may be certain that the truth will lie neither with Claudio's halting assertion of his attraction for Hero nor with the bold and self-confident denial of its validity which his critic rashly sets up in opposition to it.

It should be noted, as a first step in penetrating the true complexity of the offered pattern, that Benedick's assertiveness is from the first itself subjected to the criticism of Beatrice who, before he has spoken to Claudio or even appeared on the stage, has already referred slightingly to the quality of Benedick's wit. 'In our last conflict four of his five wits went halting off, and now is the whole man governed with one: so that if he have wit enough to keep himself warm, let him bear it for a difference between himself and his horse; for it is all the wealth that he hath left, to be known a reasonable creature' (I. i. 66). The intention of placing the pretensions of merely verbal wit in its relation to truly rational and human attitudes is clear enough and answers to an important aspect of the play. Nor is this, in turn, the last word about this relationship of seeming contraries; for it is to be noted that Beatrice, even as she expresses her contempt for Benedick, is presented as anxious to have news of him, whilst Benedick, in the very act of responding to general expectation by making his own depreciating remarks about Beatrice, pays a kind of left-handed tribute to her beauty; 'there's her cousin', he says, 'an she were not possessed with a fury, exceeds her'—that is, Hero—'as much in beauty as the first of May doth the last of December' (I. i. 199). Each in effect expresses with the scintillating verbal brilliance which is available to them in such abundant measure, and which constitutes at once their attraction and their final limitation, an attitude to the other which ministers to their respective self-conceits but which is in reality founded on something less than a true understanding of their real needs and motives.

In this way, the pattern of contrasted opinions which is to dominate the coming action is already set forth in the opening scene. We are to see whether Claudio's romantically superficial view of his new love can stand the test of exposure to reality, and at the same time whether those who so articulately and confidently defend themselves from love by asserting loudly and insistently their superiority to its compulsions can in fact maintain their declared confidence. A brief exchange between Claudio, Don Pedro, and Benedick states the future pattern in its plainest terms as they declare their respective attitudes to Hero:

CLAUD.:   That I love her, *I feel*.
D. PEDRO: That she is worthy, *I know*.
BENE.:   That I neither *feel* how she should be loved, nor *know* how she
           should be worthy, is the *opinion* that fire cannot melt out of me.
           (I. i. 238)

Each speaker's choice of words is designed to bring out the foundations of his own position and, with it, its partiality. Claudio 'feels' that Hero is worthy of his love, resting his newly acquired belief upon mere unsupported sentiment which events will prove to be powerless in the face of apparent, if perverse, reason. Don Pedro, in whom the voice of experience speaks with appropriate assurance, 'knows' upon good grounds that she is worthy of the devotion offered her, and acts perhaps with a slightly too easy confidence as a result of this rational conviction; but Benedick, strong only in the appearance of reason to support what is in fact nothing better than his own 'opinion', based on the plain incapacity, where matters of love are concerned, either to sympathize or to understand (to 'feel' or to 'know'), *thinks* that he knows that both are wrong. There, in a few words is the design of contrasted attitudes and prejudices which reflect, in the last instance, self-centred and self-justifying needs and which this comedy will be concerned to bring to a formal and harmonious conclusion.

The impulse required to set the entire intrigue in motion is provided, from outside, by the malevolence of Don John. To take this personage realistically, or to seek to provide him with adequate motivation for his behaviour, is to misunderstand the spirit which prevails in this comedy. Don John represents, in relation to the rest, the dash of bitterness required to bring out the elements of contradiction and fictitiousness which prevail in those around him. As the play opens, he has been forcibly reconciled, after undergoing a defeat which he continues to resent, to his legitimate brother Don Pedro: but the sting of bastardy remains strongly implanted in him and, after having initially declared himself as a man 'not of many words', a taciturn exception in a supremely articulate society, he soon goes on to declare his true motives in terms which closely echo the terminology of certain of the Sonnets:

> I had rather be a *canker* in a hedge than a *rose* in his grace; and it better fits my *blood* to be disdained of all than to fashion a carriage to rob love from any: in this, though I cannot be said to be a flattering honest man, it must not be denied but I am a plain-dealing villain. . . . If I had my mouth I would bite; if I had my liberty, I would do my liking: in the meantime let me be that I am, and seek not to alter me. (I. iii. 27)

The presence in this self-revelation of a number of elements common to other and more developed Shakespearean villains need not induce us to go beyond seeing in Don John the essentially flat, finally impersonal creation that he is. His attitudes are those of self-sufficiency and consciously willed isolation that constantly accompany evil in the plays; but it is not in this case required that they should reveal themselves through individual or realistic motivation. It is enough that Don John, in a spirit of envious self-sufficiency which covers his own conviction of essential inferiority, should declare through his initial self-revelation his purpose of twisting love to his own ends of defeated and embittered resentment. He is to be the 'canker', passionately inspired by his sense of social exclusion to destroy the 'rose' of natural love and normal sociability[1]; but, since this is a comedy and accordingly dedicated by definition to a harmonizing conclusion, the end of his intrigues can only be to bring out more deeply the true nature of love and to obtain, as the contrary of everything that he has desired, its consummation in personal union and social harmony. Meanwhile, and until the time comes for his designs to be unmasked, it is enough to see that the news of an intended marriage presents itself to him as an occasion 'to build mischief on', and that the decision of the brother whom he hates to woo Hero on behalf of Claudio becomes—for his perverted vision— possible 'food' to nourish his resentment.

The various relationships thus presented in the opening scenes of the action tend, according to the purpose which prevails in this comedy, to be brought together in a formal dance of balanced relationships. The true nature of this dance will not be apparent until the end of the play, when the chief actors in its development will at last be brought into a true and fruitful relationship with one another; meanwhile, the intervening state of intrigue and confusion is fittingly symbolized (II. i) in the form of a masked gathering and through the ill-assorted partnerships to which it gives rise. Before the beginning of the dance in which

it is to culminate Beatrice sums up the 'tart' character of Don John—
'I never can see him but I am heart-burned an hour after'—even as she
confirms, to her own subsequent discomfiture, her obstinate determination to avoid marriage 'till God make man of some other metal
than earth' (II. i. 63). The proviso is, of course, an unrealistic one in so
far as it is precisely to the 'earthiness' of their natures that men and
women owe their impulse to submit themselves to one another, and to
reality, in marriage. In so far as she is declaring her superiority to this
universal human condition Beatrice is taking her stand upon pride and
imperfect knowledge of herself and of life; but there is eloquence and a
true sense of reality in her pressing of her own argument: 'Would it
not grieve a woman to be overmastered with a piece of valiant dust? to
make an account of her life to a clod of wayward marl?' (II. i. 64). We
may feel at this point that the speaker is responding to the realities of the
human situation more seriously than she can yet know; more seriously
certainly than when she goes on to impose upon the diffident Hero her
own arrogant view of marriage:

> wooing, wedding, and repenting, is as a Scotch jig, a measure, and a cinque
> pace: the first suit is hot and hasty, like a Scotch jig, and full as fantastical; the
> wedding, mannerly-modest, as a measure full of state and ancientry: and then
> comes repentance, and, with his bad legs, falls into the cinque pace faster and
> faster, till he sinks into his grave. (II. i. 77)

As a principal vehicle of the comic spirit Beatrice at this point stresses
the incongruity which forms part of the spirit of love. By so doing, she
contributes an essential element to the complete effect; but she is also
indulging, through her unmatched gift of verbal brilliance, her own
precarious sense of superiority to the universal condition of that 'piece
of valiant dust', that 'clod of wayward marl' which is, even more truly
than she knows, man, and the immediate reflection, in terms of action,
of what she has said is the series of misunderstandings and mistaken
identities which constitute the first of the two formal dances between
which the main action is situated.

The pattern of confused identities which it will be the concern of the
play to unravel is, indeed, brought to a head as the various partners
address themselves to one another beneath the protection which their
respective masks afford. Don Pedro approaches Hero with the intention
of wooing her, not for himself, but on behalf of Claudio. Baltasar
presents himself to Margaret, who rejects him, and Hero's gentle-
woman Ursula truly recognizes Don Antonio, who strenuously denies

his identity; and, finally, Beatrice herself recognizes Benedick beneath his mask, but pretends to fail to do so in order to make jest the more freely at his expense. Last of all, as a fitting pendant to these various cross-purposes, real and contrived, Don John recognizes the disguised Claudio, but pretends to believe that he is addressing himself to Benedick in order to poison the mind of his victim by insinuating that Don Pedro, whom Claudio has entrusted with the furthering of his cause with Hero, is in fact engaged in wooing her for himself. The fact that these insinuations and misapprehensions, advanced in each case under the cover of mistaken identities, are taken up to disproportionate and sometimes potentially tragic conclusions lends its characteristic tone of polished and enticing bitterness to the shifting fabric of hearsay and prejudice—'Much ado about nothing'—which constitutes the material of this comedy.

With Don John's insinuation, of course, these masked cross-purposes impinge upon the main action. Claudio, confirming his inexperience and his lack of faith in the depth and reality of his own love, shows himself at once ready to take them at their declared value. His failure to believe either in himself or in the declared object of his devotion is made evident in the compound of naivety and cynicism which his own words reflect:

> Friendship is constant in all other things
> Save in the office and affairs of love:
> Therefore all hearts in love use their own tongues;
> Let every eye negotiate for itself,
> And trust no agent; for beauty is a witch,
> Against whose charms faith melteth into blood.
> This is an accident of hourly proof,
> Which I mistrusted not.   (II. i. 184)

Claudio is here engaged in persuading himself of the truth of Don John's perverse axioms, which have become for him a matter of 'hourly proof'; the cynicism of inexperience, unsure of itself and seeking assurance at the cost of its own disillusionment, is fittingly moulded to the 'canker' of Don John's craving to belittle and destroy the realities from which it feels itself excluded. To add a further complication to this pattern of perverse 'seeming', moreover, Benedick at once confirms Claudio in his unnatural belief when, speaking out of his own allegedly greater experience of these matters, he assures his puzzled friend that 'the prince hath got your Hero', even as, reflecting on the undignified manner of his own recent treatment at the hands of

Beatrice, he expresses his resentment at 'her base though bitter disposition'. Having thus uncovered the real weakness behind Claudio's too facile assumptions, we are now further shown that Benedick, for all his stressed pride in his own shrewdness, is himself incapable of declaring the true nature of love.

Benedick's own position, and that of Beatrice in relation to him, is indeed revealed by a number of seemingly inconsequential touches to be less firmly founded than either would like to believe. As much is implied in the statement of his desire to avoid at all costs 'three words' conference with this harpy' (II. i. 281), and, equally, in Beatrice's finally rueful comment to Claudio on her own position with regard to marriage: 'Thus goes everyone to the world but I, and I am sun-burnt; I may sit in a corner, and cry heigh-ho for a husband!' (II. i. 332). Even before the plot to bring them together, and to make each recognize in the other a suitable match has been set afoot, the ground is carefully prepared for us to recognize that she would be 'an excellent wife for Benedick' and he in turn, in Don Pedro's phrase, 'not the unhopefullest husband that I know' (II. i. 395). The central part of the action, which follows naturally from the several misunderstandings of the masked dance, will turn appropriately on two contrasted intrigues: one of them a positive, match-making device designed to bring together a pair who only need to know themselves and one another better to recognize that they are in fact destined one for another, the second corresponding to the darker side of the comedy and concentrating on Don John's machinations against Claudio and Hero, projects recognized to be 'athwart' and to proceed from a mind that confesses itself to be 'sick' in its own 'displeasure' (II. ii. 5).

The first plot, concerning Beatrice and Benedick, achieves its ends without much difficulty. We know that the mind of each runs upon the other, although this reality has so far expressed itself characteristically in verbal repudiation. Just before he falls, Benedick invites retribution upon himself by passing an easy judgement upon Claudio for his simplicity: 'I do much wonder that one man, seeing how much another man is a fool when he dedicates his behaviours to love, will, after he has laughed at such shallow follies in others, become the argument of his own scorn' (II. iii. 7). This, in effect, is exactly what he himself proceeds to do. Already he insinuates that marriage might, under certain circumstances become a possibility for himself: 'till all graces be in one woman, one woman shall not come in my grace' (II. iii. 30). By saying as much as this, Benedick is in effect raising the question of the nature of love, which consists largely in the ability to create the perfection of its object; for it is precisely the image of such perfection that the lover, by the very fact of being in love, creates to his own satisfaction in the recipient of his devotion. It is not surprising, in view of this, that once the comedy that is to ensnare him has been acted out for his benefit, his first words are an acceptance of the deception that, in the last analysis, answers to his intimate desires. Benedick, like Beatrice when her turn comes shortly after, is intelligent enough to know that there is truth in the judgements that he has overheard concerning his own presumption and self-love; and so he is led, like her again and in spite of his usual brilliant, if limited, range of perception, to overlook the element of deception and enticement that is also there. 'This can be no trick'; the 'wise' bachelor is caught in his own appropriate trap as he confesses that it is his destiny to be 'horribly in love'. His surrender amounts to an acceptance of his own part in the universal human condition, a recognition of the falsity both of his publicly flaunted judgements of Beatrice and of the supposedly superior insight on which he has prided himself; as he goes on to say, in rueful self-defence:

> doth not the appetite alter? A man loves the meat in his youth that he cannot endure in his age. Shall quips and sentences and these paper bullets of the brain awe a man from the career of his humour? No, the world must be peopled. (II. iii. 258)

And so, he first reacts with an excessive and finally comic modesty against his former self-confidence—'I must not seem proud; happy are they that hear their detractions and can put them to mending'—and then, when the still unconverted Beatrice comes to invite him to dine with the rest of the company, is ready, lover-like, to read the most absurd and improbable meanings into her plain words.

Beatrice, however, is by now equally ready to fall into the trap which Hero, Margaret, and Ursula have set for her. The accusation which they prepare against her, and which she overhears, is the appropriate one of self-absorbtion:

> 　　　　　　　　her wit
> Values itself so highly, that to her
> All matter else seems weak: *she cannot love*,
> Nor take no shape nor project of affection,
> She is so *self-endeared*. (III. i. 52)

This is an apt definition of the barrier which Beatrice—once more like Benedick—has hitherto been so busy erecting against nature, and which is now shown to be—as we might have expected—powerless to stand out against reality. In answer to this accusation, Beatrice—like Katherine the Shrew, with whom she has some points of contact[2]— makes her appropriate and natural submission to the reality of love, when she says:

> Benedick, love on; I will requite thee,
> Taming my wild heart to thy loving hand;   (III. i. 111)

for it is clear by now that Beatrice, again like Benedick, knows the truth of love at the bottom of her heart and is ready to recognize it:

> For others say thou dost deserve, and I
> Believe it better than reportingly.   (III. i. 115)

Once more, answering to the spirit of this most deliberately formal of comedies, disguise and the appearance of deception become instruments to lead to the recognition of 'nature' and the manifestation of truth.

On his next appearance, indeed, Benedick shows all the traditional signs of a man in love. Whilst this thread in the intrigue is being drawn to its appropriate and positive conclusion, however, the other, darker side of the comedy cuts across the newborn harmony with Don John's false substantiation of his accusation against Hero. He too makes his appeal, after his own fashion, to the 'plain' evidence of the eyes; as he says to his brother and to Claudio:

> If you dare not trust that you see, confess not that you know: if you will follow me, I will show you enough; and when you have seen more, and heard more, proceed accordingly.   (III. ii. 123)

His appeal is in effect to false sight and false certainty, and the strength of his position lies in the fact that his victim, Claudio, is ready in his inexperience to take falsity for truth and to base his actions upon his illusory conviction. Claudio's reply to Don John's insinuations against Hero is, in effect, a statement of false determination: 'If I see anything to-night why I should not marry her to-morrow, in the congregation, where I should wed, there will I shame her' (III. ii. 127). The attitude is one which, on its very different level of intensity, recalls Othello's perverse demands for 'ocular proof' and the complacency with which he contemplates the appalling and unnecessary decision to which Iago has brought him: 'Good, the justice of it pleases'.[3] Claudio's determination reflects, of course, a different situation, proceeds from one who is, by comparison with Othello, hardly a 'character' at all; but the point is that his appearance of decision, which ministers finally to a certain naive self-esteem in himself, rests in fact upon the false evidence of the eyes, upon an inadequate conception of love, and, in the last analysis, upon his own inexperienced weakness.

It is at this point, however, even as Don John arranges for Borachio to impersonate a lover in incriminating posture at Hero's window, that a further turn is given to the comic screw, as the villains are overheard describing their device and attributing it to their master. By this development, the false and the cunning, whose vision of reality is perverted to answer to their own malevolence, place themselves unwittingly in the hands of those who show, beneath their confused use of words and concepts, a certain basic loyalty and soundness of response. The attitude which we are invited to adopt towards Dogberry and his watch is not, of course, a simple one. Their verbal errors can be regarded as a deliberate comic inversion of the dexterity so abundantly displayed by most of the principal actors in this comedy; if Dogberry is far from attaining the polished brilliance which comes so readily to such as Benedick, his misuse of words is equally prompted by self-conceit, by a foolish and ignorant determination to display in the hearing of others his own imagined superiority. Some of the errors, however, and more often those of his followers than of Dogberry himself, convey meanings more profound than the speakers themselves can know. The first words exchanged by the Watch are in this respect not without significance:

DOGBERRY: Are you good men and true?
VERGES: Yes, or else it were pity but they should suffer salvation, body and soul. (III. iii. 1)

The emphasis, beneath the comic confusion, is already upon essential goodness and truth, upon the capacity for 'salvation, body and soul'; and in a situation where the perversion of keen sight in the name of ends falsely reasonable is engaged in furthering division and hatred, these are the qualities which need to be invoked from beyond the limits of sophistication to enable the truth to be declared. We shall not forget that, in Love's Labour's Lost, it was Costard, himself not above confusing meanings, who pointed to some of the firmer realities of his play,[4] and that, in A Midsummer Night's Dream, Bottom was vouchsafed his moment of 'vision'[5] even as he assumed the ass's head which his relatively simple presumptions invited.

The revelation of truth through the mouths of the ignorant is not arrived at, indeed, without overcoming a fair share of comic obstacles.

The time needed for the truth to be overheard is only obtained through Dogberry's absurd instructions to the watch to refrain from doing their obvious duty by immediately arresting the delinquents[6]; and Dogberry himself, indeed, is so taken up with what he regards as his superior command of language, so full of a kind of self-esteem which naively reflects that shown, sometimes to more vicious effect, by his 'betters', that the final exposure of Don John's intrigue comes about almost too late and runs the risk of being impatiently brushed aside, in his haste to be elsewhere, by Leonato. Here, however, it is Leonato who is displaying short-sightedness, unwillingness to wait upon the truth which is always liable to emerge from the least likely quarters; for, if Dogberry's confusions are a part of the general effect of comic incongruity, it is not less so that it is in such hands and mouths as these that the truth is finally deposited. 'Asses' though they may appear in the eyes of the sophisticated, Dogberry and his fellows yet cling to reality as they understand it, and by so doing they finally become instrumental to saving all. In spite of the self-importance which could easily make of him an officious busy-body or petty tyrant—'I am a wise fellow . . . and, which is more, as pretty a piece of flesh as any is in Messina' (IV. ii. 85)—Dogberry and his fellows are seen to be instruments of truth; the contrasted facets of appearance and fact, pretension and reality, which answer to the comic method of this play are nowhere more tellingly exemplified.

Before this revelation can take place, however, the action shifts back to its more sombre plane as Claudio and Hero meet in church for the expected celebration of their marriage. Hero has approached this moment in a typical state of apprehension. 'My heart is exceedingly heavy' (III. iv. 24), she confesses; and Beatrice in turn has given this mood a comic reflection in her own transformed state by confessing herself as in 'the sick tune' for her new love, and as being 'exceedingly ill' for a husband. In her case, however, it is the laws of life, of normal humanity, that are asserting themselves, as we may gather from the tone and content of Margaret's jesting observation:

> I cannot think . . . that you are in love, . . . or that you can be in love. But Benedick was such another, and now is he become a man; he swore he would never marry; and yet now, in despite of his heart, he eats his meat without grudging: and how you may be converted I know not; but methinks you look with your eyes as other women do. (III. iv. 83)

Against the perverse declaration of their respective inclinations, Beatrice and Benedick have in fact accepted their true natures as 'woman' and 'man' respectively; there could be no better foil to the confused tale of wilfulness, misunderstanding, and malevolence that we are now to witness.

The marriage ceremony, to which all this has been leading, is in many respects the centre of the entire pattern of the play's various 'seemings'. Offered Hero, 'this rich and precious gift', in marriage, Claudio rejects her as 'this rotten orange', making perverse appeal to what he holds to be the difference between reality and appearance:

> O, what authority and show of truth
> Can cunning sin cover itself withal!
> Comes not that blood as modest evidence
> To witness simple virtue? Would you not swear,
> All you that see her, that she were a maid,
> By these exterior shows? But she is none:
> She knows the heat of a luxurious bed;
> Her blush is guiltiness, not modesty.   (IV. i. 35)

The language at this point, and in much of what follows, notably out-strips comic convention in a way that may reasonably remind us of Shakespeare's 'problem' comedies. 'Cunning sin' covers itself, to the confusion of the simple, with the 'authority and *show* of truth', and the blush on the cheeks of the accused comes as evidence falsely 'modest' to counterfeit '*simple* virtue'. Obsessive concentration upon his own imaginings—'the heat of a luxurious bed'—impels Claudio to reply to Hero's bewildered defence of her virtue—'*seem'd* I ever otherwise to you'—with an agonized repudiation of all appearances:

> Out on thee! *Seeming*! I will write against it:
> You *seem* to me as Dian in her orb,
> As chaste as is the bud ere it be blown;   (IV. i. 56)

for, as he adds, though the former object of his love 'seems' thus, though her external aspect is consonant with the impression of remote and undeveloped chastity, the reality is brutally otherwise:

> But you are more intemperate in your blood
> Than Venus, or those pamper'd animals
> That rage in savage sensuality.   (IV. i. 59)

The exaggeration behind Claudio's new attitudes reflects itself in his hysterical concentration upon 'blood', the savage forces of animal desire which contrast so strangely with the previous remoteness of his too facile idealism. This is, in effect, the other side of the essential

inexperience we have already observed in Claudio; and we may even
feel that Don Pedro's readiness to accept the testimony of false appearance at this point throws a light of its own upon his earlier confidence in taking up the young man's errand. Claudio is now obsessed,
precisely because his previous attitudes failed to take reality into
account, with a new and distorted sense of the difference that appears to
separate 'outward graces' from 'the thoughts and counsels of the heart'.
Having begun by placing reliance too easily upon the external appearance of things he now reacts equally unilaterally in the direction of
disillusionment as to the true nature of the reality which underlies them.
The sudden change in his outlook shows a considerable insight into the
vagaries of the romantic imagination.

Something of the same kind can be said of the other characters who
participate in this surprising and unnatural inversion of former attitudes. Hero's father, Leonato, for example, falls into a hysterical excess
not altogether unrelated to Claudio's own:

> But *mine*, and *mine* I loved, and *mine* I praised,
> And *mine* that I was proud on, *mine* so much,
> That I *myself* was to *myself* not *mine*,
> Valuing of her,—why, she, O, she is fallen
> Into a pit of ink, that the wide sea
> Hath drops too few to wash her clean again,
> And salt too little which may season give
> To her foul-tainted flesh!   (IV. i. 138)

So much emphasis upon 'mine', upon 'myself' can hardly fail to bring
home to us the element of self-centred obsession which colours this
hysteria, which expresses itself in the contrast between the conventional
content of certain images—'a pit of ink', 'the wide sea'—and the bitter
emphasis on the 'foul-tainted' flesh which stands out against them. We
are reminded, in anticipation, of the way in which Leontes, in the
earlier part of *The Winter's Tale*, meditates with equal frenzy and equal
lack of a sense of reality, upon his wife's imaginary betrayal: reminded,
too, of the obsession with 'nothing',[7] vanity, intimate disaster, which
this reversal of his cherished and self-gratifying attitudes produces in
his mind.

In the face of so much accumulated unreason and hysteria, the Friar
speaks to restore the voice of sanity in the light of his own greater and
more balanced experience. 'Call me a fool', he says,

> Trust not my reading nor my observations,
> Which with experimental seal doth warrant

> The tenour of my book; trust not my age.
> My reverence, calling, nor divinity,
> If this sweet lady lie not guiltless here
> Under some biting error.   (IV. i. 167)

Benedick, too, has enough grasp of reality to ascribe the deception to its true source in Don John. To remedy matters in accordance with the general comic design the Friar proposes a new 'seeming' in the form of a public announcement of Hero's 'death'. This, he argues, will serve to bring back the natural emotion of pity, in accordance with that very inconstancy which he affirms to be a normal law of human behaviour; for

> what we have we prize not to the worth
> Whiles we enjoy it; but being lack'd and lost,
> Why, then we reck the value, then we find
> The virtue that possession would not show us
> Whiles it was ours.   (IV. i. 220)

This we may take to be, in a sense, the 'philosophic' foundation of the entire action. Claudio, whose original attraction to Hero rested on no firmly founded conception of her 'value', lost her to the accompaniment of a general depreciation of her real worth. Only through the experience of her 'loss' will the true quality of the 'jewel' thus so lightly surrendered come to be appreciated, by him and the world, for what it really is.

The news of Hero's 'death' will—to put the matter more concretely —serve, in the Friar's plan, to lead Claudio from his superficial fancies to the true 'imagination' of love as 'value' and source of life. 'So will it fare with Claudio', he says:

> When he shall hear she died upon his words,
> The idea of her life shall sweetly creep
> Into his study of imagination;
> And every lovely organ of her life
> Shall come apparell'd in more precious habit,
> More moving-delicate and full of life,
> Into the eye and prospect of his soul,
> Than when she lived indeed; then shall he mourn,
> If ever love had interest in his liver,
> And wish he had not so accused her,
> No, though he thought his accusation true.   (IV. i. 224)

The intensity of the expression here—the emphasis on 'life' at the moment when death is supposed to triumph, the stressed pairs of words ('eye and prospect', 'moving-delicate' and so forth), the emphasis laid on 'soul' and on the capacity of the imagination to render 'true' even what might appear false to the eye of reason—all confirm that we are at a crucial stage in the play's development. It is through this device, belonging to the order of comic convention, that life will finally assert itself in this play in a more mature and adequate conception of the married relationship and its implications.

Beatrice, too, as Hero's cousin, is affected by the new emotional stresses that have entered the action. Under their influence, she recognizes her love for Benedick and receives his answering surrender. As a sign of the reality of his love, Benedick declares his readiness to do for her anything she may require; and in her reply she is led by the new tragic situation, not to romantic declarations or to further jest, but to the passionate if natural excess implied in the intensity of her command to her newly found lover: 'Kill Claudio!'. At this point, the continuing demands of comedy stand delicately poised against a fundamentally uncomic situation. That Beatrice, who has hitherto shown her easy mastery of the polished and pointed phrase, should thus find herself reduced to uttering a bare and savage request for vengeance, shows an incongruity that carries comic implications of a kind; and that the reasonable Benedick, of all men, should find himself placed as a result of his new love in a situation so foreign to everything he has stood for in the past, is frankly—if disconcertingly—absurd. Newly reconciled to love, Benedick finds himself confronted with a demand that takes him far beyond the common-sense and detachment on which he has been accustomed to pride himself. To refuse his mistress' command would seem to imply turning his back on his new love, whilst to accept it means going beyond the dictates of reason and humanity; for, when Beatrice goes on to say 'O God, that I were a man! I would eat his heart in the market-place' (IV. i. 311), the intensity of her feelings is clearly leading her—and threatens to lead Benedick—into a false situation. Benedick's first reaction to this command to become the instrument of vengeance upon Claudio is the reasonable one we might expect from him: 'not for the wide world'; but his new and unforeseen love has placed him too in a new situation and he finally accepts the charge laid upon him: 'By this hand, Claudio shall render me a dear account' (IV. i. 341). By the end of this crucial scene, all the principal actors find themselves committed far beyond their original expectations; and it is from their commitment, even from their errors and

excesses—because these too are, after all, a reflection of real life—that
the final resolution will emerge.

As the action approaches its concluding stages, indeed, something of
the same kind is suggested when Leonato's otherwise self-engrossed
lamentations point to a similar repudiation of abstract, 'philosophic'
consolation:

> 'Tis all men's office to speak patience
> To those that wring under the load of sorrow,
> But no man's virtue nor sufficiency,
> To be so moral when he shall endure
> The like himself. (V. i. 27)

'I will be flesh and blood' he determines, basing his resolve on the
knowledge that

> there was never yet philosopher
> That could endure the toothache patiently. (V. i. 35)

In this mood, his own passion, and that of Antonio with him, leads them
both to draw their swords in search of vengeance upon Claudio for
Hero's despised honour; and even Don Pedro, though he speaks in
terms which are reasonable by contrast with most of what surrounds
him, is mistaken in persisting in his belief that Hero was properly
accused. When Benedick, newly dedicated to courses which his former
self would certainly have condemned as signs of unreason, makes his
appearance, Claudio, looking for relief in his friend's famous 'wit',
receives instead his unexpected challenge to a duel; for Benedick, who
is by now thoroughly out of his habitual role as a 'humourist', challenges him in the name of the honour with which his new love has
confronted him. 'You are a villain; *I jest not*', he says, as though anti-
cipating that the world will find it hard to accept him in his new guise,
and continues, with the solemnity that befits his new convictions: 'You
have killed a sweet lady, and her death shall fall heavy on you' (V. i.
152). Claudio on his side, by now thoroughly estranged from his
original role of devoted lover, directs himself in jest to love's latest
victim and is joined in this by the 'reasonable' Don Pedro, who asks:
'when shall we set the savage bull's horns on the sensible Benedick's
head?'. The 'moral' of this transformation, however, and of its opposite, as undergone by the victim of these jests, is that the merely 'sensible' also has its limitations; for both Claudio and Benedick are being
driven, each from his own very different starting-point, to acknowledge the force of reality.

Behind these confusions the moment of clarification is already approaching. Benedick has brought news of Don John's escape, and the Watch now intervene with Borachio's confession. The terms of this touch closely upon the play's central theme, the contradiction between true and deceptive vision, reality and 'seeming'; for, as the repentant instrument of villainy says, 'I have deceived your very eyes', and, more appositely still, 'what your wisdoms could not discover, these shallow fools have brought to light' (V. i. 243). As we have already had occasion to observe, it is in accordance with the intention of this comedy that truth should be discovered in unexpected ways and in unusual places. To those who find their own folly, their subjection to appearance, thus exposed, this revelation comes as 'iron' and 'poison'; and by it Claudio is led—though, as he thinks, too late—to return to the 'truth' of Hero as he once 'felt' it and as he now, on more firm and rational grounds, knows it to be:

> Sweet Hero! now thy image doth appear
> In the rare semblance that I loved it first.   (V. i. 263)

In this conviction, and sobered by the loss which he believes he has brought upon himself, he accepts 'penance' and is urged by Leonato, in return for the forgiveness offered him, to take his niece in marriage. We shall clearly not interpret this in any merely realistic sense. It belongs to the framework of the comic convention, represents a situation no more 'real', though far less moving in its effect upon us, than the 'resurrection' of Hermione at the end of *The Winter's Tale*.[8] Overwhelmed by this gesture of what he calls 'over-kindness', Claudio accepts the offer in his new and chastened mood; for he has, of course, sinned by believing too readily the accusations which envy and the desire to slander have brought against his love and which his own moral levity has induced him to accept as true.

The affair of Beatrice and Benedick, meanwhile, remains to be rounded off in a suitably lighter key. Benedick, uneasy in his new state as lover, calls upon Margaret to help him in preparing nothing less than a sonnet for his mistress: there could be no better comic proof of his 'conversion' from the man he has been. His wit has been 'blunted', subjected to that of his new mistress, which he now recognizes ruefully to be 'quick' and alive; and it is only left for him to cast an equally rueful eye upon his new state by reference to the accepted models:

in loving, Leander the good swimmer, Troilus the first employer of panders, and a whole bookful of these quondam carpetmongers, whose names yet run

smoothly in the even road of a blank verse, why, they were never so truly
turned over and over as my poor self in love.   (V. ii. 30)

Recognizing his own failure as a rhymer, Benedick goes on to confess
that he loves, in some measure, 'against his will'. The confession is
significant; in their new relation to one another, Beatrice and Benedick
both find that their former selves survive to plague them with the
distance that separates past presumption from present reality. As
Beatrice sums it all up: 'Thou and I are too wise to woo peaceably'.

In this way we move to the conclusion (V. iv), which is developed in
terms appropriate to the prevailing comic convention. Claudio marries
the veiled woman presented to him as Hero's substitute, and finds, of
course, that it is Hero herself restored to life; whilst Beatrice and
Benedick, albeit with some show of unwillingness to defend their
wounded self-respect, declare in the eyes of the world the love which so
unexpectedly unites them. Nothing less than sonnets by both of them
have been discovered and Benedick—capable to the last of playing to
the gallery—agrees to take Beatrice 'for pity', and she to 'yield' to him
'upon great persuasion'. The final word upon their union is given to
Benedick when he says: 'man is a giddy thing, and this is my conclusion' (V. iv. 109). It is also, perhaps, something like the last word on an
action which is brought to a conclusion with a formal dance of partners,
this time unmasked and truly united: a dance in relation to which even
the 'brave punishments' promised by Benedick—the humorist, be it
noted—for the villainous Don John must take second place.

2 As You Like It

At the time, approximately, of his investigation, in the second great
series of English historical plays, of the implications of the exercise of
authority, Shakespeare's comic genius reached, in *As You Like It*, perhaps for the first time the measure of its full possibilities. Through and
by means of convention, a statement about life is conveyed, without
sententiousness or undue solemnity, in the appropriate forms of
comedy: a statement centred upon the nature of love and friendship,
considered—as they had already been considered in earlier comedies
and in some of the most interesting of the Sonnets—as basic human
experiences in themselves of value, but which extends from these to
cover a concept of *sociability*, of true *civilization*.

The opening scenes of *As You Like It*, indeed, introduce us to the issues of human life in society under a variety of conventional forms which are seen to concern both the *family* and *society* as a whole. In case we should be under any temptation to think that the artificiality of these forms, their obvious dependence upon devices of literary origin, provide justification for interpreting the play as an evasion, an escape into a world of mere poetic fancy, we should note that the initial emphasis is strongly upon *disorder*, upon the sinister reversal of the most natural human relationships. The disorder thus introduced into the action at once assumes a double form. In the first place, we learn that Orlando, as the younger of the two brothers, has been subjected by his senior, Oliver, to whose care his father entrusted him on his death-bed, to a tyranny or 'servitude' which has reduced him to a status approaching that of a beast and prevented him from growing through the necessary process of education—what Shakespeare will elsewhere call *nurture*, or *art*, seeing in it the appropriate and indispensable complement of *nature*⁹ —into true gentility. 'My father', he accuses his brother, 'charged you in his will to give me good education; you have trained me *like a peasant*, obscuring and hiding from me *all gentlemanlike qualities*' (I. i. 72). It is precisely because his remains, in spite of this treatment, a noble nature—'the spirit of my father grows strong in me'—that Orlando announces his determination, as the play opens, no longer to 'endure' this subjection.

The tyrannical treatment of Orlando by his brother, moreover, takes place in relation to another equally unnatural situation. Parallel to it, and in a wider sphere, the prevalence of an essential disorder in society is confirmed in the supplanting of the legitimate and beneficent rule of 'the old Duke' by the arbitrary authority of 'the new Duke' who has usurped his position. For those who may be tempted to see, here and elsewhere in Shakespeare's comedies, no more than an elaborate game of make-believe, it is worth reflecting that these, though treated in a different and more indirect way, are the themes which will reappear in many of his greatest tragedies, not excluding *King Lear*. Though here subject to convention, transcribed as it were into a comic key, they are not on that account to be taken less seriously as dramatic reflections of real life.

The consequences of these reversals of nature and of civilized order make themselves apparent in the early stages of the action. Oliver makes use of a wrestler, a dispassionate and largely tongue-tied incarnation of brute force, to execute his plot against Orlando. In order to persuade him to this he pretends to detect an unnatural evil in his brother in very much the same terms as Edmund will later use for the discrediting of Edgar in the eyes of his over-credulous father.[10] 'It is the stubbornest young fellow of France', he says, and goes on to ascribe to him what are in effect his own unnatural faults: 'full of ambition, *an envious emulator* of every man's good parts, *a secret and villainous contriver* against me *his natural brother*', and to urge him to mingle brutality with dissimulation: 'therefore use thy discretion; I had as lief thou didst break his neck as his finger'. Before he has finished, Oliver's persuasiveness rises to even more unnatural levels of falsity: 'And thou wert best look to't; for if thou dost him any slight disgrace, or if he do not mightily grace himself on thee, he will practise against thee by *poison, entrap thee* by some *treacherous device*, and never leave thee till he hath ta'en thy life by some *indirect* means or other; for, I assure thee, and almost with tears I speak it, there is not one so young and so villainous this day living' (I. i. 155). It should be noted, however, as a most significant conclusion to this long list of what are essentially his own blemishes, that Oliver, when left to himself, is obliged to recognize the true virtue of his brother, which in fact he envies for the attraction it exercises over the rest of men: 'Yet he's *gentle*; never schooled, and yet learned; full of *noble device*; of all sorts *enchantingly beloved*; and indeed so much *in the heart of the world* . . . that I am altogether *misprised*' (I. i. 175).

These attitudes of envy and unreasonable resentment are soon seen to reflect themselves in the wider ranges of the society with which the play is concerned. In much the same way as Oliver, and on his more ample stage, the new Duke is, by comparison with his gentle and humane predecessor, thoroughly suspicious and tyrannical. He exiles Rosalind from his court in a completely arbitrary fashion—'Let it suffice thee that I trust thee not' (I. iii. 58)—and even, once she and his own daughter Celia have sought their liberty in flight, threatens his creature Oliver with the confiscation of his property if he fails to ensure the rapid return of the fugitives into his power (III. i). The tone of all these early court episodes, with their sense of a world increasingly subject to degeneration as it ages, is summed up by the courtier Le Beau when, in the act of bidding farewell to Orlando as he sets out upon his exile, he makes his own comment on what have become the sorry ways of society:

> Sir, fare you well:
> Hereafter, *in a better world than this*,
> I shall desire more love and knowledge of you.   (I. ii. 300)

The aspiration for 'a better world', and the awareness of living in a worse, are placed in the mouth of one who is old enough to remember the times when such a world actually existed. Though it may seem at this stage to be little more than a pathetic nostalgia for the impossible, it will in due course be satisfied, not by translation to an imaginary Arcadian perfection—though such a translation answers to a necessary and revealing stage in the complete conception—but by the restoration of order and humanity to the real society—'real', naturally, in terms of the conventions which the play uses—from which they have been unnaturally banished.

Even in a world of the kind so bitterly rejected by Le Beau, however, certain positives survive. Among them is the firm friendship which unites Rosalind and Celia, who might easily have been, given the situation of their respective parents, rivals, but who are in fact no such thing; for Celia declares herself ready from the first to acknowledge the wrong which has been done to her friend's father and even to offer such restitution as may be in her power in the future. 'You know', she says, 'my father hath no child but I, nor none is like to have: and truly, when he dies, thou shalt be his heir; for what he hath taken away from thy father perforce, I will render thee again in affection' (I. ii. 18); for to do otherwise would be, as she at once goes on to say, to make of herself a 'monster'. In a similar way Orlando, in the very moment of his trial, has fallen in love with Rosalind and received from her the token of true faith which he will carry with him into exile. Throughout the various stages of this opening, we may say that convention is being consistently used to reflect the complexity of real life.

It is the aim of this comedy, still working through the conventions it has chosen, to bring these tensions to a harmonious resolution which will itself answer to the genuine positives, both personal and social, of real living. This resolution is to be sought through the displacement of the action in a direction which appears at first sight (but at first sight only) to be away from common reality; by moving it, in other words, to the Forest of Arden, where love and other human relations are to be taken temporarily into the state of nature, and where the simplicities of the primitive world (itself presented in terms thoroughly and deliberately conventional) will be set in contrast to the corrupt state of sophistication which we have already seen in action. This removal, it need hardly be repeated, is not a mere 'escape' from reality, does not in any sense constitute the final answer towards which the comedy may be said to move. The 'state of nature', as the play presents it, is as artificial, as remote from the true reality of the condition it purports to represent, as the 'sophistication' which it replaces. Both, indeed, are instruments for asserting, within the limits of comedy, permanent truths about life which they do not directly or 'realistically' reflect. Rosalind, Celia, and Orlando leave the court in search of 'liberty', freedom from restraint and corruption. They will find this in the forest, and with it what is even more important, a degree of self-knowledge, a fresh understanding, itself expressed within the limits that their author has chosen to accept, of what life really is; but at the end of the action they, and with them all the others concerned, will have to return, bringing with them the insights they have acquired in the course of their adventures, to the social and civilized world, the distinctively human order of life with which the play is finally concerned.

So much, indeed, is implied in the opening presentation of the forest of Arden (II. i), which is considerably more complex than may at once appear. Our first information about life in the forest comes from the wrestler Charles, who touches upon some of the main themes in its presentation when he tells Oliver that, according to report, the old Duke has already sought refuge there,

> and a many merry men with him; and there they live like the old Robin Hood of England; they say many young gentlemen flock to him every day, and fleet the time carelessly, as they did in the golden world.   (I. i. 122)

The 'golden world' is, accordingly, set in an ideal past, presented as a compound of legendary antiquity, of the reign of the gods and goddesses in Arcadia, and of the original timeless innocence which existed in the Garden of Eden before the Fall. The ability to neglect the action of time, indeed, is essential to the conception, the key at once to its attraction and to its final insufficiency. At some period in the past, during the generation of Orlando's virtuous father, who was not accidentally named Sir Rowland de Bois, a creature by implication of the woods, the forest world of ordered harmony and simple, unchanging human happiness corresponded to an ideally natural ordering of society, which is then supposed actually to have existed in court and state; but since the passing of that mythically fortunate generation forest and court, ideal and reality have become grievously separated, and the consequent loss for mankind, tantamount to a kind of Fall from original grace, may be said to be symbolized in the figure of the faithful Adam, whose name is again not without significance and who is obliged, after his banishment from a corrupted society, to pass his old age wandering through Arden in painful search for the ideal order to which he once belonged and to the reality of which his continued loyalty to Orlando testifies. To put the matter in this way is, of course, to risk loading with abstract and theoretical meanings what is, in fact, in the play admirably light and effortlessly poetic; but the point is one which needs to be made, even with this danger in view, if the final, *unsolemn* seriousness of Shakespeare's conception is to receive its due.

The contrast between an ideal order, which those who desire it can only seek in the forest but which they will not ultimately find there, and the remembered experience of the real world to which, as human beings, they belong is one which dominates the entire presentation of the action in Arden. The forest is like the 'golden world' in partaking of a kind of timelessness, which seems indeed, to those who have recently escaped from the anxieties and mutual distrusts of their corrupted social world, to be a necessary condition of the ideal. 'There's no clock in the forest', as Orlando points out to Rosalind.[11] He goes on, however, to speak himself of that time which 'travels in divers paces with divers persons' and which necessarily accompanies the lover's awareness of his condition (III. ii); and Touchstone, an unwilling refugee on his own lower level, is expressly observed by Jacques in the act of consulting his 'dial' in the forest, and overheard by him relating the moment of time to the sense of inevitable decay which so persistently accompanies life in the real world and which no amount of dedication to pastoral make-believe can finally ignore:

> And so, from hour to hour, we ripe and ripe,
> And then, from hour to hour, we rot and rot;
> And thereby hangs a tale.   (II. vii. 26)

The reality of this 'tale' is germane to the entire conception of this comedy, and indeed to all Shakespeare's exercises in the comic form from now on.[12]

All the attitudes of those who have entered Arden imply, in fact, each after its appropriately diverse fashion, not only the attraction of an ideal aspiration, but, side by side with and consistently colouring it, the awareness of an actual fall from original innocence. The woods are said by the old Duke, who has sought refuge in them from the trials to which he was subjected by the unnatural action of his brother, to be 'More free from peril than the envious court'. This is true, and important; but the very statement implies that the memory of 'peril' and 'envy' are still very much alive in his mind as he speaks. If he is able, in his new state, to say, somewhat sententiously, that he can find

> tongues in trees, books in the running brooks,
> Sermons in stones and good in everything.   (II. i. 16)

and to declare that he feels no desire to change his condition, there is at least equal meaning in his recognition that

> Sweet are the uses of adversity;
> Which, like the toad, ugly and venomous,
> Wears yet a precious jewel in his head.   (II. i. 12)

The reality of the 'jewel', though we are asked by the very rules of the comic game to accept it, need not lead us to neglect the ugliness and poison of the toad which bears it; and the Duke's courtly companion Amiens remains fully aware during his enforced sojourn in the realm of 'nature' of what he calls the 'stubbornness of fortune'[13] which has brought him there. More than once, indeed, there are hints of real contradictions beneath the apparent simplicity of the pastoral ideal; for those who have found refuge in the forest from the pressures of a hostile world are still under the manifest necessity of living at nature's expense, of killing the deer—'poor dappled fools',[14] as they are decoratively called—upon whom their sustenance depends. Theirs is a situation into which the melancholy observer Jacques reads, not without a characteristic sense of pleasure, a moral which has a certain relation to real life, as he professes to see in his companions

> usurpers, tyrants, and what's worse,
> To fright the animals and to kill them up
> In their assign'd and native dwelling place.   (II. i. 61)

It is indeed upon the animals, the real representatives of 'nature' in the forest, that the human intruders are obliged in their extremity to prey simply to keep themselves alive. Whatever else it may be, the forest is *not* conceived as a place where the laws of common life are permanently suspended in the interests of an effortless and simple existence.

It would perhaps be nearer the truth to say that it is a place where each human actor finds what his own nature prompts him to discover. To Amiens' song, with its touching expression of the desire to believe that those who are fortunate enough to live 'Under the greenwood tree' in daily contact with nature are rendered free thereby of the less attractive aspects of life in society, finding there

> No enemy
> But winter and rough weather,   (II. v. 7)

Jacques at once responds with the disillusioned spirit of his parody:

> Here shall he see
> Gross fools as he,
> An if he will come to me.   (II. v. 55)

Both Amiens and Jacques are partially right, respond in their contrasted
reactions to elements genuinely present in the human situation; but the
central issue at stake in Arden, which is not finally to be resolved there,
concerns not these separated fragments of vision, but, in the last resort,
the complex and mutually enriching links between 'nature' and
civilization.

To the world of nature thus conceived the main actors of the play
accordingly come, to seek what is in essence a measure of self-clarification. The first to decide to join the former Duke by taking refuge in the
forest is Orlando, who is accompanied in his journey there by his
faithful servant Adam, in whose aged person the traditional ideals of
fidelity and service, which have been so harshly exiled from Duke
Frederick's corrupt and sophisticated court, are still alive. Adam, strong
in the firm and unshakeable possession of essential human values, which
his subjection to the harsh realities of old age and exile cannot obscure,
knows in the act of leaving it that 'this house'—the court—has become
'but a butchery', an abode of deception and treachery upon which he
comments without illusion:

> Know you not, master, to some kind of men
> Their graces serve them but as enemies?
> No more do yours: your virtues, *gentle* master,
> Are *sanctified and holy traitors* to you.
> O, what a world is this, where what is comely
> *Envenoms* him that bears it.   (II. iii. 10)

It is in reaction against a world of this kind that Rosalind and Celia, as
we have learnt already, have abandoned the court to go

> in *content*
> To *liberty* and not to banishment.   (I. iii. 140)

What all four find in the forest, however, is a reality in some respects
very notably distinct from any conception that they, or we, may
harbour of merely idyllic peace. The aged Adam is driven to the verge
of utter exhaustion in what Orlando, taking pity upon him, calls 'this
uncouth forest' (II. vi. 6),[15] before he finds himself forced to threaten
Duke Senior to obtain the food of which both are by now desperately
in need: forced, in other words, to sin against his own civilized and
sociable values and to make himself, in the eyes of his former sovereign,

'a rude despiser of good manners', a man 'empty' of essential 'civility' (II. vii. 92). In a way finally similar Rosalind and Celia go through much the same kind of experience; for they too are reduced to confess their weariness after long hours of wandering through the forest, and the clown Touchstone, whom they have so strangely chosen for their incongruous companion in their adventure of 'liberty' and who clearly has no illusions about the real meaning of the state of nature, has no better than this to say of his enforced surroundings: 'Ay, now am I in Arden, the more fool I; when I was at home, I was in a better place', and concludes, in a typical mood of detached fatalism, that 'travellers must be content' (II. iv. 16). We may think that the best comment on Arcadian illusion is conveyed through the shepherd Colin, when he says of his master, from whom Rosalind and Celia are hoping to get relief in their extremity:

> My master is of churlish disposition
> And little recks to find the way to heaven
> By doing deeds of hospitality.   (II. iv. 81)

The exercise of 'hospitality' is clearly under any circumstances a virtue, a distinctively human and humanizing quality; but we are not to assume that it is necessarily more prevalent in the order of pastoral simplicity than in the world of normal social intercourse. We must surely conclude, at the best, that the original dwellers in this pastoral 'paradise' are scarcely the idealized and gentle 'swains' that a more superficial use of the convention would have made of them.

It is worth noting, moreover, that those who find themselves driven by adverse circumstance to enter Arcadia bring their true, their civilized natures with them. When the Duke reproves Orlando for having so rudely interrupted his rustic feast, the latter replies that he is, in spite of the circumstances in which he now finds himself and which have driven him to this excess, a man who has 'some *nurture*', a true measure of civility, in his nature. His final appeal for understanding is made to those who have known civilized behaviour in the real world of human society:

> If ever you have look'd on better days,
> If ever been where bells have toll'd to church,
> If ever sat at any good man's feast,
> If ever from your eyelids wiped a tear
> And know what 'tis to pity and be pitied,
> Let *gentleness* my strong enforcement be;   (II. vii. 113)

for, as he goes on to imply, to 'lose and neglect the creeping hours of time' in the forest may be a temporary necessity which exile imposes, but can never be a permanent answer to the challenge, essentially sociable and human in its nature, of real life. The Duke's table, set out among the trees for the feast which Orlando has so rudely interrupted, in itself represents a *social* act and, as such, a positive good, in contrast, precisely, to the evil which has driven those who are now joined around it to seek refuge, in temporary renunciation of their full human stature, in the freedom of the forest. The final resolution of the issues raised in the course of the action must lie, in the last resort, not in Arden, which is, essentially and of its nature, a place of transition, even in a very real sense of illusion, but elsewhere.

The forest, accordingly, is to be seen above all as a place where basic human attitudes are put variously to the test; these concern more particularly love and its reflection in friendship. First and outstanding among the various pairs who meet in these new surroundings are Orlando and Rosalind, who find in Arden the love which they sought at the court, but which they were debarred from bringing to its natural consummation there. Their relations in the forest become the occasion, in the first instance, for the criticism which Rosalind, taking advantage of her disguise as the page 'Ganymede', passes upon which she calls the 'quotidian', the feverish excesses, of romantic love. It is not from this kind of love, upon which so many preceding Shakespearean comedies have passed judgement, that the protagonists of this play will derive the strength to overcome the trials to which they are respectively subjected. When Orlando, speaking of the qualities of love, asks her 'What are his marks?', she replies by cataloguing the conventional signs of the love-sick devotee which she is happy not to find in him:

> A lean cheek, which you have not; a blue eye and sunken, which you have not; an unquestionable spirit, which you have not; a beard neglected, which you have not ... then your hose should be ungartered, your bonnet unbanded, your sleeve unbuttoned, your shoe untied, and everything about you demonstrating a careless desolation. (III. ii. 397)

By the absence of all these signs, Rosalind concludes that Orlando is— to her relief and his credit—'no such man'; and, having thus established the essential sanity which makes him attractive in her eyes, she goes on, still in the light of the comic spirit, which is marked by its readiness to accept the incongruous and the irrational as aspects of life, to consider the nature of love itself, which she finds to be a madness indeed—it could not otherwise be the proper substance of comedy—but a madness both universal and necessary to life; for, if it may be admitted, in terms of realistic common-sense, that love is 'merely a madness' which 'deserves as well a dark house and a whip as madmen do', the fact remains, and is not less incontestable, that 'the reason why they'— the generality of lovers—'are not so punished and cured, is that the lunacy is so ordinary that the whippers are in love too' (III. ii. 428).

Rosalind's own attitude to love, to which these exchanges lead, and which is more directly developed in the second scene in which, still speaking as 'Ganymede', she discusses the matter with Orlando (IV. i), is a characteristic compound of humorous detachment and frank acceptance. Unwilling to take romantic love at its own incurably pretentious estimate she remarks that 'The poor world is almost six thousand years old, and in all this time there was not any man died in his own person, videlicet in a love cause', and goes on to comment sharply enough upon some of the most illustrious literary examples of this excessive passion:

> Troilus had his brains dashed out with a Grecian club; yet he did what he could to die before, and he is one of the patterns of love. Leander, he would have lived many a fair year, though Hero had turned nun, if it had not been for a hot midsummer night; for, good youth, he went but forth to wash him in the Hellespont and being taken with the cramp was drowned; and the foolish chronicles of that age found it was 'Hero of Sestos'. (IV. i. 100)

The last word, however, is not allowed to rest here. The conclusion which confirms these critical estimates goes on to lend them a deeper, even a more tragic content which is an essential part of the complete effect: 'But these are all lies: men have died from time to time and worms have eaten them, but not for love' (IV. i. 110). Real men have not, and indeed, it would seem, should not *die* romantically in pursuit of their irrational passions; but whether, and to what extent, it may be said that they should *live* for and by them is a question that still remains to be asked.

It is a question which Rosalind herself goes on to answer, at least by implication. Her attitude to Orlando is forthright, impatient of all forms of romantic excess; when he says, with a certain touch of the pretentious, that her frown might be sufficient to 'kill' him, her retort is 'By this hand, it will not kill a fly', and she goes on from this to assert against the more absurd excesses of romantic devotion her own more realistic view of the volubility of men and women alike in love. 'Men', she says, 'are April when they woo, December when they wed:

maids are May when they are maids, but the sky changes when they are wives'; and yet again, when, in his devotion, Orlando ventures to call her 'wise', her answer is conceived in the essence of the comic spirit of incongruity:

> the wiser, the waywarder: make the doors upon a woman's wit and it will out at the casement; shut that, and 'twill out at the key-hole; stop that, 'twill fly with the smoke out at the chimney.   (IV. i. 168)

It is necessary to the comic effect, however, that these sallies should not remain the last word. Orlando believes throughout that he is speaking to 'Ganymede', and Rosalind's awareness of this invariably conditions her replies. At the last she is ready, even as she continues to speak in this way, to recognize in more intimate terms to Celia her own servitude to 'that same wicked bastard of Venus that was begot of thought, conceived of spleen, and born of madness': let him, she concludes, in apparent but profoundly natural contrast to so much that she has said in her moments of purely comic inspiration, 'be judge how deep I am in love' (IV. i. 227).

Side by side with the central romantic situation, carried on by Rosalind in her disguise, other aspects of love are presented, and fall under her comment, in the story of the shepherd Silvius and the Phebe who is the object of his unreasoning and servile devotion. Silvius is the romantic lover personified in all his excess, who is content to see his disdainful mistress as his 'executioner' (III. v. 3) and who, by the very fact of so doing, ensures that this—an 'executioner'—is precisely what she shall continue to be for him. When Phebe, however, in her disdain for this abject follower, aspires beyond him to none other than 'Ganymede', Rosalind exposes the tyranny she exercises over him in no uncertain terms, stressing both the human content of love (and the equally human limitations which go with it) and the need for self and mutual respect in its conduct. To Silvius she urges the claims of a proper self-respect, based upon a genuine and necessary realism, against the excesses of sentimental self-abasement in all its forms:

> 'Tis not her glass, but you, that flatters her;
> And out of you she sees herself more proper
> Than any of her lineaments can show her;   (III. v. 54)

whilst to Phebe, on her side, she lays stress upon the positive human good of marriage, and upon the need to found this central relationship upon a true knowledge of the self and of its accompanying limitations.

'Mistress know yourself', she says, and goes on to add what amounts to a command to sanity and a proper sense of proportion:

> down on your knees,
> And thank heaven, fasting, for a good man's love: (III. v. 57)

to end, more sharply still, with a call to realism in self-assessment and in the estimate of what life may really offer her:

> Sell when you can: you are not for all markets:
> Cry the man mercy: love him: take his offer. (III. v. 60)

The mercantile form of this advice is deliberate, represents an emphatic call to realism and a proper sense of truth; but it is significant that it falls, as far as the recipient is concerned, upon deaf ears. Entrapped, little though she is prepared to recognize it, in the illusion of her supposed 'love' for 'Ganymede', Phebe ignores this advice to content herself with the considerable good which is hers for the having, and even seeks to use her victim, Silvius, to convey her impossible message to Rosalind. Silvius, by his acceptance of this ignoble mission, in reality confirms his own state of servitude, his inability to respect himself properly as a human being; the awakening of this pair to sanity, to the appropriate recognition of things as they really are, and so to the need for building their own lives upon a natural and realistic foundation, will only come with the final resolution.

Yet another aspect of love, in some sense marginal to the main action but not on that account less relevant to it, is provided by Touchstone who is brought, albeit with more than a touch of unwillingness, to recognize the place of marriage in any truly 'natural' scheme of life:

> As the ox hath his bow, sir, the horse his curb, and the falcon her bells, so man hath his desires; and as pigeons bill, so wed-lock would be nibbling.
>
> (III. iii. 85)

For Touchstone this uneasy compulsion presents itself in the forest in the ill-favoured form of the country wench Audrey. Unwilling as he is to accept even the possibility of a permanent commitment to this grotesque partner—who, however, responds adequately to his own nature—Touchstone at first sets his mind upon an uneasy and evasive compromise. He will 'marry' her through the offices of the hedge-priest Oliver Martext, and so leave open to himself the avenue for a possible escape from servitude; but when Jacques points out that this attitude cannot lead to any true or valid marriage—'this fellow', he says, 'will but join you together as they join wainscot' (III. iii. 92)—he ends by agreeing, with some unwillingness, to seek a 'true priest' to carry out the appropriate offices to unite them. In this way, he accepts the necessity of marriage, which has been brought home to him in the forest but which cannot receive its final consummation there—again to follow Jacques' phrase—'under a bush like a beggar'.[16] For Touch-stone, too, marriage presents itself with a social, a distinctively human form of challenge, and by the end of the play he will be ready to take his Audrey as she is, recognizing in her 'an ill-favoured thing', indeed, 'but mine own', and living in the hope that he too may yet find, when he returns to the real world in the company of his incongruous bride, the 'pearl' concealed in his 'foul oyster'.[17] An element of relativity, of the irreducible tendency of human nature to remain on the margin of the beautiful and harmonizing visions which the imagination proposes to it, is essential to Shakespeare's comic vision in its profounder moments, and here, in Touchstone's wry inconclusiveness, it is finely incorporated into the vision of Arden.

Finally—and at this point we are brought directly back to the wider purposes by which the action is governed, and which will eventually preside over its resolution—love plays its part in the forest by healing the original breach between Orlando and the brother who initially drove him into exile. Seeking out his banished brother in the forest, and thereby exposing himself to the kind of danger to which he had once been ready to leave Orlando, Oliver falls asleep under a tree and is rescued—and rescued precisely by a deed of courage which involves the shedding of this same brother's blood—from the dangers represented, in terms which unite the pastoral order to a kind of symbolic meaning, by a serpent and a lioness. In other words when Oliver, suitably repen-tant, carries to Rosalind a bloody napkin as a sign of his rescue he shows himself, according to his own admission, 'converted' by the 'kindness, nobler than revenge' (IV. iii. 130),[18] which he has encountered in the very person whom he once so grievously wronged. Thus finding reconciliation in the forest, the brothers make their peace and Oliver, restored to true civility as distinct from its false and sophisticated reflec-tion, given 'fresh array'[19] and 'entertainment' by the Duke, falls in love with Celia and declares himself content to renounce the 'estate' which he now recognizes that he has wrongfully administered and, furthermore, to 'live and die a shepherd' (V. ii. 14). In this way, and in accordance with the conventional pattern of the play, the natural relationship between the brothers is at last re-established for the general good of society. Orlando, bringing with him the natural virtues that have always been his, returns to the world of 'nurture' to which he truly belongs, whilst Oliver, who has previously shown himself so unnatural in his state of worldly sophistication, retires in a mood of chastened contemplation to seek true understanding of the world and of himself in the natural simplicities.

What we have witnessed through the central part of the play has been, in essence, a set of variations on the theme of love and on that of the true sociability which accompanies it and confers meaning upon personal relationships. By the time these variations have been fully worked out in the forest of Arden, we are ready for the final resolution which will be contrived by Rosalind in her understanding, now deepened by the effect upon her of her recent experiences, of the true nature of love as a cementing and positive influence, at once central and salutary, upon human life. On the verge of this resolution, the complaints of the still unsatisfied lovers strike her comically as 'the howling of Irish wolves against the moon' (V. ii. 121), residues of an excess of romantic self-centredness which can achieve only its own madness. To each of those thus situated she offers her help, in appropriate but still enigmatic form, with the end of enabling them to take up their proper places in the final dance of civilized harmonies to which the whole action is now tending. 'To-morrow', she tells them, 'meet me all together', and then goes on to distribute to each, in riddling form, her assurance that they shall find what is proper for them and what, indeed, in so far as they know themselves, they truly desire:

> (*To Phebe*) I will marry you, if ever I marry woman, and I'll be married to-morrow: (*to Orlando*) I will satisfy you, if ever I satisfied man, and you shall be married to-morrow: (*to Silvius*) I will content you, if what pleases you contents you, and you shall be married to-morrow. (V. ii. 124)

Then, after having thus announced in enigmatic form the approaching consummation, Rosalind ends by calling each of those who hear her to the appointed place of meeting:

> (*To Orlando*) As you love Rosalind, meet: (*to Silvius*) as you love Phebe, meet: and as I love no woman, I'll meet. (V. ii. 130)

The artifice of the final resolution, founded in this way upon the recognition of natural instinct and the need to incorporate it into a wider context of human realities, is set in turn against the spirit of the Page's song, with its emphasis upon the order of the seasons as the appropriate setting for love:

> It was a lover and his lass,
>> With a hey, and a ho, and hey nonino,
> That o'er the green corn-field did pass,
>> In the spring time, the only pretty ring time,
> When birds do sing, hey ding a ding ding,
>> Sweet lovers love the spring—   (V. iii. 18)

and on the need to take 'the present time', the offered moment of living experience, against the background of a mutability which originally conditions it and against which its absorbing human reality is now affirmed. The progress from winter bareness to the promise of spring—from 'Blow, blow thou winter wind' to the spring time of love reborn—answers to the general structure of the play which is now in the process of being rounded off to its natural conclusion: for love, in the concluding words of the song, 'is crowned with the prime' and the moment of its consummation is at hand.

And so, as the play is drawn to its harmonizing close, still in the forest, but with an eye now clearly directed to the reality, human and social, which lies beyond these Arcadian limits, Rosalind and Celia make their solemn entry, appropriately accompanied by Hymen, the god of marriage, who declares his intent to 'bar confusion' in the name of a conception of married union that can now reflect, in its mingling of joy and gravity, the order of nature itself: for, as the song which announces their entry puts it,

> There is mirth in heaven,
> When earthly things made even
>> *Atone* together: (V. iv. 115)

and again, when the various couplings are at last complete in the 'atonement', the restoration of unity which has made them possible:

> Wedding is great Juno's crown:
>> *O blessed bond* of board and bed!
> 'Tis Hymen peoples every town;
>> *High wedlock* then be honoured:
> Honour, high honour and renown,
>> To Hymen, god of every town!   (V. iv. 148)

No sooner have these celebrations of marriage been sanctioned by this note of due solemnity, than the time comes for all those concerned to leave Arden for the last time: to leave it in order to make their necessary return to the world of social and civilized realities to which they are at last ready to be incorporated. Duke Frederick, having declared himself 'converted' to a new and more responsible outlook upon life, restores his crown to its rightful owner and renounces the 'world' which, by his previous perverse acts, he has helped to plunge into confusion; and Duke Senior, taking up his former role, which has always been his by right, calls upon all those present to join him in the dance of married harmonies which reflects, in its grave and entranced unity, the universal harmony of nature:

> Play, music! And you, brides and bridegrooms all,
> With *measure heap'd in joy*, to the measures fall. (V. iv. 185)

The last word is left, however, not to him, but to Jacques, the detached and melancholy observer, who is now allowed to call each to the place in the dance, the harmonious 'measure', which corresponds to him. To the restored Duke he says:

> You to your former honour I bequeath;
> Your patience and your virtue well deserves it;

to Orlando, who has won his Rosalind,

> You to a love that your true faith doth merit;

to Oliver:

> You to your land, and love, and great allies;

to Silvius:

> You to a long and well-deserved bed;

and, finally, to Touchstone, who has declared his readiness to take his new-found Audrey to himself in marriage:

> And you to wrangling; for thy loving voyage
> Is but for two months victuall'd. (V. iv. 193)

In thus taking upon himself the words which distribute to each his appropriate part in the measure, it may seem at first sight that the detached and self-centred Jacques is going beyond his limitations; but further reflection may suggest to us that the last word rests thereby, as the spirit of comedy will have it, with a certain note of relativity which serves to balance and qualify the preceding statement of universal harmonies.

Some such note of relativity is, indeed, appropriate to the play's complete comic effect. To allow it a place in his conception Shakespeare has introduced into his play two characters—Touchstone and Jacques—who stand, each in his own very different way, somewhat apart from

the main unifying conception. The unwilling submission of Touchstone to the married state we have already considered; it represents, in
the typical Shakespearean way, the voice of reality qualifying the truths
and harmonies glimpsed by the imagination through the forms of
sophisticated comedy as developed in the main action. Jacques himself,
who has commented with sharp detachment on Touchstone's weaknesses, lies—contented as he is with his self-centred and self-chosen
melancholy—in a rather more fundamental way apart from the general
pattern. His comments—including those which go to make up his
famous speech on the seven ages of man (II. vii. 139), which it is too
easy to quote out of its context as a detached expression of the author's
'philosophic' wisdom—provide at all times a qualifying background to
the more positive assertions which prevail elsewhere. As such, they
fulfil a necessary role in the complete and balanced conception with
which the play is concerned; but to impose upon them a seriousness
which is certainly not intended is to falsify the author's intention and
the part assigned to the speaker in the action as a whole.

The force of Jacques' successive vignettes of representative states of
life answers, indeed, rather to a distinctively comic vision than to any
profound insight into the nature of reality. The 'whining schoolboy'
creeping, 'like snail', unwillingly to school already reflects a humorous
conception, and so, even more definitely, do the essentially satirical
comments which follow on the conventional lover,

> Sighing like furnace, with a woeful ballad
> Made to his mistress' eyebrow,

and on the soldier,

> Jealous in honour, sudden and quick in quarrel,
> Seeking the bubble reputation
> Even in the cannon's mouth.   (II. vii. 151)

We have met both these personages elsewhere in the plays, and shall
have occasion to meet them at times in other, and more serious con-
texts[20]; but the spirit in which both they and the 'justice',

> In fair round belly with good capon lined,

are conceived is one in which the comic intention, alternately tolerant
and sharply reflective of human frailties and idiosyncrasies, prevails
Slightly sententious and finally self-gratifying in tone, like nearly everything said by Jacques in the course of the play, these observations are
certainly not to be taken simply at the speaker's own valuation. The

context in which they are uttered is carefully designed to make this clear. Just as Jacques, at the end of his speech, has allowed himself the pleasure, in a final artificial flourish, of reducing the state of man in his old age to one of impotence and vanity—

> second childishness and mere oblivion,
> Sans teeth, sans eyes, sans taste, sans everything,   (II. vii. 165)

the entry of Adam, who represents visibly those positives of loyalty and faith which the melancholy 'philosopher' cannot understand or relate to his own reading of life, serves to remind us that there are other possible views of old age and, indeed, by implication at least, of human existence as a whole. It is precisely these views, based upon positive acceptance and participation, that the main comedy is concerned to advance.

For the fact is that Jacques' 'wisdom' is founded at each turn upon his limitations. He is fitted by his nature to expose the elements of vice and disorder which undeniably occupy so large a place in human existence—it is, of course, his self-declared vocation, perhaps a little too readily accepted, to 'Cleanse the foul body of the infected world' (II. vii. 60)—but the sufficiency which his every utterance implies is not in turn without its own Achilles' heel. It is worth remarking that the old Duke, as he rebukes him for his over-facile moralizing, stresses in no uncertain terms the roots of his 'philosophic' misanthropy, his complacent declaration of his own superiority to the motives of lesser men, in a very real subjection to the elements of selfishness and lust which he so readily condemns in others:

> thou thyself hast been a libertine,
> As sensual as the brutish sting itself;
> And all the embossed sores and headed evils
> That thou with licence of free foot has caught
> Wouldst thou disgorge into the general world.   (II. vii. 65)

'Brutish sting': 'embossed sores': 'headed evils': 'disgorge': the connection with the maladies of the 'infected world', and the clear statement that Jacques himself shares fully in the evils he is so apt to denounce from the standpoint of his self-asserted superiority, are too powerful for them to fail in making their point. It is noteworthy that Jacques' only defence against this accusation lies in the claim that the vices which it gives him such pleasure to expose are in fact universal attributes of human society:

                    Why, who cries out on pride,
That can therein tax any private party?
Doth it not flow as hugely as the sea,
Till that the weary very means do ebb?
What woman in the city do I name,
When that I say the city-woman bears
The cost of princes on unworthy shoulders?
Who can come in and say that I mean her,
When such a one as she such is her neighbour?
Or what is he of basest function,
That says his bravery is not on my cost,
Thinking that I mean him, but therein suits
His folly to the mettle of my speech?
There then; how then? what then? Let me see wherein
My tongue hath wrong'd him; for if it do him right,
Then he hath wrong'd himself; if he be free,
Why then my taxing like a wild-goose flies,
Unclaim'd of any man.   (II. vii. 70)

This is possibly Jacques' most truly eloquent utterance, and we need not give less than their true value to its central themes, of which echoes may be found as far away as *King Lear*; but this does not mean that we are invited, either at this point or ever, to accept this moralizing entirely at its own estimate. Jacques is laying claim here to the status of a satirist, a self-appointed cleanser of the social Augean stables; and his vision is of the kind which, though it is keen enough to penetrate to certain truths, is also limited by the element of self-satisfaction which has inspired it. We are told elsewhere of Jacques that he is one who sucks his melancholy 'as a weasel sucks eggs'; and it is there, precisely, that his final limitation as a human being lies. For his function as critic, though it enables him to mirror truly certain aspects of human nature, is none the less self-appointed, self-regarding, and incomplete, even destructive of true order. It is significant that Orlando, when the occasion arises, shows clearly that he has little use for him or for the kind of vision which he represents. When Jacques is moved to criticize Rosalind's name adversely for no more solid reason than his own unsupported prejudice, Orlando's retort is quite simple and conclusive: 'There was no thought of pleasing you when she was christened' (III. ii. 284); and when he invites him to join him in his favourite past-time of 'railing against our mistress the world, and all our misery', the reply amounts again to a reaffirmation of perspective, an exposure of the limitations of all 'philosophy' of this kind: 'I will chide no breather in the world but myself, against whom I know most faults' (III. ii. 298).

It is, accordingly, Jacques' limitation, as critic and as human being, to fail to understand the necessary truth which this observation contains. True criticism and true moralizing can only rest on the foundation of an adequate self-knowledge, which will tend in turn to make the criticism and the moralizing themselves less absolute and less self-satisfied. The 'observer' who claims the privilege of passing superior comments upon the life around him without accepting the responsibility of sharing it, finally rules himself by his own attitudes out of court. The spirit of 'philosophic' melancholy as represented in Jacques has, indeed, its moments of insight, its partial truths, to offer to the rounded and balanced vision of life at which this comedy aims; but it is *partial*, no more than a single ingredient, and by no means the most important one at that, in a more ample and positive complete effect. It is for this reason that Jacques, after having become, as we have seen, for a brief moment the spokesman of the conclusion, leaves the harmonious and 'social' order whose formation he has just confirmed to contemplate in isolation the repentance of the 'converted' Frederick:

> To him will I: out of these convertites
> There is much matter to be heard and learn'd.   (V. iv. 191)

'Much matter', in other words, to be 'sucked out', after the fashion of the weasel with the egg. As ever Jacques' motive is, in the last analysis, 'observation', the gratifying of a self-regarding curiosity based on a kind of personal impotence, an inability to participate fully and naturally in the processes of life; and, since his attitude is one which implies throughout an incapacity for genuine *giving*, for the positive acceptance of an order, at once natural and distinctively human, beyond the isolated self—the acceptance by which, in love or otherwise, the self is at last justified—he remains a mere marginal presence in the process by which that order is finally, within the scope of the distinctive comic vision, consummated.

3 Twelfth Night

Shakespeare's comedy of *Twelfth Night* seems to have been written for presentation, possibly in 1602, to a polite audience on the occasion of the religious festivity which the title recalls and which coincides with the end of the Christmas celebrations. If this is so, a good deal of light is thrown upon the different elements which combine to make up one of the most varied and subtly unified of Shakespeare's comedies. *Twelfth Night* adds to many of the qualities of a masque, an aristocratic entertainment, those of a kind of children's merry-making, an occasion for dressing up in order to mock the absurdities committed in all seriousness by their elders. Very roughly speaking, for the comedy is even less adapted than most to this kind of dissection, one could say that the element of masque prevails in the 'poetic', romantic part of the action, and that the sentiments and situations developed in this are given a comic reflection in the prose underplot which at each turn accompanies and is interwoven with it. The result is a construction notably different in kind from that of *As You Like It*, and one perhaps even more satisfying, more closely-knit and diversely subtle in its interplay of contrasted levels of meaning.

The 'serious' part of *Twelfth Night* deals principally with conceptions of romantic love derived from the literary taste, aristocratic and sophisticated, of the day. Shakespeare, as usual, transforms his material in the process of developing it, makes it the vehicle for purposes which are unmistakably his own. The play's concern with love is represented, on this level and as the action opens, by Duke Orsino and Olivia. Orsino's famous first speech—

> If music be the food of love, play on;
> Give me *excess* of it—   (I. i. 1)

together with what follows in the brief opening scene, reveals his attitude in love as a blend of sentiment and artifice, true dedication and elaborate self-centredness; it is at once an eloquent statement and, by implication, a criticism of the play's courtly romantic theme. Orsino is a fine creature, a superior being who is capable, and knows himself to be capable, of responding to the most exquisite and valuable human emotions. We shall not fail, here or later, to respond to the real beauty of the poetry in which these emotions are expressed; but this does not mean that the speaker of it is beyond criticism, or that his attitudes do not require, like those of lesser beings, to be taken out of themselves, extended beyond the sphere of self-contemplation in which they can easily lose themselves. The 'spirit of love' which dominates Orsino's heart and mind is, in other words, both a true passion and a subtle form of emotional indulgence; apprehended by him as 'quick and fresh',

possessed of a capacity that 'receiveth as the sea' and transforms all that
it touches into imaginative wealth, it is at the same time an 'appetite'
that craves its own 'excess', that tends inevitably, as it approaches the
satisfaction it so intensely craves, to 'sicken' and 'die': so that everything which it receives falls, by an appropriate law of compensation,

into *abatement* and *low price*
Even in a minute: (I. i. 13)

there is clearly a contrast here with the true love which, in the familiar
terms of Shakespearean comedy, essentially enriches and adds to the
content and value of life. In this strangely contradictory emotion, in
which Orsino's 'desires', as he confesses, pursue him 'like *fell* and *cruel*
hounds', he seeks in the last analysis a concession to sentiment, a 'surfeit'
of feeling which expresses itself most clearly in his longing for 'sweet
beds of flowers' and in the surrender to love-thoughts which 'lie *rich*
when canopied with bowers' (I. i. 41).[21] In the implications of this
'richness', half rare value and half cloying surfeit, lies the key to an
understanding of Orsino's state as the comedy opens.

Something of the same kind can be said, in a rather different way, of
Olivia, the unresponsive object of this devotion. She, too, in Valentine's
account of her, combines true sorrow for her dead brother with a
dwelling upon what have come to be for her, paradoxically, the
elaborate sweets of melancholy:

like a *cloistress* she will *veiled* walk,
And water once a day her chamber round
With eye-offending brine: all this to season
A brother's dead love, which she would *keep fresh*
And *lasting*, in her sad remembrance.   (I. i. 28)

Once again, as in the case of Orsino, we shall not be tempted to simplify this situation to produce a one-sided reading of the play's intention. Olivia, as we shall see her in the course of the action, is—like
Orsino—a creature of rare worth and strong humanity of sentiments;
she shows herself perfectly capable of living up to her position as
mistress of a great house, and there is nothing in itself unworthy about
the persistence of her genuine grief for the brother she has lost. There is,
however, in terms of the comic intention, another side to the story. To
live thus, for reasons however laudable in themselves, in the past, to
keep the memory of death alive in what is finally a self-absorbed and
self-regarding dedication to grief, is to sin against life, to close the doors
wilfully upon its necessary renovation. Orsino, like other comic

characters we have had occasion to meet, is, in a relevant if not exclusive
sense, in love with love, Olivia enamoured essentially of her own sorrow. Precisely because their potential human value, as revealed in the
intense poetic quality of their sentiments, is so great, so exceeding the
common measure, they will have to learn to go in each case beyond
these initial attitudes, to accept the experience which life offers them on
terms finally not of their own making. Throughout this opening,
Shakespeare is engaged in the characteristic task of giving courtly and
romantic feeling—and, with it, the genuine and natural human
emotions which it threatens to carry to exclusive excess—its due, at the
same time as he is limiting it, indicating the degree of selfishness which
accompanies its expression and which will have to be transformed, in
the course of the action, by exposure to more normal and ultimately
positive forms of living. These too will be expressed within the conventional limits which the comic form imposes.

The primary instrument of this transformation is, of course, Viola,
whose readiness to rely upon her own resources—like that shown by
Rosalind in a similar situation in *As You Like It*—contrasts from the
first with the attitudes that prevail at Orsino's court. This is made clear
as soon as she appears, immediately after we have seen Orsino and been
told of Olivia's grief, as a ship-wrecked fugitive on the Illyrian coast.
Her first thought for her brother is an expression of positive hope:
'Perchance he is not drown'd': a hope founded upon the Captain's
report of his last glimpse of him as one 'most *provident* in peril', whom
he saw

> bind himself,
> *Courage* and *hope* both teaching him the practice,
> To a *strong* mast that *lived* upon the sea; (I. ii. 11)

a hope which rests finally upon the quality which she detects in the
Captain himself and to which she can respond because it answers to her
own essentially realistic and positive intuition:

> There is a fair behaviour in thee, Captain;
> And though that *nature with a beauteous wall*
> *Doth oft close in pollution,* yet of thee
> I will believe thou hast a mind that suits
> With this thy fair and outward character. (I. ii. 45)

It is because she is aware of the existence of 'pollution' as a possibility
shadowing life that Viola can become the mouthpiece for its positive
affirmation. These same qualities accompany her as Orsino's messenger

to Olivia. Her attitude to the romantic terms of the message with which she has been charged is characteristically detached. 'I took great pains to study it, and 'tis poetical' (I. v. 208), and indeed Olivia herself is prepared to believe that Orsino's declarations are 'feigned'. When, in the course of the same scene, Olivia asks her how she would behave if she were to find herself in the position of an unrequited lover, Viola's reply is an affirmation, blunt and pointed for all the indirectness which her situation imposes, of the real compulsions of passionate devotion. Unlike the romantic sentiment which luxuriates in its own frustrations, true love cannot accept rejection:

> If I did love you in my master's flame,
> With such a suffering, *such a deadly life*,
> In your denial I would find no sense;
> I would not understand it.   (I. v. 285)

Romantic love is here being subjected to criticism on what are, in effect, its own terms. The implication is that passion such as Orsino's, in so far as it is self-centred and self-consuming, is finally unreal, fails to project itself in the forms which itself assumes to be appropriate. If Viola, speaking as 'Cesario', were to feel for Olivia as her master declares himself to feel, she would

> Hollo your name to the reverberate hills,
> And make the babbling gossip of the air
> Cry out 'Olivia!' O you should not rest
> Between the elements of air and earth,
> But you should pity me.   (I. v. 293)

The presence, at this point and elsewhere, of obvious elements of poetic convention in Viola's statements of love's sincerity, should not obscure the relevance of this passage to the play's main theme, which is the exploration, even within and through convention, of real life. Viola has already expressed to Olivia, in terms familiar to us from the Sonnets, her conviction that the very nature of love implies the responsibility of *giving*, in the absence of which its creative possibilities languish, turn in upon themselves to wither and die:

> Lady, you are the *cruellest* she alive,
> If you will lead these graces to the grave
> And leave the world no copy;[22]   (I. v. 261)

she now further suggests, by implication at least, that Orsino's real, though unconfessed tendency to accept the situation in which he finds himself, extracting from the contemplation of Olivia's rejection of himself a refinement of melancholy, is a sign of the unreality of his passion. It is a large part of her function in the play to act as the instrument by which this unreality is broken down and love restored to its true possibilities through a positive and life-giving contact with things as they are.

The same function emerges, perhaps even more clearly, in the course of the scene (II. iv) in which Orsino presses Viola to carry his message yet again to the irresponsive object of his desire. To his declaration, still essentially complacent, of a love 'more *noble* than the world', based upon an attraction of 'soul' which he likes to think should be irresistible, she opposes a sense of the limitations which real life, the very fact that another person, with feelings and desires of her own, is involved, may impose upon this kind of passion; she asks him quite simply: 'But if she cannot love you, sir?'. Orsino, most typically, cannot conceive that this is even a possibility. 'I cannot be so answered', he replies, precisely because his thought is fixed upon himself, in contemplation of his own situation; and when Viola, drawing now upon sentiments which she is not in a position to express openly, indicates a possible parallel with the sufferings of 'some lady, as perhaps there is', whose passion for him may be as great and as hopeless as that from which he believes himself—perhaps even a little in excess of the facts—to suffer, his reply is a refusal to believe that anyone but himself—and, in particular, any mere *woman*—can harbour so intense, so absolute a dedication. 'There is', he says,

> no woman's sides
> Can bide the beating of so strong a passion
> As love doth give my heart.   (II. iv. 95)

For Orsino, in his essential complacency, it is obvious that 'women lack retention', the capacity, upon which he so prides himself and to which Olivia's disdain allows him to give such deliciously elaborate expression, to persevere in feeling. The love of these lesser creatures is of a kind essentially different from his own superior sentiments. It may, in the conventional terms of his own poetry, 'be called *appetite*',

> No motion of the liver, but the palate,
> That suffer *surfeit, cloyment, and revolt*;   (II. iv. 100)

whereas his own feeling is, as he concludes with at least a touch of implied self-congratulation,

> all as *hungry* as the sea,
> And can digest as much.   (II. iv. 102)

The recourse to images of hunger and surfeit, rooted as they are in poetic convention, is none the less deeply significant. It is of the essence of the play's attitude to its 'romantic' theme that Orsino's own love is, in part at least, an 'appetite', cloying in its initial conception and deliberately mannered in its expression, an imposition of sophisticated and artificial attitudes upon genuine human emotion. Its final perversity is reflected in the fact that it insists in coveting the wrong object and will accordingly need to be re-dedicated before the action can be rounded off in the grouping of appropriately united couples with which the play concludes.

This transformation is brought about through the familiar comic device of an assumed disguise which involves a young woman in the temporary concealment of her sex and after exposure to the various misunderstandings to which this leads. The complications, artificial as they may appear, are an essential part of the play's complete development. Viola, as she receives the ring which conveys the awakening of Olivia to her infatuation for 'Cesario',[23] finds herself caught up in the unforeseen consequences of her own devices; as she says, in language which conveys a meaning beyond mere convention and romantic fancy:

> Disguise, I see thou art a *wickedness*,
> Wherein *the pregnant enemy* does much.
> How easy is it for the *proper-false*
> In women's *waxen hearts* to set their forms!
> Alas, our *frailty* is the cause, not we!
> For such as we are made of, such we be.   (II. ii. 28)

Something of the complexity of real life is here reflected, in and beneath the forms of convention. 'Disguise' is a reflection of Shakespeare's lifelong preoccupation with 'seeming', with the falsity beneath which men and women seek to hide, from others and perhaps most intimately of all from themselves, the intricacies of their own natures. In tragic terms this could amount to a 'wickedness', a reflection of ultimate falsity, and the fact that Viola can use this very word here is an indication that the tragic emotion is not entirely absent; but it is the end of comedy, as this play conceives it, to trace out these and similar complexities, beyond all possible human intention, to the ends of life, so that there is meaning, a significant acceptance of the way in which these ends impose themselves, in Viola's final, half-humorous renunciation of her own capacity to mould the course of events to her immediate purpose:

> O time! thou must untangle this, not I;
> It is too hard a knot for me to untie! (II. ii. 41)

It is, perhaps, the human determination to bend life, prematurely and unilaterally, to its own partial ends that produces tragedy, and the wiser readiness to wait for the unfolding of the natural pattern after its own fashion that allows the comic resolution of harmonies to grow to its completion in the fullness of time.

Viola, however, though she shows herself wise enough to admit that neither she nor any other human being can, in the long run, control the course of life, shows a very considerable capacity for understanding the nature of its operations; and that too is a part of the comic vision as this play conceives it. She can, as a sign of this realization, take up and give full value, a genuine human meaning, to Orsino's more self-centred and circumscribed melancholy. When, in urging upon her the necessity of love, he affirms, with the characteristic dying cadence of his romantic musings, that

> women are as roses, whose fair flower
> Being once display'd, *doth fall that very hour*, (II. iv. 38)

she can take up the truth contained in his observation, less in the spirit of self-immersed gloom in which it is uttered than as the reflection of a universal flaw felt to exist at the heart of life:

> And so they are: alas, that they are so;
> To die, even when they to perfection grow! (II. iv. 40)

Immediately afterwards, she goes on to set this same melancholy in relation to her own situation by referring, since the nature of her disguise makes it impossible for her to speak directly of her own state, to the 'history' of her supposed sister:

> She never told her love,
> But let *concealment*, like a worm i' the bud,
> *Feed* on her damask cheek: she *pined* in thought;
> And with *a green and yellow melancholy*
> She sat like Patience on a monument
> Smiling at grief. (II. iv. 112)

This, though it may appear at first sight to be a mere echo of Orsino's mood, is in effect different. Viola is lamenting the unnatural and apparently insoluble plight in which she finds herself, not giving it poetic decoration or luxuriating in the 'dark' thoughts which it inspires in her. Though she speaks, as always, within the limits of her appropriate poetic convention, she also speaks to ends that are distinctively her own. It is the necessity for 'concealment' that leads in her case to a melancholy conceived of as 'green and yellow', out of season and inevitably self-consuming in its effect upon the sufferer; and the way out of this unhappy state will lie, not in the romantic lover's surrender to delicious sadness, but in the advancing of love beyond this introverted stage in relation to the rest of life.

The impact of reality, indeed, makes itself felt from the moment in which Olivia is driven, in her own despite, to make open declaration of her love for 'Cesario'. In this way life affirms itself, in the characteristic fashion of Shakespearean comedy, by breaking through the barriers which artifice and pretence have been engaged in setting up against it; and, as it does so, Olivia recognizes the implications of her surrender in a speech which is itself full of disturbing and, at first sight, unexpected echoes:

> I did send,
> After *the last enchantment* you did here,
> A ring in chase of you: so did I *abuse*
> *Myself*, my servant, and, I fear me, you:
> Under your hard construction must I sit,
> To *force* that on you, in *a shameful cunning*,
> Which you know none of yours: what might you think?
> Have you not set mine honour at the stake
> And baited it with all *the unmuzzled thoughts*
> That *tyrannous heart* can think? To one of your receiving
> Enough is shown: a cypress, not a bosom,
> Hides my heart. (III. i. 124)

To respond adequately to this confession is to sense, beneath the conventional forms, a soul caught in the contradictions which its own appetites, developed in a situation of long and perverse self-concealment have imposed; those references to self-abuse, those 'unmuzzled' motions of a 'tyrannous' desire, can only be exorcised by being brought out into the open, related in a natural way to the day-light realities of life. Meanwhile, and until this can take place, the ambivalences of desire are expressed, after the fashion of this play, in which disguise habitually answers to the unavowed complexity of human impulses and appearances, through a typical interplay of double situations. Olivia, in a first tentative groping towards self-clarification, asks 'Cesario': 'I prithee, tell me what thou thinkst of me?', and the exchange is continued in these terms:

> *c* —That you do think *you are not what you are.*
> *o* —If I think so, I think the same of you.
> *c* —Then think you right: I am not what I am.
> *o* —I would you were as I would have you be!
> *c* —Would it be better, madam, than I am?
>   I wish it might, *for now I am your fool.*   (III. i. 153)

The results of a situation compounded of misunderstandings and concealment, implying a refusal on the part of so many of those most directly concerned to recognize the claims of life for what they are, become apparent when the supposed 'Cesario', herself caught, though in this case through no fault of her own, in the consequences of her own disguise, is driven by the declaration of Olivia's passion for herself to renounce the impossible mission with which she has been entrusted by Orsino:

> never more
> Will I my master's tears to you deplore.   (III. i. 175)

Not till the end of the play, when the time comes for the shedding of disguises and for the assumption by each character of the part which properly corresponds to him or herself in the whole, will the imperious and life-conferring compulsions of love find their appropriate consummation in a comic reflection of real, as distinct from artificial humanity.

The way out of this complex of misunderstandings lies through the revelation that Viola's twin brother, Sebastian, has survived the perils of shipwreck to which he was exposed at the beginning of the play. Once more the new situation is introduced through an appropriate inversion of common reality. Sebastian, meeting Olivia, who believes him to be 'Cesario' and consequently the object of her own newly awakened devotion, appears to himself to be living in a world of fantasy in which the laws which govern daily reality are strangely suspended: 'Or I am *mad*, or else this is a dream'. So might Antipholus of Syracuse have spoken in Shakespeare's early exercise in comic form[24]; but here, since the content of the 'dream' answers to his true and natural desires, he declares himself disposed to allow it to continue: 'If it be thus to dream, still let me sleep' (IV. i. 67). The 'dream' that thus answers to the intimate compulsion of real life tends, in terms of Shakespearean comedy, to merge into the reality of daylight. When we next meet Sebastian, he has received the gift of the 'pearl' which confirms Olivia's dedication to him of herself and is able to distinguish the genuine and life-giving magic of his new bewitchment from the aberrations of mere lunacy:

> though 'tis *wonder* that enwraps me thus,
> Yet *'tis not madness*.   (IV. iii. 3)

This answers to the general trend of the comic conception, which is consistent in moving away from 'madness' and the various forms of self-deception with which the earlier part of the action has been so closely concerned in the direction of sanity and normal fulfilment. To look upon life with 'wonder', a proper sense of reverence, is to be, in Shakespearean comic terms, the opposite of mad. Olivia herself is at last brought out of her self-imposed isolation, as she in turn begs Sebastian to confer upon her 'the *full assurance* of your *faith*' to the end that

> *my most jealous and too doubtful soul*
> May live at *peace*.   (IV. iii. 27)

She has come by the end of the play to understand that she is a creature whose destiny lies in marriage, that real peace will lie for her, not in surrender to the self-deceiving mirror she has set up before herself under the pretext of dedication to the dead, but in the full acceptance of life as offered in the present; as Sebastian has just said at the opening of the scene, opposing the firm grasp of reality which he shares with his sister to so much indulgence of cloistered feeling: 'This is the air: that is the glorious sun' (IV. iii. 1). Things, to put the matter in its simplest terms, are first and foremost what they are; and in a joyful acceptance of their present reality, positive, freely-given, and 'glorious', triumphant over the shades of night and over all forms of self-imposed delusion, lies the key to true living.

By the time the action has been brought to a close the ends conceived in this way have been triumphantly achieved. Neither the initial devotion of Orsino nor Olivia's reiterated sorrow emerge at their original self-estimate. When, in the final scene (V. i), Orsino marries, not Olivia, but the Viola who has conquered his true affection with her combination of self-reliance and feminine grace; when Olivia has awakened from the dream constituted by her dedication to a sterile melancholy; when, through these developments, the clear 'air' and the 'glorious sun' of life have asserted themselves to ends of harmony and fulfilment, the true purpose of the make-believe with which the play seems, on this level, to have been so long concerned is at last apparent. The romantic visions of devotion which originally inspired these courtly sentimentalists contain within themselves positive elements, emotions natural and necessary to a full and truly civilized life. They are visions, however, which now call in a new spirit for more adequate objects of dedication, and these have been provided in the course of the action. Both Orsino and Olivia have learnt that the compulsive force of the passions to which they have been respectively dedicated is such as to draw them finally beyond themselves, demanding from each the acceptance of a fuller, a more natural and spontaneous way of living.

The 'lessons' which emerge in this way from the main action of *Twelfth Night* are reinforced and diversified by an underplot which gives a new and profoundly Shakespearean content to the comedy of character which Ben Jonson had only recently exhibited in his play *Every Man in his Humour*.[25] Jonson's comedy of 'humours' is, in its essence, an attempt at psychological realism: based upon principles which purported to be 'scientific' (within the limitations of the age) it replaced poetry by prose, fancy by the realistic delineation of personality. Shakespeare, in so far as he chose to make use of this conception of comedy, modified this 'realistic' bias in the direction of the very different imaginative ends he had in view. Though the comedy of his underplot carries social implications which make their presence felt from time to time, these implications are generally subsidiary to the unifying, harmonizing purpose which dominates the play as a whole. *Twelfth Night* is more indivisible in its effect, less easily separable into elements significantly contrasted, than any preceding Shakespearean comedy; but within this imaginative unity, this uniquely pervasive 'Illyrian' quality, the comic scenes in prose make their effect by asserting a firm reality, itself suitably transformed to correspond to the general mode, against the deliberately poetic elaboration which prevails in the more aristocratic, courtly sphere of the action. No more suitable foil, indeed, could be imagined to the conventionality, the poetic artifice, which Shakespeare was in this play at once concerned to use and, as he made use of it for ends essentially his own, to criticize.

The general aim of the prose scenes is, accordingly, to balance the elaboration which so largely prevails in the courtly action with a more direct reflection of real life, comically conceived. In Sir Toby Belch, Maria, and Sir Andrew Aguecheek, as they carry on their intrigues in the backstairs region of Olivia's mansion, we may discern, in distinctively social terms, a reflection of the underside of that aristocratic life which has found elsewhere in the play its more elegant expression. Like Falstaff, with whom he has occasional points of contact, Sir Toby is no paragon of virtue. The product of a decayed feudal order, he lives by his wits and is ready to exploit the pretensions of Sir Andrew for the sake of his 'three thousand ducats a year': the means of life offer themselves as they come, and it does not behove such as Sir Toby—or Falstaff—to be over-delicate in his acceptance of them. Neither he nor Maria, however, are, like their 'betters', self-deceivers in the name of a supposed refinement; and it is here, above all, that the parallel with Falstaff, translated though it is into the very different terms of this play, holds good. In Sir Toby's presentation of him, Sir Andrew emerges as a caricature of his courtly superiors: as one who claims to play the 'viol de gamboys', to speak three or four languages, and to possess, in Sir Toby's not disinterested estimate of his social virtues, 'all the good gifts of nature', but who is also seen (by Maria, who is not easily deceived) to be a 'fool' and 'a great quarreller', saved from disaster only by his possession of 'the gift of a coward to allay the gust he hath in quarrelling' (I. iii. 33). For his intrigues and his basic cynicism, Sir Toby will be sufficiently punished when his misplaced ingenuity leads him to have his head broken for his rashness in crossing swords with Sebastian (V. i); but for the measure of genuine attachment to life which enables him to comment by implication upon his niece's self-centred and self-consuming melancholy—'What a plague means my niece to take the death of her brother thus? I'm sure care's an enemy to life' (I. iii. 1)—he is rewarded at the last (if reward it be) by marriage to his kindred spirit in humour, Maria.

Over both these personages, indeed, and over the prose episodes of the play as a whole, the comic spirit projects a light of its own, as distinct from Jonson's more explicitly moralizing genius as can readily be imagined. It produces a compound of Illyrian fancy and truth to nature which refuses either to belittle or, alternatively, to inflate into false seriousness: the spirit which finds expression in Maria's retort to Sir Andrew—'thought is free' (I. iii. 74)—and in the consistent repudiation of vain self-righteousness and officious self-approval in all their forms. These comic episodes represent—to put the matter in another way—the spirit of 'Twelfth Night', the setting free of natural instincts normally under restraint: instincts which are often absurd in the way in which they manifest themselves, but which possess—at least when set against the aristocratic pretensions which prevail elsewhere—a genuine life of their own. When Malvolio utters his protest against 'riot' in the name of the decorum and self-importance which he associates so complacently with his own person—'My masters, are you mad? or what are you? Have you no wit, manners, nor honesty, but to gabble like tinkers at this time of night? . . . Is there no respect of place, persons, nor time in you?'—Sir Toby can retort 'We did keep time, sir, in our catches', and go on to deliver the most powerful of his repudiations of pretentious and self-admiring virtue: 'Dost thou think, because thou art virtuous, there shall be no more cakes and ale?' (II. iii. 124).

The protest against pretentiousness in all its forms is maintained indeed, through the underplot in a variety of ways. Olivia's supposed letter to Malvolio (II. iv) and the form of Sir Andrew's challenge to 'Cesario' (III. iv) both carry satires of courtly conventions, of love and 'honour' respectively; and both, moreover, in so far as they involve personages from the 'serious' action, bringing them out of their usual sphere and exposing them to situations which reveal them in a certain absurdity, tend to join the play's two levels in a revealing unity. No one in the action is finally altogether exempt from the operations of this kind of comic inversion. Even Viola, who has chosen—albeit for excellent motives—to practise a kind of deception, is entrapped for a moment in the unforeseen consequences of her own assumption of disguise when she reacts in natural fear to the challenge which Sir Toby has prepared for Aguecheek; although, of course, her own attitude to the business of the duel is, most typically, one of engaging common-sense and candour: 'I am one that had rather go with sir priest than sir knight. I care not who knows so much of my mettle' (III. iv. 300). The rich and varied fusion of realism and convention in a series of comic effects which answers perfectly to the prevailing Illyrian mood is perhaps the play's supreme achievement.

The central figure of the underplot, however, upon whose person the various intrigues finally turn, is of course Malvolio. As Olivia's steward he represents her dignity, which he associates ridiculously with his obsessive sense of his own, and bears her messages to those who live in her domain; in so doing, he brings together the two worlds of aristocratic sophistication and realistic 'humour' which, by their continual interplay, make the theme of the comedy. Malvolio is admirably chosen to play this part. The comedy which surrounds his person turns upon the familiar Shakespearean contrast between reality and self-estimation; the contrast which also, under other forms, dominates the

presentation of his mistress and Orsino. Whereas they deceive themselves as to the real nature of their emotions, and choose to live in a
world of their own imagining, Malvolio, not less self-consciously
attached to 'virtue' and to his own conception of his dignity, is caught
by Maria 'practising behaviour to his own shadow' (II. v. 20) and
imagining, in the same scene, his own advancement and the putting in
his place of Sir Toby. 'You are idle shallow things', he says in his
infatuation to those who are engineering his downfall, 'I am not of
your element' (III. iv. 138). The self-love which leads him to respond
to the challenge which his enemies place before him in the form of an
illusory prospect of exaltation—'some are born great, some achieve
greatness, and some have greatness thrust upon 'em' (II. v. 159) is not
devoid on occasion of a certain crazed dignity; but it leads him at the
last to a series of misfortunes from which he is never truly delivered.

In this last respect, Malvolio is unique in the play. The presence of a
disturbing quality beneath the obvious comedy of his presentation is
most apparent when he finds himself, through the devices of Maria and
those who accompany her, imprisoned in darkness and visited by Feste
the clown in his disguise as Sir Topas (IV. ii). The essence of the comic
effect at this point lies in the fact that Malvolio, though impenetrably
deceived as to his own nature, clings to solid and tangible reality against
the illusions to which he is so mercilessly subjected. When Feste transforms the 'prison' verbally into an abode of nobility and light—'it hath
bay windows transparent as barricadoes, and the clearstories towards the
south-north are as lustrous as ebony' (IV. ii. 41)—he insists that the
place of his confinement is, as in reality it is, 'dark as hell'; and if the
comedy strikes us, at this point, as unusually sardonic in its implications,
this is related to Feste's stressing of the fact that the 'darkness' in which
he finds himself thus enveloped has a moral significance for the victim's
own nature. 'I say there is no darkness but ignorance' is Feste's retort
to Malvolio's insistence that he is in truth plunged into a real physical
obscurity; and the point of the comment is that this darkness is a
reflection of the lack of proper self-understanding which has led
Malvolio to live in accordance with a fictitious conception of his own
dignity not altogether unlike that shown by his 'betters', but from
which, in contrast to them, he shows to the last no sign of awakening:

I say, this house is as dark as ignorance, though ignorance were dark as hell;
and I say, there was never man thus abused. I am no more mad than you
are. (IV. ii. 50)

In so far as it is a matter of distinguishing truly between external realities, Malvolio's protest corresponds to an undeniable truth. The comedy of his situation—if comedy we can call it—turns upon the fact that, lucid as he is in his attitude to his physical surroundings, he is yet—like many of those who surround him, but to a far less curable degree—the prisoner of his own self-estimate.

There is, accordingly, in Malvolio's vicissitudes a note which transcends the obvious comedy of his situation and which ends by affecting with a certain uneasiness the celebration by the humorists of their triumph over him. At the end of the play Malvolio alone fails to join the final procession of characters awakened, each on his or her appropriate level, to the claims of reality. His last protest to Olivia contains a note of accusation which seems to evade the comic spirit, or at least to live unquietly in relation to it:

> Why have you suffer'd me to be imprisoned,
> Kept in a dark house, visited by the priest,
> And made the most notorious geck and gull
> That e'er invention play'd on. *Tell me why.* (V. i. 353)

The answer is, of course, that he has made his own prison, that the darkness to which he has been confined reflects his own attitude to life; but the insistence with which the question is posed, and Malvolio's invincible inability to see the answer, stand out with an odd effect of incongruity from the general orientation of the final scene. His last letter of protest to his mistress is couched in terms of a certain dignity, and Orsino himself is ready to concede that 'This savours not much of distraction': as neither, indeed, did his previous comment, addressed to 'Sir Topas' in the hour of darkness, concerning 'the opinion of Pythagoras' upon the soul's immortality: 'I think nobly of the soul, and in no way approve his opinion' (IV. ii. 61). It is Malvolio's defect to be inextricably rooted in a fixed idea of things, in which he himself occupies the centre, as he shows at the last when he responds to Orsino's efforts 'to entreat him to a peace' in the interests of the general harmony that has just been established with the bitter and uncomprehending cry: 'I'll be revenged on the whole pack of you' (V. i). This defect makes him a legitimate object for the comic derision which so abundantly overtakes him in the course of the play, and for which we need not pity him; but, for all the absurdity of his yellow stockings and cross-garters, in spite of the obvious parody of a vain self-righteousness held to be 'Puritan'—though we should note in passing that Maria

expressly denies (II. iii) that he is any such thing—Malvolio's demand
for a satisfaction that his need for self-justification craves, but which he
cannot in the very nature of things hope to obtain, places him in a
certain sense outside the play's comic spirit, relates him finally to other
and perhaps more disturbing orders of reality.

By this time, we have reached the end of the play in one of those
scenes of reconciliation and married fulfilment towards which Shakespearean comedy so insistently tends. Sebastian has been united to
Olivia, who has been thereby restored from her melancholy self-
contemplation to the claims of real life. Antonio, the sea captain, has
affirmed his place in the world of Illyrian fantasy in the name of true
friendship and honest constancy, values for which he has already
declared himself ready to risk his life in a hostile environment for the
sake of Sebastian:

> my desire,
> More sharp than filed steel, did spur me forth . . .

> . . . my willing love,
> The rather by these arguments of fear,
> Set forth in your pursuit;   (III. iii. 4)

generous sentiments nobly confirmed in action, which now find their
appropriate setting in a world where acceptance and mutual forgiveness
prevail. Having been involved, with danger of his life, in the 'Cesario'-
Viola–Sebastian confusion, Antonio emerges at the last into the light of
day, to the dawning of which his loyalty and steadfast faith have contributed. Only the remnants of Orsino's jealous resentment at Olivia's
marriage to another than himself now remains to shadow, though only
for a moment and in passing, the final resolution. In a first and typically
impulsive reaction to the frustration of his long-cherished designs, he
seeks satisfaction in the thought of revenge:

> my thoughts are *ripe in mischief*;
> I'll *sacrifice the lamb that I do love*,
> To *spite* a raven's heart within a dove.   (V. i. 133)

To this 'savage' jealousy, which prompts Orsino, even at this late stage,
to contemplate the killing of the object of his love in a last appropriate
gesture of self-torture, Viola replies by the offer of her readiness to give
her own life:

> I, *most jocund, apt, and willingly*,
> To do you rest, a thousand times would die,

even as she declares the true object of her love:

>—Where goes Cesario?
>—   After him I love
>More than I love these eyes, *more than my life*,
>More, by all mores, than e'er I shall love wife.
>If I do feign, you witnesses above,
>Punish my life for tainting of my love.   (V. i. 136)

'More than I love these eyes, more than my life': here we have, concentrated into a few intensely spoken words, the real turning-point of the whole episode. Love has at last been declared in its full truth and boundless generosity; and now the priest's revelation of Olivia's marriage to Sebastian begins to shift the clouds, whilst the return of a suitably chastened Sir Toby, with his head broken for his past presumption, finally reveals the truth in a suitably comic manner. Sebastian, restored to the sister whom he feared that 'the blind waves' had devoured, finds that the action of the waves has been less 'blind' than he had thought, and goes on to ask questions which are, in terms of the Shakespearean comic vision, a prelude to reconciliation—'What countryman? what name? what parentage'[26]—and is greeted as a 'spirit' restored:

>A spirit I am indeed;
>But am in that dimension grossly clad
>Which from the womb I did participate.   (V. i. 246)

As a 'spirit' of this kind, immortal but compact with life and corporal 'dimension', he greets 'drowned Viola' as his restored sister. In the light of this revelation, Olivia recognizes her 'mistake' and accepts Sebastian for himself; whilst, last of all, Orsino responds to the declaration of Viola's faith, waking from his own fantasies to take her for his bride:

>When that is known, and *golden time* convents,
>A solemn combination shall be made
>Of our dear souls.   (V. i. 394)[27]

The world of child-like fantasy and theatrical illusion which belongs to the spirit of this play merges here, with a delicate and ethereal intensity, into something deeper, more profound in its human reverberations, than itself. There can be few points in Shakespeare's earlier writing at which we can feel ourselves so close to the world of symbolic transformations which will prevail, at the end of his career, in *The Winter's Tale* and in *The Tempest*.

From this final restoration of harmony Malvolio, as we have already seen, is excluded. It only remains to say that Feste too stands—as he has stood throughout the play—rather outside the prevailing mood. The spirit of his own distinctive comedy, which is on occasions by no means devoid of malice, responds to constantly shifting attitudes, moods more complex and varied in their implication than may at first appear. These are related at each turn to the state of the developing action. His first song (II. iii) affirms love as natural and real. 'Every wise man's son' knows that 'Journeys end in lover's meeting', and this may perhaps imply a criticism of the love which feeds upon itself in self-contemplation; but, equally, the background of all human sentiment is impermanence, so that 'In delay there lies no plenty' and 'Youth's a stuff will not endure'. In a spirit not finally dissimilar he has already made his appropriate comment on Olivia's dedication to grief when, after asking her the reasons for her mourning, he induces her to declare her belief that her brother is in 'heaven' and concludes: 'The more fool, madam, to mourn for your brother's soul being in heaven' (I. v. 75). Feste's moods are, indeed, as varied as the constantly shifting emotional texture of this most finely woven of plays. He can respond to Orsino's melancholy—'Come away, come away, death' (II. iv)—as readily as to any other emotion which is at once true, humanly valid, and open to criticism for the excess or self-centredness with which it is sometimes pursued; equally, he can apply himself to burlesquing the pretensions of Malvolio. An element of mastery, indeed, of drawing the sources of his life from outside the main action of the play, is an essential feature of this Fool. In his position as a licensed jester, Feste is able to move freely among his superiors, and shows himself no respecter of persons when he replies to Orsino's query, 'how dost thou, my good fellow?', with the sharp and detached realism of his reply: 'the better for my foes and the worse for my friends' (V. i. 13). In this way he answers, perhaps even better than most, to the constant tendency of Shakespearean comedy to qualify its own imaginative harmonies with a profound sense of the element of relativity, of a final uniqueness and autonomy, which underlies all human experience. When the time comes for him to utter the song which rounds off the play, he conveys a mood enigmatically compounded of realism and fancy, truth and illusion, which is perhaps the last and deepest impression which we retain from Illyria. The song passes from a wistful evocation of the innocence of childhood—'When that I was and a little tiny boy'—to wry and disillusioned comment upon mature reality:

But when I came to man's estate . . .
. . . 'Gainst thieves and knaves men shut their gate, (V. i. 405)

and goes on to envelop the whole in the pervasive and intangible melancholy of the refrain: 'For the rain it raineth every day'. For Illyria, too, in spite of all the beauty of imaginative fancy which has gone to its poetic creation, is a dream; and it is of the essence of Shakespeare's mature comedy—and in this, as in other respects, *Twelfth Night* will remain unsurpassed till *The Winter's Tale* and *The Tempest*— to touch the poignant, and to extract from its sense of the passing and the insubstantial some of the deepest and most individual of his dramatic effects.

NOTES

Introduction

1. First published in 1904.
2. The stock example is provided by Charles Lamb's famous observations on the stage impression produced by *King Lear*.
3. Granville Barker's *Prefaces to Shakespeare* were published in five series from 1927 to 1947.
4. See Chapter VII below.
5. *Shakespeare's Imagery and What It Tells us* (Cambridge, 1935).
6. Published in 1932.
7. *A Midsummer Night's Dream*, I. ii:

> The raging rocks
> And shivering shocks
> Shall break the locks
>   Of prison-gates;
> And Phibbus' car
> Shall shine from far,
> And make and mar
>   The foolish Fates.

Professor Wilson Knight comments on this as follows: 'The sombre plays were plays of tempest and earthquake, and yet their shattering violence itself cleaves that confining pain, breaks it as a shell, bursting the "prison-gates" of mortality to disclose a newer life in *Antony and Cleopatra* and *Pericles*. In *Antony and Cleopatra* "Phibus' car" rises, dispelling the murk of *Macbeth* and the mists of *Lear*, and does indeed mysteriously "make and mar" the fates, which are, in that vision, by themselves "foolish".'

8. The title of my original essay was '*An* Approach to Shakespeare', not—as a choleric critic once stated—'*The* Approach to Shakespeare'.
9. These phrases are taken from the original 1938 edition of my essay. They were only slightly amended in the reprint and expansion of 1957.
10. This quotation represents the thought of the 1938 essay as slightly amended, for greater clarity, in 1957.
11. Once again the argument developed in this passage, though valid in its general aim, now strikes me as less than complete. In particular it seems to suggest a serious undervaluation of the originality and power of Shakespeare's early work: an undervaluation which I hope that the account of these plays in the pages that follow will serve to correct.

12. I am referring here, of course, to the Globe playhouse. The theatre at Blackfriars, for which the last romances were written, was different in kind, and the difference is no doubt reflected in the plays themselves: but the difference does not affect the general line of the argument here put forward.

I The Early Chronicle Plays

1. Notably the productions by Peter Hall and John Barton at Stratford on Avon in 1964.
2. Professor Dover Wilson, following earlier students of the *Henry VI* plays, has been a chief defender of the view that these represent the re-shaping for performance by Shakespeare's own company of plays written at least in part by other hands; but more recent investigation, following Peter Alexander's important study, *Shakespeare's Henry VI and Richard III* (Cambridge, 1929), has tended to give Shakespeare greater credit for originality in his early writings.
3. Compare the spirit of Hotspur's last words:

> ... thought's the slave of life, and life time's fool;
> And time, that takes survey of all the world,
> Must have a stop.
>
> (*Henry IV, Part I*, V. iv. 81)

4. *Henry V*, III. iii. See p. 252 below.
5. *Henry V*, V. ii.
6. *Troilus and Cressida, passim.*
7. See pp. 46–61 below.
8. Compare Richard II on Bolingbroke,

> Ourselves and Bushy, Bagot here and Green
> Observed his courtship to the common people;
> How he did seem to dive into their hearts
> With humble and familiar courtesy.
>
> (*Richard II*, I. iv. 23)

9. III. i. 225.
10. *Julius Caesar*, III. ii.
11. I. ii. See p. 29 above.
12. Compare *Macbeth*: 'Things bad began make strong themselves by ill' (III. ii. 55).
13. The phrase is used of Savonarola in *The Prince*, Chapter VI.
14. Compare the opening speech of Richard III. See p. 47 below.
15. See *Henry VI, Part II*, V. i, and p. 34 above.

16. A similar deal, described with immensely greater mastery, joins Caesar's sister Octavia to Antony in one of Shakespeare's finest exposures of political realism (*Antony and Cleopatra*, II. ii).

17. *Henry IV, Part II*, IV. ii. See p. 238 below.

18. See p. 41 above.

19. *The Tempest*, I. ii.

20. See p. 45 above: 'I am myself alone'.

21. See p. 49 above.

22. Compare, for the phrasing, *Macbeth*, III. iv. 136:

> I am in blood
> Stepp'd in so far that, should I wade no more,
> Returning were as tedious as go o'er.

23. Compare Macbeth's exchanges with Seyton and the Servant (V. iii).

24. *Macbeth*, V. vii.

25. Compare Macbeth's efforts to escape consideration of his true state in action, especially in V. iii, v.

26. Compare Clifford in *Henry VI, Part III*:

> The foe is merciless, and will not pity;
> For at their hands I have deserved no pity.   (II. vi. 25).

See p. 40 above.

27. *Dr. Faustus*, the last speech.

28. Compare the attitude of Clarence's murderer, quoted on p. 52 above.

29. Compare once more the spirit of Macbeth's final show of resolution:

> Ring the alarum-bell! Blow, wind! come, wrack!
> At least we'll die with harness on our back.   (V. v. 51)

30. Compare, for the vivid phrase, Biron's protest against the penance imposed on him by Rosaline:

> To move wild laughter in the throat of death?
> It cannot be; it is impossible.
> (*Love's Labour's Lost*, V. ii. 863)

II Titus Andronicus

1. Published respectively in 1593 and 1594.

2. *Macbeth*, III. ii. 22:

> Duncan is in his grave;
> After life's fitful fever he sleeps well;
> Treason has done his worst: nor steel, nor poison,
> Malice domestic, foreign levy, nothing,
> Can touch him further.

3. Compare *Richard III*, I. ii. 229:

> Was ever woman in this humour woo'd?
> Was ever woman in this humour won?

4. For *As You Like It*, see pp. 282–302 below.
5. *The Winter's Tale*, IV. iv.
6. *A Midsummer Night's Dream*, IV. i. See p. 154 below.
7. Compare Albany in *King Lear*, IV. ii. 40: 'Tigers, not daughters, what have you perform'd?'.
8. 'When did the tiger's young ones teach the dam?' (*Titus Andronicus*, II. iii. 142).
9. Compare *Timon of Athens*, V. i. 220:

> Timon hath made his everlasting mansion
> Upon the beached verge of the salt flood,

and the lines which follow.

10. Compare Lear's

> the small gilded fly
> Does lecher in my sight
> (*King Lear*, IV. vi. 115)

11. Aaron has already called the woods 'ruthless, dreadful, deaf, and dull' (II. i. 128). See p. 65 above.

III The Early Comedies

1. The main argument of this Chapter has been outlined in my essay on Shakespeare's Early Comedies, published in the *Writers and Their Work* series (London, 1960).
2. The *Menaechmi* and the *Amphitruo*.
3. See pp. 83–9 below.
4. See p. 77 above.
5. For examples and a discussion of the theme of time in the Sonnets see pp. 112–15 below.
6. Gascoyne's translation of Ariosto's play was first published, under the title of *Supposes*, in 1566.
7. *Induction*, ii. 140.
8. Act II, sc. i.
9. Act IV, sc. ii.
10. *Richard III*, V. iii. 184. See p. 58 above.
11. See pp. 303–4 below.
12. Compare, for one example among many of similar imagery, *Antony and Cleopatra*, IV. xii (IV. x. 33 in Oxford University Press edition):

> All come to this? The hearts
> That spaniell'd me at heels, to whom I gave
> Their wishes, do discandy, melt their sweets
> On blossoming Caesar.

13. Compare, more especially, the spirit of the exchanges between Pompey and the judge Escalus in *Measure for Measure*, II. i.
14. See p. 178 below.
15. See p. 96 above.
16. *A Midsummer Night's Dream*, V. i. See p. 157 below.

IV The Sonnets

1. See Leslie Hotson's book, *Shakespeare's Sonnets Dated* (1949). Hotson's arguments have, however, been strongly contested.
2. Among many examples of this device, we may quote these from the Prologues to *Henry V*: 'the *invisible and creeping wind*' (Act III): 'the *quick forge and working-house* of thought' (Act V). Many other examples could be found in the plays, and very notably in *Hamlet*.
3. Compare Angelo's

> it is I
> That, lying by the violet in the sun,
> Do as the carrion does, not as the flower,
> Corrupt with virtuous season.
> (*Measure for Measure*, II. ii. 165)

4. Compare Lucio in *Measure for Measure*, I. iv. 40:

> Your brother and his lover have embraced:
> As those that feed grow full; as blossoming time,
> That from the seedness the bare fallow brings
> To teeming foison; even so her plenteous womb
> Expresseth his full tilth and husbandry.

5. Sonnet IV.
6. Sonnet IV.
7. *The Merchant of Venice*, II, ix. See p. 190 below.
8. For example, in *The Two Gentlemen of Verona*. See p. 92 above.
9. Sonnet LXV.
10. The fact that 'devouring time' is a translation of this classical commonplace does not, of course, invalidate the point here made. It is the relationship between the two elements in the complete concept—'devouring time' and the 'lion', respectively—that produces the poetic effect, which is not in any way modified by the origin of the elements which compose it.

11. This aspect of the Sonnets has been well studied by L. C. Knights in his essay published in *Explorations* (London, 1946).
12. See pp. 117–42 below.
13. For this play see *An Approach to Shakespeare*, Vol. II (London, 1969), Chapter 1.
14. Notably the so-called 'problem' plays, including for this purpose *Hamlet*.

V From 'Romeo and Juliet' to 'Richard II'

1. See pp. 106–15 above.
2. Sonnet CXVI. See p. 113 above.
3. Compare the treatment of the same theme in the Sonnets quoted on p. 111.
4. Compare *A Midsummer Night's Dream*, I. i. 141:

> Or, if there were a sympathy in choice,
> War, death, or sickness did lay siege to it,
> Making it momentary as a sound,
> Swift as a shadow, short as any dream;
> Brief as the lightning in the collied night,
> That, in a spleen, unfolds both heaven and earth,
> And ere a man hath power to say 'Behold!'
> The jaws of darkness do devour it up:
> So quick bright things come to confusion,

and p. 145 below.

5. It is interesting to compare these two lines, stylistically, to those, at least equally famous, from *Hamlet*:

> But look, the morn, in russet mantle clad,
> Walks o'er the dew of yon high eastern hill.
> (*Hamlet*, I. i. 166)

6. It is hardly necessary to point out the relationship between these themes and those raised by the resolution of Navarre and his companions in *Love's Labour's Lost*. See pp. 95–105 above.
7. We have had occasion to note Shakespeare's concern with 'doting', as a one-sided and self-centred perversion of true love in relation to *The Comedy of Errors* and *The Two Gentlemen of Verona*. See pp. 79 and 92–3 above.
8. See *Romeo and Juliet*, II. ii, quoted on pp. 125–6 above.
9. The poetry of Puck has a good deal in common with that of the Mercutio of the 'Queen Mab' speech. See *Romeo and Juliet*, I. iv, and p. 120 above.
10. Compare *The Two Gentlemen of Verona*, IV. ii, quoted on p. 93 above.

11. The relevance to this of Helena's 'blind Cupid' speech (I. i), quoted on p. 146, is obvious.

12. There is some anticipation here of Touchstone's attitude to the Forest of Arden (*As You Like It*, II. iv) quoted on p. 290 below.

13. We are reminded of the repeatedly expressed determination of Antipholus of Syracuse, in *The Comedy of Errors*, to escape from the 'madness' which surrounds him in Ephesus. See p. 78 above.

14. See p. 79 above.

15. See p. 94 above.

16. The implications of poetry of this kind in Shakespeare's final romances are discussed in my book *Shakespeare: The Last Phase* (2nd Edition, London, 1965).

17. St. Paul's *First Epistle to the Corinthians*, II. ix.

18. See pp. 102–3 above.

19. They can be compared, in spirit and purpose, to those of the song which marks the entry of the god Hymen, with Rosalind and Celia, at the end of *As You Like It*. See pp. 297–8 below.

20. The later plays in the series are discussed in Chapter VII.

21. See pp. 248–60 below.

22. *Henry VI, Part III*, II. v. See p. 40 above.

23. See, more especially, pp. 130–1 above.

24. Compare *Hamlet*, I. ii. 76.

> I know not 'seems'. . . .
> . . . I have that within which passeth show;
> These but the trappings and the suits of woe.

25. See Chapter VII.

26. A more exhaustive account of *Richard II* is given in my book *Shakespeare: From 'Richard II' to 'Henry V'* (London, 1958).

VI 'King John' and 'The Merchant of Venice'

1. *Richard III*, V. iii. 184. See p. 58 above.

2. *King Lear*, I. ii.

3. This, perhaps, is not altogether different from the attitude of Prince Hal, in *Henry IV, Part I*, who is ready to draw his own lesson from proximity with dissolution and to wait for the suitable moment to declare his reformation to its best effect. See p. 203 below. In saying this, I am not implying that Hal and the Bastard are similar creations: rather, that a common political vocation, exercised to patriotic ends in times not altogether dissimilar, produces results that show some affinity.

4. There is an obvious parallel between the situation of Arthur in this play

and that of Henry VI in the chronicles devoted to his reign. See, especially, the remarks on Machiavelli's 'unarmed prophet' on p. 40.

5. The exploitation, in such passages as these, of a consciously 'theatrical' element is one of the most interesting features of the rhetoric of this play.

6. The last and most distinguished example is the deal between Antony and Octavius over Octavia (*Antony and Cleopatra*, II. ii).

7. Here again the terms in which the problem is presented, if not the problem itself, are of some significance to the very different character and situation of Prince Hal.

8. John Bale's 'morality' play on King John can be dated, in its final version, to 1561.

9. *Henry IV, Part I*, I. i. See p. 200 below.

10. *Henry IV, Part I*, V. i.

11. See pp. 303–4 below.

12. *The Taming of the Shrew*, V. ii. See p. 89 above.

13. Written in or about 1590.

14. For *Henry V*, see the debate with Williams and Bates before Agincourt (IV. i, and pp. 254–6 below): for *Hamlet*, the exchange with Polonius concerning the players: 'use every man after his desert, and who shall 'scape whipping' (II. ii. 561): and for *Measure for Measure*, the double confrontation of Isabella and Angelo (II. ii, iv) and especially:

> Alas, alas!
> Why, all the souls that were were forfeit once;
> And he that might the vantage best have took
> Found out the remedy. How would you be,
> If He, which is the top of judgement, should
> But judge you as you are?   (II. ii. 72)

15. This account of *The Merchant of Venice* rewrites and slightly expands the section devoted to the play in my essay on *Shakespeare's Early Comedies* (*Writers and Their Work* series, London, 1960).

VII 'Henry IV'—Parts I and II, and 'Henry V'

1. We may suppose that some three years separate *Richard II*, which must have been written round 1595, from the three later plays.

2. Shakespeare made considerable use of such works as Hall's *Chronicle*, published in 1548, and Holinshed's, first published in 1577.

3. The argument developed in this Chapter has been worked out, in considerably greater length and detail, in my book on these plays: *Shakespeare: From 'Richard II' to 'Henry V'* (London, 1958).

4. See p. 175 above.
5. *Henry IV, Part II*, IV. v. 233.
6. Compare, in this same opening scene, Henry's words to Westmoreland:

> Yea, there thou makest me sad and makest me sin
> In envy that my Lord Northumberland
> Should be the father to so blest a son, ...
> Whilst I, by looking on the praise of him,
> See riot and dishonour stain the brow
> Of my young Harry.   (I. i. 78)

7. Compare the words spoken by Hotspur at the moment of death. See p. 223 below.
8. These elements have been well studied by J. Dover Wilson in *The Fortunes of Falstaff* (Cambridge, 1943).
9. See references as far apart as Richard II's hostile description of his rival's 'courtship to the common people' (*Richard II*, I. iv. 24) and Henry's own account to his son, quoted on p. 215 below, of his 'politic' wooing of public opinion.
10. It is noteworthy that even Henry V, on the eve of Agincourt, is unable to throw off entirely this sense of impending retribution for sins committed in the past.

> Not to-day, O Lord,
> O, not to-day, think not upon the fault
> My father made in compassing the crown!,

which, after listing some acts of reparation, leads to the desolate conclusion:

> More will I do;
> Though all that I can do is nothing worth,
> Since that my penitence comes after all,
> Imploring pardon.   (IV. i. 312)

Claudius, on his knees in *Hamlet* (III. iii), could well have spoken in this way, which does not mean of course that his fault is equal or that he is the same kind of character.

11. See p. 252 below.
12. Compare, again, Henry V's reaction to the Dauphin's gibe, quoted on p. 250 below.
13. 'I am not yet of Percy's mind, the Hotspur of the North; he that kills me some six or seven dozen of Scots at a breakfast, washes his hands, and says to his wife "Fie upon this quiet life! I want work"' (*Henry IV, Part I*, II. iv. 116).
14. Compare Aufidius:

> Let me twine
> Mine arms about that body, where against
> My grained ash an hundred times hath broke,
> And scarr'd the moon with splinters.
> (*Coriolanus*, IV. v. 112)

15. See pp. 113–15 above.
16. Professor J. Dover Wilson, in his studies already referred to, has argued that the two plays are to be regarded as forming a single dramatic unit. His arguments, however, have been strongly contested by other scholars.
17. The discussions between Agamemnon, Ulysses, and Nestor (*Troilus and Cressida*, I. iii) are notably similar in conception.
18. Numerous examples of this type af imagery may be found in the Sonnets.
19. I have discussed this aspect of *Troilus and Cressida* in Vol. II of *An Approach to Shakespeare* (London, 1969), Chapter 1.
20. *Henry IV, Part I*, V. iv. 86. See p. 224 above.
21. Something like an approach to it is contained in the Prince's parody of his father (*Henry IV, Part I*, II. iv. See p. 211 above); but Falstaff's reaction and the final disposition of sympathy are there very different.
22. *Henry IV, Part I*, I. ii. See p. 203 above.
23. *Henry IV, Part I*, II. iv.
24. *Henry IV, Part I*, II. iv.
25. This carries us forward, by its phrasing, to Troilus': 'This is the monstruosity in love, lady, that the will is infinite and the execution confined, that the desire is boundless and the act a slave to limit' (*Troilus and Cressida*, III. ii. 85). The echo is striking testimony to the continuity of Shakespeare's thought in the plays of this period.
26. See *Richard II*, V. i. 57.
27. *Henry IV, Part I*, IV. ii. 72.
28. *Henry IV, Part I*, V. iii.
29. Compare Henry's references to 'rank diseases' (III. i), quoted on p. 235 above.
30. Compare Northumberland's reception of the news of Shrewsbury, quoted on p. 226 above.
31. See, more especially, pp. 248–9 below.
32. *Henry IV, Part II*, V. iv.
33. See pp. 223–4 above.
34. See, especially, Sonnet XCIV: 'They that have power to hurt, and will do none'.
35. See Vol. II of *An Approach to Shakespeare* (London, 1969), Chapter 1.
36. Compare

> Now we are well resolved; and, by God's help,
> And yours, the noble sinews of our power,

> France being ours, we'll bend it to our awe,
> Or break it all to pieces.   (I. ii. 222)

37. Compare *Coriolanus*, II. ii, and especially the feeling behind such a phrase as:

> with a sudden re-inforcement struck
> Corioli like a planet.

38. The conception has, of course, a traditional foundation of which Shakespeare was well aware and which is closely connected with the mediaeval view of monarchy; but the use made of it in this play also connects it with other, and more 'modern' reflections upon the nature and implications of princely authority.

39. *Hamlet*, III. i. 76.

40. *Hamlet*, I. ii. 136.

41. Theobald's famous emendation has, of course, its difficulties; but in the absence of an alternative which shall appeal both to sense and the poetic instinct we may perhaps be allowed to retain it.

VIII The Great Comedies

1. For the use of similar imagery in the Sonnets, compare Sonnet XCV:

> How sweet and lovely dost thou make the shame
> Which, like a canker in the fragrant rose,
> Doth spot the beauty in thy budding name!

2. See pp. 88–9 above.

3. *Othello*, III. iii.

4. See p. 97 above.

5. See p. 155 above.

6. Act III, sc. iii.

7. *The Winter's Tale*, I. ii.

8. *The Winter's Tale*, V. iii.

9. For a mature Shakespearean statement of the relationship between *nature* and art, compare Polixenes to Perdita:

> nature is made better by no mean,
> But nature makes that mean: so, over that art
> Which you say adds to nature, is an art
> That nature makes. You see, sweet maid, we marry
> A gentler scion to the wildest stock,
> And make conceive a bark of baser kind

> By bud of nobler race: this is an art
> Which does mend nature, change it rather, but
> The art itself is nature.

(*The Winter's Tale*, IV. iv, IV. iii. 89 in O.U.P. edition)
See also *An Approach to Shakespeare*, Vol. II (London, 1969), Chapter 4.

10. Compare Edmund to Gloucester in *King Lear*, I. ii.
11. III. ii. 321.
12. Compare Polixenes' remarks on 'innocence' and 'the doctrine of ill-doing' (*Winter's Tale*, I. ii). I have discussed this in my *Shakespeare: the Last Phase*, pp. 262–4.
13. II. i. 19.
14. The words are Duke Senior's, II. i. 22.
15. For this attitude to the forest we can look back as far as *Titus Andronicus*, where Aaron describes the woods, scarcely less conventionally conceived, as 'ruthless, dreadful, deaf, and dull'. See p. 65 below.
16. III. iii. 90.
17. V. iv. 63.
18. Compare Prospero in *The Tempest*:

> the rarer action is
> In virtue than in vengeance.
> (V. i. 27)

19. Compare the 'fresh garments' with which Lear is clothed on his awakening (*King Lear*, IV. vii. 22).
20. Jacques' description of the soldier may remind us in spirit of Hamlet's reflections on Fortinbras and his men,

> Whose spirit with divine ambition *puff'd*
> *Makes mouths* at the invisible event,
> Exposing what is mortal and unsure
> To all that fortune, death and danger dare,
> *Even for an egg-shell.*   (*Hamlet*, IV. iv. 49)

21. Compare, for a more extreme statement of this kind of attitude to love Troilus' appeal to Pandarus:

> give me swift transportation to those fields
> Where I may *wallow in the lily-beds*
> Proposed for the deserver.
> (*Troilus and Cressida*, III. ii. 11)

22. For expressions of similar sentiments in the Sonnets, see p. 111 above.
23. It is scarcely necessary to stress the value, symbolic in kind, given to rings and their exchange in the development of Shakespeare's 'romantic plots'.

We have already touched upon a slight example from *The Merchant of Venice* (see pp. 197–8 above), and the bracelet stolen by Iachimo from Imogen to 'prove' her infidelity to Posthumus (*Cymbeline*, II. ii) is a device similar in kind.

24. See p. 81 above.

25. Jonson's play may be dated to 1599.

26. Compare Pericles' question to Marina restored:

What countrywoman?
Here of these shores?

(*Pericles*, V. i. 103)

27. For the various overtones associated with the Shakespearean use of the adjective 'golden', implying at once the ideally remote and the precious, compare the reference to 'the *golden* world' of Arden (*As You Like It*, I. i, see p. 286 above), and the refrain from the song in *Cymbeline*:

Golden lads and girls all must,
As chimney-sweepers, come to dust.

(*Cymbeline*, IV. ii. 262)